Everyday Inspiration for Change

HOW DAILY EXPERIENCES CAN BE YOUR BEST MENTOR FOR CHANGE IN LIFE

Minola Jac

Copyright © 2023 Minola Jac.

All rights reserved. No part of this publication may be reproduced, distributed, or transmitted in any form or by any means, including photocopying, recording, or other electronic or mechanical methods, without the prior written permission of the publisher, except in the case of brief quotations embodied in critical reviews and certain other noncommercial uses permitted by copyright law.

Every effort has been made to obtain permission for, give proper attribution, and cite each quotation within this book correctly. Express permission for each quote has been obtained where possible, and where not possible, only brief quotations have been used with complete attribution for the nature of commentating on these quotations and providing readers with further resources on certain topics. No effort was willingly made to copy quotations without attribution or use a quotation with the intention of this book being a replacement for the source material. If you find any errors in the use of these quotations, please contact Flying Wings LLC at contact@flyingwings.llc. Some quotations, including all of those from Wikipedia, used under the Creative Commons license.

Published by Flying Wings LLC.

ISBN: 978-1-7376243-4-9
Printed in the United States of America.

To everyone who has been found by this book, I hope it will inspire you to look for the big magic in the small moments.

Contents

Section 1. Start. Just Start.
Section 2. Tuesday Change Management Random Thoughts

7	What Baking Bread Teaches Me about Change Management
10	What My Mom, a Pediatrician, Taught Me about Change Management
14	We Are Not Born to Be Docile. We Are Born to Be Meaningful!
18	Why the Words We Struggle with Most Seem to Come in Sets of Three.
22	On Happy Feet and Dealing with Different, Differenter, Differentest
26	What Adopting a Stray Cat Taught Me about Change Management
29	What Getting Tattoos Taught Me about Change Management
33	The Fundamental Difference between "Not Knowing" and "Not Knowing Yet"
36	What a Beautiful Zulu Greeting Teaches Me about Change Management
39	What Wearing Glasses Teaches Me about Change Management
43	What a Difference a Blink Makes!
46	What Wishlists Teach Me about Change Management
50	What Doing Laundry Teaches Me about Change Management
54	What Eating Alphabet Cereal Teaches Me about Change Management
58	What Collecting Fridge Magnets Teaches Me about Change Management
62	What Caring for Plants Teaches Me about Change Management
66	What Eating Street Food Teaches Me about Change Management
70	What Listening to Music Teaches Me about Change Management
74	What Hiking Teaches Us about Change Management

78	What Giving Gifts Teaches Me about Change Management
83	What Taking a Break Taught Me about Change Management
87	What Preparing Lunch for a Friend Teaches Us about Change Management
90	What Charging My Phone Teaches Me about Change Management
95	What Traveling by Train Teaches Me about Change Management
99	What Washing Dishes Teaches Me about Change Management
104	What Wearing a Mask Teaches Me about Change Management
107	What Dealing with Writer's Block Teaches Me about Change Management
111	What Improv Teaches Us about Change Management
116	What Watching the Sky Teaches Me about Change Management
120	What Tying My Shoelaces Teaches Me about Change Management
124	What Changing the Toilet Paper Roll Teaches Me about Change Management
129	What Stopping at Gas Stations Teaches Me about Change Management
133	What Losing Loved Ones Teaches Me about Change Management
137	What Buying Jewelry Teaches Me about Change Management
141	What Binge-Watching Television Shows Teaches Us about Change Management
144	What Swimming Teaches Me about Change Management
149	What Living and Working in a Foreign Language Teach Me about Change Management
154	What Enjoying Cartoons Teaches Me about Change Management
158	What Choosing Health Insurance Teaches Me about Change Management
162	What Shopping at IKEA Teaches Me about Change Management
165	What Getting Used to a New City Teaches Me about Change Management

169	What Walking in the Rain Teaches Me about Change Management
173	What Looking at X-rays Teaches Me about Change Management
177	What Reading Books I Don't Like Teaches Me about Change Management
181	What Sitting on the Couch Teaches Me about Change Management
185	What Shopping Online Teaches Me about Change Management
189	What Changing Bags Teaches Me about Change Management
193	What Removing Sticky Labels Teaches Me about Change Management
198	What Living in an Apartment with No Lights Teaches Me about Change Management
201	What Unpacking the Moving Boxes Teaches Me about Change Management
205	What Cleaning Windows Teaches Us about Change Management
208	What Hanging Out in My Hanging Chair Teaches Me about Change Management
212	What Getting WiFi Boosters Teaches Me about Change Management
216	What Eating Pancakes Teaches Me about Change Management
220	What Choosing Poster Frames Teaches Me about Change Management
225	What Watching the Moon Teaches Me about Change Management
229	What Being Totally and Crazily in Love with Penguins Teaches Me about Change Management
234	What Cooking and Eating Spaghetti Teaches Me about Change Management
239	What Drinking Prosecco Teaches Me about Change Management
243	What Playing Tetris Taught Me about Change Management
247	What Struggling with Chronic Insomnia Teaches Me about Change Management
250	What Collecting Swatches Teaches Me about Change Management

- 254 What Sewing Buttons Teaches Me about Change Management
- 258 What Living Right Next to a Tram Stop Teaches Me about Change Management
- 263 What Making New Friends Teaches Me about Change Management
- 268 What Speaking about Silence Teaches Me about Change Management
- 272 What Getting Lost on the Way to a Memorial Service Taught Me about Change Management
- 276 What Dog-Sitting over the Holidays Taught Me about Change Management
- 281 What Struggling with an Unstable Internet Connection Teaches Me about Change Management
- 286 What Being Stuck in Back-to-Back Zoom Calls Teaches Me about Change Management
- 291 What Delivering Presentations Teaches Me about Change Management
- 295 What Coloring My Hair Teaches Me about Change Management
- 299 What Enjoying Candlelight Teaches Me about Change Management
- 303 What Making Peace with Broken Dreams Teaches Me about Change Management
- 307 What Crossing Bridges Teaches Me about Change Management
- 312 What Celebrating My Birthday Teaches Me about Change Management
- 317 What Drinking Coffee Teaches Me about Change Management
- 322 What Learning to Meditate Teaches Me about Change Management
- 326 What Experiencing Moments of Being Absent-Minded Teaches Me about Change Management
- 331 What Knitting and Crocheting Teach Me about Change Management
- 336 What Repotting Plants Teaches Me about Change Management
- 341 What Shopping at Farmers Markets Teaches Me about Change Management
- 347 What Getting Scars Teaches Me about Change Management

352	What Loving Watching Waves Teaches Me about Change Management
357	What Enjoying the Solar Lanterns on the Terrace Teaches Me about Change Management
362	What Taking Myself Out to Restaurants Teaches Me about Change Management
368	What Renewing My Passport Teaches Me about Change Management
373	What Putting Things in Storage Teaches Me about Change Management
378	What Eating Ice Cream Teaches Me about Change Management
382	What Watching Water Teaches Me about Change Management
388	What Having Surprise Late-Night Conversations Teaches Me about Change Management
392	What Cooking with Chocolate (and Eating It!) Teaches Me about Change Management
397	What Changing Bed Sheets Teaches Me about Change Management
403	What Getting to the ER Teaches Me about Change Management
409	What Loving Thunderstorms Teaches Me about Change Management
414	What Visiting the Zoo Teaches Me about Change Management
419	What Loving (and Eating!) Pizza Teaches Me about Change Management
425	What Looking for Daily Celebrations Teaches Me about Change Management
430	What Making Sense of a Breakup Teaches Me about Change Management
436	What Hosting People in My Home Teaches Me about Change Management
441	What Writing 100 Tuesday Change Management Random Thoughts Taught Me about Change Management
446	What Getting Obsessed with Jamón While in Spain Teaches Me about Change Management

Section 3. More Change before Change Management   **450**
Sources   **455**

What Readers Have to Say about
Everyday Inspiration for Change...

"The journey of transformation is a complex one but it is also deeply personal. That is why Everyday Inspiration for Change *is such an important and meaningful read. It not only is a prescriptive guide to making change, but it goes where a lot of other books don't—it delves into the intersection of how vulnerability and trauma inform how people transform and respond to change and is refreshingly open and authentic, just like its author. I highly recommend this book, I got a lot out of it and know you will too."*

—Colin H. Mincy, Co-Founder and Principal of Going Beyond the Work, LLC and CNBC Workforce Executive Council

"Minola's storytelling of change experiences touched my heart and captured my curiosity with an authenticity that drew me in to listen more about how we are always living and learning and growing. A personal and natural way to better understand how to build resilience."

—Kerry Brown, Change and Future of Work Strategist, Customer Transformation Advisor - Celonis, Former Global VP Transformational Change – SAP

"Minola is a brilliant thinker. She studies the benefits and blessings of personal and organizational change. I read her thoughts and think and then smile!"

—Robert Hamilton Owens, Keynote speaker, Leadership and Management Development Coach, Mediator and Crisis Coach, Author of *Beyond Average: Developing Yourself Through The 20X Principle*

"Congrats Minola for authentically and vulnerably highlighting how your life experiences can be applied to the complex and challenging task of changing human behavior. I particularly enjoyed the lens of stakeholder engagement that accompanies this read throughout, and how that applies to supporting and influencing stakeholders on their own change journey within our organizations."

—Bhushan Sethi, Strategy & Partner, PWC and Adjunct Professor NYU Stern

"Listen to the whispers of wisdom in this book, as it converges change management clutter into memorable conversations, shaping meaning late at night or during a stroll around town, inviting you to experience change as a friend you recognize, approach with curiosity, and embrace with love."

—Wagner Denuzzo, LCSW, Coach, Start-Up Advisor, Speaker

"With honesty, humanity, humor and insight, Minola reminds us that change isn't primarily about frameworks and tools, but about the incremental impact of connection, conversation and intention in every-day action. Her musings on all things change are a worthwhile read for leaders, practitioners and other humans!"

—Ricardo Troiano, Global Change and Organizational Development Senior Leader, Growth Discomfort and Disruptive Thinking Advocate

"Minola's writing style and lessons on change are truly magnetic! This is the kind of book designed to challenge your thinking and give you plenty to reflect upon in a healthy way. Her stories and experiences will not only educate you, but grow you in ways you hadn't thought about. If you're lost, tired and stressed in the wilderness of change, this is the compass and map you're looking for!"

—J. Scot Heathman, Executive Coach, Leadership & Development Jedi, Owner of Elevating Others.

"There are many, many books out there on Change Management. It is rare that a book makes me immerse myself but this one did just that. Minola hooked me with her first sentence! Seamlessly weaving together new perspectives on change challenges with thought-provoking stories. A new lens on change—a required reading for everyone interested in organizational and personal change!"

—Bernhard Stieger, Practice Leader Leadership & Organizational Advisory, Kincentric, Making Transformation Work — Empowering Leaders to Reach Their Full Potential and Create Change That Sticks

"Few people in the world are ever as inspired and passionate about a craft as Minola is about change management. Minola's passion is evident in her writings and the work she does on a daily basis to enlighten us about the ins and outs of change management. This book gives voice and expression to her passion and, in many different ways, will make you feel as inspired as she is about change. If there's one ultimate guide about both the theoretical fundamentals and practical insights regarding change management, conveyed in a serious, yet exciting and witty way, it is this book."

—Enrique Rubio, Founder at Hacking HR

"Minola humanizes 'change' in this book as something we all go through in everyday life, yet we make it such a big deal when we see it through the lens of an organization, only to realize that if we embrace it with courage, compassion, humility and curiosity, the journey becomes so much more enjoyable…just like the journey of our life!"

—Anoop Chaudhuri, Award-Winning Global HR Leader, Mentor and Coach

"Transformation and change management are generally complex. If you are looking for a lighthearted humour and authentic narrative on how to spot and experience transformation and change in your everyday life, this masterpiece of Minola is the right pick! I am sure you will enjoy reading it as much as I did, and it will make you curious and intentional in the way you approach life and transformation, with vulnerability and authenticity."

—Bala Asirvatham, Global Head of CoE Talent & Learning, Global DEI Officer, Vanderlande Industries B.V. a Toyota Company

"Most of us are exposed to 'change management' in the workplace, most often in a way that is formal and scary. Which is exactly why Minola Jac's book is so important to read. In Everyday Inspiration for Change: How Daily Experiences Can Be Your Best Mentor for Change in Life and Work, *she takes daily experiences—taking public transportation, home decorating, chatting with a friend—and writes about these shared experiences through the lens of change management. Even if—and especially if—you aren't a change management practitioner, you can take inspiration from Minola's excellent book. Change Management is everywhere. As she tells her friend in the book: 'You actually know more about this change management thing than you think, and you do it more consistently and more meaningfully than you give yourself credit for.' Once you read this book, you will see that you do as well! And you will start seeing the lessons change management teaches you with your very next cup of espresso, like I did!"*

—Tracie Sponenberg, Chief People Officer, The Granite Group

"It's much more than an essay on change management! It's an enjoyable read that talks joyfully about life and the wisdom it takes to live it well. . . ."

—Giuseppe Natale, Co-Founder and Board Member at Valagro, Busy to Turn Dreams into Reality, Passionate about Nature, People, Technology

"Minola's superpower—and gift to her readers—is packaging the simplicity, depth, and beauty of life's smallest intricacies in a way that connects to a simple, clear, and purposeful framework of high-level principles that facilitate better change. Minola's light but thoughtful nature shifts our beliefs about change from overwhelmed to overjoyed. Here, she helps us find not just our unique ability to change—but to transform and evolve."

—Joe Jacobi, Olympic Gold Medalist, Performance Coach, & Author of Slalom

"Living a full and happy life is only possible if you're able to handle life's one constant which is change. Minola Jac has written a groundbreaking field guide to help anyone navigate their personal and professional life by illustrating change in digestible, insightful, thought provoking and oftentimes humorous antidotes taken from the most relatable things in our lives. She writes with a clarity and wisdom that makes this a must-read. Absolutely remarkable!"

—Scott MacGregor, Founder & CEO of SomethingNew LLC & The Outlier Project, 4x Author, Record 8x Winner of The American Business Award for Innovation

"Minola's storytelling is mesmerizing both because the journey she gets you immersed in but also because of how it has you constantly learning and reflecting on the art of 'managing change.' A must-read."

—Salvador Bernardo Segura Ortega, Senior HR Digital Transformation Global Leader

"If you don't want to spend time reading thick theoretical books, articles and videos, then here is your simple solution: Minola's book on change management and self-help is all you ever need. Her content delivers value and her ability to inject this value into the content is nothing less than an art. Storytelling at its best, an absolute masterpiece!"

—Khalil Zafar, HR & Management Professional, Author, Speaker & Humble Lifelong Learner

"Minola's orientation and perspective on change has been one of the most pragmatic, insightful and delightful I have come across! Whether in life or our organizations, it seems as though we only embrace, resist, celebrate or expect the meteoric changes and overlook the small moments. Minola's Tuesday Change Management Random Thoughts and now this book are both a meditation and an invitation to embrace the 'big magic and small moments,' to remind us that change is not episodic, but has the generative power to help us evolve. If we are not moving, we are simply standing still."

—Terry van Quickenborne, VP, Talent Development

"In the artful words of Greek philosopher Heraclitus, 'Change is the only constant in life.' In her debut book on change management, Minola Jac masterfully explores this profound reality, taking us on a transformative, soul-affirming, and often laughter-filled journey through its pages. With an exquisite blend of relatable storytelling and insightful wisdom, Minola teaches us how to better navigate the ever-changing tides of life and business using an arsenal of practical and immediately applicable tools. As we embark on this empowering journey, Minola reminds us that one of the keys to actualizing the realities we seek is to ignore perfection and to 'Start. Just start.' So whether you're seeking transformation in your business or any aspect of life, Minola's book is the beacon of light you've been waiting for to guide your way."

—Charmaine Green-Forde, Founder & CEO, Chapter tOO, LLC

"Over the years, I managed different organisational change initiatives, trained senior leaders on how to lead their teams through change, and managed my own life changes. One lesson that stuck with me throughout the years is that paying attention to how our physical body & mind react is a good first to step to 'finding comfort in discomfort' during change. Take the time to notice when your heart is beating like crazy because you don't know what's coming next. Observe your thoughts as you imagine different scenarios, like you're directing a movie. Practise managing these two things and you will view change differently. Change is a marathon, not a sprint. Remember that finding comfort in discomfort is a process that requires time and patience. You will find a lot of inspiration for this in Minola's book."

—Florencio "Rhency" Padilla, Globally Recognized HR Leader, Culture Champion and People-Centric Workplace Experience Designer, Founder and Managing Partner of Perky People

"Get ready to embark on a transformative journey as you dive into the remarkable book crafted by Minola, a dear friend whom I lovingly call my sister from another mother. With her kind heart, captivating soul, and unique perspective, she infuses every situation with a wealth of positivity and inspiration.
In her book, she draws upon the rich tapestry of her relocations, adventures, and diverse experiences, unveiling the unchangeable truths about life through the lens of the constant changes that surround us. With masterful craftsmanship and creativity, Minola delves deep into the essence of change, inspiring and challenging readers to embrace transformation.

Immerse yourself in the pages of her remarkable work and prepare to be enlightened, as Minola's words have the power to ignite profound personal growth. Let her wisdom guide you on a journey of self-discovery, inviting you to embrace change and experience the transformative power it holds."

—Kofi Douhadji, Author of *Unbroken Optimist*,
serial entrepreneur, and coach.

"In this insightful and empowering book, change expert Minola Jac takes you on a transformative journey where ordinary experiences become extraordinary teachers. Drawing on personal anecdotes and professional expertise, Minola reveals profound lessons hidden in daily life's small joys, victories, and challenges. From baking bread to navigating relocations and heartbreak to new beginnings, you learn the importance of mindfulness, compassion, and consistency in change management. In her distinctive Minola-esque way, her authenticity, courage, and fierce introspection leaves you wondering, "How did I not think of this before?"

—Stephen Matini, Organizational Consultant,
Host of the Podcast Pity Party Over

"This book reminds us that, while we brace ourselves for major change in our work or home lives, there is 'big magic in small moments,' the everyday and sometimes imperceptible changes that make up a full and meaningful life. Read this book to see how we can embrace change and live each day with wonder, intention, and joy."

—Angela Champ, Bestselling Author
of *The Squiggly Line Career: How Changing Professions Can Advance a Career in Unexpected Ways*

"Are you a Change enthusiast, a change specialist, a change agent or just looking to implement change in your life, organization, institution, or church? Minola Jac, authentic and as real as can be, brings out the real meaning of 'change management' through ordinary, everyday life happenings, in this inspiring and engaging book. A powerful resource for change work."

—Terry Shiundu, Organizational Culture Enthusiast

"A Truly Inspirational & Generational Book—And One That Will Prepare You to and for Change. Packed with both knowledge and wisdom, Everyday Inspiration for Change *reflects the real-time challenges of the COVID pandemic, coupled with the 'little moments, small joys, and everyday victories' of the Millennial generation bouncing back to a new post-COVID world. Minola Jac captures the essence and heart of the 'big magic in small moments' and the true meaning of 'being present' in one's own life and experiences. Created by a self-proclaimed 'change enthusiast,' Minola makes the appreciation of change her personal and professional crusade. And she can help you appreciate how meaningful and sustainable change is something welcome, a healthy mindset that captures life's key moments in critical snapshots of everyday living, coupled with an appreciation for the*

profound change coming our way. Change your perspective and you'll change your perception. Become more 'meaningfully present' in your own life, get comfortable with change, and lead the way. The whole world is waiting to see the gifts you bring!"

—Paul Falcone, Bestselling Author of *"The Paul Falcone Workplace Leadership Series"* (HarperCollins)

"For me, Minola represents one of the most practical coaches for change. Her thoughts have depth and inspire others to think about their own change journey. Her positive attitude is predominant in her book and is an example for many who struggle with change in their personal life and/or in the workplace. Showing empathy for others is key. However, this you can only reach after having empathy for yourself. One of Minola's strengths is converting complicated theories into practical solutions that take away hurdles and at the same time touch your heart. This book is the start of a powerful journey that will change your life."

—Prof. Dr. Theo Bosma, Senior University Lecturer at The Hague University of Applied Sciences

"This work is an oasis of peace. A fun, effortless inspiration for gathering our thoughts and finding 'big magic in the small moments.' Minola Jac artfully blends work life experience with personal transformation, by sharing how to pause, cherish the moment, notice and reflect in her daily encounters with reality. For those of us that forgot how to look out the window while the train is traveling from point A to B, this book illustrates how to integrate and grow from daily life lessons; from any encounter, activity and unexpected storm."

—Sam Yankelevitch, Author of An Interview with Failure, Problem-Solving Coach and LinkedIn Learning Instructor

"As I'm writing this, I'm going through some milestone changes and I can't help but think of my dad's mantra—for mere mortals like us, there are three things granted in life: death, taxes and change. Perhaps change is the one in this triad that consistently instills most fear in us. But it doesn't have to be this way! The inevitability of change and its omnipresence can be a phenomenal catalyst for good, for progress and for designing and creating a better future. You will learn plenty from this book but perhaps the biggest lesson of them all will be about yourself and the role you play in the daily act of shaping the world you want to be a part of. Minola offers surprising perspectives, her sharp and witty eye will make you think differently about the surrounding world and ways in which we can all apply and use change management as a force for generating value, both in and outside of the workplace. Relatable, practical, dazzling, calming yet stimulating—you will find it all within the carefully crafted pages of this wonderful journey through the brilliant mind of this keen-eyed author!"

—Mary Glowacka, Strategic Practitioner,
Hands-on L&D and Talent Leader, HR Domain Researcher,
Leading Leadership Development at Rolls-Royce

"Minola and I have had many fun interactions, fascinating conversations and shared many stories on calls and on panels over the last few years - in a pandemic-induced world. Even across the Zoom screen, I could feel her being 'in the intensity of the moment.' When she mentioned that she was compiling her articles into a book, Everyday Inspiration for Change: How Daily Life Experiences Can Be Your Best Mentor for Change in Life and Work, *I knew it would be a must-read. Minola's book is the quintessential Minto Pyramid for thoughts around Change work—her ability to find common strands of thought and pull out*

insights that can be applied back to Change work is truly amazing. She has the ability to find innovation and creativity where you least expect it and thus be able to overcome 'functional fixedness.' Spoiler alert: A frame is not just a frame. :) The book is a must hold, savour and read for everyone, especially for people engaged in Change work—a lesson on how to hold on to the small moments and do big work. Wishing her big magic at all times!"

—Soundari Mukherjea, CEO, Soundbytes11 - Organizational Consultant and Business Storytelling Coach

"Minola has a unique way of finding meaning in seemingly mundane, everyday tasks but also the skill to articulate that in a humorous yet moving way. I have loved reading her weekly columns and so pleased that she has written her first book. Looking forward to seeing where her journey takes her!"

—Harsha Boralessa, Founder & Host of
Reframe & Reset Your Career Podcast

"In this captivating piece of writing, Minola takes us on a journey through the transformative power of revealing insights into the nature of change management that uncover intriguing patterns. With personal anecdotes and introspection, she delves into the complexities and nuances of various change experiences, sharing her journey of understanding and redefining meanings. Minola challenges societal norms, questions the overuse of beliefs, and discovers the empowering nature of reframing. She cleverly questions the true essence of change management, leading to a revelation that change is already ingrained in our everyday lives, disguised as high-stakes communications, strategic engagements, and transformative experiences. This thought-provoking exploration will make you reconsider the significance of the *experiences in your own life and relationships. With gratitude and warmth, Minola invites readers on a captivating journey of self-discovery, connection, curiosity, courage, and compassion as you embrace change as a constant force shaping our existence."*

—Marinela Tănase, Executive & Leadership Coach and Mentor, HR Transformation Advisor, Former Global Head of HR Global Business Services at BAT

"During my work experience that focuses on supporting organizations to redesign the organizational and people strategy and coach the leaders, I have experienced people reluctant to change. Change requires moving from one situation to another. In such a way, change becomes evidence of motion and life. Yet, several people are less comfortable with this move; despite life being universally appreciated. This book brings back the concept of change to its destined dimensions; to be part of everyday life. It also mentors readers with captivating and pleasurable little stories related to everyday activities. The author, Minola Jac, discusses how to deal with change in trivial routine matters and models these situations to prepare the audience for dealing with more significant life or workplace changes. It will change the way you see change!"

—Anna Mamalaki, Organizational Transformation & Workforce Strategy Consulting, Executive Coach

"Minola's book will create some of the most exciting change possible...it will change the way we feel, think about, and experience the process of change. Her insights will allow people to understand that change is connected to everything we see and do. She has a compassion about the humanity of change that rings out loudest through her stories and examples. She has experienced extreme change in her own day to day. Through this book she offers

us the opportunity to understand and manage some of the complex (and at times painful) feelings that change can create.

This book will change everything, one page at a time."

—Isabel Pollen, Performance Under Pressure Coach, Facilitator, Professional Actress

"These are Real Life Change Stories. This is what makes Minola's insights into change so powerful. Honest, vulnerable with a dash of humor, blended with a practical approach to navigating change. You owe it to yourself to read this book. Change happens to us all, why not be well equipped for the change? Minola Jac is my go-to source for change leadership and she will be yours, too."

—Denise Beers-Kiepper, Principal, DBK Coaching & Consulting, ICF Certified Coach, Career Chaos Sherpa

What the Co-Authors Have to Say about This Journey

"I met Minola during one of the most challenging times of my life. An expat trying to find her way in a new country with all the personal stuff that goes along with life. Minola shared her passion for 'Tuesday Change Management Random Thought' *with such vigor that I couldn't help but be drawn to discussions on change management. I've always loved writing and when Minola asked me to co-author an article with her, I jumped at a 'yes.' As we shared ideas of what we would want to write over a bowl of pesto, it dawned on us, this was it! To me, that's exactly what* Tuesday Change Management Random Thought *is. It's these small moments that we can use to look at life more critically and think about how we can be a part of positive change. I am honored and humbled to be a part of this journey with Minola. Most of all, grateful for her incredible energy. Minola, I love you, I miss you, I can't wait to see this on shelves!"*

—Allison Tanner, Digital Transformation Enthusiast, Technology Sales and Business Insights Advocate

"Minola is one of the most prolific thinkers I have met. Her love of life and deep insights serve as a ray of hope in this world."

—Jerome Huggup, Talent Acquisition and Development Global Leader, Coach and Mentor, Podcaster

"It was a scrolling for inspiration on LinkedIn in August 2020 that introduced me to Minola Jac. I was drawn to one of her earlier musings that related bread-baking and change management—a great picture of freshly baked bread packaged well with a well-written and descriptive article demystifying change management in a relatable way. I immediately showed my support

of the post and sent an invitation to connect. In true Minola spirit, she quickly responded with gratitude and an interest to learn more about me and my professional aspirations.

Meeting Minola Jac was serendipitous for me. I was at a career crossroads, eager and terrified to transition from a 20+ year career in higher education to explore the possibilities in the areas of talent development and organizational psychology. Not only did Minola directly expand my professional network through thoughtful introductions and professional collaborations, she inspired me through her courage to share her creative talents and meditations through writing.

I am grateful for the opportunity to collaborate with Minola on a few articles and that Minola has expanded accessibility of her writings and collaborations with others in book form. Prepare to be inspired to wonder, empowered to relate, and equipped with a fresh perspective to navigate change in life and business."

—Scott Lyons, Ed.D., Learning and Development Leader, Educator, and Executive Coach

"One of the highlights in my professional life these past few years has been meeting Minola. Her unique combination of unwavering positivity, seemingly boundless energy, creativity, and kindness have lifted my spirits and made me a better professional. She's a tremendous resource, both for valuable professional guidance and friendly conversation. It's been a pleasure collaborating with her and it brings me great joy knowing that her gifts will now be shared with a wider audience."

—Alan R. Slavik, Lifelong Learner, Co-Founder at Insight Revenue, Writer & Mentor

Acknowledgments

Giving proper, meaningful and full acknowledgment and expressing my gratitude to everyone who got me here today would mean writing a full book in and of itself.

I am grateful for each and every person who has ever touched my life in any way, shape or form. You all left a mark on my mind, heart and soul, and I would not be who I am today without our interactions on our journeys.

I am grateful to each and every person who has ever supported my work and content, cheered me on, challenged me, pushed me out of my comfort zone, hugged me, sat next to me in my moments of joy or pitch-black pain, showed me respect, appreciation, trust, unconditional love, kindness and compassion.

I am grateful to each and every person who "saw" me when I tried my best to be invisible.

I am grateful to each and every person who "heard" me when I tried my best to stay silent.

I am grateful to each and every person who believed in me and told me I could do whatever I put my mind, heart and soul behind. I needed to see myself through their eyes when I believed in myself less than they did.

I am grateful to each and every person who told me I had absolutely no chance to do what my mind, heart and soul yearned for. I had to see myself through their eyes when I needed just a tiny bit of extra fire to prove them wrong.

All these being said, I do want to express my forever special gratitude to a few people, in no particular order.

My maternal grandparents. They taught me about unconditional love and made me unbelievably happy and carefree throughout my childhood and well into my adult life. They got me forever fascinated by stories while reading to me by candlelight during endless power cuts in Communist Romania while hungry and cold. Their legacy is my strongest belief that dark can make everything brighter. I miss you every single day, and I love you forever!

Cristina Pop—"Chris" in everyday life, my best friend, my soul sister, closer than any family by blood I have ever had. You have been my lighthouse for two decades now (but who is counting?), and I cannot imagine my life without you in it. I actually absolutely refuse to run this creative exercise. I know sarcasm is how we hug, and our bond is nothing short of magic! Thank you!

Tatjana Tasan—you started holding my hand, literally, on an ICU bed in a hospital in Tallinn in October, 2016, when you barely knew me, and you never let go. I believe I still have to fully understand why you found me in this life. I am beyond words grateful you did. Thank you!

Helena Jeret-Mäe, I would not be alive today without you. Had you not called the ambulance years ago, against my quite incoherent resistance by that stage, I would not be here today, and this book would not have happened. Your own resilience is an inspiration to me, and it keeps me accountable and true to my own journey. You and your unwavering friendship have been life-saving in more ways than one. Thank you!

Wagner Denuzzo, where do I start to express my gratitude? Our connection was instantaneous, and over the years I feel we have been discovering its various layers and nuances with each conversation. You have been my mentor, coach, thinking sparring partner, true friend, safe space, mirror, unconditional supporter in ways I didn't even know I needed to be supported. Thank you!

Ricardo Troiano, Over the years I have heard people saying that the relationship we have with our boss is the most important one within the workplace. I always felt I didn't have "enough data points" to get behind that. Until we started working together. If I didn't feel we had an unwavering safe space of mutual trust, respect, appreciation, insatiable appetite for intellectual confrontation, infinite curiosity and deep kindness, I wouldn't be who and where I am today. And this book would not have been possible. Thank you!

Biba Kocevski, my absolute favorite "partner in change crime." I have always thought that change work is quite a lonely work. And every now and again you find someone from your tribe, who truly "sees" you, and embraces the whole you—the crazy ideas, the craving for adventure, the quest for deliberate discomfort, the thirst for growth mischief. You have been feeling like a big inspiring, energizing, healing and validating hug for my mind, heart and soul from the very first conversation. I cannot imagine my life today and tomorrow without our shared ideas, laughs and Thai meals. Above everything else, your steady and unconditional friendship is the most precious gift. Thank you!

Allison Tanner, Scott Lyons, Jerome Huggup, Alan Slavik, all amazing human beings whom I am blessed and honored to call "friends" and "co-authors" of a handful of pieces in this book. I treasure, cherish and take great joy, inspiration, comfort and safety from our connection, above and beyond the writing together. I am humbled by your trust to join and support me on this journey. Thank you!

Kofi Douhadji, my brother from another mother, my publisher, and an infinite source of joy and inspiration. I will forever be grateful for our paths having crossed, for our friendship that felt like family right from the start, and for how you took a publishing chance on me and this book with an open mind and an open heart. Thank you!

E.J. Robison, the world's wonderfulest, loveliest, most inspiring, curious, considerate and compassionate editor! You have been the best writing adventure companion, and I want to take a moment and acknowledge, appreciate and celebrate your amazing, heart-hugging work! Special gratitude for how you made my "voice" clearer while keeping it "very mine," allowing my "accent" to come through in my writing. Thank you!

Start. Just Start.

There is no other journey worthier of our curiosity, courage and compassion than living everyday life with awe, wonder, grace, purpose, intention and joy.

It took me two decades of change work to realize I had been making the same mistake in my professional life as I did in approaching my birthday while growing up (who am I kidding, I still do this, so count that as four and a half decades of "birth-daying"). I have this expectation, as in an unrealistic, unspoken and undefined hope, that something biiiiig will happen. Life-altering. An immense surprise that would feel like a universal burst of never-ending joy. If you ask me to tell you what exactly I am envisioning, two things I know with absolute certainty: I haven't the faintest clue, and it has never happened. Yet! And while I hold my breath and festive awe for this celebratory Big Bang, I am not fully present for all the wonderful moments filled with meaning, joy and, quite frankly, life. My "festive radar" has simply not been set to sensitive enough to pick up on life, while waiting to beep for the "All-Time Celebration Meteorite" entering my atmosphere...

Time and time again, research proves that organizations

buckle up for "transformations," "major shifts," "strategic turnarounds," yet almost entirely fail to mindfully and intentionally address everyday changes that occur within the very fabric of their environments and ways of working. And guess what? The jet fuel of (organizational) resistance to change and change fatigue is not the big upheaval. It is the ever-increasing series of small, almost imperceptible changes and challenges occurring every day, piling up. Slowly but surely chipping away at our change resources of time, energy, patience, focus, decision-making resilience, commitment, head- and heart-space.

This book is my way of advocating for the best of both worlds. For the big magic in the small moments.

As a matter of fact, this book didn't start out as a book. It was July of 2020, I was living in Luxembourg at that time, and like most of you, I was just about to conquer new heights of glamor and thrill in lockdown life: baking bread! While mixing the ingredients together, I had this idea to write about what baking bread teaches me about change management. I wrote it out as a sheer stream of consciousness and barely re-read it before posting it on LinkedIn. I wrote it out of isolation and weariness more than anything else. Very much to my surprise, it got good reactions, and people told me to keep on writing. Challenge accepted! I thought I would write three, maybe five more. What happened next is living (writing, actually) irrefutable proof of how bad I am at math: I ended up writing 102 weekly pieces on what random everyday experiences teach me about change management. They became the "Tuesday Change Management Random Thought" series.

For 102 consecutive weeks (with small 3-week long breaks around Christmas in 2020 and 2021), I woke up at 4:00 AM on Tuesday, listened to music for one hour, and then opened my laptop. I took a few deep breaths and let my mind wonder and wander on what the past week taught me about change management. The little moments. The small joys. The everyday victories. These writing sessions became my "sanity milestones," and I needed them as I made sense of starting a new job, sorting out an international relocation that felt more like an exchange of lockdowns, buying furniture for the first time in my life, losing friends to suicide, going through a breakup, bracing myself for impact during two Swiss tax seasons, learning to read utilities bills in German (if you can't understand what an achievement this is, reach out and I will send you a scan!), using Google Translate for grocery shopping, taking the wrong tram and ending up in France at 9.30 PM. I came to rely on my writing while trying to build a new life from scratch. As I am writing this now, I realize this journey made me more meaningfully present in my own life!

Getting everything together in a book wasn't even my idea. I sort of grew into it after hearing it more and more often from people reading my weekly pieces. Many years ago, I came across the best definition of conclusion from Arthur Bloch, an American writer, author of the Murphy's Law books and a self-help satire called *Healing Yourself with Wishful Thinking*: "A conclusion is the place where you get tired of thinking."[1] I believe this is what happened to me—I got tired of thinking of all the reasons why the Tuesday Change Management Random Thoughts would not be a book. So, I concluded I would give it a try.

It is my deepest and fiercest hope that this book will speak to you (without my Eastern European accent in the voice-over. At least until the audiobook comes out—what a blooper galore that will be!!!). Please allow it to tell you a few things I have learned on my journey, equally applicable to change in life and work:

Start. Just start. Start even if you do not know where the journey will ultimately lead you. Had you asked me a while back which random thought was my favorite, I would have said "The last one." Along the journey, I changed my answer. Now it's "The next one. Always the next one." I learned to crave, create, nourish and enjoy a space of curiosity more than a place of certainty.

Your voice doesn't need to be perfect to be used and heard. The most meaningful conversation for this book to be in your hands now was with my wonderful editor. My ask was to edit it in such a way that it was still me and my "voice." I didn't want it to be native speaker perfect, but it was paramount to me that it would be perfectly easily readable for native speakers. The obsessive strive for perfection before starting something is the second biggest killer of dreams, second only to "What would people think and say?" As you will see, it also took a few attempts before the weekly writings settled into their format. I didn't want to retro-curate them. That is an integral part of my journey and an essential piece of my message.

Stay true to yourself. If you fear losing something, make losing yourself your biggest fear of all. If you think that I love change unconditionally, think again! There are days when I believe change is great. There are also days when I believe change is great—when it happens to other people!!! I try to be honest, first and foremost with my own self, on what kind of day I am experiencing. I also try to show up fully and authentically in both life and work. One of the things I say often to people I work with is "I want to be comforting, not comfortable." I had to learn to "uninstall the screensaver functionalities" I had built growing up and to constantly unlearn and relearn who I have become along my journey through life and change work. I did lose myself a few times. Getting my true self back…hmmm, let me rephrase this: getting back to my true self took everything I got, and a little more, every single time.

Over the following pages, you will get to read my everyday stories and how they inspired me for my change work. There is a quote, misattributed to St. Francis of Assisi and said to raise historical, theological and biblical questions, but it strangely speaks to me (an agnostic of all people) about showing up and role-modeling: "Preach the Gospel at all times; when necessary, use words."[2] My everyday experiences and interactions are my equivalent of "at all times;" this book brings the "necessary words."

What Baking Bread Teaches Me about Change Management

First published on July 28, 2020

There is something so comforting, so deeply satisfying about savoring a slice of freshly baked bread. Even more so in a kitchen still warm from the oven and filled with the unmistakable smell of one of the best comfort foods known to mankind.

For some reason, baking bread has always been my go-to activity when I need to think about something. Like a magic mind balm. Because it resonates so deeply within me, it made me think about what it really means to me and if I can transfer that little "something" it gives me into other areas of my life.

After quite a few loaves, I realized that baking bread also spoke to me about my professional love: change management. Below are a few of my random bread-fueled thoughts on how baking bread constantly reminds me to be a better professional:

It takes the time it needs to take. For the yeast to work its magic, for the baking, for cooling off so you can cut it without breaking it to pieces. Same in change management—it takes time. You can incorporate accelerators and speed up some parts of the process, but it will take the time it needs to take to yield the best and most sustainable outcome. *It teaches me respect, patience and resilience.*

It is even tastier when shared. A few days ago, I experimented with a new recipe. One of my best friends stopped by and we shared a slice of still-warm bread in my kitchen. I had already tasted it before, but her smile added a whole new world of flavor when we shared our afternoon snack. *It teaches me altruism and joy.*

Sharing the recipe builds connections. As consultants, we often have a slight apprehension when sharing our tools, methodologies and methods. Whenever I have shared a bread recipe, I've gotten surprising little messages like: "Just baked your bread for the third time this month, thinking of you every time." And even better: "Would you happen to have a recipe for chocolate chip cookies?" I feel like I gain people's trust, make them comfortable with revealing their needs for help. That is where value is created. *It teaches me trust and gratitude.*

Simple ingredients are best. I love to experiment, but it all comes down to four basics: flour, salt, yeast and water. Understand and respect your basics; they are your "bread and butter." Everything else can be…a nice-to-have marmalade. And slice your bread with Occam's razor. *It teaches me the ultimate sophistication: simplicity.*

There are rules you absolutely need to follow, but there is always room for creativity. I have learned not to compromise on the basics—in terms of ingredients, but also steps. But I also like to try new flavors—especially some that would not usually go together. *It teaches me intelligent disobedience.*

Taste is a very personal thing. I could bake the most amazing whole wheat, honey and thyme bread (which I actually do…), and there still is going to be someone who prefers a baguette. Or is gluten intolerant. It is important to keep in mind that it is (almost) never just about you. You need to meet people where they are. Bake the bread they can savor to the fullest! *It teaches me empathy.*

Translation is important. Whenever I moved to another country, I needed to (re)learn the ingredients, the names, the characteristics, get familiar with a new oven and adapt everything accordingly—quantities, temperature, time, etc. I ask for recommendations and opinions, listen to and learn my new baking environment. *It teaches me open-mindedness, adaptability and agility.*

One of my favorite expressions is also bread-related: to break bread. All definitions agree that "breaking bread" is about more than just eating; it's about sharing who you are and meaningfully experiencing others as they share themselves, too. As a change manager and consultant, what else could I wish for?

What My Mom, a Pediatrician, Taught Me about Change Management

First published on August 4, 2020

When recently asked during a conference "Who has most influenced you professionally?", I said, "My mom and Mumble from *Happy Feet*." You'll see a future article on *Happy Feet*, but for now, here are some of the ways in which my mom shaped me as a change manager and professional:

When people are scared or stressed, they need to hear the language of comfort. My mom's practice is back in my hometown, a lovely city in the northwest part of Romania, right on the border of Hungary. The population is mixed, so it is quite often that my mom has Hungarian-speaking patients. She has been learning the Hungarian words for illnesses, body parts, medicines and medical terminology so she can best relate to children and parents who are scared, stressed and sick with worry. She has even purposefully hired native Hungarian nurses so she can rely on their help and support.

I am always extra careful when communicating in the mother tongue of people going through a change process as much as possible. And I always ask for help and guidance from native speakers. It is not always about different national languages. Teams, business units, companies—they develop a language of their own, they fill words with their own meaning. I always try to listen to them, understand them and learn to speak their language.

Time is important, chocolate is importanter. My mom's practice is literally five minutes away from home on foot. She leaves at least half an hour early and arrives at least half an hour late back home. At the same time, from as far back as I can remember, my mom has always had chocolates wrapped like golden coins in her purse and pockets. I never knew these two facts were related until she explained the connection to me. She always met some of her patients on the way to and from work, and she wanted to take time to speak with them and give them chocolates.

This taught me to always build pockets of extra time in my interactions with the people I work with. And to have some "chocolates" for them: a remark on their intervention during the last meeting, a kind word, a genuine question about how their weekend went, a joke, a smile or just 30 seconds of comfortable silence while we wait by the coffee machine.

Invest five seconds to save five minutes. Especially during winter, my mom always warms up the stethoscope between her hands before putting it on a child's skin. When I was really young and asked her why, she told me: "It takes me five seconds to make it warm so that the child will not feel it cold, get scared and start crying for five minutes." Change is hard and uncomfortable. I constantly ask myself what can I invest five seconds in so that whatever it is that needs to be done will not have the effect of a cold stethoscope on a baby's skin.

There is always more than just one way to heal someone. My mom always carries around this green, ancient-looking notebook. Ever since medical school, she has been collecting recipes of alternative remedies from her travels, usually from old ladies in some village or another. Teas, herbs, potions, combinations of who-knows-what. She is also a very active participant in pharma seminars and buys medical books. And she keeps telling me that these "worlds" are not mutually exclusive. They are mutually enhancing.

There is no single miracle-working change management framework, methodology, method or tool. Depending on what needs addressing, it can be one or another, or it can be a combination building on strengths from its parts.

"I am only as good a doctor as the mother helps me understand her child." My mom once told me that a child's mother was the best doctor for that particular child. She is there with him/her 24/7, can pick up a nuance in his/her cry, the slightest disturbance in sleeping patterns, a smile slightly less bright than the day before. The mother is the one helping my mom understand the symptoms, context and any possible constraints.

Same in change management—the leaders and people "on the ground" enable me to understand the situation, teach me how to pick up on early signals, interpret them accurately and determine how the company will react to potential solutions. My knowledge, experience, tools and professional comfort zone should never be a pair of Cinderella's shoes!

My mom hit retirement age two years ago. She applied for and was granted an extension of her medical license. Ever since COVID happened, she has been at her practice every day, putting in extra hours, making house visits to those who could not or would not go to a hospital. I asked her once if she was okay, and she told me: "It is easy to treat people when you deal with a sore throat from ice cream or a skin rash from chlorinated water in the swimming pool. I did not choose to be a doctor to have an easy life. I chose to be a doctor to make life easier for others."

My mom is my inspiration.

My mom is my mentor.

My mom is my HERO!

We Are Not Born to Be Docile. We Are Born to Be Meaningful!

First published on August 11, 2020

"You are not docile!" This is to date one of the best compliments I have ever received in a professional setting. Only, it was not meant as such, more like "constructive feedback" during a performance review meeting.

It immediately triggered two things. The first one was a very conscious decision to hear: "You are different, you stand up and stand out; the dress code did not become a mental uniform." Pretty much like in that post I saw a while back on social media: "Somebody called me 'pretty' today. Well, actually, they said 'pretty annoying,' but I concentrate on the positive."[3] Which, by the way, happens a lot if you are in change management—you do get called "pretty annoying," but let's focus on the positive and read on.

The second thing that statement triggered was a quest for answers to the following questions:

- How much of who we really are is expected, accepted and safe to bring into our work life?

- How can I put my lifelong "NDS: Not Docile Syndrome" to best use in my change management work?

Whenever I am in a situation to talk about organizational culture and engagement, I use two oversimplified definitions to drive a point across. Culture is "this is how we do things around here," and engagement is "this is how I feel about how we do things around here." Oftentimes, when executives are asked how they want their people to feel about their work, the answers fall into the following big categories: engaged, motivated, driven, dedicated. But how about inspired, aligned with their personal selves and values? How about safe to bring up ideas, improvements, all the way to making mistakes sometimes? How about empowered, enabled? How about heard, valued, respected—even for the things that set them apart?

If we were freed from all our constraints, how many of us would still—intentionally and happily—choose our current work situations?

These rollercoaster times we've all been braving over the last several months have sparked and (re)fueled conversations around what a "healthy and safe environment" means, what the "work-life blending" is supposed to be and what the "new normal" should look like. Over the past several weeks, I have come across a few extraordinary and totally unexpected insights that gave me ideas, hope and renewed resilience in my change management work.

Equally inspiring and healing reading. One book I recently read resonated deeply on its core message of how, when and why to break the rules—*Rebel Talent: Why It Pays to Break the Rules at Work and in Life*, by Harvard Business School professor Francesca Gino.[4] Through science, practical advice and most relatable stories, this book advocates for restoring the bad reputation of rebels, and for deriving inspiration from their life-changing and equally life-enriching unconventional outlooks. This reading made me go back and leaf again through Adam Grant's *Originals: How Non-Conformists Move the World*[5] and Malcolm Gladwell's *Outliers: The Story of Success*.[6] Dots were starting to get connected in my mind...

While letting these readings marinate in my mind, I remembered a study described in Johann Hari's *Lost Connections* in the chapter "Cause One: Disconnection from Meaningful Work."[7] In the 1970s, an Australian psychiatrist named Michael Marmot ran a study on the British Civil Service, looking to understand the ways in which work life affected overall health. The British Civil Service was the ideal environment with comparable roles and conditions of the subjects but with real differences in status and in how much freedom people got at work. The outcome of this study scientifically proved that the worst stress for people is when they can't put their soul into their work, when they dread going to work because it feels meaningless or trivial. In other words, feeling the full impact of your "say" is better than feeling you have no say at all.

The rise of design thinking. One of the principles used during the ideation phase of a design thinking process is "focus on extreme users," where extreme users are those at either end of the spectrum of users of a product or service. Typically, extreme users need less or more of something to fulfill their needs and some will find workarounds to existing problems, unlike the average users. Let's agree for the sake of this conversation that the "outliers," the "originals," the "not dociles" are the extreme users of a company's culture, processes and ways of working. Especially when driving change, speaking to the extreme users and understanding their amplified needs can be particularly helpful in pulling out more meaningful insights. This ultimately helps spark creativity by uncovering hacks and use cases we wouldn't have previously imagined. As explained during any and all design thinking workshops, it's easy to design something too generic when attempting to appeal to the average users.

There is still a small smile on my face when reading an article in *Harvard Business Review*: "The role of a manager needs to change in 5 key ways," written back in 2018, but now more valid than ever: from directive to instructive, from restrictive to expansive, from exclusive to inclusive, from repetitive to innovative, from problem solver to challenger.

Do I advocate for breaking or bending rules just because? Absolutely not. I do strongly advocate for unexpected, innovative, empowering ways to increase accountability, ownership, empathy, learning and creativity. And I believe in all my NDS fellows out there who stand for absolute positive intent and unwavering integrity.

Why the Words We Struggle with Most Seem to Come in Sets of Three.

First published on August 18, 2020

As a journalist by trade, I must admit in all honesty that words represent the greatest and truest love of my life. Going through these months of lockdown and social distancing and having to use more words to make up for the lack of physical interaction (handshake, hug, pat on the back, light touch on the arm) made me think a lot about the words we use and how we use them. About meaning and meta-meaning.

A few weeks ago, I started thinking about words that are difficult to say. Then I reached out to people to talk about their relationships with words. Quite soon, a few patterns emerged. And for some strange reason, my empirical list of the top three things people struggle with most is entirely made up of sets of three. Here they are below:

"I love you." Because of the most amazing grandmother ever, I have never had real difficulty in saying "I love you." I was used to hearing it and feeling it, so it was something natural for me. During my wild early twenties, I said this quite easily. In retrospect, I most profoundly apologize to my younger self. Over the past several years, I have very consciously pushed myself to become comfortable with saying this in non-romantic settings to people who are most meaningful to me. It is a process and I am still practicing, but I'm happy to say it has transformed some bonds into something deeper and stronger. About a month ago, I also had a very interesting conversation with a friend about why it is still somewhat uncomfortable and strange to use this word, totally void of the romantic dimension, within professional settings. This is something I will look more into.

"I am sorry." Almost four years ago, an ambulance rushed me to a hospital emergency room in Tallinn through a fairy-tale-like snowfall in mid-October. It was late in the evening by the time I got parked in the intensive care unit and got a healthy dose of sleeping juice with my IV drip. I woke up after midnight and felt that somebody was holding my hand. One of my closest friends was there, and the only thing I kept repeating was "I am sorry." At some point she looked at me, squeezed my hand a little bit tighter, smiled and said: "What are you sorry for? Being human?"

That memory stuck with me and I started considering what "I am sorry" really meant. Soon, I realized that it was one of the most overused expressions, and I totally agreed with the huge amount of inspiring articles advocating for breaking the "sorry cycle" of over-apologizing. This put me on my journey of replacing "I am sorry" with what I really mean, whatever that is. And oftentimes it turns into a "thank you."

I have been doing this for years now, both in my professional and personal interactions. Instead of "I'm sorry I'm late," it is "thank you for waiting for me;" "apologies for the late reply" is "thank you for your patience and understanding;" "I am sorry" as a reflex answer to a complaint or negative input is now "I hear you, thank you for the opportunity to address this;" "I'm sorry to interrupt" during meetings is "that is a very valid/valuable point, I would like to add to it."

This also made me additionally mindful of how words are used for communication during change management interventions. I once asked a client whether there were words that had been overused and emptied of meaning in that particular organization. He paused a moment, then replied: "Please do not use 'honest' and 'open.' We keep using them, but the reality is there are very few, if any, honest and open conversations around here." I had to bite back a reflexive, empathy-filled "sorry." Instead, I took a breath and said: "We now have the opportunity to make these words relevant again."

Another time, I got a comment after a presentation: "You used 'transformation initiative' in your talk. We are quite technical around here. Please say 'project'—to us that means that somebody is (hopefully) driving it, a clear start and end date, a pressure to deliver against a budget." Again, I bit back a reflex "sorry," and said: "Thank you so much for the feedback, appreciated and truly helpful." Now I keep my "I am sorry" for when that is exactly what I mean. It is a difficult thing to say when you stand behind its whole humbling power.

"I need help." This has been my lifelong nemesis. Because of things I was told during my childhood. Because moving around so often put me repeatedly in a situation where I had to do everything by myself, usually from scratch. Because twice it was decoded in a professional setting solely as "I cannot/do not know how to do it," and it made for a very "honest and open (please see reference above)" conversation. But it turned out to be one of the best change management tricks in my toolbox.

A few years ago, I was working with someone who emanated potential and creativity but was struggling with a lot of (mostly self-imposed) doubts and limitations. One day, while waiting around the coffee machine, I smiled at her and said: "I need your help. Could you give me five minutes to discuss something?" She was puzzled at first, then smiled and nodded. We discussed some steps in a communication plan that needed to happen, I asked her to do a couple of things, gave her a bit of direction and guidance and we agreed to follow up the next day. She did a brilliant job. And I got a question at the end of our meeting the following day: "Can I help you with anything else?" She did. After a few such collaborations, the question became: "Is there anything else I could do?" I realized that when she had the opportunity to step up into a place where she could help, that was bigger than whatever had been holding her back. So I kept using the "I need help" strategy in my change management work as an engagement and empowerment tool. But I am still struggling with it "outside working hours." No, I will not say "I am sorry…"

Reading this now, just before pressing the 'publish' button, I realized that "I love you," "I am sorry" and "I need help" is not the most positive progression. So here is a happy set of three words to close off: Thanks for reading!

On Happy Feet and Dealing with Different, Differenter, Differentest

First published on August 25, 2020

One quote that I like to use in my change management workshops is: The secret of change is to "focus all your energy not on struggling with the old, but on building the new."[8] I also mention that it is attributed to "Socrates." Then we start discussing what this focus might be about.

A few years ago, I came across an article I sadly can't recall the name of that advocated for (almost complete) removal of mentioning previous/current ways of working in communication and training content when going through a change. By referring to or making comparisons between "as is" and "to be," the author said, we keep things anchored in the past, and take the focus away from the future state. I often think about this perspective and can find some merit in it. Most of the conversations around change end up sooner or later in a "comparison" phase—how is this "new" going to be a "more or less in some way" version of the current situation. Sometimes, I try to slice the answer into three parts: things people need to stop doing, things they need to start doing differently, and new things they need to learn how to do. Sometimes, I try to say "It is going to be different, just different." And then, without exception, this question pops up: "How much different? Like a lot different or not so much different?" And this is the moment when I remember the precious lesson from *Happy Feet* on how people can react to something/somebody being different.

And, as promised, I am sharing it now, as one of the ways in which I have been trying to help people deal with their perception of something or somebody being "different, differenter, differentest."

Make them laugh. Eva Hoffman, an editor and writer with *The New York Times*, once said a line about how humor reminds us that we're all human.[9] This rings so true to me! Among the questions for an ice breaker for workshops or meetings, there is always the classic "your favorite movie." And I always pick it. Very openly and honestly, I tell the others that *Happy Feet* is my favorite movie because it teaches people a valuable change management lesson: how some people (some of you might say "most" people) react to something different.

The cartoon is about a dancing penguin born into a colony of singing penguins and he gets teased and looked down on. When pushed by his father to forget dancing and become good at singing to be able to fit in and get accepted, Mumble replies that even if he's asked to change, he simply can't do it. He eventually gets rejected by his colony. After a series of adventures and some life-and-death-situation-induced mindset change inside his colony, all is good. It is a story about a cartoon with singing and dancing penguins, so it makes people laugh. But they get the point every single time. Use humor as often as you can. As Mumble puts it: Be "spontan-you-us." And watch people's reactions. You can also learn a lot about people based on what makes them laugh.[10]

Tell them the stories they are ready to listen to. *Powered by Storytelling*, written by Murray Nossel, Ph.D., has an amazing chapter dedicated to obstacles to listening. He says that listening is like a container and stories are like liquid put in that container.[11] The lesson for change management here is that we all have our own container, and therefore the same "liquid" will end up shaped in different forms. We are different even in regards to the quantities of liquid we can contain. Our different experiences drive different lenses of judgment towards what we hear. Try to get the best understanding possible regarding the different containers you need to fill and pour accordingly.

Look at the difference differently. A few years ago, I was working for a company going through a series of changes. In addition to the scope of each separate project, the transformation agenda also listed "cultural turnaround" aimed at breaking down silos and addressing biases driven by language, geography, business unit, type of product, and the list went on and on and on. While visiting all the offices, the thing I heard most often was "We are so different."

I had an idea to write an article called "We Are So Different Myth Bust." It acknowledged the fact that they were indeed very different: they spoke different languages, lived in different cities and serviced different clients with very different needs for which they developed different solutions. Yet, they were fundamentally the same in more meaningful ways: how they approached their work and clients, how they built and respected their teams, how committed they were to making a difference, how they supported each other, how they stepped up to claim accountability and ownership. That article sparked the setup of a company-wide change community, and many different good things started to happen.

Remember the quote at the beginning: The secret of change is to "focus all your energy not on struggling with the old, but on building the new"? It belongs to Socrates. Not the renowned Greek philosopher Socrates, but a gas-station attendant character in the book *Way of the Peaceful Warrior* (p. 105) published in the 1980s by the world-class gymnast Dan Millman.

Now, has this "different" Socrates' identity changed the validity of the quote?

What Adopting a Stray Cat Taught Me about Change Management

First published on September 1, 2020

When I moved from Tallinn to Luxembourg, I went for the "change trifecta": different time zone, different country, different everything. The change came with downgrades—there is no sea in Luxembourg—but also with upgrades: there is Starbucks in Luxembourg. Perspectives, perspectives…

 I was incredibly lucky to find an amazing apartment on the ground floor with a tiny terrace, right on the edge of one of the parks in Luxembourg City. Two years ago, after coming back from a long-term project in Malta (I left again barely one month after moving to Luxembourg, welcome to my geographically-challenged life!!!), my new home gave me one of the best presents ever: a cat! He was, to the best of my knowledge, the stray cat of the park. Some people told me they had seen him for at least five years before I came here. Our relationship has evolved to the point where sometimes he brings his cat friends home for a snack and cat milk drink. I am also happy and proud to celebrate the third round of my grand-cat-children—yeah, life happens, and it is purrrfect!!

As we were spending a quiet evening on the terrace, I started thinking about all the things Orange, as I named him, has brought into my life over the past two years. And below I am sharing some of his change management teachings:

Be consistent. When he started coming onto the terrace, as soon as he sensed movement in the kitchen, he would hiss and run off. It was quite fortunate that it was the beginning of summer so I had the chance to spend more and more time outside and leave the terrace door open. He got his own bowl of fresh water that I changed twice a day, at least. Then his bowl of food that I changed and refilled daily. I started speaking to him whenever he was close by. For some strange reason, I spoke to him in French at the beginning—of course that didn't work, my accent was just painful to listen to! Then English—slightly better results. In the end, I just kept on talking to him in my native Romanian.

Orange became used to my voice and presence. Then I moved his food bowl inside the kitchen, right by the terrace door. In about one month, he got used to going inside to eat. Fast forward to late October, I found him napping on the sofa in the living room. Adoption completed! It took five months of daily routines to get here, having him totally comfortable and relaxed in my presence. And this is the consistency lesson. It also made me think about how important it is to keep doing the good things on bad days when the reaction is disappointing or altogether missing.

Trust the timing. Orange started visiting the very next week after my own cat of fifteen years died of a stroke. She was back in Romania, and I was literally on my way to see her when it happened. She passed away almost one year to the day after I lost the most important person in my life, my grandfather. Add into the mix an ongoing breakup, and you can understand why getting attached (to any form of life!) was highest on my "Do not even dare to do it, you idiot!!!" list.

I thought and felt I wasn't ready. Just like all the people in all my projects asking at some point: "But why this? And why now? No." Change doesn't happen when we are ready. It doesn't happen when everybody is ready. When you ask people "Why not now?", listen to their answers. But listen to understand, not to reply. There is always value in their perspective. Acknowledge, respect and address change fatigue. And grab hold of your "now."

Create "the best of both worlds." Of course I would love to have Orange with me all the time, but he is used to roaming around in the park. Keeping him inside would be cruel, selfish and soul-destroying. So each of us has our own separate lives, and we get together when it happens. He knows he has his safe home here, I know he is out there and comes home when he wants to. It is a good feeling knowing you are chosen over and over again.

The question "What needs to be preserved?" doesn't come up that often in change management conversations, and it should. Because change is about keeping the good things and creating new things around these so that the whole is even better.

Be grateful. I have no idea what the "hooman handover process" is up there in cat heaven, but I am grateful it happened. In all honesty, I am more Orange's rescue than he is mine. I learned to be comfortable with not knowing why it happened when it did. It makes me happy just being able to pet him, hug him, be there for him when he comes home. And this is enough to make me smile.

What Getting Tattoos Taught Me about Change Management

First published on September 8, 2020

About ten years ago, in early summer, I was out with a friend when some of his work colleagues joined us. I ended up having a conversation about vacation plans with one of them. "So, what are your plans for this summer?" she asked. "I am getting tattoos," I replied honestly. Her jaw dropped. "OMG, you are crazy!! But come on, you are over thirty, that is not responsible adult behavior. What would people say?" There it was, the sentence that has killed more dreams than anything else in the world. I started laughing and said, "Hmmm, now I am curious. What would they say indeed?"

Quite surprisingly, I was reminded of this conversation at one point during this summer. At the end of a Zoom call, the lady I was speaking with said: "We definitely need to talk again. I am curious about the stories of your tattoos." That made me remember that initial reaction from ten years back and consider what people had actually said over the years. The most common reaction was: "I have been thinking of getting a tattoo myself.

But I am not sure what I want... What if it doesn't turn out like I want it? What if I get bored after a while? And honestly, I am quite afraid of the pain." This sounds so much like reactions you get during change management conversations.

While pushing for yet another 500k steps monthly achievement, I came up with some answers on what getting tattoos taught me about change management. And my random thoughts are here below:

There is always a "point of no return." For some people, the point of no return is when they have their first full sleeve done. For others, when they sit on the tattoo chair. For me, personally, the point of no return is when the needle hits the skin for the first time. Even if we stop right there and then, I will always have an "odd-looking freckle" for the rest of my life.

I have seen different points of no return during change management interventions. Sometimes, it took seven months into the project, one-third of the budget spent, and two IT platforms decommissioned. I also remember one project when the point of no return was a five-minute informal conversation that planted an idea into a senior executive's mind.

The "body pain map" is real. On most tattoo-related websites, you can find a lot of information explaining how different bodies experience pain differently. The pain you are most likely to experience while getting inked depends on how well-rested you are, on your consumption of coffee and alcohol the day(s) before and your overall emotional and physical state on the day. But strictly speaking of the "body pain map," here's the general consensus: the least painful places to get tattooed are those with the most fat, fewest nerve endings, and thickest skin. The most painful places to get inked are those with the least fat, most nerve endings, and thinnest skin. Bony areas usually hurt a lot. Once you know this, reassess your decision of getting that tattoo you have in mind for your feet/inner wrists/around your knees or elbows/along your spine and get ready for the extra pain.

In organizational design, there is the principle of "contingency planning," which basically means very purposefully reinforcing the parts of your organizational structure most likely to be under extra pressure from external and/or internal forces. Think of the Compliance and Regulatory Departments of companies active within highly regulated industries, or the Research and Development Units within high-paced, innovative domains.

Getting a tattoo is easy, but how do you live with it? After I got my first tattoos, all my professional attires changed into long sleeves, regardless of the season. I bought wide bracelets in all available colors—okay, I admit to using my forearm and wrist tattoos as an excuse to go crazy on these accessories… Even when I meet clients or colleagues in less formal settings, I consider whether the long-sleeve navy blue shirt is better than my favorite green t-shirt…

I spent a few days debating with myself and some close friends on the timeliness of this article. Because, whether we like it or not, tattoos still raise quite a few eyebrows and can trigger biases. All these things made me think of two change management points. The first one I already touched on in one of the previous articles: how much of who we really are is expected, accepted and safe to bring into our work life? The other one is related to how we follow all the rippling effects of the changes occurring in an organization.

Depending on the organizational context and structure, as well as on the project and type of changes, the rippling effects can reach into the governance framework, organizational structure, roles and responsibilities, various policies/processes/procedures, onboarding strategy and training, career progressions, PR and marketing strategies and plans, suppliers agreements, client SLAs, office layout… Making a change stick is sometimes more challenging than making the actual change.

Cover-ups are more painful. When you want to cover up a tattoo, getting the new ink is more painful because the needle needs to go deeper into the skin. The colors will most probably need to be darker, definitely more intense than the previous ones. And in order to be able to create a meaning for the new tattoo, the ink will take up a larger area of your skin. These things will happen regardless of why you want a cover-up, but additional frustration comes on top of the pain if you want to "hide" a tattoo that was done badly. All these points apply to change management work. Just take a moment to think back to all the times you had to deal with displacing, replacing or repairing outcomes of previous initiatives.

Getting tattoos also means getting comfortable with people asking questions and sometimes having a deeper, better understanding of who you are and things that mean a lot to you. The stories behind your tattoos are like little glimpses into your soul. There is a wonderful book called *Pen & Ink: Tattoos and the Stories Behind Them* by Wendy MacNaughton and Isaac Fitzgerald where they talk about how all tattoos share the story of the wearer, no matter if the ink was considered a mistake later on or came from thoughtful intention, whether it's displayed for all to see or hidden away. They are important, personal keepsakes that the wearer carries with them always.

One particular story resonated with me a lot: a now-famous writer and blogger got a very naïve-looking bunny tattoo on his left shoulder blade many years ago. But it wasn't a mistake—he did it to "mark time." Now, 17 years later, the tattoo reminds him that he and his thoughts are always changing.[12]

The Fundamental Difference between "Not Knowing" and "Not Knowing Yet"

First published on September 15, 2020

Many, many years ago, after a client meeting, my direct manager at that time told me, while we were waiting outside for the taxi: "You know, there is a special place in hell for consultants who say 'I don't know' in client meetings." It is true that, during the meeting, I very honestly answered one of the questions with "I don't know, let me get back to you on this one by noon tomorrow." The meeting went on naturally after that, but there I was, outside the client's office building, searching for something more meaningful to say to this other than "Hmmm, okay." I didn't know what else to say.

This remark lurked at the back of my mind for years, and it became front and center one February morning three years ago. I was passing some time in one of the bookstores in the Arlanda airport and a turquoise cover caught my attention: *Nonsense: The Power of Not Knowing* by Jamie Holmes. My buying decision was made right there and then. And what a lovely reading it turned out to be! It was a witty and well-researched argument that in an increasingly unpredictable and complex world—even more so now than ever before—it turns out that what matters most isn't IQ, willpower, or confidence in what we know, but it's how we deal with what we don't understand. Saying "I don't know" is just a temporary snapshot, context- and topic-driven. And not in any way an eternal life sentence.

Last summer, I stumbled upon another inspiring book: Karen Rinaldi's *(It's Great to) Suck at Something*. It is an eye-opening book on the reality that we prioritize work and productivity to a damaging degree. We see high aspirations as equivalent to success, but in not allowing ourselves room to fail or even rest, we're all more mentally, emotionally and physically exhausted than ever.[13]

Very often during change management-related conversations, I get the opportunity to mention the Dunning-Kruger effect. In the field of psychology, the Dunning–Kruger effect is a cognitive bias in which people with low ability at a task overestimate their ability. But, surprisingly, this effect also comes into play with experts who undervalue their ability—so, neither the most or least skilled groups can accurately assess their skills. As blogger Jason Kottke put it: "Confidence feels like knowledge. I feel like that simple statement explains so much about the world."[14]

My favorite tote bag has one of my mantras printed on it: "It's not hoarding if it's books." Also, it was a festive day for me and my best friend when Marie Kondo clarified her decluttering advice regarding the number of books one can have on one's bookshelf. For the record, you can have more than 30 books as long as you first "wake them up."[15] Our books are wide awake and keep us happily awake, too! Following Karen Rinaldi's teaching, I found what I suck at: decluttering. But I excel at tsundoku, the Japanese term used for the habit of buying reading material and piling it up. A few years ago, I read a wonderful article that said that practicing tsundoku is a great exercise in self-awareness: having unread books around you shows you how much there is that you still do not know, and it can serve as a reminder to stay humble.

"I don't know" used wisely, with the right people, in the right situations, with the right frequency, is a very honest answer. And oftentimes it goes from an honest answer to a starter of meaningful conversations and relationships.

Over the last months, I have had several conversations about the effects of saying "I don't know" during job interviews. Whenever this topic comes up, I think about a powerful scene in *The Pursuit of Happyness*. The lead character Chris Gardner, played by Will Smith, sits in a job interview, a bit dirty and disheveled after one night in jail for failure to pay parking tickets, and tries to win over the "senior executives" with wit.

Being bold and honest about his work ethic, Chris tells the executives that if he's asked a question he doesn't know how to answer, he'll always be honest about what he doesn't know—but he also adds that he's the type of person who will always find out the answer. One of the executives responds by asking Chris what he would think if they hired someone who interviewed for the job without a shirt on. Unfazed, Chris replies that he'd think the guy must have been wearing "some really nice pants."[16]

This scene always makes me wonder why being honest and being impressive are perceived, sometimes, as mutually exclusive. Honesty is always impressive. And if I had to choose, I'd rather be honest than impressive.

I do hope that my direct manager was right about that special place in hell for consultants saying "I don't know." Because I am very much looking forward to having a nice chat with Chris Gardner and many other people I have come to admire, respect and trust implicitly over the years. Mainly because they have been honest over impressive.

What a Beautiful Zulu Greeting Teaches Me about Change Management

First published on September 22, 2020

On my birthday back in 2008, I came very close to missing my flight because of my (one and only) superstition: I never board a plane without a book to read. While running around a bookstore inside Henri Coanda Airport, I saw a book with a bright turquoise cover and Egyptian motifs, grabbed it, paid for it, and shoved it in my backpack as I ran toward the boarding gate. And this is how, totally by chance, one of my favorite writers entered my life: Wilbur Smith. The book I bought that day was *Warlock*, part of the Ancient Egypt series which follows the fate of the Egyptian kingdom through the eyes of Taita, a multi-talented and highly skilled eunuch slave. I fell in love with Wilbur Smith's writing, and soon I discovered the Courtney and Ballantyne series, which follow the lives of several generations against the majestic backdrop of the African continent.

One of the very first things that fascinated me was a Zulu greeting that kept popping up in the books: "sawubona." It felt like a very special thing that contributed in some way to the relationship dynamic between the characters, so it got me really curious. I started reading and talking about it with different people in different settings, and the things I have discovered over the years hugely impacted my life, both professionally and personally.

"Sawubona" literally means "I see you." I've even heard people take the definition further with something like: "I see you, I take the time to understand your needs, faults and fears, and I accept and value who you are." It is a way to make the other person visible and to accept them as they are with their virtues, nuances and flaws. This greeting can also mean something for both parties: "We see, value, and appreciate each other. We see each other's journey and are willing to help wherever we can." "Sawubona" allows us to communicate that we truly see each other. And listening to a TED Talk, I learned that in the Zulu tradition, the "I" is the connection to the lineage of ancestors. So "sawubona" not only represents the speaker, but their ancestors as well.[17]

Over the years, I also came across "sawubona" in *The Fifth Discipline: The Art and Practice of the Learning Organization* by Peter Senge, a professor at Stanford University. The way in which the author spoke of the Zulus and the magnificent way they interact with one another, and also how they handle problems, sparked my own journey to making "sawubona" part of both my professional and personal interactions with people.

"Sawubona" symbolizes the importance of directing our attention to another person. It exists to remind us to understand others without prejudice and to leave grudges behind. The term reminds us to be aware of other people's needs and to give importance to individuals within a group. It also helps us think about integrating ourselves into our communities and valuing them. I keep asking myself what I "see" when I look at organizations and their people, how my "ancestors"—meaning all my past experiences—contribute to my sense-making. Are my experiences helping me add valuable insights, or are they blurring my vision? And equally, what do I let others see in me?

Last week I participated in an online conversation on cultural competence, and one of the key takeaways was being reminded that self-reflection is the foundation for meaningful communication and relationship building. I was also inspired by hearing that "seeing," listening and accepting suspend judgment and drive actionable sense-making. One particular bit of wisdom resonated deeply and reminded me of "sawubona": Treat people how THEY want to be treated. See people for who they really are, acknowledge, respect and value them accordingly.

In a business world where "customer experience" and "employee experience" are present in every piece of messaging, what can we learn from the ancient Zulu greeting? "Sawubona" is a word that reminds us to trust one another. It reminds us to see the other person as they are and pay attention to them. We have to authentically understand them and see their needs, desires, fears, sorrows and virtues. Equally, in our personal lives, especially during these times, who wouldn't want to be seen this way? And how comfortable are we with allowing others to really see us?

I also researched how to reply to "sawubona" and found several answers, depending on translation nuances and geographies of use. One version is "shiboka," which means "I exist for you." I also found reference to "yebo, sawubona": "yes, we see you, too." The possible response I like most is "ngikhona," which means "I am here." The inherent meaning is that until you saw me, I didn't exist. By recognizing me, you brought me into existence. A Zulu folk saying clarifies this: "Umuntu ngumuntu nagabantu," meaning "A person is a person because of other people."

What Wearing Glasses Teaches Me about Change Management

First published on September 29, 2020

There is a long-standing joke in my family about me getting eyeglasses not because of poor eyesight, but sheer ignorance. I have been a city girl all my life. I hated "how I spent my vacation" essays in school because all the other children had wonderful stories about life in the countryside while the highlights of my summer were the long walks on the beach with my grandmother when she took me every year across the country to spend ten days on the Black Sea coast. As the story goes, my parents took me to the optician when I was about three and asked to have my sight tested. Since I was no prodigy and did not know the letters yet, I got to look at the chart with the animals. And the eye doctor, instead of prescribing me a long stay in the countryside to learn more about ducks, geese, chickens, dogs, and cows, sent me off with my very first pair of eyeglasses.

Fast forward 38 years and I now have a collection of glasses in all different colors and shapes, which I enjoy wearing. As I read recently on the Zenni blog, I have become a "fashionable frame wearer" and I enjoy "multiple glasses personalities"[18]—it sounds equally posh and worrying…

And in case you are wondering, it still takes me a little conscious effort to differentiate between geese and ducks!

What we "see" and how we create meaning have been a lot on my mind lately. After "sawubona," this week's random thought is about wearing glasses and how that contributes to my change management perspective.

You get glasses even when/how you don't want them. The short story of how I got to wear glasses is one perfect illustration. We are not always in the situation to drive change, but to go through it. Sometimes, we might be in a situation where we don't even have a say about how change happens. You know how kids have big dreams of becoming doctors or pilots or explorers? I didn't dream of that. My biggest dream was to grow up and, as an independent adult, get to choose the frames that I liked. I used to rebel—I broke a pair of hideous glasses and got something even more horrible instead because it was the only option available in the store at that moment. It was one of my first lessons in picking my battles; how I wish I knew about intelligent disobedience back then! Revolution is not always the best solution—evolution might work out better.

Not all positive change feels positive in the beginning. It is a particularly insightful metaphor for me how, when you change your glasses, at first you get headaches and you feel off-balance. Although the prescription is the right one for you and you even chose the frame you liked most, the change comes with discomfort. Wearing your new glasses as much and as often as possible will speed up your eyes' prescription adjustment. No matter how comforting and comfortable your old glasses seem to be, wearing them occasionally only makes the adjustment more difficult. Change doesn't necessarily need to be as significant as new diopters to feel uncomfortable. Eyes need to adjust to different lenses, frame shapes and sizes, as well as new lens types and materials. When you have multiple glasses and you switch between them, you also need to factor in some adjustment time. And this always makes me think of multitasking and an article I read on how much focus, energy and productivity are lost with constant switching and adjusting. It also makes you "see" change fatigue a bit differently.

Constant care is important. You know how mothers, when you pick them up at the airport when they come visit for Christmas, give you a looooong look over and ask: "When did you have your last proper meal?" Mine never asks that. It is always: "When did you clean your eyeglasses last?" As a glasses wearer herself, she is totally OCD on this issue. Now it's like our own ritual. She asks, and then I reply: "Come on, you know these are my creativity development glasses. I need to imagine the world in front of them."

Just like you clean your glasses, it is necessary to clean the filters through which you look at your environment—recheck assumptions, expectations, biases, information and rumors, levels of motivation and frustration. As Aaron Hill, a 17th-century English poet, said: "Don't call the world dirty because you forgot to clean your glasses."[19]

Glasses become part of who you are. We all have at least one person in our life whom we could not imagine without glasses. In my case, the first one that comes to mind is myself. How we look at the world, what we are open and able to see, how we create meaning through our vision and sight speaks volumes about who we are—what we value, what we overlook, what we focus our attention on, how well we train our eyes to improve our visual perception across all types of eyesight fields.

Don't turn sight into your only source of information. When we experience headaches, blurred vision and unsteady balance with new glasses, we need to rely on other senses and/

or reflexes to stay safe and function normally. It can be relying on other senses a little more, muscle memory or merely automatisms we developed for routine tasks performed within fixed environments. In my own kitchen, I am perfectly capable of making a cup of coffee not only wearing new uncomfortable glasses, but in pitch black conditions.

When we cannot "see" properly, how much can we rely on experience, knowledge, reflexes, faith, hope and resilience in ourselves and those around us? How comfortable are we with relying on other "senses" and people around us? How long before we say "I need help?"

There is infinite wisdom in a famous quote from *The Little Prince* that says the most important things are only seen with the heart, not the eyes.[20]

But, just to be on the safe side: keep calm and wear cool glasses!

What a Difference a Blink Makes!

First published on October 6, 2020

The "rainy season" started in Luxembourg two weeks ago. Not surprisingly, I came down with a bad cold and had to spend several days in bed. I spent the weekend before last looking and feeling like a "several-times-dropped-on-its-head-during-international-shipment" Egyptian mummy and couldn't do anything. The overwhelming thought in my mind during those three days was: "I am wasting time. I am doing nothing, just wasting time I do not have."

I got two short notes from two very special people who don't each other and yet sent me the same message: "Find your balance, just let go." I have been trying really hard to learn this "letting go" bit over the last year. I can count on one hand all the times in my life when I was told that maybe something was not meant to be. And I totally lost count of how many times I heard: "Maybe you just did not try hard enough. Are you sure you did everything possible?" "Doing" has always been my default response. And it took quite a lot of painfully honest conversations over the past year to make me understand that it can also be a toxic coping mechanism sometimes.

While sick, in between hot milk and antibiotics, I pushed myself to "do" some research for last week's article on wearing glasses and eyesight. I ended up reading medical articles on blinking and it got me fascinated. We blink to keep our eyes clean and moist so that they can focus properly. It is a physiological phenomenon that also happens during our sleep. We blink like we breathe: unceasingly. An adult blinks at least 12 times every waking minute. These momentary lapses into darkness come at the cost of blocking 10% of our daily visual input. Scientists have found that the human brain is set up so as to ignore the momentary blackout. The very act of blinking suppresses activity in several areas of the brain responsible for environmental changes so that we experience the world continuously.

This was when I made a decision. Since I am having a hard time taking a break, I will talk myself into being more intentional with my "blinking"—small mental "disruptions" to help me refocus properly.

It also got me thinking about several things. If I am to use "mental blinking" as a refocus mechanism, what should go into that 10% of daily blocked input? What are the things that I can ignore? At this point, I remembered a mug I got years ago from one of my best friends customized with the following text: "I've got 99 problems and 86 of them are completely made up scenarios in my head that I'm stressing about for absolutely no logical reason." When I got it, the number of my problems went straight to 100 because I stressed over being so bad at math. Blinking, blinking, blinking…

What do I need from and within my environment to experience my world continuously? In my case, the "constants" I need are all people. And maybe salted caramel ice cream. There is a quote I absolutely love, and it reminds me of a walk in Kadriorg Parc in Tallinn with one of the meaningful "constants" in my life: "Some talk to you in their free time, and some free their time to talk to you. Learn the difference."[21]

Speaking of people talking, here are more interesting facts about blinking. One study assessing blink rates during different tasks found that people blink most during conversation. Even more tellingly, another study found that when listening during a conversation, rather than blinking randomly, we tend to blink at the end of sentences and at points when we believe the speaker may have finished what they are saying. Researchers also believe that blinking helps disengage our attention. The first thought that popped into my head when I read this was that I should just "blink" to disengage my attention when the "wasting time" self-conversation happens to start again. Self-conversations should be at least as intentional as conversations with other people. And we should free our time to talk to ourselves.

Meditation is, to me, pretty much in the same category as "taking a break"—my personal best ever is 43 seconds, including one sneak peek at my wristwatch. I also tried yoga and left the session perfectly at peace with contemplating taking up Krav Maga classes. But after reading about blinking, I realized something. Back in early summer, I attended an online event that had a mindfulness moment included. After hearing the agenda at the beginning of the event, my plan was to be an active participant until that activity, and when it started, switch to audio-only, have a glass of wine and crochet—my kind of meditation. Instead, I got one of the best surprises in a very long time. It might have been the voice of the yoga teacher, or the words of the meditation, most likely the combination of these two, but I can still hear them. Quite often I replay them in my head whenever I feel the need to quiet my mind. And it was last week that I realized my mind has been "blinking" for a while with these words: "May I be happy, may I be healthy, may I be safe, may I be at peace."

What Wishlists Teach Me about Change Management

First published on October 13, 2020

693. This is the number of items currently on my Amazon wishlist, 679 of which are books. I also have wishlists on the websites of my favorite jewelry brand from The Netherlands, an online bookstore in Romania, a yarn manufacturer in Lithuania, a coffee syrup producer in Germany and a shoes and boots manufacturer in Spain. Plus IKEA and Yankee Candle. And lists of saved courses on LinkedIn Learning, Coursera and Udemy.

My dearest wishlist of 2020 is the one with all the people I want to hug from all the places I long to (re)visit as soon as times will be kinder and safer.

Last week I was in a mind-boosting, heart-warming conversation where we ended up discussing acknowledging, directing and harnessing energy, about how the things towards which you focus your energy are a testimony of how you have processed past experiences and create future possibilities. This got me thinking about my endless wishlists and whether there is some learning here for my change management work.

Below are some possible takeaways which make the time spent building and managing wishlists a good investment:

Pay attention to how you define your reality. There is an anecdote into which Albert Einstein's name was inserted to give the story an air of credibility and a bit of celebrity traction where a student (Albert Einstein) humiliates a University Professor during a debate on the existence of God. The student argues that cold is the absence of heat, as darkness is the absence of light, and ultimately proves that evil in itself does not exist, but it is the absence of God and love.

While the story is fictional, the principle it describes is valid. How do we define our reality: by the absence or presence of something? Is a wishlist the inventory of things we do not have in our life, or rather of our desires, hopes and aspirations? Is it an expression of frustration or a statement of faith in a life safe, kind and long enough to enjoy everything we want? When we build a change story, a stakeholder engagement strategy, a communication strategy, don't we want to give people a "burning aspiration," rather than a "burning platform?"

Celebrate patience. In a world so keen on instant gratification, quick wins and overnight success stories, practicing patience is almost rebellious. About 12 years ago, I was getting ready for a meeting where I knew things would get tense because all participants had been complaining about deadlines and project timelines, cross-finger-pointing each other for "unreasonable expectations." I asked a graphic designer friend to help me with a handout and we made a one-pager with descriptions of the following roles, all quite popular among project managers: "A Project Manager is a person who thinks nine women can deliver one baby in one month. An Operations Manager is a person who thinks one single woman can deliver nine babies in one month if she works hard enough. A Marketing Manager is a person who convinces everybody that one baby can be delivered even if no man or woman is available." The meeting agenda became "defining our roles" and we ended up having a constructive conversation after a good laugh.

Wishlists teach me patience and how to use time to check whether what I wanted three months ago is still valid, wanted and/or needed today. Anticipation also adds to the joy of receiving a delivery. Wishlists teach me to define value and filter through "urgent" and "important." They teach me to practice intentional re-contracting.

Balance between "Big Bang" and small incremental steps. There are times when I go for a "Big Bang" retail therapy episode, others when I celebrate both patience and restraint. While thinking about this article, I asked myself whether the "volume" of my purchase influences the way in which I perceive the individual value of the items. This reminded me of a very nice visual with a turtle walking across a beach and these Plato-inspired words written across it: "No matter how slow, forward is forward."

A few years ago, I discovered a book that tremendously influenced my professional life: *The Progress Principle: Using Small Wins to Ignite Joy, Engagement, and Creativity at Work* by Teresa Amabile and Steven Kramer. Through extensive research, the writers discovered how fundamental the power of progress is to human nature: They found that the key to enhancing personal motivation and well-being during the workday is simple, consistent, meaningful progress. The more a person feels like they're making progress, the more driven and creative they'll become in their work.[22] In case you are curious about how long *The Progress Principle* was on my wishlist, let me clarify that this was a total impulse buy.

Lists create the illusion of hierarchy. Unless otherwise clarified, many people perceive lists as some sort of progression, either on an importance scale or across a timeline. This makes me particularly careful when using lists in change management-related communication. My wishlists are also constant reminders of the "serial-position effect," a term coined by the German psychologist Hermann Ebbinghaus who pioneered the experimental study of memory. The serial-position effect is the tendency of a person to recall the first and last items in a series best and the middle items worst. When asked to recall a list of items in any order (free recall), people tend to begin recall with the end of the list (the recency effect). Among earlier list items, the first few items are recalled more frequently than the middle items (the primacy effect). The most recent item on my Amazon wishlist is a book on Agile HR added over the weekend, while the first one dating back almost two years is a set of ergonomic crochet hooks… Only Jeff Bezos knows what is in between.

Just like change and change management work, wishlists are never-ending and oftentimes self-generating. They are fluid, and anticipation and (re)prioritization require constant management. But, as the Ancient Chinese philosopher Lao Tzu said: "Nature does not hurry, yet everything is accomplished."[23]

What Doing Laundry Teaches Me about Change Management

First published on October 20, 2020

According to research, it can take anywhere from 18 to 254 days for a person to form a new habit and an average of 66 days for a new behavior to become automatic. It's been 84 days—and counting!—since the first article in the #tuesdaychangemanagementrandomthought series, and I must admit I've developed the reflex of looking at my everyday life through the lens of "article potential." For once, I am happy to be part of good statistics.

Last week felt like "laundry week," and my new reflex prompted me to think of whether there were Change Management teachings in this very necessary domestic activity. I was just a girl, standing in front of her laundry, asking it to fold itself, and these thoughts were running around in my head:

There are two ways to ignite change. Change can occur naturally and be embraced accordingly—usually in high-paced industries and/or dynamic environments. There are people out there in the big wide world who do their laundry regularly, at a steady pace, just another routine. At the opposite end of the change ignition reality is the "for things to remain the same, everything must change" approach, so brilliantly described by Giuseppe Tomasi di Lampedusa in his book *The Leopard,* where he chronicles the struggle of the Sicilian aristocracy to survive in the face of social change brought on by Risorgimiento, the Italian unification.[24]

In laundry equivalent, this is a very straightforward "laundry today, or naked tomorrow," as a social media meme summed it up quite eloquently. Changing (at least some of) your plans and focusing your willpower toward loading the washing machine are the guarantees of your immediate decency, cleanliness and joy of being able to keep on matching clothes to accessories as inspiration strikes instead of as availability allows.

"No man is an island." This year, and specifically the lockdown and social distancing measures, made me quite comfortable—and potentially overconfident—in my rather self-sufficient, self-reliant bubble. All good and nice, until I really needed to wash a load of whites and the washing machine refused to start. While reaching out to my network of friends and acquaintances to get recommendations for reliable service and repair people, I thought about a rather new concept that brings a lot of value into stakeholder engagement and change community conversations: "allyship," or fostering meaningful, honest relationships with marginalized people, as it was described in an inspiring article in Forbes magazine. The article also spoke about how allyship is defined and approved not by you, but by the people you are allying with. It's a chance to learn more about others while growing and learning about ourselves.[25]

Diversity is natural, inclusion is intentional. I have heard stories of extraordinary people who manage to finish their shampoo at the same time as their conditioner! Mind-blowing! And also of some superhumans with program management capabilities that enable them to have the perfect loads of separate, specific laundry. Based on the research I referenced at the beginning of this article, I am average, and it is time I make peace with my limitations.

While loading the washing machine with colored and white items and shoving in a color catcher sheet, I started thinking about the power of diversity and inclusion and how, when harnessed properly, they create the "perfect load." At first, I thought that using the color catcher stands for change impact assessment and risk management, but it felt like there was more to it. I realized that the color catcher speaks to me about the commitment and care to preserve, value and repeatedly celebrate the individual, specific characteristics of the items. To make sure they do not become "all the same" and lose their very essence. Nothing like dull, washed-out colors to ruin your day.

It never ends!!! Don't you just love those 12 seconds when the laundry is done??? A good lesson in starting over again and again. A good lesson in resilience. I recently found this nice saying, and I believe anyone who has ever done some kind of change management work will resonate: "Sometimes I feel like throwing in the towel but that would only mean more laundry for me."[26]

Making change stick lacks glamor, but safeguards value. Washing I get, drying I get, but folding… Maybe because it has some sort of "administrative" vibe to it. Like doing the expense reports after the traveling and actual work are done. The potential equivalent of folding in change management work is everything around updating and upgrading procedures, role descriptions, specs of any kind, supporting documentation, where you follow and document rippling effects of the actual change. It might lack the challenge and "glamor" of the change itself, but this is what makes it stick, what ensures sustainability.

A lot of value is lost when the "folding" is not done properly. It might ruin a clothing item completely. It might make the item take up more space in your closet than necessary and force you to keep some other pieces of clothing scattered around the house. It makes ironing more difficult—and here is a great one about ironing, it made me laugh to tears when I found it: "Irony is the opposite of wrinkly."[27]

We've all heard the famous words of Heraclitus: "Change is the only constant." The laundry equivalent might very well be: "Whoever said death and taxes were the only guarantees in life obviously never had to do laundry."[28]

What Eating Alphabet Cereal Teaches Me about Change Management

First published on October 27, 2020

Many years ago, I discovered my human equivalent of "boot from CD:" spending Sunday morning in bed, eating cereal and watching classic *Tom and Jerry* cartoons. For me, it doesn't get any better than that.

Because of some recent developments, and also due to the rainy weather in Luxembourg, this kind of "me time" had been in the planning for a while. And it finally happened this past Sunday. Inspired by a fascinating conversation over coffee on Thursday morning, I went for alphabet cereal. As I was twisting and turning the spoon around in the bowl, I started thinking of any possible change management teachings.

And here they are below. Bon appetit!

Stay childlike, forever curious. Eating cereal speaks to me about staying childlike for as long as possible. Even Albert Einstein advocated for never growing old and constantly staying curious like a child.[29] This curiosity lesson is probably the most important for change management—never ceasing to question, to look for new questions as soon as we get answers.

The other meaningful reminder is that fear, discrimination and judgment are all learned behaviors. Children are born into infinite wonder and potential. They learn all their limitations. Whenever you do innovation or change management work, if you are fascinated by a question that is ridiculed by others, don't be afraid to pursue it, even if you do this on your own. A dominant group thought should not quell questions that can lead to fundamental shifts.

You need all the letters of the alphabet for meaningful communication. On Thursday morning, I had the opportunity to catch up over coffee with a dear friend, one of those rare individuals that forever touches your mind and soul. We ended up talking about professional profiles, trendy competencies, dreams and hopes for the future, mostly on the professional side. At some point, we mentioned "T-shaped professionals," then "H-shaped."

That conversation made me decide to go for alphabet cereal on Sunday because I realized that organizations are bowls of alphabet cereal. The most popular letter-shaped professionals are T, H, M, E, I, but I am convinced that with a group of creative talent acquisition people and a big carton of ice cream, we can come up with profiles for all the letters. And some special characters as an extra topping of inspiration.

Over the last few months, whenever I had the opportunity, I spoke about the importance of moving from "safe recruitment" towards "meaningful recruitment," from requirements-based bullet-points mandatory "grocery-list" recruitment, to potential-seeking, transferable competencies-enhancing recruitment. Just like people do not go into supermarkets, open alphabet cereal boxes and take out specific letters, recruiters should go for as many letter-shaped professionals as possible, then create inspiring words. How can you hope to win at Scrabble with a limited number of letters?!? Get the alphabet cereal, put it in milk (could this be the organizational culture?) to enhance the flavor and enjoy your meal!

Value curiosity over history. Many years ago, I took part in a shadowing program for high school students and I remember when a young, hopeful soul asked me to go through a questionnaire with him, a deliverable for his school assignment. When we got to the question "What are the most helpful and useful things you learned in school?", I was very honest and replied: "Reading and writing. They tried their best with math, but it was never meant to be." He started laughing and said, "But, seriously now." I stood by my answer. There is nothing we cannot learn if we put our minds to it and if it is important enough to us. Nothing!

Moreover, we can unlearn things we have absorbed and which are no longer useful. Or which are downright toxic. A job interview or a performance review where the focus is solely on achievements, tasks, deliverables and questions like "What inspires you?", "What motivates you?", "What makes you happy?", "What does work mean for you?" do not get raised are just not good enough.

One of Albert Einstein's most famous quotes is about education. He reminds us that after time has passed and we forget all of the lessons we were taught in school, education stays with us.[30] Later, he went on to criticize modernized education by suggesting it was in danger of snuffing out our natural curiosity.[31] Curiosity, imagination and a genuine drive to discover and explore are the basis of education, learning and development, performance improvement and, ultimately, innovation.

Not all truth lies in figures. No matter the project, one debate always pops up: quantitative or qualitative key performance indicators (KPIs)? Both. Always take the "if you cannot measure it, it doesn't exist" saying with a pinch of salt. Figures are important, they provide a snapshot, a trend when measured iteratively, in incremental developments. But do they really tell the whole story? How about context? Nuances? Interpretations? Sociologist William Bruce Cameron made an amazing statement in his 1963 text *Informal Sociology: A Casual Introduction to Sociological Thinking*, which said: "Not everything that counts can be counted, and not everything that can be counted counts."[32] I often use this in the KPIs definition conversations. "Letters" are just as important as figures.

All this being said, my key takeaway for change management from eating alphabet cereal is: "If Plan A didn't work, the alphabet has 25 more letters. Stay cool!"[33]

What Collecting Fridge Magnets Teaches Me about Change Management

First published on November 10, 2020

There are a few things that remained unchanged for me throughout this year, and I consider myself very blessed, lucky and grateful for them. They kept me grounded, safe and sane. My inner change manager is quite happy celebrating this statement. There is one constant, though, that has been having quite the opposite effect: my fridge magnet collection. This is "the year of least travel" with no new addition and my fridge has been looking frustratingly the same every single morning.

A while back, while waiting for coffee to be ready, I found myself staring at one of my favorite magnets: "Once a year, go someplace you've never been before," and then thought to myself, "You haven't thought about what fridge magnets teach you about change management. Why don't you give it a try?" And I did.

Awesome stuff stops being awesome. During the early days of lockdown, I got curious about a course everybody talked about, "The Science of Wellbeing" from Yale University. So I took it and was reminded of something very important for change management: "miswanting." The definition is quite simple: the act of being mistaken about what and how much we are going to like things we want in the future. We get used to stuff over time. It's not like we get a stimulus check and we notice it all the time. We just get used to it. The phenomenon is called Hedonic adaptation. It works on the same principle when applied to my fridge magnets collection, motivation and incentive packages and buying a house or a car. This is the process of becoming accustomed to both positive and negative things and events so the effects you experience emotionally don't work as well over time.

In his book *Stumbling On Happiness*, psychologist Daniel Gilbert notes that wonderful things are especially wonderful the first time they happen, but this "wonderfulness" wanes with repetition.[34] Hedonic adaptation. The new things that you get or changes that you make feel great, they're awesome, they stick around, you get used to them. They become the new normal. They stop bringing you the happiness that you expect. And they reset your reference point for the future.

Value interactions over actions. While staring at my fridge, I had an unexpected thought about systems thinking, about how each and every magnet is filled with a meaning of its own but contributes to this wider story of my traveling adventures. I have always found systems thinking meaningful for change management; it's a discipline for seeing interactions, relationships, interdependencies, for identifying patterns and trends, not simply static information in isolation/in and of itself. All this helps with understanding the points of highest impact, where the smallest of interventions can yield/trigger the widest/largest impact (similar to the snowball or domino effect).

The "Wholeness and Interaction" principle of systems thinking speaks about the product of interactions, not the sum of actions of the parts. This reminded me of Niklas Luhmann's theory that any social system (like a company or any type of organization) is a system of communication with actions and interactions where interactions are crucial in providing context and meaning.[35] It speaks to me about stakeholders' engagement, based on interactions, where they bring their own individual truths and create a higher meaning. Actions yield "deliverables" that are subject to Hedonic adaptation, while interactions create meaning, an outcome that is further filled with life and can evolve as the system progresses and changes.

The most important stories are the ones we tell ourselves. It was an absolute joy to attend a webinar on storytelling a few weeks back. It brought me the realization that the most powerful storytelling is the kind we perform for and to ourselves. Every time we make a memory, when we revisit it, when we recreate meaning. Writer Joycelyn Campbell claims that the stories we tell about our past influence us more than the past itself.[36]

Every time I look at the fridge magnets, I retell myself the story of that travel, and maybe I can even remember the story of buying that particular souvenir. The same principle applies to any and all communication artifacts, PowerPoint decks of slides, answers we give during business meetings or recruitment interviews. These are our sense-making stories. And they are particularly important because they define our expectations.

Joycelyn Campbell, creator of the website Farther to Go!, puts it best in her article "The Anticipation Machine Isn't All It's Cracked up to Be": "Philosopher Daniel Dennett describes the human brain as an 'anticipation machine.' He says that 'making future'[37] is the most important thing it does. Unfortunately, the process the brain uses—adding the past to the present to equal (predict) the future—is far from a fail-safe method for figuring out either what actually lies ahead or how we will feel should what we anticipate come to pass. Our 'anticipation machine' creates what we experience as expectations: estimates or forecasts of future situations based on present or past experiences. Expectations are beliefs we have about what should happen or about the way things should or will be. Our visions of what may be possible in the future are heavily constrained by what has already been—or rather, by the stories we've constructed about it. We're not influenced by the past as much as we're influenced by our stories about the past." So what are the stories we tell ourselves?

While researching for this article, I found out that a collector of refrigerator magnets is called a "memomagnetist." It is derived from the words "memorial" (Latin for "memory") and "magnetis" (Greek for "magnetic"). It is somewhat unusual to finish an article with something that sounds like an introduction, but a bit of change never hurt anyone. "Hi, my name is Minola, and I am a memomagnetist." I have been called worse. Like…change manager…

What Caring for Plants Teaches Me about Change Management

First published on November 17, 2020

Sunday is my gardening day. There are quite a few plants in my apartment and most of them traveled with me here from Estonia. Some "locals" have been welcomed, and one of my biggest achievements this year is growing three Saint Paulias from leaves sent by my mom in one of the care packages from home.

This past Sunday, I decided to give it a go and look at my gardening time through my change management glasses. Finding this quote from the American horticulturist and botanist Luther Burbank helped a lot: "Flowers always make people better, happier, and more helpful; they are sunshine, food and medicine for the soul."[38]

Environment is key. It is never (just) about the plant. It is about the light, the air, the water, the quality of soil, patience, and maybe even a bit of luck. One of my favorite quotes comes from H. Jackson Brown, Jr., author of *Life's Little Instruction Book*: "Remember that children, marriages, and flower gardens reflect the kind of care they get."[39]

Whether the flower is a team member or a project, look at the environment when they do not "bloom." It is always, always, always a cumulative effect. Learn as much as possible about the ideal conditions for your plant. Does it like sun? Place it on the windowsill. Shade? Move it, or place it in the shade of a sun-loving plant. Your apartment is not sunny enough? Maybe change your choice of plants. What water do you use? Do you filter it? Get it straight from the tap? Do you live in an area with heavy water? Do you have pets that might chew on the leaves or get jealous of the time you allocate to your plants instead of them? Are your plants toxic for your pets? All of these questions have their equivalents in organizational culture, ways of working, team dynamics, individual profiles.

Routines are important. I cannot say I have always been a huge fan of routines. And there were times when I considered them downright boring, rigid and stifling. Over time, I gained a lot of respect for them and learned about surprising ways in which they can be best of allies. Gardening was one great teacher. Plants require consistency and sticking to a routine is the best way to give it to them. Finding a routine is one part training your plants, but also requires discipline on your end. My Sunday morning gardening routine actually gives me something nice and steady to look forward to, helps me "reduce the weekend planning" and it is a fun and rewarding way to mark the passing of time, especially when I spot a new bud or leaf.

Organizational routines are equally important. And they are great for change management—they provide a steady, comforting, reliable structure, act as pacesetters and keep the "action mode" on.

All conversations are worth having. All of my plants have names. And I do talk to them quite a lot. They haven't replied yet, in case you are wondering… In a study performed by the

Royal Horticultural Society (UK's leading gardening charity), researchers discovered that talking to your plants really can help them grow faster. They also found that plants grow faster with the sound of a female voice than the sound of a male voice. Charles Darwin himself suspected a link between plant growth and vibration. In an informal experiment, he had his son play the bassoon to seedlings, but the results were inconclusive. Fun fact: his great-great-granddaughter, Sarah Darwin, participated in the Royal Horticultural Society's study, and read from *On the Origin of Species* to her tomato plants. The TV show *Mythbusters* conducted a study on 60 pea plants to see whether they responded differently to compliments and insults. The results were roughly equal, but I choose to see some hopeful difference in "roughly."

Speaking to plants is my way of saying all conversations are worth having, even those that might feel like a monologue. It is not always about getting a reply—it is about saying what you have to say, speaking your mind, speaking up. Then you get to decide whether "no reply is a reply." Difficult conversations are worth having. And plants are living proof of that. Research published in the BMC Plant Biology journal reveals that (certain) forms of mechanical stress actually help plants grow. Plants frequently have to deal with mechanical stress, be it caused by rain, wind, animals or even other plants. But plants also respond to more delicate forms of mechanical stress, such as touch. Some responses are obvious, some more discreet. Rubbing some plants' leaves triggers a strong, transient immunity to a whole series of fungi and other parasites.

Not all friction is bad. Immunity and evolution need a bit of nudge, just like communication needs a bit of "shaking." Here's additional support for this statement: if you have a fiddle leaf fig and want it to grow big and tall, you should give the stem a good wiggle every few days, or at least once a week. This mimics the wind and helps your plant develop a stronger root and stem system.

What is your "why?" This is a question that sparks many interesting—and sometimes difficult—conversations. "Why" is a word hugely associated with Simon Sinek, but given the topic of this article, here is a great quote from author and humorist David Hobson: "I grow plants for many reasons: to please my eye or to please my soul, to challenge the elements or to challenge my patience, for novelty or for nostalgia, but mostly for the joy in seeing them grow."[40] Why, what and whom do you grow with your projects and conversations within your environment?

If my plants could reply, I really do hope they would quote Spanish athlete Bojan Krkić back to me with: "It is important to find a place where you feel trust, you feel belonging and stability."[41] And I do hope you get to hear this, in various ways, from the people whose lives you touch with yours.

What Eating Street Food Teaches Me about Change Management

First published on November 24, 2020

With the looming lockdown in Luxembourg, I felt like having some comfort food on Saturday. There's a lovely place here selling kumpir, a Turkish baked potato with various fillings and toppings, and I was a girl on a mission. You know that saying that goes: "In love with street food isn't a statement, it's an emotion?" I found love in a hopeless plate…

The weather was nice. Cold, but dry. As I was eating my late lunch outside, I started thinking about any takeaways for change management and a few ideas popped up in my mind. Bon appetit!

It takes practice to get to a level of "decently messy." One of my earliest childhood memories is walking with my grandmother and stopping to get donuts on weekends back in my hometown. My favorites were the apricot jam-filled Berliners. I managed to get jam and sugar all over my face, some on my t-shirt and a bit on my grandmother's favorite skirt. According to some very old black-and-white photos in one of the family albums, that was not my first attempt at enjoying those donuts… Thank goodness I got to live a Facebook-free childhood! My first hot dog wasn't a particularly "clean" experience either. The first kebab…not enough wet wipes in the world… My first change management project was definitely not the smoothest ride. Second one still a bit bumpy.

As you learn by doing, trying, failing, then doing again, things get a bit easier each time. You learn how to manage the strange dynamics of the "apricot jam" and you end up enjoying it to the fullest. If you are really lucky, you get to teach others, too. And you will have wet wipes ready for when they need them.

Always pay attention to the "one stop shops of insight." Street food spots are great places for observing and getting to know people. Do they go for the places with longest lines, or are they in a rush? How do they wait in line? Do they talk with the people around them? Do they first check out the food offered or wait to make their decision until it's their turn to order? Do they ask for information about the different options? Do they make the effort to say "hello" and "thanks" in the local language, if they are tourists? Do they go for the same thing, or order different meals, and then happily share? (Sharing is caring, people, sharing is caring!!!) Do they sit down or eat on the go? Big meal to keep them going for as long as possible, or small, curiosity-driven bites to get them to the next street food stall? Are they "experienced street food eaters" or not?

All these questions have their own change management-relevant equivalents in the business world. Develop a habit to pay attention to how people behave around the coffee machines or in the elevators. Spend some time in and around the reception areas, see how they greet each other. Do they say "hello" and "bye" to the reception staff and the security guard? You can also learn a lot by paying attention to how people make small talk at the beginning and end of their business meetings. Or how they ask for coffee, tea or water for or from other people. How much do they volunteer to "take more work on their plate?" How and when do they ask questions? How many?

Hemingway was an awesome change management teacher. In *Across the River and Into the Trees*, he advocated for intentional listening whenever anyone else is talking—really focusing on what is being said and not what you're going to say, paying attention to your surroundings, living in the moment.[42]

Frustration is a matter of when, not if. You know how awesome cheese and some impossible to pronounce, yet divinely tasty sauce always get stuck to and wasted on the napkin or wrapping paper? Always say "yes" to more cheese and sauce. You'll need it. Sometimes accidents happen and you drop some of the food. Other times it gets even more frustrating.

I was spending a very lazy Sunday in Helsinki, enjoying a bowl of salmon soup on a bench in the South Harbor Market Square. (Whenever you happen to be in Helsinki, go have a salmon soup and send me a "thank you"/"kiitos" note after!) The day was sunny and warm and the market was full of people. I was working my way towards that perfect last spoonful—a small piece of salmon, potato, some corn, a bit of rye bread—when a seagull passed by and decided to "drop its food critic opinion." OOOH, did I unleash my inner Samuel L. Jackson on that bird!!! Years later, I found a nice quote from Kurt Vonnegut on how one can respond to frustration with laughter or tears. He said he liked laughing better because there was "less cleaning" involved.[43]

In every single change management piece of work, some things get dropped. Every one! But how you handle frustration—whether your own or others, oftentimes both—is key to moving forward. It will happen. It is purely a matter of when and related to what, not if it happens. Let writer Anthony J.

D'Angelo be of help when that happens: "Realize that if you have time to whine and complain about something, then you have the time to do something about it."[44]

Street food has been teaching me to enjoy the moment. To stay curious and adventurous, and always go for extra cheese. To learn to say "hello" and "thank you" in as many languages as possible. Street food reminds me to make the journey towards death as wholesome and whole as possible, to truly live with all my might, to eat, laugh, and love as much as I can and enjoy every second of it.

What Listening to Music Teaches Me about Change Management

First published on December 1, 2020

Merely 500 steps into my daily walk on Sunday, my iPod's battery decided to give up on me. My plan was to go for a long walk, listen to music and write this week's Tuesday Change Management Random Thought in my head, then come home and type it out. Not meant to be. I needed the music to think. I cannot think or work in silence—a bittersweet reminder of my days in the newsroom.

It was a crisp day, good for walking, so I decided not to return home. Instead, I kept on walking, parked my initial idea, and started thinking about any potential change management teachings from listening to music.

"I wish my life had background music so I could understand what the hell is going on."[45] This is such a great saying, and it popped up in my social media news feed quite a lot. Music clearly establishes the feeling of what the story is about. The soundtrack of a movie helps set the atmosphere, it provides insight into a particular character or event, it intensifies the overall impact of the film. If 2020 were a movie, what would its soundtrack sound like?

A simple definition of music is that it is sound organized in such a way as to evoke various types of responses. It often involves the use of instruments or vocals (or both) and contains elements such as pitch, rhythm, harmony, and timbre, all of which determine the overall experience for the listening audience. Music doesn't just come from thin air. The creators and performers of music are inspired to do so for myriad reasons. Furthermore, the different sounds of music are influenced by factors such as technology, individual creativity and available resources, among other things.

Doesn't this sound a little like the organizational culture? Any organization has its own music, and even every team plays its own soundtrack. Sometimes it sounds like Rammstein, other times like Rachmaninoff. There is no such thing as "silence" in an organization. And there is always some style of underground being played. The term "underground music" has come to be defined as "any musicians who tend to avoid the trappings of the mainstream commercial music industry"[46] and always tells the truth in whatever music they produce. And who knew Frank Zappa had an inner change manager? He attempted to define "underground" by noting that while mainstream music just happens naturally, you have to choose to seek out the underground.

"Music is the shorthand of emotion."[47] I would still be a big Leo Tolstoy fan if he wrote nothing but this short sentence. One great thing the year 2020 did was normalize conversations about emotions in the workplace. We are emotional beings, we make (most of) our decisions emotionally, then use reason to justify and support them, or to make them happen. A study performed by scientists with McGill University in Montreal found that when we listen to tunes that move us, our brain releases dopamine, a chemical involved in both motivation and addiction. Keep in mind the parallel between music and organizational culture when you read the following finding of this study: the reason that we feel so good while listening to music is because as our brain processes it, it tries to figure out what will happen next. The nuances trigger the release of dopamine.

Think of your onboarding programs as the opening notes of your organizational song, creating anticipation in the "listeners." How will their anticipation be answered through their overall experience within the company? What does the "music" of the open space sound like? And the "coffee machine playlist?" Are the team meetings "music to your ears?" Songwriter Frank Ocean said, "When you're happy, you enjoy the music. But when you're sad, you understand the lyrics."[48] How do you write your organizational lyrics? What words do you use? Do you sometimes feel like you need "real-life-inspired subtitles" added to your corporate PowerPoint slides? What words do you use to make things simple, especially when they are not easy?

People who show you new music are important. My playlist is a musical legacy built by the people I have met. At its most basic nature, music is a communication tool. It is a way to share information, ideas, and feelings. With that said, many people find it difficult to communicate with others, especially if they are shy or introverted. Music provides an avenue for these people to communicate, whether by writing down their thoughts in the form of song lyrics or by using songs from other artists to make a point. Whenever I get a song recommendation from someone, I listen to it right away—both music and lyrics. And I always learn something new. New music speaks to me about curiosity, keeping an open mind and an open heart, about lifelong learning. About vulnerability and authenticity, empathy and compassion.

In my change management work, my playlist is built by recommendations from stakeholders across the board, and the underground vibe comes from within the change community. Even when you think you have come to know a "song" inside out, after several projects within the same company or industry, there are always new "covers" ready to surprise you.

When thinking of music and organizations, I remembered a blog post on the roles of music in human culture that I read a while back on tunedly.com. The first one listed was providing a voice for the masses. In various movements and protests throughout history, artists have created music to give voice to certain people or groups who need to be heard.[49] And here is my small musical change management confession: one of my all-time favorite songs is Sam Cooke's "A Change is Gonna Come." Speaking of "covers," I listen to Seal's version.

Maybe because I am writing this article on the first day of December, the festive month of the year, and am thinking of going into the new year with a little bit more hope, I remembered a quote from Napoleon Bonaparte on music, which fits in quite nicely: "Music is what tells us that the human race is greater than we realize."[50]

What Hiking Teaches Us about Change Management

With Scott Lyons
First published on December 8, 2020

With the end of the year approaching, I started thinking about what 2020 has been feeling like. A rollercoaster? Definitely. A friend suggested an Ironman competition. Could be. To me, it feels mostly like an arduous hike—up, up, up, the only way to move forward is up. Purposefully. Resiliently. Mindfully. Quite often painfully. Resting when you get tired, but not giving up.

One of the best parts of hiking is meeting fellow hikers. It's just a brief "hello" encounter with some of them. But keep an open mind and an open heart, "stay true to your path," and with a bit of luck, you get to meet people that will truly keep you company and amplify your experience—oftentimes, for the roughest part of the hike. During my "2020 hike," I met Scott just around a bend on my "LinkedIn path." And what a great hiking company he turned out to be!! During our conversations, we realized we both enjoy real-life outdoor hiking and started thinking about what change management teachings were there.

Below are some of our joint thoughts; we hope you will enjoy the "mountain views" with us.

The more we appreciate nature, the better we understand the whole world. Similar to the origins of hiking, the origin of change management is tied to the practice of understanding and testing the limits of interaction and reaction to seek new possibilities. Like trails, models and best practices have been established and evolved over time to pave the way for greater possibilities and deeper challenges and understanding of ourselves and our ecosystem. A change management initiative or project can be just the escape for discovery, growth and a new mantra that we need.

"Mountains have a way of dealing with overconfidence."[51] A great, humbling lesson in change management from Austrian mountaineer Hermann Buhl, one of the best climbers of all time. While hiking, some mistakes can be debilitating or even lethal. Injuries. Encounters with wildlife. A loose stone rolling the wrong way. Unexpected turn of weather. A moment of distraction. Overconfidence.

Just like for hiking, you need to set limits and prepare with suitable gear and timing in any and all change management adventures, regardless of how many previous similar projects you have run. There are always things that will fall outside of your control. Be prepared. Always. Enhance, yet at the same time balance your taste for adventure with experience, common sense and preparation. Critical thinking is a must for greater challenge and, in many cases, survival.

A great hike is good for the soul. What makes a good hike great? Mountain views? Yes. Good company? Yes. Nice weather? Yes. Also, yes for a new, exciting trail, or an old, familiar one with dear memories. Hikers often speak about persistence, about a difficult trail that builds character and agility for future adventures. They speak about hikes reconnecting them with purpose and passion. Mindfulness is something both Scott and I mentioned when talking about hiking. American naturalist Henry David Thoreau said it beautifully: "Methinks that the moment my legs begin to move my thoughts begin to flow."[52]

A positive experience with change management is good for the soul. For people's souls, for the organization's "soul." It builds common purpose and creates meaningful, shared experiences. A great hike is also one that fulfills the need for adventure. One with the excitement of the unexpected. You do not need to have everything figured out to the slightest detail to start on the mountain trail. Respect the mountain and equally respect your inner resilient self. Start walking on the path of change management and the path will appear. Trust yourself and trust the journey. And always think of your fellow hikers. Trails are forged and require maintenance to keep the path open and safe for future adventurers. Create a great hike for those coming after you.

Presence is the best gift you can give yourself throughout the adventure. As the late French novelist Marcel Proust conveyed in his most celebrated novel, "The real voyage of discovery consists not in seeking new landscapes, but in having new eyes."[53] Anyone who has endured a challenging hike knows the dance of emotion and self-doubt. To endure the many challenges, we divide the trek into manageable chapters, like a good project manager. However, planning and execution do not beget mindfulness and presence. Presence powers our ability to conquer self-doubt and frustration with false summits and the most challenging of obstacles. Be sure to permit yourself presence in each moment that leads to your targets along the way; it's where the good stuff is! Greater presence on today's adventure can greatly maximize our preparation and responsiveness for future endeavors.

We leave you with one final quote for inspiration, originally stated by Sir Edmund Hillary, the New Zealand mountaineer who was one of the first to officially reach the summit of Mount Everest: "It's not the mountain we conquer, but ourselves."[54] Maybe we've even inspired you to go for a hike before your next change management adventure. If you do, be present and safe and you'll be sure to find some welcomed inspiration and grit. Maybe you'll even find a new hiking buddy in the process. May your journeys be eye-opening!

What Giving Gifts Teaches Me about Change Management

First published on December 15, 2020

This past week, I received several surprises from my best friends. One was a box filled with a little bit of everything I love: a candle, a book, sweets and accessories. It arrived the very next day after an Amazon gift card landed in my inbox with the "festive request" to use it for books on my wish list and something for Orange, my furry flatmate. I know of at least a couple more on their way. And, with my own gift shopping going on, it made me think of any "insight gifts" for change management that I could get from our gift-giving traditions.

Every Christmas, birthday, anniversary and special occasion, we carefully choose and offer gifts to our loved ones. It's something we do naturally and most of us don't think about its deeper implications. Yet, the gift we choose and how we present it says so much about us, our relationships and the complex social structures within our community. Behind every perfect present lie social, psychological and emotional currents.

Some of the most lavish gifts possible have already been

given. Between 605 and 562 BC, King Nebuchadnezzar II built the Hanging Gardens of Babylon for his wife, Queen Amytis. In 1772, Russian Empress Catherine the Great received the 189-carat Orlov diamond from her lover, Count Grigory Orlov. France gifted the United States of America with the Statue of Liberty in 1884. Fast forward to 1968, Paul Newman gets the Rolex Cosmograph Daytona watch for his wife, which went on to become the most expensive watch ever sold at an auction.

With humankind's rich history of gift giving, started by cavemen presenting each other with unusually shaped rocks or animal teeth to strengthen social connection and show their appreciation to others, going through the Middle Ages with the rise of the practice of dowries, all the way to our time with an oftentimes confusingly wide spectrum of possibilities, we should find inspiration, rather than consolation, in the words of French tragedian Pierre Corneille: "The manner of giving is worth more than the gift."[55]

As in any change management endeavor, let's start with our "why." Why do we give gifts? As gifting plays such an important role in our social fabric, we give gifts for many, sometimes conflicting, reasons. At times our culture requires it—for example, Christmas or birthday presents. At other times, it builds and reinforces relationships with family members and potential mates and can be done for a variety of reasons. Giving a gift to someone we care about allows us to communicate our feelings and appreciation for them. In fact, some sociologists think that we only give gifts to people we want relationships with. In his book *The Gift*, French sociologist Marcel Mauss argues that not giving a gift or rejecting it is essentially a dismissal of the relationship.[56]

Always assume positive intent behind the gifts. People communicate through the use of symbols, says the "symbolic interactionism" theory. Have you been given a gift that has filled you with joy? Or perhaps you've been unlucky enough to receive something that left you feeling deflated and upset since it didn't meet your expectations. But why would this irritate you? It's the thought that counts and that's precisely it. When you look deeper into the matter, it's because we attach symbolic meaning to gifts. This means that a gift you are not overly enamored with can be interpreted as thoughtless in spite of its altruistic motives. Pretty much the same in change management. If the "what" is not necessarily our dream come true, what do we think and how do we feel about the "why" behind it?

Give gifts that appreciate people for who they are, not for what they do. The most meaningful gifts are those symbolic of the giver's knowledge of the receiver. If we have challenges choosing gifts for our closest loved ones, how exponentially difficult does it become to send the right message within an organization with hundreds and thousands of people? And, with all the written and unwritten behavioral rules in the business world, how well do we really get to know the true selves of our colleagues?

In an article titled "The Real Point of Gift-Giving," published on December 15, 2010 in the *Harvard Business Review*, the writer talks about his 43rd birthday. I absolutely love his opening point that we give gifts to show appreciation, but it's not actually the size or value of the gift that matters—it's the intention behind it, the person showing their appreciation. Someone can receive an enormous gift and still feel under-valued because the gift wasn't heartfelt. A gift can't express appreciation unless the person giving it does, too.

He goes on to write about the gifts he appreciated most on his birthday. His wife asked family and friends to write him a note of appreciation, and then comes the best part of the article where he talks about gratitude in the corporate world. He says that this kind of sincere appreciation is almost nonexistent within businesses; yes, there are performance reviews, end-of-the-year parties, and bonuses, but they all fall short in actually showing individual appreciation. Performance reviews cover both strengths *and* weaknesses (praising someone and then telling them how they still need to measure up), parties include a thankful speech by a leader in the company that's overall generic and impersonal, and bonuses are simply transactions with no personal thankfulness behind them.[57]

This article reminded me of a great quote by Patti Digh, an organizational storytelling coach and diversity and inclusion strategist: "Generosity has little to do with giving gifts, and everything to do with giving space to others to be who they are."[58]

Don't use special occasions to "settle the caring bill." Don't wait for special occasions to show appreciation and express love. Don't wait for company events to express gratitude through a well-crafted speech, or a performance review to say "well done" and, if you feel extra generous, "thank you!" Every day and every interaction is a special occasion. Do not overdo it either. Be present, mindful and genuine in all of your interactions, listen to understand, and you will find the right way to go about it. Make every day feel like a mini-Christmas for yourself and those around you.

I love the poem "Let Everyday Be Christmas" by the American design engineer Norman Wesley Brooks where he claims that Christmas is not just one day, but every day; the spirit of giving and unity that we feel on Christmas should last throughout the whole year as we always treat others with love and respect.[59] And remember, the message is not in the size of the gift, but in the intention behind it. Give someone a smile the next time you are waiting together by the coffee or copy machine. You never know who is silently fighting a battle you know nothing about. A smile is a great gift, says motivational writer William Arthur Ward: "A warm smile is the universal language of kindness."[60]

You have no control over the opening and impact of your gift. The different customs regarding unwrapping gifts have been puzzling me since forever. They are culture-sensitive, context-driven, based on personal preferences. Some of us open our presents right away. Others experience some sort of anxiety, going over thoughts like: "But what if I don't like it? What if it's embarrassing? What if I already have it?" When you add on the layer of a public opening, there is some level of "performance" required. We know people expect us to like the gift, so we're worried about what to do if something goes wrong.

Same with change management. Some people are comfortable expressing themselves openly and in public. They ask questions, challenge answers, are comfortable with having uncomfortable conversations. Others are not. For a number of reasons, they also feel compelled to "put on a mask" and pretend to enjoy "the gifts." Some read their emails right away and don't think twice before hitting the "reply" or "reply to all" button. Others, not really. If we assume positive intent behind our actions, we care in between special occasions and give people the space and safety to be themselves. Even if we "do not like the presents," we feel more open and safe to have a conversation about it. Nobody likes an elephant in the room; let's not make it a white elephant.

I know I kept advocating for the meaning of the gift over its size, and yet somehow this turned out to be the longest article so far… Wrapping it up now with a last bit of inspiration from Lao Tzu: "Kindness in words creates confidence. Kindness in thinking creates profoundness. Kindness in giving creates love."[61]

What Taking a Break Taught Me about Change Management

First published on January 5, 2021

While taking a walk sometime between Christmas and New Year's, I realized what I have been missing the most since last March: traveling, and more specifically, flying. Not so much for the airplane food and drinks (did you know that, with so many flights grounded because of the pandemic, surplus airplane meals and snacks have become available to buy??), but for the opportunity to take a break.

I never work while flying. It is with the greatest of joy that I turn my mobile off, and even leave it in my hand luggage or jacket in the overhead bin. Well, most of the time. If I see beautiful clouds, I take it out, turn it back on, set it on airplane mode, and take pictures. Looking out the window, reading and listening to music are the only things I ever do while flying. And it always feels like taking a break.

Working from home throughout 2020 made it a bit more difficult for me to get into the "break mode," mainly because there was no major change in my surroundings or routines. I still went to the office, meaning I sat in my favorite spot on the couch, and there were always Post-it notes around me. I ordered books as Christmas presents for myself. And because I made a promise, I was thinking about this article. As a result, below are my takeaways from a break that did not feel like that much of a break.

Stopping is just as challenging as starting. And it needs to be just as intentional. A *Harvard Business Review* article titled "How to Convince Your Boss You Need Time Off" highlights the challenge that many workers think they will make more progress in their career by not taking breaks. For various reasons—guilt, fear, etc.—they feel like they can't stop working if they want to show full dedication to their jobs. Remote work makes things even more difficult, as it can be harder for managers to see the amount of work their employees are doing. Therefore, these employees work even harder to impress and take even less breaks.[62]

Identifying and challenging assumptions and beliefs is core to change management. So do your own change management work. Purposefully. As the previously mentioned article says, we often don't realize that we harbor inner beliefs and misconceptions about using those vacation days. Once we actually identify and think about the reasons behind our aversion to taking time off, we can start to break free from this endless cycle.[63]

Write a new change story for yourself. One of my personal favorites is from Russell Eric Dobda, writer of *Spin the World Around: One Man's Mission for Intention and Unconditional Love*: "Taking a break can lead to breakthroughs."[64] I also learned the hard way, twice, that if you don't pick a day to relax, your body will pick it for you. And just like any change, build habits for stopping, just like you do when you start something. What is your equivalent for turning the phone off and storing it in the overhead bin? Use behavioral design for fun, for a change.

If "taking a break" is not specific enough, break it down into behaviors and build a new routine. Put *I'm Afraid Debbie from Marketing Has Left for the Day: How to Use Behavioral Design to Create Change in the Real World* by Morten Munster on your reading list for your next break.

It resets the baseline for "urgent" and "important." Oftentimes, with the hustle and bustle of everyday work, everything becomes "urgenter" and "importanter," and then under their own snowball effect, you blink and you've got "urgentest" and "importantest." Guilty, guilty, guilty of falling into the "productivity-at-all-costs mindset" as it is described by anthropologist James Suzman in his book *Work: A History of How We Spend our Time*. He explains that while work is so important to us now—influencing our value, identity, and social status—humanity's past proves that it wasn't always this way. Work was historically never the top priority in our lives. Suzman wonders how this "glorifying" of work has changed our culture and questions why, in a time when we have more "stuff" than ever, we're also working more than ever before.[65]

Taking a break allows for things to settle, get put into perspective, and gives you an opportunity to reassess "urgent" and "important." It gives you better visibility into where to best allocate your time, attention, and energy.

It teaches me patience and presence. It is especially difficult for me to refrain from sending emails during the Festive Season knowing that they will most probably not get answered with anything more than a cheery "out-of-office." As is normal. Patience is still loading into my system…

As a result of thinking about this article, I moved Celeste Hadlee's *Do Nothing: How to Break Away from Overworking, Overdoing, and Underliving* from my wishlist straight into the basket. Now I can't wait for it to be delivered! According to the short description on the author's website, *Do Nothing* strives to offer answers to questions like "Why do we measure our time in terms of efficiency instead of meaning?" and "Why can't we just take a break?" Spoiler alert: the answer is to accept and live out our "humanness," our thoughts, happiness, creativity, and capacity to love.[66] Some future articles might be in the making after reading this…

Thank you for taking a break to read this. As a start-into-the-New-Year gift, here's a bit of Anne Lamott wisdom: "Almost everything will work again if you unplug it for a few minutes, including you."[67]

What Preparing Lunch for a Friend Teaches Us about Change Management

With Allison Tanner
First published on January 12, 2021

"Lunch break" has changed dramatically over the past year with "going out with colleagues" or "meeting a friend" replaced with a "Zoom break." It has become a rarity and a luxury to dine with someone who is not your spouse/partner or young children over the lunch hour. So, in the age of nothing normal, I was ecstatic to be hosting lunch for a beloved friend and business collaborator earlier this week.

I believe that people and ideas come together over meals. There is a reason business dinners exist/existed, and the reason is that eating together is more than sharing a meal; it is an opportunity to connect at a deeper human level. As Greek philosopher Epicurus says so eloquently, "We should look for someone to eat and drink with before looking for something to eat and drink."[68] I would go so far as to say that eating together is one of the most human characteristics we possess.

As I eagerly organized the house in expectation of my guest, I began thinking of how preparing lunch teaches me about change management. Over lunch, the idea grew from a passing thought to a fascinating conversation with Minola.

Find a common meal. Taste buds vary from person to person and while I pride myself on being willing to eat anything once, not everyone eats all foods. Like super-taste items such as coriander/cilantro—an entire meal can be ruined for someone with just one wrong ingredient!

Just like you pay attention to check for potential food allergies or strong likes/dislikes when preparing lunch for a friend, you try to learn as much as possible about the boundaries of your change management work. Ask questions and listen to understand the appetite for change, and also to figure out how much room for customization there is. After all, you can always add cheese on top of your pasta on your own plate; some people like cheese, some are intolerant to it, some just happen to live for cheese.

For any human interaction, be it lunch with a friend or change management, ensuring a safe, comfortable, judgment-free environment is key to creating a meaningful experience. I was adding lettuce to the salad when I heard "I am really not that big on that, could we skip it?" I smiled, said, "Absolutely," and put the lettuce back into the bag. Strive to create an environment where people can speak up about their likes and dislikes, and accommodate their preferences as much as possible so as to ensure a meaningful common experience.

Be willing and able to make quick adjustments. Sometimes things come up; that is life. The bus was missed, the car needed fuel, or a last-minute meeting popped up. Keeping room in the schedule for adjustments will ensure you have adequate time to sit down and enjoy quality time together. Take a moment to ask yourself what is more important: the timetable or the outcome? And make adjustments accordingly.

Just because something is simple does not mean it isn't

the best. Do not get me wrong, I like fine dining as much as the next person, but not all meals can be extravagant. The goal is for the food to taste good and for the experience to be enjoyable. One of my favorite chefs and a dear friend of the late Anthony Bourdain, David Chang, has said that you don't have to reserve fine dining to eat well; a plain old greasy hamburger can be worthy of a Michelin star![69] Being able to make things look and feel simple, especially when they are not easy, is the kind of magic any change management endeavor needs.

Imperfect pairings can still make a perfect experience. It is such a great feeling when your friend asks "What should I bring?" when invited for lunch, and you know they are genuinely open to anything from wine, sweets, to just their self and sense of humor. And this opens up the possibility of not having the perfectly gastronomically paired wine or dessert with your simple, honest-to-God pesto pasta, but what is the most valuable here is their commitment to share the experience and contribute to it. Give people opportunities—and space!—to be part of the change experience, and most of them will be genuinely up for it.

As the "closing dessert" for this article, here are the words of Swedish-born American sculptor Claes Oldenburg, best known for his public art installations typically featuring large replicas of everyday objects, just as every day served as inspiration for this change management random thought: "I like food because you can change it. I mean, there is no such thing as a perfect lamb chop; you can make all types of lamb chops. And that's true of everything. And people eat it, and it changes and disappears."[70]

What Charging My Phone Teaches Me about Change Management

First published on January 19, 2021

There has been an increase in both the quantity and quality of the conversations about how navigating the pandemic has been impacting people's energy, motivation, and overall mental health and well-being. The effects of social distancing, lockdown, the loss of loved ones to the virus and the over-consumption of stress-inducing media reports are taking a huge toll on our mental health and well-being and will continue to have lasting effects long after lockdown is over. In addition, the inevitable recession that lies ahead will affect all of us.

All of this has been on my mind while preparing for an event on "Employee Experience and Engagement in 2021 and Beyond." And while reaching for my phone charger sometime this past weekend, the idea of writing this week's Tuesday Change Management Random Thought on what charging my phone teaches me about change management popped up. I went along with this self-challenge, and here below are my key takeaways.

Learn where you get your energy from and how you can best manage it. So many awesome *Harvard Business Review* articles have stayed with me over the years. One of my top three favorites to date goes back all the way to October 2007: "Manage Your Energy, Not Your Time" by Tony Schwartz and Catherine McCarthy. In a nutshell, it says that in response to rising demands at work, employees are working more and more hours. This, of course, results in burnout, which not only harms the employee, but the entire company. The answer isn't to make more time, but to keep track of our energy. According to the article, there are four aspects to energy: the energy itself (our physical bodies), plus its focus (our minds), purpose (our spirits), and quality (our emotions).[71]

This perspective can be applied to any change management endeavor. What is the physical energy of the organization and its people; what is their appetite for change? What is the quality of this energy—what emotions are people experiencing while going through the rollercoaster of an organizational change, and even as they go about "evolution as usual" (replacing "business as usual")? According to research included in the article, we physically cannot experience strong positive emotions indefinitely without frequent recovery periods. When we face roadblock after roadblock, our brains enter that "fight or flight" mode and default to negative emotions.[72]

How often do we ask people how they feel in addition to what they think about a project, an activity, a task? In addition to storytelling, a powerful ritual that fuels positive emotions—both in us and others—is expressing appreciation. It can be something as simple as a conversation, email, or heartfelt note, but the more specific you are in your appreciation, the greater impact it has.

The article goes on to say that multitasking turned out to

be not so great at supporting productivity. Incessant switching between tasks and allowing constant interruptions in the flow of our work negatively impact our focus. People struggle to concentrate, and distractions are costly.[73] How is the focus of your change initiative impacted by strategic reprioritization? Or constant people and resources reallocation across projects?

Finally, there's the energy of the human spirit. It is mind- and heart-warming to hear conversations about belonging and purpose being created above and beyond the definition and printing of company values, mission and vision. When a person's work aligns with what they personally value, when they feel like their work is meaningful, they naturally feel more positive and perform better.[74] So what is your organization's "why?" How does it touch on and build on the energy of people's individual "why's?"

Pay attention to what drains your energy. A lot of things can cause a phone battery to drain quickly. After spending some time on websites dedicated to mobile device performance, I realized that, while some of those things are totally out of my control, there are a lot of ways to better manage the battery on my phone. According to feedback gathered and streamlined from service centers, there are five main culprits for draining a phone battery. First one up there is cold weather—both charging the battery in the cold and using the phone in low-temperature environments. So how is the "weather" within your organization? Does the "sun shine" on the project team, or is there a "snow alert" in the forecast?

Second culprit: screen size and brightness. What are the "visibility" and "exposure" of your change initiative? How can you turn on the "auto-brightness" option to make sure it adapts to ambient lighting conditions automatically? And can you better manage notifications settings so that the display is not turned on constantly to drain the battery?

Poor cell phone coverage coming in at number three. We could add poor Wi-Fi to this too, but poor coverage has a far greater impact on battery life because the phone is constantly hunting for a better signal. How easy is the access to senior leadership? How "stable" is the connection to the project sponsor? What is his/her "coverage" across the organization? How "stable" is your stakeholders' management?

Moving on to apps next: rogue apps, as well as increasing number of used apps at any given time. In close connection to this, here comes number five: lots of notifications coming in on the lock screen, causing the display to switch on constantly. All the change managers out there, does this sound familiar?

Once you identify the things that drain your energy, it's up to you to change the way you approach them; no one else can do it for you!

"The phone takes only the current it can handle." As explained on www.consumerreports.org, when you plug a fast-charging phone into a normal phone charger, it won't charge as quickly. But as long as you use the cable you got with your phone, it should be safe to plug it into any USB phone charger. All technical tests prove the same thing over and over again: a fast charger will not charge a non-fast-charging phone quickly. For rapid charging to work, the phone and charger must both be able to quick charge. Also, while you can use the same charger for multiple devices, you probably shouldn't. Not unless you want to ruin your gear or wait a lifetime for it to recharge. Sounds like multitasking in the phone world, right? You can use accelerators during change work, yet keep in mind while managing expectations—your stakeholders', as well as your own—that "the phone takes only the current it can handle."[75]

Before "pulling the plug" on this week's piece, here is a summary of the *Harvard Business Review* article's conclusion, still very much valid and relevant today: There is a silent agreement between all employers and their employees that the only goal of the relationship is to take as much as possible from each other before quickly moving on. The authors state that this mindset is "self-defeating," as employer and employee both end up gaining little but burnt-out frustration. In other words, the relationship becomes mutually destructive rather than mutually edifying. Employees are left feeling empty and exhausted, while employers waste resources constantly hiring and training unenthusiastic employees to replace the ones that are leaving. But what if we all settled on a new agreement? Instead of draining each other dry, this new contract would have employer and employee working together to build each other up. Employers would support their employees in all aspects of their lives to nourish growth and stability while employees would happily bring their complete energy to work each day. In the end, both parties grow and increase in value.[76]

What Traveling by Train Teaches Me about Change Management

First published on January 26, 2021

Trains have always fascinated me. One of the reasons I always looked forward to school vacations was that there would always be some traveling by train involved. Until I left my hometown of Oradea in the northwest of Romania, I lived on Locomotive Street, three minutes away from the train station, and the sounds of trains were part of my childhood everyday music. While growing up, I had an uncle who was hearing and speaking impaired, and sometimes we used to go to the train station in my hometown and watch the trains come and go. The horns and whistles of the locomotives were the only sounds he could still faintly perceive, and that made me look at trains as something nothing short of magic.

Whenever rail is an option for my travels, I take it without hesitation. There is something about that "clickety-clack" sound that is deeply calming and comforting. Taking the Trans-Siberian is way up there on my bucket list, and traveling by train from Rome to Palermo is one of the first things I am going to do when lockdowns and restrictions are over.

While passing by the train station a few days ago, I started wondering whether there were any teachings for change management in traveling by train. With all these changes unfolding around us, I was thinking about our "destination," and also about the train "engineers." There is a beautiful quote by Dutch watchmaker and writer Corrie ten Boom: "When a train goes through a tunnel and it gets dark, you don't throw away the ticket and jump off. You sit still and trust the engineer."[77]

How you mark progress makes a big difference. One of the first things that made me fall in love with physics was when I understood reference points and how choosing them changed your perspective. I often think about that when I travel by train and pay attention to whether I think about the journey relative to where I am from the departure or the arrival point. The stations along the way are my "moments of change," moments of awareness and realization as to how far I have come, how close I am to arriving. I often try to pinpoint the moment when I start to think that I am closer to the destination than the start of the journey. The amount of time a train spends at certain stations catches my attention, too. And it makes me think about how we mark and celebrate progress. Recognizing success stories and lessons learned is critical for change management, and it goes well with this saying I picked up a short while ago: "Don't let the train of enthusiasm run through the station so fast that people can't get on board."[78]

Feeling stuck or feeling lost? Having "sampled" both situations of missing a train and taking it in the wrong direction made me think about which one is the "easiest" to fix. And the answer is a very typical "consulting" one: it depends. If I miss the train in a place I am familiar with, or where I speak the local language at least, I only perceive the pressure of time. If I take the train in the wrong direction somewhere I have never been before and I get "loster" by the mile, that makes it a bit more complicated than just being late. Lutheran pastor and anti-Nazi dissident Dietrich Bonhoeffer said it best: "If you board the wrong train, it is no use running along the corridor in the other direction."[79] It also depends on whether I travel for business or pleasure, and on how many other people are impacted in any way by my being late and/or lost.

These are thoughts also related to change management work, and my preferred instance when they arise is during conversations regarding communications. Some people are hesitant about communicating something very early on when things are yet not fully clear and information might change dramatically. Others are preoccupied with the speed and efficiency of the "rumor mill." "When is the best time to start communicating?" and "What and how are we communicating?" are popular questions among "change engineers."

Every time these conversations happen, I think about traveling by train. If you sleep at the station, you might miss the train, and if you sleep on the train, you might miss the station. So which one is easier to fix: feeling stuck or feeling lost? The answer depends on the organization, overall context, nature of the project, composition of the team… It depends.

Luggage matters. Without the comfort of checked-in luggage for flights, the experience of traveling by train can be significantly impacted by the amount of luggage you bring along. I find it a tiny bit more challenging when there are train changes happening along the journey. Dragging luggage is not my favorite thing to do, and in order to avoid it as much as possible I often find myself in situations when I need to "supplement resources" along the way, revisit my wants and needs, or simply improvise. Sometimes even compromise. I am sure any random group of change managers needs a very looooooooooong train ride to have the opportunity to discuss "project luggage" experiences.

I will hop off this week's train of thought leaving you with the words of Charles Dickens: "I am never sure of time or place upon a Railroad. I can't read, I can't think, I can't sleep—I can only dream. Rattling along in this railway carriage in a state of luxurious confusion, I take it for granted I am coming from somewhere, and going somewhere else… I know nothing about myself—for anything I know, I may be coming from the Moon."[80]

Bon Change Voyage!

What Washing Dishes Teaches Me about Change Management

First published on February 2, 2021

One morning last week, making coffee didn't feel that good. On top of reaching for the decaf (even typing the word hurts!!), I had to start the day by washing my favorite mug. I usually do it right after using it, but the day before was a total blur of emergencies, so I broke the "no dishes in the sink at the end of the day" rule. My best friend loves washing the dishes; she says it calms her. What great living proof of "opposites attract," and supporting "case study" for all the research advocating for best friends being polar opposites!

Speaking of research, I recently found an article about a study conducted in 2015 at Florida State University proving that people who washed dishes mindfully (they focused on smelling the soap, feeling the water temperature and touching the dishes) upped their feelings of inspiration by 25% and lowered their nervousness levels by 27%.[81]

While realizing I have been going through my "lime-scented dishwashing detergent" phase for a few months now, I also started to think about whether there were any takeaways for Change Management in this "mundane task with potential for mindfulness" activity. It was fun giving it a go!

Success is a series of small wins. There was a post in my social media feed a while ago that made me laugh, saying that "you know you are an adult when you get excited about a new sponge at the kitchen sink."[82] This is so true, and it makes me think about the importance of small changes, small differences, small wins. And about the fact that there is still hope for responsible adulthood for me!

Meaningful change doesn't always happen with a Big Bang, or through a large-scale project. There's a famous quote by Harvard University professor Rosabeth Moss Kanter that reminds me it's oftentimes the smallest things that make the biggest differences.[83] Speaking of sponges, a Forbes Daily Quote signed by Cecil Baxter raises a meaningful point: "You don't get anything clean without getting something else dirty."[84] An extraordinarily good insight to identify and follow dependencies and rippling effects in any and all change management work. Displacing the problem by moving it away from your intervention is not solving it. And it sure doesn't count as a win, not even a small one.

How you present information is just as important as the information itself. Many years ago, I very seriously entertained the big idea of opening a small bistro. Part of my daydreaming was researching the importance of food presentation as it became more and more apparent with the rise of social media and its impact on the perception of the restaurant itself. Of particular relevance for change management is how food presentation is not just an art form, but also made up of science to make your dish and the perception of it more tasty and delicious.

Not only is a spotless clean plate is mission-critical for the overall dining experience, but shape, size and color also play a major role. Round plates are suitable for hearty foods, while angular shapes give the food a sleek, modern vibe. Using a plate that is too large will make the quantity of your food feel scarce and not enough, whereas a small plate will make the food look cluttered and messy. Different colors send different messages to the psychology of your customers, and they are also highly culturally sensitive. Red plates are a difficult choice, as they can trigger subconscious reactions related to interdiction. Historically in Chinese tradition, red plates were only served to the most prominent guests. Blue activates diet and a controlled eating sense in human psychology. You can never go wrong with white plates as they accentuate the variety of color in your dish and elevate it. A study carried out at Cornell University showed that people who used plates with colors that highly contrasted the color of their food (for example, red pasta on a white plate) served themselves 22% more. Those whose plates were low contrast (red pasta on a red plate) tended to take less.

All these elements have their equivalent in change management work. What is the "shape" of your interactions and communication items? Are they whole and round, or do they feel more angular? If you could describe your communication with a color, would it feel red, blue, constructively contrasting white? How about cleanliness? Always, always, always check for spelling, especially for names. It sounds so common sense, yet the tragedy with common sense is that it is not always common. How do you harness the power of storytelling in your interactions?

Here's a bit of "food for thought": different kinds of ingredients belong in different spots on a plate. You can follow the clock method in presenting where main ingredients such as chicken or ribs are placed between 3:00 and 9:00 on the imagined clock, starchy carbohydrates like fries and potatoes between 9:00 and 12:00 and vegetables between 12:00 and 3:00. There is a trick where you can put food such as shrimps or scallops in odd numbers to create an illusion of extra quantity while making it easier to plate at the same time. Be intentional in your "information plating," and the whole experience is elevated.

Clean as you go. Within the HORECA industry, a "clean as you go" policy is a cleaning strategy used to minimize risks to hygiene, health, and safety. The "clean as you go" method involves taking opportunities to clean continually throughout the working day and making cleaning part of your daily routine to ensure that surfaces, equipment, waste, and the premises are clean, hygienic, and clutter-free. There are two types of cleaning under the "clean as you go" method: urgent and non-urgent. Urgent cleaning is anything that may pose an immediate risk to health, hygiene, or safety, whereas non-urgent cleaning is a part of your daily processes. Formalizing a "clean as you go" policy is part of any role in retail, hospitality or catering, and it leads to a consistent attitude to cleaning. It also helps less experienced staff members feel confident taking the initiative to clean during downtime and know that doing so is part of the role.

We can all relate to the "clean as you go" policy—tying up loose ends, follow-up on emails and meeting memos, sometimes filling and archiving info. Checking, correcting, updating and upgrading info. It is not the most glamorous part of change management, but it is critical. Pay attention to whether your "sponge" is still suitably clean, and if you are dragging "health hazards" such as change fatigue, unchecked and/or outdated information, wrong assumptions, sometimes even personal biases, from one phase of the project into another. Do you dread washing pots and pans? This comes in the form of a joke, but it is totally relatable: When washing dishes, 98% of people think: "Gosh, there's also a pan to wash!!!" Well, yeah, it might not be all fun, but it needs to be done. Get a new sponge, add extra dishwashing detergent, and make it spotless.

While washing dishes will not become my favorite mindful stress relief activity during this lifetime, there is a key takeaway for change management in it, in the form of this quote from American illustrator Maira Kalman: "Washing dishes is the anecdote to confusion. I know that for a fact."[85]

What Wearing a Mask Teaches Me about Change Management

First published on February 9, 2021

It was just a matter of time until wearing a mask made me curious to explore any takeaways for change management. In all honesty, I am quite surprised I did not pick up on it sooner. Every time I leave the house, I go through the usual mental checklist: wallet, keys, and the "pandemic upgrades" of mask, hand sanitizer, and a tissue or paper towel to defog my glasses. Oh, the joy! The only time when fogged glasses were funny was in this post that popped up in my social media feed: "If you have to wear glasses and a mask, you may be entitled to condensation."[86]

After getting a brand-new box of lens-cleaning wipes, I see clearly enough to be able to type this week's list of takeaways. Here they are.

"The chief virtue that language can have is clarity."[87] I can't think of a better context to use this quote from the "father of medicine" Hippocrates. With the mask muffling and distorting words, I realized the need to go for simple, straightforward, "fluff-free" communication. I also have more difficulty understanding what other people are telling me. Very often, messages need to be repeated. What strikes me most is how much "communication value" is lost when we cannot use a smile to ease and enhance the conversation. How slightly less touching a "thank you" feels like without seeing the smile that (often) goes with it.

This is all such a great reminder about how important it is to keep communication clear, especially when the context and conditions make it difficult. To ask for clarification until we are sure we understood what was said, and to make sure what we said got through. To have patience if we are asked to repeat ourselves more than once. And we can always smile under the mask; the genuine, heartfelt smile will travel all the way up into our eyes, and it might just make somebody's day a little bit better.

Frustration can be turned into a foundation for creativity and the birthplace of new insights. This is my favorite takeaway from wearing a mask: the importance of reframing the relationship with frustration if we seek to spark creativity. There is so much frustration associated with this regulation: fogged glasses, skin irritation, lipstick and lip balm smudges, all sorts of ear discomforts from the elastic cord, difficulty breathing, to name just a few. Little by little, people turned masks into fashion accessories, or advertising space for awareness messages like "wearing is caring" and "I don't know how to explain to you that you should care about other people." Even plain advertising space for products and services.

Compliance-driven projects are definitely not glamorous. They also come with additional layers of frustration and are generally "drier" than other change management interventions. Yet, with a reframed relationship with frustration, they can be used for great insights. While driving compliance, a lot of improvement opportunities can surface. You can use compliance projects creatively to drive organization-wide communications. Understand what the compliance boundaries are, what is regulated and what is not, and get creative. Frustration is a part of the process, and that's not necessarily a bad thing.

"Behind every mask, there is a face, and behind that a story."[88] When author and journalist Marty Rubin made this statement, he could not possibly have seen the pandemic coming, yet his words are quite appropriate from across the years. Wearing a mask throughout these months is a timely reminder of how everyone is fighting a battle we know nothing about, and kindness is the greatest gift to ourselves and those around us. It's a good opportunity to ask ourselves what "mask" are we wearing, that could "fog our glasses" with assumptions, blind spots, or "muffle" our words? Amit Abraham, the Indian author and psychologist who served as Deputy Vice Chancellor at the Mount Zion International University of Rwanda, said that wearing a mask is nothing new; everyone wears masks all the time, but it becomes obligatory when our lives are in danger.[89]

Wearing is caring. You don't need a full-on stakeholder analysis and mapping exercise to understand who your stakeholders are in this project of getting through the pandemic. It is about everyone. And this is how you show you care. Whenever you need to reframe your frustration, here's a good kick-start courtesy of Marty Rubin: "The desire to change things must begin with accepting things as they are."[90]

Take care, stay safe, and happy wearing!

What Dealing with Writer's Block Teaches Me about Change Management

First published on February 16, 2021

Writer's block popped up unexpectedly in two totally separate conversations over the last week. It is not the most common of topics, so it stood out to me. While walking over the weekend, I came up with the idea of challenging myself to write this week's article about how dealing with writer's block teaches me about change management.

The first thought that came into my mind was: "How ironic it would be if I got it while trying to write about it?!" Not the most inspiring of thoughts, but I do love a good challenge. Especially writing-related. So, here it goes…

Don't fight it. Understand it. There are loads and loads of opinions out there on writer's block and whether it is a condition or just an excuse. According to research, it is indeed a serious condition primarily associated with writing but also manifested across many other creative endeavors. It stands for when an author is unable to produce new work or experiences a creative slowdown. A writer may simply run out of inspiration or get distracted by other events. Oftentimes, a block is caused by adverse circumstances in an author's life or career: physical illness, the loss of a loved one, financial pressures, etc. The pressure to produce work may in itself contribute to writer's block, especially if they are compelled to work in ways that are against their natural inclination—for example, with a deadline or an unsuitable style or genre. A sense of failure or fear of what other people might think of the work produced are often cited as key sources of writer's block.

Each and every one of these potential causes for writer's block manifests itself through equivalents in any and all organizational change projects. Competing events, shifting priorities, a stifling history filled with rules, restrictions, and even failures, fear of judgment, disengagement, lack of motivation, disappointment. To me, writer's block speaks of a symptom, giving me the opportunity to go on a mindful (self) journey for the deeper cause. The more I fight it, the less I understand it. British philosopher Alain de Botton said, "'Writer's block' is an emotional or logical incoherence in a future work slowly working its way through our unconscious."[91] It sounds like change as it unfolds around us.

You need to show up. Every. Single. Day. There is no way around it. You must show up every day, good day or bad day, and do the work. With no judgment. I found some great advice on a writing website that is sadly no longer around: "Start writing whatever comes to mind, free from any judgment. Tell your inner critic to hush. . . . Basically, shake up the dust in your head like a snow globe. Eventually the particles will settle back down, but everything will have shifted, rearranged itself. Finally, those trapped words will start spilling out."[92] Start writing whatever comes into your mind. Just lay words one after another. Be intentionally inclusive with your thoughts and surprisingly awesome things might come out of it. American screenwriter John

Rogers said it best: "You can't think yourself out of a writing block; you have to write yourself out of a thinking block."[93] If we only replace "writing" with "change" in this statement, it rings so true for any transformation journey!

The big secret is "don't break the chain," as explained by comedian Jerry Seinfeld in his (very serious) productivity hack. When Jerry Seinfeld was an up-and-coming comedian, he made a commitment to write one joke a day. Not an entire routine or monologue. Just one funny line. He had a big calendar of the whole year on a wall in his apartment. Every time he wrote a joke, he put a red X on that date. Before long he had a growing chain of red X's on the calendar—a visual reminder of the consistent work he put in.[94]

Do something related to your craft every day, no matter how small. Do something related to change every day, no matter how small. Do not break the chain! "Discipline allows magic," urban fantasy author Lilith Saintcrow says, explaining further: "To be a writer is to be the very best of assassins. You do not sit down and write every day to force the Muse to show up. You get into the habit of writing every day so that when she shows up, you have the maximum chance of catching her, bashing her on the head, and squeezing every last drop out of that bitch."[95]

Ask for help. There are a lot of proven strategies for coping with writer's block: class and group discussion, journals, systematic questioning, free writing, brainstorming and encouragement, to name just a few. The range of solutions also includes altering the time of day to write, setting deadlines, lowering expectations, and using mindfulness meditation. It's also important to evaluate the environment in which the writing is being produced.

Psychologists who have studied writer's block have concluded that it is a treatable condition once the writer finds a way to remove anxiety and build confidence in themselves. One of the best ways to do this is to engage with fellow writers. Reach out to people, share your journey—your complete, whole journey, with the good, bad and ugly, and listen to their own struggles and victories. Ask people questions to understand their own creative processes and find out what worked for them when they got stuck.

One of the best, most meaningful outcomes of the pandemic is people's increased willingness to open up, to share their experience and knowledge and offer support and encouragement. Over the last year, I have connected and talked with more people, including professionals within the change management field, than in the previous five years combined. I heard "I need help" more often than ever. I heard myself say "I need help" more often than ever. Ask for help—people are willing, able and happy to give it. And you will have your chance to pay it forward.

My closing thought for this week comes from one of my all-time favorites: Ernest Hemingway. Even as an incredible writer, he still struggled with writer's block and was honest about how it hindered his writing process. His solution to simply write something true proves that writer's block is an opportunity to go back into ourselves and look for our own truth.[96] A journey of vulnerability and authenticity, full honesty, no judgment, looking for our truth and our voice. And our words will follow.

What Improv Teaches Us about Change Management

With Alan Slavik
First published on February 23, 2021

I was first introduced to live improv and sketch comedy in my early twenties at a wonderful theatre in Minneapolis called Brave New Workshop. I was amazed (and entertained, I might add) by the ability of the performers to adapt to any situation that was thrown at them and create something magical, all in real-time. Whether it be random suggestions from the audience or a playful suggestion from another member of the ensemble, the performers took everything in stride and were able to create wonderful scenes seemingly out of thin air. It truly was magical.

My love and appreciation for improv grew stronger when I lived in Chicago and frequently attended performances at The Second City, the world's premier comedy club, theater and school of improvisation.

Years later, as I was exploring ways to improve my stage presence and agility as a public speaker, someone recommended I attend an improv workshop. Little did I know that this short workshop in Paris with a group called the Improfessionals would have such a profound impact on my life, both personally and professionally.

For over ten years I've been practicing and applying many of the teachings and techniques of improv in my daily life. In partnership with Minola (which has been a great example of "Yes, And"—see below) we've listed below just some examples of how improv can be applied to change management.

Yes, And. This is the simplest and probably the most powerful concept I've learned from improv training. At its core, "Yes, And" is about being deliberately and consciously open to new ideas and opportunities and making an effort to *not* shut down ideas and contributions from others. This means replacing the words "no, but" in all forms with "yes, and" on all occasions with no exceptions. Building on other people's ideas to ignite and keep conversations going is key for change management. Acknowledging and recognizing their contributions, while supporting their involvement, is what enables anyone doing change management work to harness people's energy for meaningful transformation. It is as much about being open-minded as it is about staying open-hearted, curious, mindful and intentionally inclusive.

Side-note: Yes, And is so central to improv that it's the title of Kelly Leonard & Tom Yorton's wonderful book about improv. It's a great read for those interested in knowing more about the benefits of improv.

Make others look good. In an ensemble or team, if you focus on making others look good, magical things can happen. It also takes the pressure off when you consider your primary role to be making others look good. This is even more powerful when you see and feel that others take this approach while collaborating with you. This principle is also beautifully illustrated by

Benjamin Zander, an English conductor, currently the musical director of the Boston Philharmonic Orchestra and the Boston Philharmonic Youth Orchestra. In his "Shining Eyes" address to head teachers during the 2011 conference organized by the National College of School Leadership, he speaks about his "eureka" moment of realizing a conductor's mission. The conductor doesn't make music themselves; instead, their power comes from being able to make others powerful.[97] Making others look good, empowering those around you to grow into their own space and "make their own sound" in a way that gives out "music" happens at the intersection of the science and art of change management.

Failing fast. Not everything works in life and in work. Failure is a part of the process. Expect it, embrace it and even enjoy it. Just do it quickly and move on to the next thing. This attitude and philosophy can be both liberating and extremely productive. A great way to think about change management is like it's a dolphin, not a whale. Dolphins are agile, curious, playful and quite chatty creatures—they would make for great improv artists and change managers. They jump out of water, enjoy the waves, take unexpected swift turns, and they look like they enjoy it tremendously.

Plan for and embrace the unexpected with open arms. We cannot plan for every eventuality in life. And if we spend too much energy doing so, the result will not only be disappointment, but utter exhaustion. The alternative is to be prepared for the unexpected and roll with it. American playwright and actress Tina Fey has a saying about improv that could be inserted into change management workshops just as well: improv basically happens by accident![98] Just as under-planning is an issue, over-planning can turn out just as potentially damaging. The "management" bit of "change management" should not be used to stifle people's creativity, their natural ability to react in the moment, their space for failing fast. Do we have a change management strategy and plan? Yes, And…

Creating something out of nothing. Every day, managers and teams must create something out of nothing. We're often thrown into new teams, situations, meetings or projects where we must take on the unknown and produce something of value. Understanding this idea alone opens us up to many possibilities. Oftentimes, lack of clarity feels like "nothing." Too many possibilities might feel to some like "nothing," inducing analysis paralysis. Change management works its magic when it is harnessed to take "nothing" and turn it into an understandable, actionable, communicable "something." It doesn't need to generate clarity all the way. As 13th-century Persian poet Rumi's wisdom goes, "As you start to walk on the way, the way appears."[99]

No change manager starts out with "nothing"—there are expectations, aspirations, knowledge, experience, expertise and a genuine will to contribute available all around any organization, within any given team. Start out by listening, move forward with "Yes, And," don't be afraid to fail fast, embrace the unexpected, and "nothing" is turned into common understanding and potential.

While doing some research on improv for this article, a Pinterest post popped up with a quote from Del Close, an American comedian and teacher, and this will definitely be one of the key takeaways of future change management workshops: "Don't bring a cathedral into a scene. Bring a brick. Let's build together."[100]

Don't take things too seriously. This speaks for itself. It's always easier said than done. Perhaps Amy Poehler, American comedian and co-founder of the improvisational-comedy troupe Upright Citizens Brigade, said it best: "No one looks stupid when they're having fun."[101] There's also Benjamin Zander's famous "Rule no. 6", described in detail in his *The Art of Possibility* book.[102] Yes, And... what are the other rules, you might ask? There aren't any! Humor is very serious business. The capacity to express or perceive what's funny is both a source of entertainment and a means of coping with difficult or awkward situations and stressful events. It plays an instrumental role in building social bonds and releasing tension. What you laugh at and when you turn to humor teaches you a lot about yourself. How people react teaches you a lot about them. Some who have sought to explain humor point to the fact that many jokes or funny events contradict one's sense of how things are supposed to be. Other theories of what makes things funny focus on the role of tension-relief, suddenly "getting" how incongruous details fit together. Humor is quite possibly one of the best change management tools, and it should be seriously put into action.

Typing the word "improve" brought on the realization that it requires typing "improv." We are always improvising. Improv, in essence, is a beautiful part of who we are as humans. It's a part of our improvement process, literally and figuratively. **You cannot spell "improve" without "improv."**

If we can all understand, embrace and apply the spirit of improv to our everyday lives, the results can be spectacular. If nothing else, the process will certainly be more enjoyable, rewarding and even entertaining.

What Watching the Sky Teaches Me about Change Management

First published on March 2, 2021

A couple of years ago, after a deep and heavy conversation with one of my closest friends, we started the habit of sending each other photos of the sky. It is very rare now that a day goes by without the two of us exchanging sky photos, oftentimes without any other words. It is our reminder that as long as we can take a few seconds and look up, we are alive and, therefore, we have everything we need to be happy. Ironically, watching the sky became one of my most grounding rituals.

The habit spread around us, some people knowing the story behind it, some not. Regardless, everyone gets hooked on watching the sky and sending photos. Fun fact: I had to buy extra space "in the cloud" for my photos, consisting mainly of the sky...

While out for a walk last week, I looked up and enjoyed one of the clearest, bluest skies ever. And one question popped up in my head: what is watching the sky teaching me about change management? I had to give it a try...

Blink, and it's changed. There is constant change up there, on some days more visible than on others. Just like in life and in the life of any organization. When you do change management work, you are in the middle of it, and hopefully you even get the feeling of driving it every now and again. For most of the people inside the organization, change must be like watching the sky—they look up from their daily tasks, and while they blink, everything has changed again. And again. When the wind moves the clouds around, we do not "see" the wind. We can only feel it and see its effect.

People must have the same experience while going through change. Most of them do not "see" it, but they feel it and see its effect. It is important for anyone doing Change Management to give out "weather forecasts and alerts" so people understand what weather they are most likely to experience. The concept of the leader bringing the weather is explained in *Scaling Leadership: Building Organizational Capability and Capacity to Create Outcomes that Matter Most* by authors Robert J. Anderson and William A. Adams. When a leader walks into the workplace, research proves one of two things will happen: either the mood and performance of the team and individuals will be boosted, or the mood and performance of the team and individuals will be lowered. The organizational culture is the climate.[103] Which one is yours? Tropical? Dry? Polar? Temperate? Is it prone to sudden, drastic weather changes? Does it feel like wonderful Malta, with an average of 300 sunny days a year and only seven snowfalls registered since 1858?

There is no single truth, but an infinite number of true perspectives. We look up at the same sky, yet we see different things. In some parts of the world, the sky is cloudier or clearer. Or maybe there is fog. Under my sky, it was winter, while under the same sky, people enjoyed summer Down Under. This is a key lesson for change management: meet people "under their sky" to be able to see what they see. And how it all changes when you are on a plane! The first time I flew, it was a cloudy day, and when we were above the clouds, to me it looked like we were flying over a giant bowl of whipped cream. I can't wait to get my fix of "sky dessert" soon... I will savor it while remembering this amazing quote from Konrad Adenaeur, the first Chancellor of the Federal Republic of Germany: "We all live under the same sky, but we don't all have the same horizon."[104]

Direction is a choice. Some ancient Buddha wisdom is needed at this point: "In the sky, there is no distinction of east and west; people create distinctions out of their own minds and then believe them to be true."[105] When the "organizational true north" is set in a "high-level strategy document," make sure everybody can adjust their compasses accordingly. Make that choice and communicate it, set direction and give out maps. And also keep in mind that people are prone to binary thinking. It is not so much about good or bad, as it is about "being aligned." "Develop a mind that is vast like space, where experiences both pleasant and unpleasant can appear and disappear without conflict, struggle or harm. Rest in a mind like vast sky," adds Buddha.[106]

Change of focus clears the vision. In our busy lives, we rarely look up to observe the wonders in the sky above. According to research, this is mainly due to two reasons: we don't have access to clear night skies, and we are too busy looking at our computers and smart devices. Guilty as charged! Though we don't always think about it, our eyes need breaks from all that staring, scrolling, reading, and just plain seeing they do. And not just while we're asleep. Anything that asks a lot of our eyes can lead to eye strain. Think: long stretches of reading, driving, or bright lights.

These days, the most likely culprit is screen time—eyeballs glued to mobile phones, tablets, laptops. Eyes that need to twinkle with infinite curiosity and interest during back-to-back Zoom calls… In fact, the American Optometric Association created a special category for this flavor of visual exhaustion: digital eye strain (DES). The number one quick fix for eye strain is to reset your vision. One lesser-known way to reboot our eyes is to look off into the distance. Resetting our eyes from close-up to far-off gives them a rest and helps reset our focus. Experts recommend the 20-20-20 rule: every 20 minutes spent at a computer or device, turn your eyes toward something 20 feet away, for 20 seconds. Those mini-breaks are great, but your eyes need more time off. A few times a day, get up, take a walk, stretch, and do some deep breathing exercises. Why not look at the sky while you're at it? Like every muscle, our eyes need regular rest. You are not wasting time. You take time to clear your vision.

Look up at the sky as often as you can and enjoy what you see, no matter what that might be in that moment. Remember: you blink, and it's changed. Just breathe, enjoy the wind on your face, or the sun, and know you are the best part of something bigger. Take the wise, comforting advice of A. P. J. Abdul Kalam, the Indian aerospace scientist and politician who served as the 11th President of India from 2002 to 2007: "Look at the sky. We are not alone. The whole universe is friendly to us and conspires only to give the best to those who dream and work."[107]

Work. Take a break. Watch the sky. Dream. Be happy!

What Tying My Shoelaces Teaches Me about Change Management

First published on March 9, 2021

When the heart-warming story behind Nike's first hands-free shoes hit my social media news feed in mid-February, it touched me deeply. According to an article published on ndtv.com, dated February 2, 2021, Matthew Walzer, a 16-year-old with cerebral palsy, contacted Nike in 2012, telling them that it was his dream to go to college without worrying about someone having to tie his shoelaces day in and day out. Matthew was born two months premature with underdeveloped lungs that led to cerebral palsy, according to Nike. While he overcame many physical obstacles, tying his own shoelaces remained a challenge and his parents had to do it for him. As a teenager, this kind of dependence soon became both frustrating and embarrassing. Matthew's letter inspired Nike designer Tobie Hatfield to create a shoe that would address his specific need. This journey led to the development of Nike FlyEase, a range of no-lace footwear launched in 2015 that culminated with Nike Go FlyEase, its most innovative design to date.[108]

This story made me think about what tying my own shoelaces means to me. An everyday taken-for-granted activity that can make such a difference in someone's life. On a lighter note—yet not so much, according to my knees and lower back—tying my shoelaces is something I perceive differently as I move forward in life. Pretty much like reading Jane Austen novels… "Knot funny," yet it looks like I am not alone in this realization. "You know you're getting old when you stoop to tie your shoelaces and wonder what else you could do while you're down there," as American comedian George Burns put it quite rightly. While tying my shoelaces over the last few days, I started to think about any teachings for change management, and here they are below.

Always honor your legacy. My grandmother taught me to tie my shoelaces. Most of my friends also learned to do this from senior members of their family—grandparents, older aunts, uncles. It seems like something that is passed on through generations. It feels like a legacy. It took the Nike story for me to look at tying my shoelaces as an act of independence, continuously honoring one of the sweetest legacies in my life.

And this is the key takeaway for change management. Through one of the most life-changing conversations of last year, I realized that a change manager navigates a fluid journey between being an innovation manager and a stability manager. The new doesn't discard the old. The new should honor the old.

It always looks more complicated to the people watching you do it. As the designated "crazy aunt" to most of my best friends' children, I was in the situation to teach some awesome kids how to tie their shoelaces. So much potential for stakeholder engagement, communication and training delivery exercise right here!!! There seemed to be a breakthrough when I took them in my lap and we practiced together while looking at our hands under similar angles.

It is the same with change management work—it often looks more complicated to the people watching you do it. Don't just stand in front of people and watch, show them or talk with them. Welcome people by your side, even behind you, and let them watch you work. Then you go and stand beside them, behind them, watch and learn. Welcome their questions. Acknowledge their effort. Respect and encourage their curiosity. Next time you tie your shoelaces, think about what it teaches you about communication. Here's a hint from Donald Arthur Norman, an American researcher, professor, and author of *The Design of Everyday Things*: it's almost impossible to describe how to tie shoelaces with words alone![109]

They always seem to come undone at the worst possible time. When you carry two or three bags of groceries and your hands are just otherwise unavailable. When it rains or when it is muddy. Whenever it is most inconvenient, at the worst possible time. Every. Single. Time. There is such a thing called "the shoelace factor," a close cousin to the concept of Murphy's law. The "shoelace factor" is the concept that anything you really need, especially small things like shoelaces, will break at the most inopportune moment. It relates to small errors occurring when you most depend on something to work.

Remember this factor when you plan and carry out change management work. It is not a matter of if, but a matter of what and when. Prepare for it and check the fabric of the shoelaces; if they are silky, they will come undone sooner. Maybe go for a double-knot. Or go for flip-flops or Crocs boots if you want to eliminate the risk altogether.

Believe it or not, there is research carried out on the roles of impact and inertia in the failure of a shoelace knot. According to an article published on The Royal Society Publishing website, the single act of shoelaces coming undone happens in seconds, but only after a long time of buildup. The simple impact of the shoe hitting the floor with each step makes the knot looser, as does the inertia of the swinging ends of the laces. Multiple details, including the knot's structure, have an impact on how quickly the shoelaces will come loose.[110]

Both impact and inertia are critical factors in change management work. It turns out shoelaces are greater teachers than people give them credit for. Hal Higdon, an American writer and runner, has a great piece of advice: "I double-knot my shoe laces. It's a pain untying your shoes afterward—particularly if you get them wet—but so is stopping in the middle of a race to tie them."[111]

Next time you tie your shoelaces, maybe you get to smile and have a sense of great achievement. Think a bit about change management, and remember: Life's a trip, don't forget to tie your shoelaces!

What Changing the Toilet Paper Roll Teaches Me about Change Management

First published on March 16, 2021

It was bound to happen sooner rather than later, I guess... I lost a bet to a couple of friends and had to come up with a far-fetched idea for the Tuesday Change Management Random Thought. And, well, here it is—the lucky winner out of a shortlist of three. Inspiration is everywhere around us, and oftentimes humor is our only serious ally.

What started out as a funny challenge and a creativity exercise turned into a series of serious takeaways for change management work. I hope you will enjoy reading it. If nothing else, you will see there is research backing up the "right way to hang the toilet paper" and settling one of humankind's longest-standing debates...

We take basic things for granted. I am sure we can all remember the shortage of toilet paper from a year ago. As a "pandemic anniversary" post on social media put it: "This March is like last March, only with toilet paper."[112] The shortage was induced by panic shopping which depleted the inventories of a very lean industry. People got nervous and bought way more than they needed. What a great example of how we take basic things for granted! Next time you engage in change management work, remember how rumor mill, miscommunication, panic and open-ended scenarios can create havoc even upon the very basic, foundational things we all consider "a given."

What happened a year ago was also a real-life survey of (civic/collective) responsibility and selflessness. While I will leave the "data interpretation" to each of you, American professor Brené Brown, a leading researcher on courage, vulnerability, shame and empathy, reminds us that the pandemic has been a massive test in vulnerability. Fear can make us brave or turn us into our worst selves with not much in between—which of course is due to our "flight or flight" mindset. But this is a choice we make, and we can still choose to be brave and kind. "We don't have to be scary when we're scared."[113]

Never underestimate logistics. Toilet paper teaches you the importance of logistics—in quite a humbling manner, I might add. Well, I guess we've all "been there" at some point… Logistics is not even remotely as "glamorous" as vision and strategy, yet it is equally important.

Change management work is no exception. Here's a great piece of wisdom from Tom Peters, an American writer on business management practices, best known for co-authoring *In Search of Excellence*: Vision and strategy are important, but wars are won with logistics—making sure the right resources are available in the right places at the right times.[114] Many change management conversations are about ensuring (senior) stakeholders understand and facilitate the availability of the right resources (capability, capacity, time, decision-making authority) at the right time. Sometimes, a critical "resource" is visibility over the other ongoing or foreseen initiatives that might have an impact on the resources and prioritization of a given project. Whatever impacts logistics ultimately affects vision and strategy.

Keeping an updated view of your resources is an act of responsibility and professional maturity—arguably, an equivalent of "adulting," or acting like the perfect mature and responsible adult. This informal term was coined by Kelly Williams Brown, a New York Times-bestselling American writer and author. In her book *Adulting: How to Become a Grown-up in 468 Easy(ish) Steps*, she even makes a reference to toilet paper that is quite relevant for this point on the importance of logistics, pointing out that until the first time you run out of toilet paper as an adult, toilet paper has always just been there—now, you have to actually keep track of it like it's some kind of near-extinct species.[115]

Also, bathroom etiquette varies across cultures, so it might be useful to do some research before you leave for your first post-COVID holiday destination so you can "know before you go."

There are debates never meant to be settled. According to Eric Rosenberg, a keynote speaker on finance topics and a contributor to the *Huffington Post*, *Business Insider* and *Investopedia*, we have all had to make an integral decision at some point in our lives ever since the invention of toilet paper: does it hang under or over? In a lengthy article on his blog, dated October 28, 2014, he presented extensive research in support of settling the great toilet paper debate once and for all. You have to consider both usability and decoration and which one you're willing to sacrifice. The "over" hang is superior in that it's easier to grab and more sanitary, too. However, the "under" hang can be better for pet owners, especially cat owners, as it makes it a bit more difficult for the playful creature to unravel and waste the precious commodity. It is also the better way to hang the toilet paper in an RV—while driving over bumpy roads, "over" hanging toilet paper can come unrolled.[116]

What a great example of a debate never meant to be

settled! And yet life goes on, despite paralysis by analysis or not reaching a consensus. Although inclusive decision-making is great, life and businesses need to move forward even when there are unsettled conversations. As the great toilet paper debate proves, while all team members "agree" to support a consensus decision, the decision may not, in fact, be the optimal decision for the team or the business, given a set of particular circumstances. Business writer Erik Sherman spoke about the idea that while people can have bad ideas, committees can truly create catastrophes.[117] Groupthink is real—the desire to reach a consensus can cause people to ignore indications that what is proposed is a bad idea. The team pushes aside any data that may derail the consensus decision. Aiming for consensus also causes delays in decision-making and indecision. Remember the words of Roman Consul Marcus Tullius Cicero: "More is lost by indecision than wrong decision. Indecision is the thief of opportunity. It will steal you blind."[118]

It is always someone else's task. Nothing like the sight of a desolate toilet paper tube to speak about (shared) accountability and ownership... Changing the toilet paper roll is always someone else's business. One of those tasks that should be outsourced, delegated, or even better, inspires the "bring in the consultants!" moments. I wished somebody else had done it even during the long times I lived on my own... While change management work benefits greatly from new, fresh, complementary (from the outside) perspectives, role modeling accountability and ownership is key for meaningful, sustainable transformation.

The way you hang your toilet roll could reveal whether you have a controlling or laidback personality. Relationship expert and personality coach, Dr. Gilda Carle, devised an experiment to uncover key traits that can be directly linked to which direction you choose to unravel your roll. It turned out "over" hang people are usually the more assertive, fierce leadership types, while "under" hangers are often more submissive, empathetic, and adaptable.[119]

Regardless of how you roll your toilet paper, I hope you found something amusing, something insightful and something helpful for your change management work in this week's article.

What Stopping at Gas Stations Teaches Me about Change Management

First published on March 23, 2021

One of my most vivid childhood memories is waiting for hours on end for gas, sharing time, stories and loads of laughter with my grandfather. And with tens of other people waiting in line just like us. Many friendships were formed during the endless waiting, and going to get gas always felt like a joyful, slowly unfolding adventure to me.

Every single time I pass by a gas station or happen to stop at one, my childhood memories put a smile on my face—my memories *and* the fact that, for someone without a driver's license, being fond of gas stations is quite ironic. There are several gas stations that I pass by on my regular daily walks, and I thought it might be high time I gave it a go at what stopping at gas stations teaches me about change management. Stumbling upon Eddie Vedder's quote that likens nostalgia to stopping at a gas station fueled my creativity.[120]

And here below are some takeaways that might fuel your excitement for change work.

The proximity of the gas station seems to be inversely proportionate to the amount of fuel in your tank. I guess it all comes down to perceptions, personal preferences and risk appetite. Based on this, there are two types of people in this world. The "I need gas as soon as the tank is not almost overflowing" type and the "I know my car" category. My grandfather sat squarely and proudly in the latter. I swear the green Dacia 1330 he drove all his life sometimes ran on nothing but his larger-than-life willpower. And probably a bit of healthy fear, too. He was the poster boy for careful driving, in the sense of this saying: "If you don't swear while driving then you are not paying attention to the road at all."

Think about this next time you are doing change management work and pay attention to how you perceive the distance to your milestones depending on the resources you have available—time, capability, capacity, team members, support and decision-making power, budget and even your own enthusiasm and motivation. These constitute your "change gas." And remember what the late psychology professor William Frederick Book said: "A man must drive his energy, not be driven by it."[121]

Sometimes, being at the same place at the same time is the only common denominator. Gas stations are one of my favorite places for people-watching. I find it fascinating how they interact with each other and how they customize their gas station experience. At one point, I came up with this theory of three categories of people: Single C—people who only get coffee, Double C—people who get coffee and croissant(s), and Triple C—people who get coffee, croissant(s) and engage in some sort of light conversation with the fellow drivers or gas station staff.

All of these have their equivalents in the types of profiles you need and want on your change management journey. Being challenged on my perceptions of gas stations as purely a passenger and never a driver, I realized that the common denominator is not coffee—especially where people can pay directly at the pump and don't even need to come into the station to pay for the gas. The common denominator for all the people at a gas station—drivers, passengers, and staff—is that they happen to be at the same place at the same time. They all have different needs and wants, and they all go about fulfilling them differently. And I am sure they all have different thoughts about their different journeys. Sometimes, "being present" is the only common denominator.

It is not about having all the answers but about asking all the questions. Writing about gas stations without having ever driven in my life challenged me to question what I didn't know that I didn't know. I started asking my driving friends what they pay attention to when they stop at gas stations. How they decide what gas stations to stop at. Some of them prefer gas stations with a car wash. Others have fond memories of full service with a human touch, whereas now you can wash your own windshield and check for tire pressure yourself. Some of them take the "no cell phones" more seriously than others. Some pay attention to the brand of gas available. My biggest stress would definitely be filling the tank with the wrong fuel.

All these conversations made me think about the fact that, as a change manager, sometimes—arguably oftentimes—the job is not about having all the answers. It is, however, about asking all the questions and challenging yourself and those around you on what you don't know that you don't know. And avoid "mis-fueling" by asking people "what they run on." Listen to their answers, "be present" with them and send them safely on their way.

Throughout most of my life, one of my biggest regrets was not inheriting my grandfather's amazingly blue eyes. As a consolation prize, his risk-taking gene did get into my DNA. I am one of those "I know my car" people (and, by the way, also a Triple C—coffee, croissant, and conversation).

Until next week's "gas station," Happy (re)Fueling!

What Losing Loved Ones Teaches Me about Change Management

First published on March 30, 2021

Since the start of this year, I've lost a few loved ones. To the natural progression of life. To distance and silence. To "versions of truth," as Jack Nicholson's character in *Something's Gotta Give*, Harry Sanborn, said with a spin when confronted with his lies.[122] Regardless of what took these people out of my life, their loss is something beyond words. With three painful anniversaries coming up over the month of April, grief has been in my soul and on my mind over the last several days. And when a post popped up on my social media feed with a quote saying that "grief is just love with nowhere to go," I decided to see if there is some teaching in it.

Remembering Ernest Hemingway's encouragement to write about the most difficult things,[123] here it goes, my attempt to make some sense out of everything that has been happening.

Conversations not had are truths not told. Two weeks ago, one of my closest, oldest friends sent me a "Happy Birthday" note. I did acknowledge it with an emoji, but got caught up in the festive rush and never properly replied. Two days later, on a Wednesday morning, I learned he passed away. There is a "Love you loads" message in my Inbox that never got answered. That will never get answered. I can think of several other conversations that got postponed, and most likely they will never happen.

When you have something to say, say it. Open your mouth and let the words out. Write a note and hit "send." Dial the number and start with, "Hi, I need you to listen, do you have a minute?" The time might never be perfect.

Oftentimes, in change management conversations, questions regarding when to start communication are raised. "We don't want to start communicating too early when things are not clear enough," is the version I hear most often. How about starting too late, when people have already made up their minds and filled in the gaps with assumptions, rumors, scenarios, bits and pieces of information that create alternative puzzles? People don't have to pass away to become "unreachable." They just need to get into a space (mentally, emotionally) where they are no longer willing, able, open to listen. You can always go back to clarify, confirm, correct, expend, but some instances of "too late" are just "nevers" waiting to be acknowledged.

Be kind on the journey from an end toward a beginning. Sometimes, when I pass by the bookshelves in my living room, I take out the first book that catches my eye and open it randomly. Last Friday, this book happened to be *Transitions: Making Sense of Life's Changes* by William Bridges.[124] It opened at the beginning of Chapter 6, "Endings," and there it was, a quote from T.S. Eliot's "Little Gidding" about how beginnings are often endings and endings are often beginnings.[125] When the pain of the loss is overwhelming, we can only see the end. Yet the beginning is waiting patiently. The beginning has time to happen. For many people, autumn is the perfect expression of an end promising a new beginning come spring. There is this beautiful piece of writing from blogger Shira Tamir (livinginmyownworld.com): "Anyone who thinks fallen leaves are dead has never watched them dancing on a windy day."[126]

About two years ago, a good friend of mine with whom I share a passion for change management came back from a dedicated course and told me something that has stayed with me ever since. One of his professors said during a class: "Project management starts at a beginning and goes towards an end. Change management starts at an end and creates a new beginning." I was reminded of this over the past several days and it made me realize, yet again, the absolute importance of being kind to oneself and all the others as we are on the journey from an end to a beginning.

Grief is personal. Especially as we still navigate through the pandemic, we are all grieving. Loved ones. The "old normal." Opportunities to meet and hug, and just "be there" for each other. A sense of security. Jobs. Dreams and plans. Hopes that will never get to become reality. I spoke with a friend over the weekend whose grandson will soon turn two, and a new baby is on the way. She said: "My grandson doesn't know who I am. I will not be there when the new baby will come into this world. I will never have these memories with them." She is grieving.

Whenever we do change management work, we need to be mindful and intentional with acknowledging a sense of grieving over some loss—familiarity and comfort of ways of working, knowledge made redundant, a sense of security, sometimes status and authority, professional identity. We can never know what people perceive as being lost, taken away, forgotten, unacknowledged. And we must always seek to understand. Never assume. Grief is personal. No rulebook. No timeframe. No judgment. As David Kessler says in *Finding Meaning: The*

Sixth Stage of Grief, everyone grieves differently, but we all need someone there with us as we do it—not to lessen the pain or try to point out the positives, but just to truly be there.[127]

Over the last few days, I wished to just go numb. And I would have missed out on filling my soul with the joy of walking in the sun with a friend and feeling comfort, safety and reassurance in his hugs. As Brené Brown points out in her book *Rising Strong,* if you get rid of the dark, you get rid of the light, too. Grief is scary, but it's also what helps us to heal.[128]

I hope the end of this article is a beginning for you to see a great change manager in the Roman philosopher Seneca: "Every new beginning comes from some other beginning's end."[129]

What Buying Jewelry Teaches Me about Change Management

First published on April 6, 2021

There is no excuse left unused by yours truly to buy jewelry. My birthday. Christmas. Graduation. Some work anniversary. A real special occasion…like…uhm, Wednesday… "At least it's silver," I keep telling myself as I "add to cart," feeling my "magpie gene" activated.

Recently, I had to take a few items to the jewelers for some cleaning. And, while waiting to have them done, I roamed around the shop, trying my best not to add to my collection. To keep my mind distracted, I challenged myself to come up with what buying jewelry teaches me about change management, and here are the shiny ideas.

The temptation of "the next shiny thing" is real. I lost count of how many times I told myself, "This is it, the last one, at least for this year," or: "Wait until the winter sale." Not even, "Sleep on it, check it out again in the morning" works. Guilty as charged. "Shiny object syndrome" is a real thing, and it stands for the situation where people focus all their attention on something that is current and trendy, yet drop it as soon as something new takes its place. The term "shiny object syndrome (SOS)" is often used when people make the mistake of focusing on something small and fixating on it to the extent that they lose the big picture. You can come across it within management literature, popular psychological literature, and the social and computer sciences.

In change management, where progress happens one individual at a time, SOS is very popular amongst the stakeholders. Is there a new framework available? A methodology, method or tool? Something "buzzwordy" mentioned in the latest business newsletter? Does it have some "agile" in it? Design thinking elements? It must be good. It must be implemented. At least "as an accelerator to what we have going at the moment." Pretty much like the "mix and match" jewelry style.

There are many risks associated with SOS, two of them change management realities. The inability to finish projects is one, caused by the excitement to jump from one type of intervention to another, not having the patience to wait for sustainable progress. Confusing your people is, for me, the biggest risk. You aren't the only one affected by your decisions and constantly alternating momentum. When people see the projects they work on suddenly changed, or plainly become irrelevant, when they feel their goals shift almost unpredictably, they will ultimately question the big picture. Productivity and loyalty? They were nice and shiny once…what is the next shiny thing now?

"If you don't know jewelry, know your jeweler." I simply love this quote from Warren Buffet, American investor and philanthropist. It is the title of Chapter 10 in *Buffett Beyond Value: Why Warren Buffett Looks to Growth and Management When Investing* book by Prem C. Jain.[130] It speaks to me about how we all have our unique talents and how magic happens when we work together, respecting what each of us brings to the table. It is like a more sophisticated version of the good old "everybody is a mechanic until the real mechanic shows up" saying—like "shiny wisdom."

Change management should be developed and enabled across the organization as a critical literacy at all levels. And dedicated change managers have their part to play in any and every transformation. The type of relationship they create and nurture with all their stakeholders is, most of the time, what "makes or breaks" their contribution. The key currency for change management is trust. This is the best safeguard against "the next shiny thing," and it takes both (all) sides to work at its best. It requires (self) awareness, honesty, courage, persistence and a bit of sparkle.

It is all about being unique. We should just be honest and admit that "unique value proposition," "competitive edge," "differentiators" were on our list when we entertained the thought of starting a game of "corporate bingo." This is what we are all after: being unique. And how we can best express it. Jewelry reminds me of this quest for uniqueness. As jewelry designer Jennie Kwon puts it, "Jewelry has the power to be this one little thing that can make you feel unique."[131] This is why businesses keep on changing: to stay unique. And it is generated from within. It doesn't come from the "next shiny thing."

Oftentimes, when being asked what change management is, I am inspired (as in, "tempted to steal with pride") by a quote about design from Erik Adigard, a communication designer, multimedia artist and educator. He says that design is a mix of things like science, propaganda, stories, philosophy, and creativity.[132] Change management is the same kind of mix. It also started out as "the next shiny thing" to help in the search for being unique. Let me leave you with a final sparkle from Belgian fashion designer Diane von Fürstenberg: "Jewelry is like the perfect spice—it always compliments what's already there."[133]

Until next week, keep on shining!

What Binge-Watching Television Shows Teaches Us about Change Management

With Scott Lyons
First published on April 13, 2020

What's the easiest way to break the ice when connecting or reconnecting with others? Ask them what shows they are binge-watching these days! Sadly, it could be argued that a prominent shared experience for humans today is being pulled into the vortex of watching an entire season (or two) of the latest rage on Netflix or Disney Plus. We share the feeling of turmoil that comes with the grueling decision to watch one more episode or go to sleep. Have we even come up with a name yet for the predicament of leaving our fate to locating the remote control before the countdown to the next episode reigns over the near future?

Whether or not you watch television as part of your daily routine, there is much to learn about the phenomenon of binge-watching, just as there is to the fascinating experience and realities of change management. This week, two recovering binge-watchers join forces to explore what binge-watching television shows can teach us about change management.

Remember WHY? There's ample research to inform us about the pros and cons of binge-watching television shows. To state it simply, binge-watching cultivates a mixture of pleasure and self-doubt. How much is too much? What will we do when this six-season series is over? Binge-watching too many shows at once can be disconcerting, as is the case for change management and prioritizing projects that maybe shouldn't be concurrent. Like any activity, we can moderate our behaviors when we know why we are participating in an activity and how it fits into our bigger picture and purpose.

It's easy to focus solely on change management and miss out on the importance of socialization; spending time only with your project managers and other change managers like we do when binge-watching snuggled up with our pets can be unhealthy and even damaging. Take a break and test your *why* by having open conversations with other people. Try to do a little "binge-watching" through their eyes and perceptions. Who knows, it might feel like an entirely new season…

Manage your state of flow. Like binge-watching, embracing the change management process can help us get into a state of flow, which research associates with raised levels of creativity and well-being. Viewing experiences are most often designed for anticipation and time to reflect before the saga continues. Binge-watching can easily summon the evil spirits of impatience within us, or the need for instant gratification. And there is always the risk of unnecessary conflict created by leaving others behind.

In *The Progress Principle: Using Small Wins to Ignite Joy, Engagement, and Creativity at Work*, Amabile and Kramer offer the answer to the question on top of every manager's mind: *how do you truly engage people?* The answer is simple: help them see their own progress.[134] One key action to do this is to take your foot off the gas—once in a while. We should never fall into the trap of thinking progress is burning through the project plan, milestones and deliverables. Progress is also time to reflect, to let things settle, to go back and question assumptions, to recontract, to wait up for others, to pause and breathe. You cannot binge on progress.

Navigating complexity feeds our intelligence. Television narratives have become more complex, and as such, it's possible that watching more of these shows could make you smarter. According to recent research, binge-watching activity has been related to greater dissatisfaction and less enjoyable viewing experience, even though viewers may have retained more information in short-term and long-term memory.

Similarly, we learn from change management experts that stakeholders will respond to incremental change more than they will for radical change. Like anything, moderation is key! We can define our own pace and rhythm of binge-watching. Similarly, clear targets and purpose for change management projects set the stage for a healthier immersive experience for stakeholders in the change process.

If we happened to pull your attention from a current binge-watching session, let us know what resonated with you. Hurry up, before the next episode starts!

What Swimming Teaches Me about Change Management

First published on April 20, 2021

Maybe because I am a Pisces, I have always been fascinated by water. Give me a river, a lake, or even better, a sea or an ocean, and I am the happiest girl in the world. Not water in a bathtub, that is just plain frustrating! My father was a water polo player, and he used to take me to the swimming pool even before I could walk there on my own two feet. It started out as play, but slowly it turned into discipline—his coach began to pay attention to my splashing around, and I was in training without even realizing it.

One of the phrases I heard a lot while growing up was: "You don't care how deep the water is, you are not swimming towards the bottom. You swim forward. Breathe, and swim forward." It sometimes went on with, "And don't splash so much, you are not a water fountain." As I look back to almost two decades of swimming and four of just enjoying water, I am grateful for a few valuable life lessons. "You are not swimming towards the bottom" is one of them. The importance of breathing is another one. Knowing your limits, pushing them, acknowledging your fears and thoughts, instead of just "drowning" them—this is the swimming legacy in my life.

There are a few teachings for change management work, too. And we can dive straight into them.

Each stroke counts. And count each stroke. Monitoring stroke count is not the most common way in which swimmers keep track of their performance, yet it might very well be the most meaningful one. It gives you almost instantaneous feedback on your performance lap-by-lap, alerting you to loss of efficiency or variation in your stroke length. The distance you travel on each stroke and your stroke length have been shown repeatedly to correlate more closely with performance than any other aspect of swimming. When stroking efficiently, you should travel between 55% and 65% of height on each stroke. Counting strokes is the simplest, most convenient way to monitor swimming performance in real-time. And it is also a great enabler for mindfulness. It tracks progress, and it keeps focus—something that every change management intervention needs.

Over the years, I have been involved in or simply witnessed debates on the relevance and "weight" of change management in comparison to other more "concrete, tangible and actionable" disciplines. Most often, the term of comparison has been project management. One of these recent instances reminded me of these words from the late Dusty Hicks, a high school swimming phenomenon and spinal cord injury victim: "It's been told that swimming is a wimp sport, but I don't see it. We don't get timeouts! In the middle of a race, we can't stop and catch our breath; we can't roll on our stomachs and lie there; and we can't ask for a substitution."[135] Courage and trust are the currencies of change and change management. You cannot take a break from these. In change management, each interaction counts. Count each interaction, and make each interaction count.

Fundamentals over fluff. To swim smoothly, coordination of the entire body is a must. And it requires mastery of five basic skills. Breathing is the one that is frequently overlooked or downplayed, yet it is the most important one. If you are not comfortable breathing while swimming, you won't be able to enjoy it completely and learn new things. Floating cannot be highlighted enough. Before you start kicking and stroking, first learn to float in the water. Floating helps you to get used to the habit of moving through water properly. Coordination of your body movements, kicking and stroking complete the list of critical skills. These are your swimming fundamentals. Everything else is…"moving fluff."

All these have their equivalents in change management work. Learn to "breathe," find your state of "float" that can give you some needed rest and helps you manage the vertical buoyant force when immersed, coordinate all the moving parts, and be purposeful and mindful about your kicking and stroking.

Slow is smooth, and smooth is fast. Apparently "slow is smooth, and smooth is fast" is a Navy SEAL saying. The meaning is pretty clear: practice slowly so that the correct motor patterns are ingrained. And perhaps equally important, execute "slowly," meaning "don't rush." Pushing your nervous system to perform faster than it's trained to will simply cause you to fumble what you're doing, and the end result is that your rushed performance is slower than if you had attempted a measured cadence in the first place.

Like in a number of other sports and disciplines, this also applies to swimming: practicing at reduced speeds will make you faster when you go full speed. Competitive swimmers, especially the freestyle ones (like yours truly), go for super slow swimming, a technique that allows for a different focus on fundamentals and an improved relationship with water. It is painfully hard at times to resist the urge to just crank up the speed. It almost feels counterintuitive as you "swim a thin line" between precise technique and feeling like you could almost sink between strokes. Many swimmers hop into the water and do the assigned swim practice with the sole intention of getting it over with or getting their hand on the wall first. Guilty! Or we get lost in the need to swim fast all the time, forgetting the fundamentals that got us there in the first place. Been there, done that! Not as efficient as advertised.

Find your own change management "super slow swimming" drill, focus on the fundamentals and believe that you will be as efficient as needed when you hop into the water next. And breathe! Train yourself to relax and perform the steps with efficient precision. Train to relax, train to focus, train to "muscle memory." When you're relaxed and calm and need to move fast, you'll cut through the water like a happy dolphin on an adventure.

It is not just about what you do when you go into the water. Not surprisingly, outside of the swimming pool, training includes core strength exercises, weight training, mobility and flexibility drills, and also nutrition, rest and recovery.

Over the last few days, "intention" came up in several unrelated conversations, and it made me reflect on why I get into the swimming pool. Intention is as important as breathing and it influences your sense of progress and focus just as fundamentally. What else is as meaningful and fundamental to change and change management as intention? Australian (now retired) swimmer Ian Thorpe, five-time Olympic gold winner, said that his personal definition of losing is not coming in second, but failing to give his all.[136]

Also remember that, although you are alone in the water, your swimming is an expression of a team—who made it safe for you to discover your love for water, who took you to the swimming pool for the first time, who taught you how to breathe, float, stroke and kick, who encouraged you every stroke of the way. One of my best friends from growing up drowned while saving two younger kids and also took me to the river a while after and sat on the bank while I swam the fear out of my head. He is on my team.

When speaking about relay, Ian Thorpe also beautifully spoke about how you can perform better when you're working to help others than you can if you're working for yourself.[137] Think about the relay team you are on with all your former selves and the relay team you are building with everyone around you during change management work.

Since my mid-twenties, I have been having a recurring dream. I am at a beach (what a surprise, right?), enjoying a perfect day. Not too hot, not too chilly. And not too many people. The waves become taller and taller until suddenly there is this wall of water coming onto the beach. People start running away, while I just stand and watch it coming. And I remember all the swimming training and I hear these words in my head: "You don't care how tall this is. You breathe and swim forward. Just breathe!" The reflex kicks in and I start concentrating on my breathing. I always wake up at this point, and the feeling I experience every single time is one of peace.

Until next week, train to relax, focus on fundamentals and breathe! And do splash if you feel like it—water fountains make people happy.

What Living and Working in a Foreign Language Teach Me about Change Management

First published on April 27, 2021

In the second half of last week, I received an invitation to speak at a change management conference in June. Beyond being happy and honored by the opportunity, what excites me most is the fact that I will deliver the speech in Romanian. It dawned on me that I have never spoken about my passion in my mother tongue in a conference setting. Over the past several days, I have caught myself pausing and trying to translate bits and pieces of my work into Romanian, and it is not the easiest of tasks.

Also last week, one very delightful conversation surfaced a surprise: a fellow Hungarian speaker. Coming from a mixed family from the northwest of Romania, I was blessed with a mother tongue and a "father tongue." Not a lot of occasions to use either of those on a regular basis over the last years ("decades" might be a more accurate term). English is the language in which I have been living and working for the past 25 years. Which makes it…what? My "everyday reality tongue?"

These two recent events prompted me to think about any takeaways from speaking foreign languages for change management. And you can read them below, using whatever accent you fancy for your "mind voice."

Psychological safety starts with speaking before speaking up. There is an ever-increasing amount of research pointing to a worrying reality: a new addition is to be made to the list of "isms," or prejudices we have been alerted to—"voiceism," a coinage that refers to the destructive stereotypes and preconceptions triggered by the way people sound when they speak. As described in an article in *The Walrus* titled "Accents, Dialects, and Discrimination: From surfer-dude drawls to Valley-girl upspeak, how we talk still defines how we're seen" (adapted from *This Is the Voice* by John Colapinto[138]), voiceism doesn't just cover accent; it includes every tiny detail of the way we speak. Something as small as the volume or pace of someone's voice can lead us to make quick conclusions about who they are and where they come from. As someone who has carried some sort of accent all their life, I can totally resonate with the writer's experience; they're very conscious about what assumptions other people are making just because of their voice.[139]

It cannot be emphasized enough how change management starts with creating a safe space for listening and speaking. It is my choice to believe, and hopefully role model, that acknowledgement, respect and trust are language- and accent-agnostic. At the same time, I have a loooooong list of instances when English, for example, remains just a common denominator in the workplace and fails to become the enabler of a level playing field. There is English, and there are the "languages of small talk." Sometimes there is even a "language of power." The working language within an international environment (be it English, French, German, you name it), oftentimes fails to be the "belonging language." People who are aware of the fact that they speak with an accent do experience "voiceism" in one way or another, at some (various) point(s) during their life.

Speaking a foreign language also teaches you to honor silence. When someone is searching for their words, it is a sign of respect. For you and themselves. Whenever possible, translate as much as you can, and make information available in various languages. A quote adapted from the words of Nelson Mandela, the South African anti-apartheid revolutionary, political leader and philanthropist who served as President of South Africa from 1994 to 1999, holds a valuable lesson for change management communication: "If you talk to a man in a language he understands, that goes to his head. If you talk to him in his language, that goes to his heart."[140] Keep in mind all the time that if someone is speaking to you in a foreign accent, they are smart enough to know at least two languages and were brave enough to do their job in their second. Psychological safety starts with speaking. Speaking up comes after.

Honor the differences. Never judge them. There is a beautiful Arab proverb that says: "Learn a language, and you'll avoid a war." As explained in *The Walrus* article previously mentioned, voiceism is part of how our brains are wired. The limbic part of our brain processes *how* something is said before it even considers *what* was said. Additionally, when we hear someone speaking, our amygdala will instantly tell us whether or not that someone is a trusted individual or an unknown element, a quality passed down from early humans. But—this is not an excuse to make quick judgments![141]

In our moments of deepest honesty, we can all admit to being guilty of letting our amygdala get the best of us. As it also happens in change management work—and the first step to changing something is acknowledging it. How intentionally inclusive are we when listening to other people? It is not always about foreign languages. It is sometimes about different "organizational languages"—the industry/company/team vocabulary, the acronyms. To someone from another environment, this sounds just as foreign as a foreign language. Add the buzzwords into the mix. Are they "cool" or "cold"? Do they "warm up" the conversation or "freeze" it?

Marcus Fabius Quintilianus, a Roman educator and rhetorician from Hispania, left us with a beautiful quote: "One should not aim at being possible to understand, but at being impossible to misunderstand."[142] Whenever you feel the amygdala acting up, practice a bit of self-awareness, courtesy of Austrian-British philosopher Ludwig Wittgenstein: "The limits of my language mean the limits of my world."[143]

Make mistakes a natural, necessary part of your learning process. Learning a new language can be daunting at times. It takes time, practice, dedication, and patience. Whenever you get frustrated on your linguistic journey, just take a second to remember how long it took you to master your own language! Give yourself enough time, enough space, and enough kindness. Regardless of the preferred means of learning, practicing with native speakers is recognized as one of the keys to success. While being a learning accelerator, this also brings an additional layer to a classic challenge: exposure to mistakes.

Whether it is about vocabulary, pronunciation or grammar, making mistakes is a natural, very necessary part of your learning process. How people react to mistakes, including how you yourself react, is a very telling sign. How an organization reacts to mistakes is a mark of its culture. Pay attention to how mistakes are being addressed, including how they are addressed by yourself. Clarify in public, correct in private. And whenever you feel your motivation and courage dwindling, remember these words from Flora Lewis, American journalist and *The New York Times* contributor: "Learning another language is not only learning different words for the same things, but learning another way to think about things."[144]

Self-worth is a universal language. Being fluent or good in a foreign language is not irrefutable proof of intelligence or character. Being intelligent is not simply about being educated and smart enough to use an international language. Learn to respect first, before you claim yourself to be an intelligent person. And learn to respect yourself for all the things that make you unique—like your accent. Celebrate it, honor it, use it to tell your full, unaltered truth. Use your accent every day to run meetings, support your team members and express acknowledgment and respect for all the things that make them unique.

Canadian psycholinguist Frank Smith makes a great point: "Language is not a genetic gift, it is a social gift. Learning a new language is becoming a member of the club—the community of speakers of that language."[145] Whatever foreign language(s) you speak and/or are currently learning, make it a language of acknowledgement, respect and acceptance.

What Enjoying Cartoons Teaches Me about Change Management

First published on May 4, 2021

Last week, an incredible book found me when I needed it most: Charlie Mackesy's *The Boy, the Mole, the Fox and the Horse*, an amazingly touching collection of drawings with gentle life encouragements on each page. The boy is trying to make his way home, and on his journey he meets the other characters. All of them are unique, and uniquely human. The writer himself said that he could see bits of himself in all four characters, each with their own peculiarities and weaknesses. Even the setting is relatable—it's springtime, where the weather can change drastically from day to day…a little like life.[146] It is one of the most thoughtful goodbye gifts I have ever received, as it was given to me a couple of days before I left Luxembourg for an adventure: a new beginning, a journey to a new home.

The first thing that caught my eye when I entered my Airbnb accommodation in Switzerland was a cartoon poster. The fact that it had a turquoise frame really made me notice it—there is not enough turquoise in the world!

With these two recent nudges, I started thinking about what enjoying cartoons teaches me about change management. Since my drawing skills are somewhere in between "not worth mentioning" and plain "retina damaging," I will simply write them below. If there are any cartoonists out there reading this and you feel like having some fun drawing these takeaways, please reach out.

The best nation is imagination. During the Toastmasters District 80 Annual Convention in Hong Kong in May 2007, the 1999 World Champion of Public Speaking, Craig Valentine, shared the story of how a homeless lady used to ask him: "Sonny, do you know what is the best nation?" When he replied that he did not know, she said, "Imagination is the best nation!" A few years ago, I saw a post on social media with graffiti from Crete, Greece, saying: "The only good nation is imagination." And I couldn't agree more.

According to Wikipedia, imagination is "the production or simulation of novel objects, sensations, and ideas in the mind without any immediate input of the senses. Stefan Szczelkun characterizes it as the forming of experiences in one's mind, which can be re-creations of past experiences, such as vivid memories with imagined changes, or completely invented and possibly fantastic scenes. Imagination helps make knowledge applicable in solving problems and is fundamental to integrating experience and the learning process."[147] Cartoons speak to me about imagination, about what the human mind can create and find the means to express.

And this is the most meaningful association with change management for me. In order to change things, we need to first imagine them (a)new. And then find the means to express what we have imagined, and subsequently the means to turn them into reality. Also, cartoons leave a lot of room for different people to "see" different things in the characters and the plot. People need their own space for imagination. The nation of imagination is not so much about "one single imagination" as it is about a collective intention to acknowledge, respect and encourage the individual freedom to imagine. Belonging is driven by choice, not conformity.

Unrealistic expectations oftentimes stem from realistic challenges and concerns. Amongst all the pearls of wisdom out there in the whole wide world, there is an anonymous saying that I can totally resonate with, and this week's change management random thought gives me the perfect context for making this confession: "I don't care about Disney lying about my Prince Charming. I'm more upset about forest creatures and their unwillingness to clean my house."[148] How we, as human beings, choose to go about assessing "unrealistic" is simply fascinating. It is subjective to the core.

If I had a cent for every single time I heard "But this is just unrealistic!" in a change management conversation, right about now I'd be on a quiet, pleasantly windy beach on my own little island. Before discarding expectations as "unrealistic," it is helpful and useful to understand what triggered them. They might stem from very real challenges and concerns. And what turned them into "unrealistic" might be emotional overload. Or lack of relevant information. Or a combination of both, and many other valid factors. Unrealistic expectations are oftentimes a symptom of something realistic that needs immediate addressing. Not judging and dismissing.

Rule no. 6. In his book *The Art of Possibility*, Benjamin Zander, an English conductor, currently the Musical Director of the Boston Philharmonic Orchestra and the Boston Philharmonic Youth Orchestra, explains that rule no. 6 is essentially not to take yourself seriously)! What are rules one to five? There aren't any.[149] At first glance, this rule speaks about humor and taking things easy. It also gives me a great solution to a math problem: "I've got 99 problems and 86 of them are completely made-up scenarios in my head that I'm stressing about for absolutely no logical reason."

Cartoons are often described as exaggerated and humorous drawings; one could argue that rule no. 6 is a good source of cartoon inspiration. Oftentimes, we take ourselves, and our position (in both our professional and personal lives) too seriously and lose our ability to laugh at ourselves. If there is anything that could significantly improve our quality of life and the ability to lead in uncertain times, it is this gift to not only laugh at our own mistakes, but to also learn from them. At the same time, we can learn from anyone around us, just as much as they can learn from us. Beyond humor and lightheartedness, rule no. 6 speaks to me about kindness and self-compassion. It might just be my imagination creating unrealistic expectations, but I will take kindness and self-compassion over anything else on any given day.

The final takeaway for change management comes as an excerpt from Charlie Mackesy's introduction to his own book, and it summarizes beautifully everything I wish you could take with yourselves from enjoying cartoons: "As the horse says: the truth is everyone is winging it. So I say spread your wings and follow your dreams."[150]

What Choosing Health Insurance Teaches Me about Change Management

First published on May 11, 2021

New country, new health insurance…oh, the many joys of relocation!!! The only thing that makes me feel more ignorant and confused than buying a laptop or filling in my tax declaration is choosing a health insurance plan. One of the very few instances when figures make more sense to me than letters—it usually comes down to what I need to pay every month, because after reading the coverage of at least two options my brain just cannot compute. I get the human version of the "blue screen."

This past weekend was *THE* weekend; I could not postpone making a decision on the new health insurance plan any longer. After reading three different options, revisiting my medical history and trying to make an educated guess about my (immediate) future needs, I didn't necessarily feel like an empowered, responsible adult. On top of the "analysis paralysis," I realized I was older than the last time I got a health insurance plan, and the various things covered by the detailed plans did not sound as much like sci-fi as they used to…

Oh well, after making peace with the sad reality that I am not Wonder Woman (although I do things that make you wonder…), I thought about what choosing health insurance teaches me about change management. While you read the takeaways below, I will resume my hoping beyond hope that one day I will find a health insurance plan that covers retail therapy.

Conversations about your vulnerabilities are the foundation for safety. Reading the health insurance plan options raises a lot of questions about vulnerabilities. What basic and extra coverages make more sense—optical, dental, hospitalization? A thorough risk management plan is a given in any project—and many argue that is squarely a project management tool, and change management should not take any credit for it. Where do you have the conversations about vulnerabilities, then, when you do change work? Pretty much everywhere, if you do it right—stakeholder analysis and mapping (push to cover beyond your "usual suspects"), change impact assessment, change readiness assessment, engagement and communication strategies and plans, training needs assessment.

Build a dedicated resistance management strategy and plan. Be as clinical (not cynical) about it as possible. And challenge what it is you are dealing with: resistance to change, immunity to change or change fatigue? As choosing health insurance teaches me, different risks and medical histories come with different investments for future safety. Although made with humor, there is serious truth behind one of Dave Carpenter's cartoons: a patient is sitting on a hospital bed and the doctor holding his chart tells him that they'll first run a few tests to watch how his insurance reacts.[151]

Health care above and beyond health insurance. My health insurance-dazed brain raised the question of whether there is also a distinction to be made between "change management" and "change care." Oftentimes, "change management" sounds purely operational to me, inducing the expectation that if there is a framework set up, a methodology followed and tools applied, change is guaranteed to happen. A structured approach definitely helps, yet over the years I learned there is a lot of "care" needed around the purely "managementy" part. Every project should have change management. Every employee should have change care.

View health as an investment, not a cost. During the weekend, my health insurance decision felt a bit more on the "cost" side, but I am sure it will shift heavily towards "investment" in a few days, right after my dentist appointment.

Change management work is perceived sometimes as a cost—of time, focus, and other resources taken away from "concrete work." However, when adoption rates of a new process or technology are not exactly skyrocketing, then "some change management intervention" seems like a timely investment. John Quelch, the Charles Edward Wilson Professor of Business Administration Emeritus at Harvard Business School, once talked about how most companies are so focused on the "cost" side of health that they don't even consider how they can help to prevent rising healthcare costs.[152]

Especially after what we all have been experiencing since the pandemic started, I believe this goes beyond ergonomic chairs and good ventilation (over-simplifying here to save some mental bandwidth for choosing a home insurance plan tomorrow). There is an undeniable and ever-increasing societal cost incurred from organizational cultures. Investing in curating the people experience within organizations in all its aspects and manifestations will have a positive impact on overall societal healthcare costs.

Sir Winston Churchill, British statesman and former Prime Minister of the United Kingdom, believed that healthy people are the biggest strength of any country.[153] Equally applicable when we substitute "organization" for "country."

Until next week, keep calm and stay healthy! Get a good health insurance plan—just in case…

What Shopping at IKEA Teaches Me about Change Management

First published on May 18, 2021

Over the weekend, I discovered the most dangerous feature of my new home: a direct tram line to IKEA from right in front of the building. I wish I had known this last week while I was looking into insurance plans and could have covered for this type of accommodation hazard... Suddenly, the very empty apartment seemed like the best thing ever—not simply a mere retail therapy excuse, but the perfect business case for shopping at IKEA.

It goes without saying that I successfully reconfirmed most of the IKEA sayings on social media, except those involving using cars to get the goods back home. If there is one instance that makes me entertain the idea of getting my driver's license, it is the bit of returning home looking like an overly-committed Santa Claus with blue bags.

Part of my recent "IKEA penitence ritual" was looking at this experience and trying to get any takeaways for change management. You can hopefully assemble them into something useful for you from the elements below.

"There is no such thing as scope creep, only scope gallop."[154] ...says an anonymous quote commonly misattributed to Cornelius Fitchner, the host of *The Project Management Podcast*. Nothing better to illustrate this than a shopping trip to IKEA. The only things I needed were a shower curtain and a wine bottle opener. You know, basic priorities... I ended up dragging home (almost literally) plants, cushions, bed throws (currently only having a rented single bed), vases, candles, a set of mixing bowls (just because one of them was a light shade of turquoise, but not in natural light as it turned out). I did get a shower curtain and a wine bottle opener eventually; I remembered them while already standing in line for the cashier... The moment I placed the first candle in the shopping cart, I knew I would not stop there, and I braced myself for the walk back to the tram station.

We all know that buying only what you came for at IKEA is not a real thing. Yet somehow, realistic expectations management fails again and again. I personally never seem to take the lesson learned, only the success story of sheer physical strength and credit card resilience. IKEA also creates scope creep in the future, as now I am looking for bookshelves for the books I do not have yet... Let me check that wish list on Amazon...

Be equally intentional about both "fuel" and "friction." Two simple forces can explain human behavior, in an attempt to simplify the conversation: fuel and friction. Dan Ariely, Professor of Psychology and Behavioral Economics at Duke University, uses the metaphor of a rocket ship to explain this. For a rocket ship to fly through space, it needs to not only bypass atmospheric friction and avoid debris, but also consume fuel to propel itself up and out of the atmosphere. Too much friction, and it won't fly. Not enough fuel, and it won't fly either.[155] Supplementing fuel doesn't automatically decrease friction. Simply telling people more often why change is good doesn't automatically make change easier. Reliving the enjoyable part of my weekend IKEA trip—getting more and more excited about the items in my shopping cart—did not bring the tram station any closer. It sure didn't make the cumulative weight feel any lighter, either...

Results are good, the experience is better. The IKEA effect in change management demonstrates that we appreciate more what we made ourselves or put our own effort into rather than what was created by someone else. In other words, we accept change by creating it. This effect was proven in 2011 in a joint study run by Harvard, Yale and Duke Universities, led by Professor Dan Ariely. Co-creation has been gaining traction over the past several years, bringing significant value into organizational change work. As detailed in an article on changedesigners.eu, employees are more motivated when they play an active role in the change process. When they successfully complete a task related to that process, that's when the IKEA effect comes into play: they now find more value and are willing to further invest in the change.[156]

I hope next time you do change management work, you get some good inspiration from sitting on a comfortable sofa (which you assembled yourself!) or from a nice-smelling candle. Also, while you roam the IKEA maze, think about how much that experience resembles a change journey.

And always remember: there is still hope in this world, but not for sticking to IKEA shopping lists!

Until next week, happy shopping and happier changing!

What Getting Used to a New City Teaches Me about Change Management

First published on May 25, 2021

It is equally exciting and daunting getting used to a new city, even if you have done it several times before. You brace yourself for the administrative rollercoaster and learn to prioritize discovering the absolutely necessary places like Starbucks, closest supermarket, utility companies, bank, ice cream shop, IKEA, post office…

Starting to discover a new city after ten days of quarantine is a whole different adventure. Everything seems more intense, and there is also a little feeling like you have already missed out on something. While spending the quarantine in a lovely (getting smaller by the day) studio in the Old Town Center of Basel, I felt what American writer Judith Thurman described so beautifully accurately: "Every dreamer knows it is entirely possible to be homesick for a place you've never been to, perhaps more homesick than for familiar ground."

As soon as I was allowed to roam free, I went to get the keys to the new home and started walking around as much as humanly possible every day. While thinking about this week's article, I decided to try and see what getting used to a new city teaches me about change management, and here below are my wonderings and wanderings.

Replace fear of the unknown with curiosity. No matter how many "homes" you have changed, a new city, especially in another country that you have never visited before, is intimidating. It comes with loads and loads of questions, and Google Maps only has limited answers. You experience the whole range of emotions, and telling yourself that it is all part of the natural change curve doesn't make them any less intense. What has been helping me is to train my "knowledge emotion"—curiosity. Replace "I don't know" with "I don't know yet."

Travel books author Bill Bryson described something like this in *Neither Here Nor There*, an account of his first trip around Europe, when he spoke about how being in a country where you know nothing is like being a child all over again. You can't understand the language and have no clue how anything works, so every choice becomes a guess.[157]

No matter how many times you have done change management work in similar projects, every single initiative is a work of discovery. And it comes down to a series of interesting—and, in time, hopefully educated—guesses. You have a good engagement and communication plan? Great! You never know what you might discover as you "turn a corner," regardless of how well it is marked on your "map." Replace fear of the unknown with curiosity. Help those around you do the same. Trust that whatever comes, it can be dealt with, one meandering street at a time. Herman Melville, author of *Moby Dick,* has a great piece of wisdom for all change managers out there: "It is not down in any map, true places never are."[158]

Take things as they are, do not make comparisons. Without exception, every single time I move, people start asking me,

"So, how is it, do you like it better than where you lived before? Is it more or less something or other than the previous cities you lived in?" I used to make comparisons. Until I realized that kept me anchored in the past, and it only made me miss things, taking away from the wonder of discovering new ones. So, I stopped comparing cities and started to take experiences as they came. I enjoy some more than others, but I try to limit comparisons as much as possible. The reasons why I choose specific cities are different, the filters through which I experience them are different, so it would be like comparing apples to oranges. You might end up with an apple faulted for not being a good orange. In my native Romanian, the saying refers to comparing apples and pears…which brings me to a line from one of my favorite movies, *My Big Fat Greek Wedding*: "We are all fruit."[159]

In change management work, avoid making comparisons as much as possible. Ask yourself and people around you how the plan, situation and outcome serve their intended purpose, whether they solve the problem or fulfill the ambition and expectations. Not if it is more or less of something, but if it is fit for purpose. Being intentional and mindful about seeing things as simply different, not as more or less of something, gives you new perspectives.

Give it time. While I was in quarantine, the weather was really nice. Ever since I resumed freedom…yeah, you guessed right: mostly gloomy skies, rain… And everybody tells me this is unusual in Basel for this time of year. Every single change requires adjustments, and that takes time. Do not jump to conclusions and wait until you experience the new city in all kinds of weather and situations. Let your emotions stabilize. Stay aware of how your emotional journey influences your perceptions. On the day you discover your residence registration will take longer than expected or that the delivery of the rented furniture was mis-scheduled, everything will seem a bit off. Even if the sun is shining.

Do not feel bad if there are days when you do not feel like going out exploring. This is part of adjusting, too. Taking a break is just as important as taking a walk. Just like you need time to get used to a new city, people need time to adjust to organizational change, whatever it might be. Some don't mind the "weather," others need sunshine and blue skies to feel inspired to go explore. The emotional journey is not laid out in any strategy or plan, and it is deeply personal. Do not make comparisons, and give it time.

Getting used to a new city puts your curiosity, resourcefulness and resilience to the test. Pretty much like change management work. And it rewards you with the magic of new beginnings. Until next week, here's a wholehearted truth wrapped in words by French novelist Marcel Proust: "The real voyage of discovery consists not in seeking new landscapes, but in having new eyes."[160]

What Walking in the Rain Teaches Me about Change Management

First published on June 1, 2021

Last week marked a milestone: I met a colleague in person! We decided to meet up for coffee and a walk and talk, regardless of the weather. It was raining when we met, yet we kept true to our plan, got coffee and went for a walk.

I have always enjoyed walking in the rain, regardless of whether it is a summer shower or a fall drizzle. As we were walking, I found myself extremely grateful to the person who invented the lids for to-go cups, saving us from having to deal with "coffee spritz" on rainy walks. And slowly but surely, I started thinking about any change management learnings from walking in the rain.

It is not lost on me that I am writing this during a small series of particularly beautiful sunny days. It makes me wonder whether I would have been inclined to give this article a go had it still rained… Somehow, we always seem to assess people, things and situations more accurately in retrospect, through a lens of smiling nostalgia when we end up in a good place.

While appreciating the hindsight, I hope you will be left looking forward to your next walk in the rain after reading the thoughts below.

There is no such thing as bad weather, only inappropriate clothing. This saying is true for all kinds of weather—think snow and extreme cold, or sun and heat wave, yet people associate "bad weather" most often with rain.

The first time I remember going out for a walk in the rain on purpose was when I was a little kid on vacation at the seaside with my grandmother. We woke up to a rainy day and I started feeling sad about not going to the beach. My grandmother looked at me and said: "Come on, get ready, we are going to the beach." "But it's raining," I said. "So what? We are not going to swim and sunbathe, we are going for a walk. The beach is still there, why not enjoy it anyways?" I went for my light jacket instead of my swimming suit and got super excited about this new adventure.

In retrospect, this might have been my first early lesson in reframing. Walking in the rain is a great teacher for acceptance—a key milestone, arguably the most important one, on the change curve. American poet Henry Wadsworth Longfellow advocated for acceptance: "The best thing one can do when it's raining is to let it rain."[161] Don't give up on your plans when it starts to rain. Put on your jacket or grab an umbrella and go out. Change happens, and oftentimes it feels as beyond our control as the weather. Why not deal with it the same way? Accept it, make adjustments, big or small, and ride with it. Find some inspiration in this bit of reggae wisdom attributed to Bob Marley: "Some people feel the rain. Others just get wet."[162]

"A single gentle rain makes the grass many shades greener."[163] ...and not just on the other side, according to American essayist, poet, and practical philosopher Henry David

Thoreau. This quote makes me think about feedback—when we give it (so it doesn't feel like "raining on someone's parade"), and mostly how we give it. It is true that a storm serves a different purpose, equally beneficial under a specific set of conditions, yet "Criticism, like rain, should be gentle enough to nourish a man's growth without destroying his roots," as former American politician and lawyer Frank A. Clark put it.[164] Why go for a storm when a gentle rain might serve you better? Be patient, consistent and persistent when you give feedback. One gentle rain might not be enough in most cases, though. Take inspiration from nature, like Titus Lucretius Carus, an Ancient Roman poet and philosopher, whose only known work is the philosophical poem "On the Nature of Things": "The drops of rain make a hole in the stone, not by violence, but by oft falling." Be intentional and very careful about not letting your "drops of gentle rain" turn into Chinese dripping torture.

It is not just about your picnic. Every now and again, change management work teaches me to live vicariously. There are moments when it doesn't feel like the most pleasant of endeavors, yet it does make someone else's life easier or simpler—hopefully! While doing a bit of research for this article, I came across this quote from Tom Barrett, an American politician who served as the 44th Mayor of Milwaukee, Wisconsin, that expresses this thought beautifully: "If the rain spoils our picnic, but saves a farmer's crop, who are we to say it shouldn't rain?"[165]

Sadly, at some point, last week's coffee and walk and talk through the rain had to be cut short. Both my colleague and I had to get home to our Zoom calls-filled reality. As I tried to take a shortcut, I had to cross a small patch of grass—definitely getting greener from the rain, and, as I soon discovered, muddier, too. Which brings me to a moment of truth, after trying to convince you to enjoy rain to the fullest. So, here we go, the closing thought, courtesy of actor, director and producer Denzel Washington: "You pray for rain, you gotta deal with the mud, too. That's a part of it."[166]

Until next week, keep calm and enjoy walking in all kinds of weather!

What Looking at X-rays Teaches Me about Change Management

First published on June 8, 2021

Sitting in my dentist's office and trying to make sense of a "grinning zombie" type of X-ray was no fun. Nobody really expects fun after hearing, "Well, we need X-rays;" does good news need that level of investigation and confirmation? I did my best to talk myself into breathing deep and taking everything as it would come, yet I wasn't as ready as I thought I'd be when I heard, "Okay, we need to discuss the surgery plan." The room got a little bit darker, and the grays in the X-ray a whole lot more confusing.

There is a slide I use in all my change management workshops that says "People fear what they don't understand," and that got a new layer of meaning while I was looking at my X-ray two weeks ago. In a matter of seconds, my mind was filled with questions. "How many surgeries?" "When?" "What does this mean, a surgery plan?" "How painful will it be?" "Is there really really really no other way?" "How intrusive and painful will the invoice be?" "What if I say no?" "Do you mean *surgery* surgery?"

"How many anesthesia shots can I get in one sitting?" I even caught myself thinking, "Are we absolutely sure that is my X-ray we are looking at?"

As I was walking home trying to process this bit of news, it dawned on me that my questions were not fundamentally different from many points raised during change management conversations. And I started thinking about any takeaways for my work—why would I let a confusing conversation in a dark room go to waste?

Critical information lies in shadows and shades of grey. My X-ray had a bit of white, a bit of black, and a whole lot of grey. There I was, looking at it and only seeing a tiny fraction of the things I was hearing about. There were moments when the more I tried to concentrate to see what I was hearing about, the less I could actually perceive visually. It was all shadows and shades of grey to me. To all intents and purposes, I was "blind" to an entire world of critical information right there in front of my own eyes. I've felt like that at certain points along the journey of navigating some changes in both my professional and personal life. I am sure we all have been there, felt that.

Organizational changes make no exception. They hold critical information in shadows and shades of grey, and this confusion is exactly what people experience every now and again. In this context, X-rays come in different shapes and forms—conversations, detailed stakeholder analysis and mapping, risk assessments, change readiness assessments, change impacts assessments, "temperature checks" and surveys, points under "Any Other Business" on a meeting agenda, low responding rate to employee (dis)engagement surveys, even moments of silence on Zoom or Teams calls. It is all there, ready to be seen.

Nobel Prize-winning British chemist Dorothy Hodgkin gave an inspiring lesson on change management when she spoke of the X-ray's amazing ability to shed light on something unexpected with total certainty. The challenge is being able to explain the X-ray to the patient in a way the patient can understand.

Question and clarify what you see. As it was explained to me, a dental X-ray works on the principle that harder, more mineralized tissues will block more of the X-ray radiation. Due to this, hard tissues like the enamel and dentin will appear light in color. Spaces between teeth and tooth pulp appear dark because they are non-mineralized. One easy way to understand it is the harder something is, the lighter it appears. The softer something is, the darker it appears. It does sound a bit funny and borderline counterintuitive to me, yet it made me realize how wildly inaccurate my initial perception of the X-ray was. And it reminded me that sometimes, flipping something on its head is the only thing that makes sense.

Question and clarify what you see, make sure you understand shadows and shades of grey for what they are. Double-check a shadow is darker for real, and not the result of an accidental fingerprint. Make sure you look at the X-ray in all the possible ways, from all perspectives, from all angles. Flip everything on its head. Remember that some X-rays require contrast paint. I need to go for a 3-D X-ray.

Go to the level of detail and accuracy you need in your change management intervention. Question and clarify until you are as sure as you can be. Don't always trust what you see; remember that even salt looks like sugar. And just like X-rays teach us, there is always the possibility that the harder something is, the lighter it appears, the softer something is, the darker it appears.

Looking within comes at a price. The first way to interpret this is that X-rays are not necessarily cheap, and the more complex and subsequently more accurate they are, the more expensive they get. The kind of price that is particularly relevant for change management work covers the mental and emotional toll taken by being confronted with (potential) confirmation of a negative situation. A "full of shadows and shades of grey" situation. It also comes with a significant investment of trust in someone else to make (better, more) sense of your own X-ray for you. Add to this the vulnerability of sometimes saying, "I don't understand, could you explain this to me again?" Looking within comes at a price, whether it is a dental X-ray, therapy, or equally organizational change management work.

There is a beautiful quote from former President of the United Federation of Teachers Randi Weingarten where she states that tests can help teachers see where their students need help—but, just like an X-ray, tests are not a cure.[167] Before I left the dentist practice, I got the best, most comforting, yet most surprising part of the treatment plan: a hug. A genuine "let's try and squeeze all the shadows and shades of grey away" kind of hug. And that is the best takeaway for change management work: kindness. We do not have X-ray vision to know what shadows and shades of grey organizations and their people are trying to cure. Be kind. Be kinder than necessary. Always.

What Reading Books I Don't Like Teaches Me about Change Management

First published on June 15, 2021

As I was scrolling through my social media account while waiting for coffee to be ready one morning, I stumbled upon a post that made me laugh: "Know why an empty bottle of wine is better than a full one? It shows you know how to finish what you start. That's an achievement. Be proud."[168] Filled with this new sense of pride, I started to look around for other achievements. I saw a bar of chocolate… which reminded me of strength, according to American writer and newspaper journalist Judith Viorst: "Strength is the ability to break a bar of chocolate into four pieces with your bare hands, but only eat one of those pieces."[169] I am not strong. Just proud.

Moving on, and out of the kitchen, I passed by a coffee table filled with the books delivered the day before. And there it was, the inspiration for this week's piece: what reading teaches me about change management—and to make it more challenging, what reading books I don't like teaches me about change management.

Just in case it turns out you don't like it, I do hope you will stop for a second to ponder whether to quit or keep on reading… Who knows, it might just grow on you.

Be intentional in learning about what you don't like. Your taste is shaped on the go by every book you read. And there comes a point where you can predict quite accurately whether you would like a book based on genre, author and/or topic. You learn to spot small differences across the bestsellers' lists, therefore you will be more inclined to follow some recommendations and celebrated pieces over others.

My high school history teacher used to give us reading recommendations. He would go around the class asking us what we read and whether we liked it or not. If the answer was "Yes, I liked it," he would smile and move on. He only asked more when the answer was "No, I didn't like the book." He would come sit down close to you and ask you to tell him more about what you didn't like. That taught me to be intentional in learning about what I don't like and understand it. Little by little, I started to be able to say whether I found the plot interesting, but the writing really bad. Or that the characters were too cliché. Maybe the dialog felt…off, like something a person would not say in real life.

Reading books I don't like teaches me to frame and define issues and problems. To look at "why" a little differently. And these are good lenses for change management. Understanding what doesn't work and going deeper to uncover why it doesn't work are critical for transformations. They say life is too short to be spent reading bad books (or the ones you realize you don't like). Reading (any kind of) books is a waste of time only if you don't let them change you.

Do you quit or keep going? When is it fair to make the final decision that you do not like a book? Before you even buy it, based on reviews and your taste? After the first ten pages?

The first one hundred pages? Do you quit reading or finish the book no matter what? I do agree with mystery writer and poet Edgar Allan Poe on setting reading boundaries: "I intend to put up with nothing that I can put down."[170] Yet this would have made me give up on a book that had a most meaningful impact on my life. The first fifty pages were pure torture, I felt like a "squirrel pushing through jam" (an expression I picked up from a book, and I found it quite vivid), but then I hit the life-changing motherload.

At the same time, Thomas Mann's *The Magic Mountain* is my absolute Sisyphus reading. I started it seven times, and the furthest I got was page 314. Can I ever read it? Maybe, if I get stranded on a deserted island with nothing else but this one book…after I counted—and named!!!—all the sand particles on the beach…

There is always a change curve, and it takes some time to adjust. As you grow to understand what it is that you like or not about a book, the same happens with change and organizations. Some projects simply have those initial fifty pages that feel like "a squirrel pushing through jam." One common trait of great novels is the writer's ability to hook readers and keep them hooked. Letting readers wander around in their own heads is like letting them off the hook. Does this sound like change management work to you? Understand that people get hooked to different things, and even more importantly with different speeds. Whether you quit or keep going also depends on how well you understand what people don't like and why they don't like it. There is always the possibility of a plot twist.

Sit through the conversations you don't like and stand by your "because." My inner teenage rebel was on such a high every time I had the opportunity to say in history class, "Yes, I read that book, and I didn't like it. Because…" Years later I realized those reading assignments taught me patience and resilience to sit through things I didn't like, understand what I didn't like, and stand by my "because."

Just like you come across books you don't like, you find yourself in conversations or situations you don't like. If you choose to sit through these and not walk away, make sure to sit by your "because." Really listen and understand, and then say what you think, what you agree or disagree with. Reading books I don't like teaches me I first need to read them to be able to have my "because." We have two eyes and one mouth. We also have two ears and one mouth, and we should use them in this proportion. Read and listen, then speak. And just to clarify, there are conversations and situations where you absolutely must stand up and quit. All the (self-)discovery work going through as many diverse books and situations as possible will help you fine-tune your filter.

A great takeaway for change management work comes from American writer and journalist Lionel Shriver, who said that reading a bad book, or even one you're not ready for yet, can make you not want to read at all.[171] Remember this the next time you deal with "change resistance" on your project. Maybe people went through bad experiences or badly-timed initiatives. Help them rediscover change. Just like you would recommend a great book to someone you care about, tell them why this particular change is good for them.

Until next week, happy reading, and…be proud!

What Sitting on the Couch Teaches Me about Change Management

First published on June 29, 2021

One of my most recent discoveries is that furniture delivery time seems to pass by in loooooooooooonger days. Moving into a totally empty apartment redefined my relationship with furniture. I can think of very few things I ever wanted in my life more than I have been longing for a couch over the last two months. I miss that feeling of home, a couch corner, a cushion keeping my back happy, a book in my lap, and a large mug of coffee within easy reach (make that a glass of wine, as the book pages keep turning)… After all, it does not seem like too much to ask.

Couches always make me smile ever since the *Friends* episode with the legendary "pivot, pivot, pivot" and "I'd like to return this couch, I'm not satisfied with it" scenes.[172] "Couch potato" never made it on my list of "things I want to be when I grow up," but now that is all I dream about. One weekend, one glorious full weekend of doing nothing, maybe just imagining Benedict Cumberbatch whispering in my ear his famous "I can feel infinitely alive curled up on the sofa reading a book."[173]

Until my furniture gets delivered, I thought I'd keep myself busy by thinking about what sitting on the couch teaches me about change management. And here we go, with some thoughts on how people might find comfort during change. Sit back, relax, and maybe you can read this in Benedict Cumberbatch's voice…

Comfort is relative. Choosing a couch reminded me that different people define comfort differently. Some like deep, soft couches. Some go for loads of cushions, throws, and blankets. Then you have the ones more on the minimalist, fit-for-purpose side. There are "wide sitting couch" people, and then you have the "narrow couch" tribe. The "love seat" romantics. Upholstery fabrics make the conversation even more complicated. Leather, cotton, synthetic microfiber, linen…somebody please get me a fainting couch! Climate is also important, as humidity, temperature and overall weather conditions might impact your "couch experience." How people define comfort and then subsequently go about their choice of couch is very similar to how they define and perceive change. We all need a place to sit, yet we define being comfortable based on different factors.

A change manager is sometimes a furniture sales consultant. You need to understand what people are actually looking for in a comfortable couch, how many seats, what type of fabric. Always ask about budget, and pay attention to the timing of this question within the overall buying conversation. Sometimes it helps to get this information up front, sometimes you feel the buying decision will ultimately be made based on something else. What type of home does your customer have? What's the interior design style? Expected timeline for delivery? Custom-made requirements? Before they feel comfortable sitting on their new sofa, your customers need to feel comfortable with you, so smile, listen to understand their needs, and make a meaningful sale.

Company matters. When I got the furniture order confirmation, one particular figure stood out for me in the middle of the fourth page: six. And not just because it is my lucky number, but because I realized I have never bought a six-seat couch before. It made me feel good to imagine having friends over, talking and laughing and feeling comfortable in all the meanings of the word. In my definition of "comfortable," company matters. The people you interact with shape your perception of comfort and comfortable. Who do you spend time with, how close do you sit, how "far apart," who can reach the coffee table easiest, who leans over to turn the lamp on, who sits on the remote…

All these have their equivalents in organizations and teams. Look around and really pay attention to who is on your "organizational couch." Are they comfortable? Are you comfortable in their company? Are they comfortable in yours?

"The hardest distance is always from the sofa to the front door."[174] —a good change management teaching from Estonian politician and decathlete Erki Nool. Making the decision to stand up and get into action requires not just energy, but intention and purpose—mission-critical for change. For me, this distance also speaks about those moments of goodbye after some time spent in the company of friends, a nice evening come to an end. American comedian Demetri Martin said that "The sofa is the enemy of productivity."[175] Not necessarily, if you use your "couch time" to build intention, purpose and energy for what you want to do when you get up and walk out the door.

Be mindful and spend some time with your thoughts as you sit on your couch. Having done this for some time now, I got one of my key takeaways for change management work: sometimes, the couch is uncomfortable because of what you think while sitting on it. And then you know you need to stand up, walk out the door and do whatever you need to do to come back home and feel comfortable on your own couch again.

Until next week, enjoy the comfort of your couch—and of your thoughts!

What Shopping Online Teaches Me about Change Management

First published on July 6, 2021

This upcoming Wednesday is "cardboard and paper recycling day" on my street, a monthly occurrence I have been looking forward to. What started with two cardboard shipping envelopes pushed to the side of my desk silently grew into three large boxes of neatly cut and folded cardboard extravaganza occupying one corner of the hallway.

One of my key reflections sparked by the pandemic was that the worst part of online shopping is having to get up and get the card out of the wallet. This past weekend, during two hours of cutting and folding cardboard envelopes and boxes, I challenged myself to reflect on what shopping online teaches me about change management. A few recent conversations made me think about how the pace of change within many organizations feels like an "add to cart" spree, with the entire spectrum of associated emotions. The rush of anticipation right after placing the order, the joy of receiving it and ultimately the frustration of dealing with the leftover packaging piling up until recycling day.

Can I afford it? Yes, and… The first question I asked myself when reflecting on my online shopping behavior was how I perceive it differently from the offline experience. In both instances, "Can I afford it?" is a critical question. The fundamental difference for me is that, when in a shop, I immediately move to "Can I carry it home?" Shopping online removes this constraint, and consequently dilutes the quality of my decision-making process by not triggering (inner) conversations around prioritization, timeliness, logistics.

The organizational equivalents of "Can I afford it?" and "Can I carry it?" should be used together in this sequence in any and all change management conversations. And here's an additional reflection: just because I don't do the carrying myself doesn't mean that deliveries happen by magic. It took less than one month for the Swiss Post and DHL people covering my residence area to start recognizing me on the street. All thanks to "their carrying" prompted by "my affording." Who are the "delivery people" for the change initiatives your organization perceives as affordable? And how much organizational recycling do you generate with your business "add-to-cart" decisions?

Easy return policy doesn't guarantee return. I wish I could say that I do take full advantage of the easy return policies most online shopping offers. Unless the value of the purchase is significant, I cannot say I have a spotless track record of returning stuff. While cutting and folding the cardboard boxes this weekend, I started thinking about the cumulative effect of not taking advantage of return policies. Just like small shipping envelopes pile up and ultimately occupy a big space, small amounts add up and create significant impact. Some buying decisions are made easier when a "no questions asked, 30 days return policy" guarantee tips the scale in favor of "add to cart."

What is the return policy on your change interventions? Do you have one? How consistent are you in making sure you take advantage of it and not letting "stuff" pile up? How would your decisions be different if they all came with the disclaimer "All sales final. No returns. No refunds"?

It is convenient to shop online. It is inconvenient to return it—repackage it, take it to the post office, possibly wait in line to get it shipped. So you "tolerate" the buy and accept the cost, even as it becomes a "write-off," while the seller goes on believing you accepted the product. After all, they did make it easy for you to return it. Not taking full advantage of the return policy is on you, not them, right?

The convenience of 24/7 shopping availability turns into inconvenient expectations management. Shopping online creates and maintains the illusion of everything being available all the time. If no big, bold red letters scream at you "currently unavailable" or "out of stock," everything is "add-to-cartable." I have been reflecting on how shopping online is an expression of "living/working online behavior"—"orders" piling up into my Outlook calendar, oftentimes overlapping, the green dot next to people's names marking them as available at all times, the underlying expectation that time saved by not commuting or having to actually come to the office and go back home is automatically repurposed into more "available time."

How the expectation of having everything "one click away" turns into so much more disappointment and frustration when the delivery time turns out to be longer than expected, or delays occur, or deliveries get lost… Many people say that "offline is the new luxury," and they are right. How does shopping, working and living online influence your perception of availability? How do the red, yellow and green dots next to people's names drive your expectations management? How about your trust management?

As I make a Post-it note to remember to take out the recycling this evening, the lingering reflection over my shopping online is how the overall experience defines the difference between "price" and "value." Is convenience the enemy of responsibility? And I have already started to think about ways to prompt these reflections through some of the upcoming change management conversations.

Until next week, keep calm, add to cart and take advantage of the return policies!

What Changing Bags Teaches Me about Change Management

First published on July 20, 2021

Two weeks ago, I had my appointment for the first COVID vaccine shot. As I was waiting for the vaccine center staff to come and check my documents, I experienced a most feminine adrenaline rush: "My passport…where is my passport??? Oh no, I must have left it in the other bag!!!!" I have no idea why I decided to change my usual everyday backpack for a crossbody bag that day, but I did. And for the first time in more than a decade, I forgot to check whether I moved my passport from one bag to the other.

A quick inventory of the contents of my bag made me question my overall life priorities… A backup mask, two disinfectant bottles, a receipt from a flower shop, a notification for registered mail waiting for me at the post office, my keys, a pen, Post-it notes and a mango-flavored lip balm. And my wallet, where I had my residence permit with a photo (a way more normal-looking photo than the one in my passport, by the way) and all my identity details. So, I thought I could use that as Identity Plan B. And it worked, thank goodness!

On my way home, while ruining my lip balm with ice cream, I started wondering whether I could take any teachings from the changing bags episode into my change management work. I hope I get to move all my ideas from my head and onto the below list.

Between utility and accessory, how many bags do you really need? In all honesty, this is a painful question to even type out! If I define "need" strictly through the lens of "needing something to carry my stuff around in," then the answer is pretty simple. The real "counting" starts when I define "need" as a means to say something about myself through the choice of my bag, handbag, purse, backpack... It is not just a fashion statement. It is an identity statement.

This is a good takeaway for change management work. Between utility and accessory, how many transformation initiatives does an organization need? What identity statements do projects make beyond being within the "fashion trends" of digital transformation, culture turnaround, future of work, organizational redesign? There is no one single answer to this question. And definitely no "one size fits all." American writer of legal thrillers Lisa Scottoline gave us a real-life inspired change management reflection: "Let's talk about a decision women have to make every morning—big purse or little purse?"[176]

What are the statements of your identity? The most important item in my "bag of the day" is my passport. I keep my ID card tucked inside the cover of the passport. Unless I forget them "in the other bag," these two are always with me. Luckily, I have other means to prove my identity, like the residence permit—which, thankfully enough, I keep separately from the passport. Needing to prove my identity without having my passport with me prompted me to think about the various "statements of identity" and how important, helpful and even safe it is to keep them separate.

More often than not, change management work is perceived as managing some kind of loss, hopefully before gaining something new. If we try to imagine organizational equivalents of a misplaced or lost identity document, what are the other statements of organizational identity you can rely on? How many ways does one organization have to prove their identity? How many and what types of these identity statements can one organization afford to misplace, forget or lose without losing any means of proving what they are and what they stand for?

What do you match your bag with? The spin-offs of this seemingly simple question are virtually infinite… Should your shoes match your bag? Typically, people match their handbag to the shoes they are wearing. If you are wearing gray shoes, you can choose a bag with fun colors or designs—but your shoes and purse don't have to match. Just like with any style choice, you can mix and match as long as your overall look is cohesive. If one piece is a true statement, then tone down on the others. Match your purse to your dress and have a pair of brightly colored shoes.

Should bag and shoes match for a wedding? Here's a tip from the article "Mother of the Bride: Getting your outfit right for the big day" by Beverley Edmondson Millinery: it's more important that your whole outfit goes together, so there's no need to match your shoes, bag, and hat. In fact, there's such a thing as over-matching![177] It is never simple, is it? It looks like it all comes down to a "coherent look" and not so much a rigid set of strict rules.

Could the same be true for organizational transformation? I would venture to agree. It is a bit of systems thinking at work here. Value interaction over action and reaction, the coherence of the whole over the strict matching of the parts. However, do not lose the matching part completely. Here is a good piece of advice from whowhatwear.com: choose a color palette for your outfit rather than trying match everything. If your purse matches your clothes, you should pick shoes that stand out—and vice versa.[178] Do not be afraid to mix and match—in your fashion choices as well as in your organizational transformation decisions. As long as the outcome is comfortable, consistent and true to who you are, dare to make bold decisions!

It is almost frustrating that today, after writing this article, I chose to work from home, and there is no immediate "need" for a bag… On this note, my closing thought is that we all look more put together with a cup of coffee and a new bag!

Until next week, take care, and add that bag to cart…

What Removing Sticky Labels Teaches Me about Change Management

First published on July 27, 2021

There is nothing, absolutely n-o-t-h-i-n-g that drives me insane faster than a sticky label carelessly stuck on the front cover of a book and just WILL. NOT. COME. OFF!!! Or, when it does, it leaves a sticky surface that gets the book glued to anything and everything—wrapping paper, an older-than-life receipt you have forgotten in your bag, some other book you have on your coffee table. You just do not do that to people!!! Oh, sticking it on the back cover right in the middle of the writer's bio doesn't make me happy either. And if you think this is the perfect opportunity for you to tell me to get a Kindle, please don't. Just don't!

Because it is not just about labels on books. It is about labels on pretty much everything. You know those long, plastic sticky labels with the size on the front of clothes? Every now and again, they leave a nasty trace behind. Or those labels on nice-shaped wine bottles that make perfect vases. They take forever and a decade's worth of hot water, soap and vinegar to come off. There is no "get a Kindle" solution for those, is there?

Last week, I finally took the time to go downstairs to try and remove the temporary label with my name that I put on my mailbox when I moved into the new home in mid-May. The use of "temporary" is one of my most sarcastic comments to date, since that little thing will live to see the end of all worlds. And, in case you are wondering, I did have professional label remover spray, a scraper and some other…"tools." I also had a life to live, and after half an hour, I admitted "temporary" defeat and came back inside. It felt like such a waste of time, and the only way to turn that into a "research investment" was to think about what removing sticky labels teaches me about change management.

Hopefully, you will enjoy the thoughts below, and they will "temporarily" stick to your memory.

Other people's actions aren't an excuse to do a sloppy job. I was in a bookstore a few years ago and saw one of the employees carelessly sticking price labels on books before putting them on the shelves. He didn't even look where the label went, just grabbed a book from a box, put the label on, put the book on the shelf, job done. I walked up to him and asked why he went about his task so casually. "People take these labels off, so why bother, right?" No, not right. What other people might or might not do with the end result of your work is never an excuse to do a sloppy job.

Sadly, there are organizational equivalents to "temporary stickers" where "we need to get something up and running for the moment and we can sort it out later, there is so much change going on right now, people will not pay that much attention." Sometimes the word "agile" gets thrown into the conversation, and quite a versatile little sticker this is… Whenever I hear this, a bit of change management inspiration courtesy of American poet and civil rights activist Maya Angelou runs through my mind: people may forget everything else, but what they won't forget is "how you made them feel."[179] People will remember whether they felt inspired, curious, comfortable and comforted, or simply frustrated. How do you want to make people feel? How can you help them feel that even through seemingly temporary, casual and sometimes smallest things in the bigger scheme of (organizational) life?

If you can't control how something gets labeled, what can you control? As a writer or the designer of a book cover, there is no real way that you can influence how the price label will get stuck on your book in a store. But then, what can you control? Well, design, for starters. Make it airy, try to mitigate the risk of having relevant information getting lost under a pesky sticky label.

What, how, and how much can you put forward in a change initiative that stays relevant when different bits and pieces get lost or unintentionally covered? Make that information available via multiple channels. Go for a dust jacket, the detachable outer cover, usually made of paper and printed with text and illustrations. The dust jacket protects the book covers from damage. However, since it is itself relatively fragile, and since dust jackets have practical, aesthetic and sometimes financial value, it may in turn be wrapped in another jacket, usually transparent. So many layers, you might say. Yes, layered information is an everyday reality, in both our personal and professional lives. It prompts the reflection on what is temporary or permanent information.

While writing this paragraph, it dawned on me that one of the most temporary bits of information put on sticky labels is price, the "value" of something. And how excited we get when we can enjoy a "sale," "promotion," "discount" or "final offer." We can control what information we put out there, our intention behind it and our mindful and intentional care to protect it. We cannot control how people label it later. And this is equally true about a book, a relationship, a transformation project. We cannot control the quality of the label and glue and how easy it might be to remove the label afterward, or other people's intention to remove it at all.

Labels change. Do you clean them, or pile them on top of each other? When sticky labels found me as a hopeful pre-teen in post-communist Romania in the late 1990s, it was a life-changing discovery. Much more so than free access to Coca-Cola, chocolate and bananas… I started putting them on everything. Preserves and jam season was forever changed as I helped my grandmother label tens and tens of jars. But, most of all, I could label my school notebooks. Patience has never been my strength, so scrapping the labels of the notebook plastic covers every year was not an activity I excelled at. Year after year, the labels piled one on top of the other—math, biology, geography, history… If you ever needed a concrete, tangible proof that "change is the only constant," there you go!

I was reminded of this a couple of months ago when I bought a box of permanent markers with a rather thick pile of price labels, a testimony of the pricing policy history. Yeah, the irony was not lost on me—temporary price labels for permanent markers. How do we go about changing labels? Do we clean them or just pile them on top of each other?

How do we go about "changing labels" in change management work? Do we "clean" the environment or pile changes one on top of the other? Just for the fun of it, I tried to peel the price labels off the markers box and plotted the prices on a graph (former corporate consultant having fun…). The visual looked like a most irregular EKG. If people could plot the change interventions of your organization, what kind of EKG would they get? Would it speak of a healthy heart with a steady rhythm or would it alert you to an impending heart attack?

How I can peel the label off an item is very much a part of my customer experience. A few years ago, I came up with a theory that great companies make an effort, financial or otherwise, to get good quality labels and carefully place them on products, so people can enjoy their purchase without the pain of removing sticky bits and goo.

The definition of a label is "a brief description given for purposes of identification."[180] How "sticky" are your labels—the ones you attach to yourself and others? The labels we attach to people and various parts of our life are the topic of a future random thought.

Until then, keep calm and enjoy mindful labeling!

What Living in an Apartment with No Lights Teaches Me about Change Management

First published on August 3, 2021

The last three months have been marking a most unusual and unexpected stroll down memory lane. Growing up in communist Romania meant a lot of time without power filled with stories told by my grandparents, so I would associate the dark with something comforting. I learned to write and read mostly by candlelight. And television never really became part of my daily routine.

When I moved into my new home in Switzerland in mid-May, the last thing I expected to be reminded of was my childhood. Yet, this is exactly what happened. The "empty apartment" bit in the renting ad meant exactly that. With impressive Swiss precision and accuracy. An apartment with no furniture, and…no lights. Well, with one light: the one in the fridge. It reminded me of that joke that goes: "If we are not supposed to have late night snacks, then why is there a light in the fridge?"

The first night I spent here in a new home, in a country I had never visited before, felt strangely familiar. In the dark.

With one thing I didn't have while growing up: chocolate. Three months later, there are still no lights installed. Because the lamps took forever to be delivered. Because it got to vacation time and it became quite a challenge to find someone to install them. Because, maybe, I needed to be reminded of enjoying stories in the dark. Only this time I did my own storytelling, and it got to be about what living in an apartment with no lights teaches me about change management.

You need light to show other people things you are familiar with. The only instance when it is really frustrating not having lights is when I want to give my friends a virtual tour of the apartment, and with all these time zones we are spread across, it's already dark for me. I fell in love with this apartment the first split second I saw it in a set of five blurry photos in mid-March. It felt like home the moment I opened the door. I just want everybody to see it like I see it. And for that, I need light.

American film director and exhibition curator Aaron Rose summarized this change management takeaway beautifully: "In the right light, at the right time, everything is extraordinary."[181] This is what change needs: right light and right timing. So how do you make sure you have these in your interventions? Communication is a critical source of light. The power of your words translates into voltage, warm light or cool light, natural or artificial. Do you want the light to be turned on automatically when it gets dark or there is movement? Or do you want to have full control over the switch? My apartment taught me I need light to show other people things I am familiar with. The same applies to organizations. Turn the light on!

"The electric light did not come from the continuous improvement of the candle."[182] I have always loved this quote attributed to Oren Harari, a former business professor at the University of San Francisco. It speaks to me about positive disruption, so critical to innovation. As I enjoyed a glass of

| EVERYDAY INSPIRATION FOR CHANGE

Prosecco by candlelight this past weekend, I was reminded of it. No matter the number of candles in the apartment, ceiling lamps did not materialize into existence. Hopefully, this week will see some positive disruption in my home.

Continuous improvement is a fine balancing act between evolution and revolution. How do you go about it in your organization? Having lights at home speaks to me about the power of choice. I will be able to make a choice on the kind of light I want: electric or candle. Or none. That is also a choice. Innovation creates options. Choices. Which bring accountability, ownership and commitment. All essential to change management.

"There is nothing in the dark that isn't there when the lights are on."[183] —an ever-inspiring thought from screenwriter and narrator Rod Serling. The first time I read this, I thought of comfort and safety. And then, every time this came to my mind, it pulled me into the direction of self-awareness and authenticity. How do you create comfort and safety for yourself and those around you? By making sure there are no surprises in the dark. By making sure light will not make you or others face something dreadful. No bad surprises. Not to yourself, not to others. Know yourself and your organization just as well as you know your home in the dark. Authenticity creates comfort and safety. Personal and organizational authenticity is what makes people trust "there is nothing in the dark that isn't there when lights are on."

As it is morning now and the apartment is filled with the light of a new day, my closing thought before pressing "publish" comes from German writer Ruth E. Renkel: "Never fear shadows. They simply mean there's a light shining somewhere nearby."[184] It is always easier to write about shadows in the light of day. Yet another lesson learned for change management, courtesy of my home.

Until next week, keep calm, and make your own lighting choices.

What Unpacking the Moving Boxes Teaches Me about Change Management

First published on August 10, 2021

After experiencing roughly four months of transition associated with the joys and challenges of an international relocation during the COVID pandemic, the time for unpacking the moving boxes finally arrived. Most days over the past week felt like small Christmases with opening boxes and unwrapping things.

Getting my things out of the boxes after a long time felt like, all of a sudden, I got new things. As the weekend passed and I had the time to walk around my home and think about the best way to use the space and the furniture, I started to look at my things more mindfully. And suddenly it hit me: nothing was new. It might certainly feel like that after everything was packed for so long—and especially when I found items that, with all the commotion, I mistakenly thought lost about three relocations ago. Once the joy of unpacking and the comfort of the familiar dimmed down, I realized—there is nothing new in an old box.

Prompted by this realization, I started to think about any takeaways for change management. And, as I unpack them from my mind-box, please find them below:

From the moving box to the final place is not always a straightforward, one-step process. The unpacking spree was sparked by the confirmation of the last furniture order delivery for this week. And I needed to vacate the room that was designated as the "residential warehouse" for the past few months. So, while keeping my fingers crossed that the delivery would actually happen (if there is one thing this change taught me, it's that no matter how many confirmations, it is not really yours until it is in your home…), I took the things out of the boxes and put them in temporary places. Books on the bookshelves in no particular order, clothes in the wardrobes and in no particular drawers. Just get them out of the boxes and get the boxes down in the basement storage space. Sometimes, the most important thing is to just start and make small progress.

What is the equivalent of moving boxes taking up a space you need vacated in your organization? Do not use the excuses of not having time, energy, resources or clarity of the final setup, to put off unpacking. Just start. Sometimes, the most important thing is to make space— in your life, as well as in your organization—for new things to come. Space that has been occupied by old boxes. Get rid of the boxes one at a time and know you can make final, better decisions about the things in the boxes later.

Good unpacking starts with good packing. My moving boxes were not labeled properly. It was definitely not the best packing experience of my life, but this is a story for another time and a good bottle of wine. I had no idea what to expect as I opened one box at a time. This contributed to my joy and excitement last week, but it had been a source of big frustration over the last months. I knew I had things I needed in the house, but I did not know which boxes they were in. In most cases, it was easier to buy quick solutions than to open who knows how many boxes.

The takeaway here for my change management work is

that good unpacking starts with good packing. Make things easy to find, especially when they are needed. Avoid unnecessary spending of time and money and do a proper job packing. One organizational instance that comes to my mind is knowledge management. How do you pack and store information in your organization? Is it easy to find? Do people spend resources on temporary fixes?

On a more personal note, thinking about packing reminded me of a wonderful quote from American naturalist and wildlife photographer Richard Proenneke where he speaks on the inherent sadness that comes with packing, wondering if the new place ahead of you will be as good as the place you're leaving behind.[185] This is equally applicable in life and organizations. Every packing brings some sadness. It is okay to pack some of it. Do not forget to also pack the hope that the new destination will be awesome. Do not forget to pack the courage to find out. Make hope and courage easy to find.

Nothing stays in a box forever. I heard this as a reply in a pirate treasure hunt movie when I was little and it came to my mind as I started writing this piece. It made me smile, and I accepted the challenge from this memory. The first thought it sparked related to change management is about emotions. Particularly negative ones that are triggered during transitions. People choose to keep their emotions in a box for an infinite number of reasons. Because of education. Maybe cultural influences. Perceived lack of psychological safety. But nothing stays in a box forever. It comes out as resistance, low and slow adoption rates. Even, sometimes, as updated CVs and LinkedIn profiles marked as "open to recruiters."

Nothing stays in a box forever. Especially not emotions. There is no use putting more duct tape around the box or taking it down in the basement. Open the box. Take everything out. Clean the items that were inside. Clean the box, cut it, take it to the recycling center. Make sure you build open and safe spaces so that people will not need to look for boxes and duct tape for their opinions and emotions.

As I am writing this, I am living proof that there is a stage in unpacking during house moves when it feels like auditioning for *Hoarders*. For days, I thought to myself "Just go around it!" I will think about this again tomorrow. And the day after, and some more days after that. I also think about the fact that "home is where the heart is"…even if you can't remember which box you packed it in.

Until next week, keep calm and just start mindful unpacking!

What Cleaning Windows Teaches Us about Change Management

With Jerome Huggup
First published on August 17, 2021

It was a beautiful, still chilly spring morning in Luxembourg when we met for a coffee and a walk. As usual, our conversation flowed from one topic to another as our steps took us to turn corners randomly. And the best gift of that morning started with Jerome saying, "Hey, I got some ideas for your Tuesday articles."

Life happened, and it took a while for this article to come together. A lot of sun and rain touched our windows in the meantime and made us see that morning's idea in the right light it needed before it was written.

We hope you will enjoy our takeaways for change management from cleaning windows. And may it open your windows to new perspectives.

Listen to understand how people see through your windows. I invited a couple of friends over for dinner and happy hour at my house because I am still reluctant to go out to restaurants due to COVID. While we were enjoying a few beverages, one of my guests asked, "When was the last time you cleaned your windows?" For those of you who are outside of Europe, cleaning your windows seems to be a weekly tradition here (I am making this up). You can see the pride of clean windows everywhere you go in Europe, from the shopkeepers cleaning the windows at 6:00 AM before customers arrive to old ladies and those still working at home pridefully cleaning their windows in the morning.

The question from my guest caused me to stop for a minute and examine the windows in my house and to my surprise, my windows were in need of a good cleaning. At times while we are working on a project or in a situation, we often do not see the issues (dirty windows) or we get complacent and accept things the way they are. Sometimes bringing in an outside viewpoint highlights the problems that we could not see or helps us to get unstuck.

Take time to look from the outside in. The next day, I went out, bought cleaning supplies and cleaned all the windows in my house. Beaming with pride, I stopped and admired my wonderful window-cleaning job. Later that afternoon, I went for a walk basking in the wonderful sun of Luxembourg (my home "by the sea") and thinking to myself what an amazing job I did. As I returned from my walk, I stopped outside my home to admire my cleaning masterpiece. As I stared at the windows of my house, I could see nothing but streaks in the windows and they looked worse than before. That is when I decided to call an expert and seek advice on how to properly clean the windows and not end up with streaks. I received some great advice and then cleaned the windows once again. In the end, my windows were beautiful and without streaks.

When nearing completion of a project, you sometimes realize that the outcome you were going for is not attainable. This does not mean your efforts were in vain and that you should abandon the project. It simply means that you might have to seek expert advice to help you adjust and complete the project. Always take a step back from your project, reassess, re-evaluate to see if you are on the right path, and never be too embarrassed or prideful to bring in an expert to evaluate your project before rolling out the final product.

You are your own window. There was a little bit of a change manager in Irish playwright George Bernard Shaw, who put it beautifully: "Better keep yourself clean and bright; you are the window through which you must see the world."[186] We see the world through our own "window," cleaned and equally dirtied by our experiences, hopes, expectations, knowledge, biases, and judgment errors. The "view" we allow ourselves to have from the inside out as well as what we allow others to see from the outside in are the result of how we care for our window through self-awareness, self-compassion and self-care.

This is as true for our personal life as it is for our professional journey. When light that is traveling through the air hits a glass window, some of the light is reflected off it. The rest of the light passes through the window but it bends (or refracts) as it enters your home. Keep this in mind next time you look through a window and know that reality reaches different people through their own windows in different ways.

Until next week, keep calm, may your windows be clean and streak-free and may all your projects be a success!

What Hanging Out in My Hanging Chair Teaches Me about Change Management

First published on August 24, 2021

It was a late Saturday evening in early March 2016, a little bit before midnight, and about halfway through my nine-month-long stay in a hotel in Tallinn. I was having a Bailey's at the hotel bar, letting my mind wander freely as I watched the snow fall outside the big windows. I still have no idea where the thought came from, but it appeared as clear and crisp as the big snowflakes clinging onto the glass: if I ever feel like "making a home," I will get myself a hanging chair.

Five years, four addresses and three countries later, it happened. The very first thing I bought for the new place, while still in quarantine in the temporary housing, and before even setting foot in the new apartment, was a hanging chair. It felt like the timing was perfect. From the moment I saw the photos of the place in the online renting ad, I knew there would be a hanging chair on the terrace. I remembered that late evening thought in Tallinn, and a bottle of Bailey's was the first thing that made it into the new fridge as soon as I could move in. Because…hopes and dreams, you know, priorities.

There hasn't been a day when I have not spent some time hanging out in my hanging chair. Reading, watching the sky, listening to the birds, letting my mind wander and wonder freely. And I guess it was just a matter of time before it started wondering about what hanging out in my hanging chair teaches me about change management. I hope you will hang on to reading the list below until the end. And if you so feel like getting a glass of Bailey's, cheers!

"Stillness is where creativity and solutions are found."[187] —a great insight from preacher Meister Eckhart, a Dominican monk considered the inventor of serenity, and whose work was deemed as misleading and partly heretical in the 14th century by Pope John XXII. I totally love the rocking motion of the hanging chair. Yet, every single time I sit in it, what I crave most is that first moment of absolute stillness when the motion stops and I delay reaching out for the nearest wall to give it a new push. The moment is pure bliss. Oftentimes, without even realizing it, I hold my breath just before it happens, close my eyes, and live it to the fullest.

There have been loads of conversations about stillness, and the topic has gained special interest during the turmoil we have been navigating over the past 18 months. An interesting read is Ryan Holiday's *Stillness Is the Key*, inspired by the wisdom of the ancient stoics. Stillness, he argues, whether physical, spiritual or mental, is the art of finding inner peace, and it can save us from the chaos.[188]

Transformations in our life—equally personal and professional, feel like chaos. And with the wild pace of technology, the feeling that no matter how quickly we move, how much we accomplish, it's never enough can be exacerbated. Whatever inner peace means for each of us, we need to be intentional about building pockets of stillness into our lives. That reset brings about creativity and solutions we could never see while running, running and running faster.

"When nothing is sure, everything is possible."[189] For many people, comfort and safety are described by words like "grounded," "anchored," "settled," "rooted." For others, yours truly included, comfort and safety come from what Dame Margaret Drabble, an English novelist, described as "When nothing is sure, everything is possible." My hanging chair reminds me of this. There is nothing "grounded" about it, and everything is possible—a perfect moment of stillness, an unexpected gust of wind, a soothing rocking motion.

There are moments like this in every bit of change management work and the ones who can make the most out of it are the ones who believe that everything is possible. Look for a moment of stillness and find a way. Find *your* way! One stillness practice that I have found particularly useful in my change management work is to weigh advice against the counsel of my convictions. Always ask for advice. And always, always, always keep in mind that advice represents the perspectives of another person who has lived an entirely different experience from you, who has formed a different outlook on the situation than you. Trust your intuition, give your mind time to process and remember: "When nothing is sure, everything is possible."

Suspend above, with the lower portion swinging free. While looking through the many definitions of "(to) hang," I realized that the primary meaning is to be suspended above while the lower portion swings free. I will skip the next definition involving rope and necks and capital punishment and stop for a second at the mention of "hang" being used as an expression in South Africa to cover a range of strong emotions from enthusiasm to anger.

These meanings are so rich with takeaways for change management work! They make me think of stakeholder engagement, first of all. How the work should "be suspended above," meaning anchored in the firm vision and buy-in from the senior stakeholders, while the "lower portion swinging free" is the freedom, compassion, and trust in creating a space to be filled with the energy, commitment, hopes and experiences of the people within an organization. In terms of emotions, enthusiasm and anger and all the emotions in between are fully present and lived throughout any change journey. Think of a hanging chair—secured above, with the seating part dangling free to find its own rhythm of movement and moments of stillness.

I put the hanging chair together myself—which, knowing that my superpower is definitely not the wielding of a wrench, made me a little uneasy to sit in it at first. And soon the jokes started to appear: "So, are you still enjoying your temporarily hanging chair?" Slowly but surely, I gained confidence. "When nothing is sure, everything is possible," remember? So why wouldn't it be possible for my hanging chair to stay... well, hanging?

And here is an additional takeaway for change management, courtesy of social media: "A bird sitting on a tree is never afraid of the branch breaking, because her trust is not on the branch but on her own wings. Always believe in yourself."[190]

As I am writing this, the bells of the church nearby started tolling. After years and years of soul-searching, I made peace with myself as an agnostic. Yet, without exception and most certainly without looking for it, I always ended up living close to churches. Which now makes me remember a part of one of Meister Eckhart's sermons: "If the only prayer you said in your whole life was 'thank you,' that would suffice."[191] And I realize that I am, indeed, grateful—for my hanging chair, for my moments of stillness, and for my hope and belief that everything is possible.

Until next week, keep calm, hang in, hang on and hang out with yourselves!

What Getting WiFi Boosters Teaches Me about Change Management

First published on August 31, 2021

After months of getting frustrated with having to pay attention to where I was in my home to make sure I enjoyed proper WiFi coverage, I finally decided to order two WiFi boosters. I so wish it had been as easy as advertised—"plug and play"—but it came down to a lot of furniture rearrangement (for direct access to the only wall socket in the living room), some electric work on the sockets in two other rooms, and, overall, me getting to the point where I wished I had chosen a much, much, much smaller apartment.

Then, of course, moving on to the joys of getting help from the technical support center. 47 minutes waiting on the line to get transferred to an English speaker, then running in between the rooms to connect and sync the devices… I am totally convinced I was born in the wrong era. Although, with my luck, if I ever do manage to use time travel, I might get thrown back into the "corset age"… WiFi troubles are so much easier to breathe through; I guess I should be grateful for small mercies…

While hearing Ross from *Friends* in my head with "Why do bad things happen to good people???" on heavy rotation, I tried to shift my train of thought. And, no surprise by now, I started thinking about any takeaways for change management—boosting my thinking with a glass of Prosecco savored in my hanging chair. Now that I have good coverage on the terrace, I tried to put together the thoughts below.

Meaningful conversations are the everyday life equivalents of WiFi boosters. One thing that comes up quite often in change management conversations is scalability —how can we scale change interactions? There are methodologies and tools that can definitely help with increasing the volume and amplitude of change. Yet, after nearly two decades of change management work, I have come to believe that the single most significant way to trigger deep, sustainable and exponential change is through meaningful conversations. Each conversation that adds value to someone's life, be it personal or professional, acts as a WiFi booster, strengthening the signal and expanding the coverage area so that the signal can be picked up and transmitted further by another WiFi booster, and another one after that.

Grow fully into your own space and own it unwaveringly. For the past month, I have been struggling with deciding on a personal issue. A "connect and sync" situation as old as time, I guess, between my mind and heart. Wouldn't it be wonderful to have some sort of WiFi booster on the collarbone, press "sync" for ten seconds, and get it done? I would happily wait for longer than 47 minutes on the phone with a technical support center for that!!!

The takeaway from my latest technology adventure is related to self-awareness and growth into one's full space until there is no room and no corner left uncovered. While spending time mediating between my thoughts and feelings, I remembered a most unexpected, life-changing conversation last year about vanquishing remorse. The advice that stayed with me came in the form of very touching parting words that resonated deeply within my very core: "Be aggressive in pursuit of yourself." Until recently, that "aggressiveness" spoke to me about how water makes its way through a rock—steadily and persistently. The WiFi boosters made me think about a different kind of "aggressive pursuit": stable and strong. Ensuring that the WiFi signal is stable and strong throughout the entire home made me think about how we should come into any transformation with an unwavering intention to grow fully into the new space and own it from wall to wall and corner to corner.

During every conversation about stakeholder analysis and engagement, I make sure I ask one question towards the end: "How long does this list need to get before you list yourselves?" Without exception, the answer comes in the form of silence, and then some smiles. How do we make sure that we stay "aggressive in pursuit of ourselves," that we enable ourselves to grow fully into our own space, stable and strong as the WiFi signal? And who are the people that we trust to be our WiFi boosters when we need to stay unwavering in our intention, yet agile in implementation?

Offline is the new luxury. A few years ago, while looking into solutions to best manage my insomnia episodes, I pushed myself to keep my bedroom free of any technology—no cell phone (I used the alarm excuse for longer than I am comfortable admitting, then I got a beautiful, simple, regular clock, perfect for my bedside table), no TV, and no laptop. Now I have a perfectly stable and strong WiFi signal, yet it is my choice not to use it. Okay, not all the time—I do walk into the bedroom talking on the phone every now and again and I do enjoy some Netflix chill up until sleep time. Then everything technology gets banished.

Offline is the new luxury. But it should be so by choice, not by poor coverage. There is one quote I totally love from Ezra Taft Benson, an American farmer and government official who served as the 15th United States Secretary of Agriculture: "You are free to choose, but you are not free from the consequences of your choice."[92] When I started telling my friends about my new routine, they all asked me whether this gave me the famous FOMO, fear of missing out on good news, latest updates on social media, even people trying to get in touch for emergencies. First of all, the people who need to reach me at all hours know how to get in touch—they can call my number and I will come and answer no matter what my bedside table watch is telling me. Second of all, for everything else, I actually developed JOMO, the joy of missing out and having a really good time catching up on all the news over my morning coffee. What are you afraid of missing out on when not online? What routines—personal or organizational—do you intentionally develop and implement to turn FOMO into JOMO?

Until next week, keep calm, make any conversation a spark of change, use your hopes and self-awareness to create JOMO routines and stay stable and strong in the aggressive pursuit of yourselves.

What Eating Pancakes Teaches Me about Change Management

First published on September 7, 2021

One of the "love languages" of my childhood was based on crêpes with apricot jam. Before I even learned the days of the week, I knew it was a special day when I woke up and it smelled of freshly made crêpes. That divinely smelling day was usually a Sunday.

When I got a scholarship in the USA in my late teens, I discovered pancakes. With maple syrup, of course. And, as they say, my life has never been the same again. My first trip to Brussels brought waffles into my life, those "pancakes with syrup traps," as American comedian Mitch Hedberg quite rightly described them.[193] Russian blinis were up next on my discovery list. And the most recent addition to my addiction is aebleskiver, the Danish pancake ball.

With all these milestones along my life's journey, it should come as no surprise that one of my favorite sayings ever involves pancakes: "Never let your toes or your pancakes get cold."[194]

This past weekend, I felt like having some "Sunday kind of love"—and yes, Etta James goes just as well as maple syrup or

Nutella with pancakes. While humming along with the music and getting busy at the stove, I started thinking about any tasty takeaways for change management out of making, eating and (now that my secret is out…) worshipping pancakes. And here below is your serving, I hope you will enjoy it.

"No matter how flat you make your pancake, it still has two sides."[195] —for this statement alone, I would nominate American comedian Daniel Tosh for the Change Management and Communication Hall of Fame! There is no such thing as "flat" communication. It is never one-sided, no matter how simple or straightforward you think it is. There are always at least two sides to every story, and they can be as different as the sides of the same pancake—one brown and fluffy, the other one, well, burnt. Even if you think you came up with the perfect, foolproof way to package and deliver your change story, check for the individual subtitles people put to it. Clarify and confirm, again and again. Acknowledge and strive to understand where the different meanings come from and what contributed to their creation. Remember: we all flip our pancakes differently.

Embrace drama and learn to harness its energy. Every bit of change work comes with a tremendous amount of emotions, both positive and negative, more or less openly displayed and acted upon. Whether it is enthusiasm or anger, curiosity or a sense of loss, they are right there waiting to be seen, acknowledged, validated and respected. Telling people that "emotions are for outside working hours" (sadly, I've heard this more often than I thought I would) or that the best fix is a resilience workshop has never yielded the expected results—shock of shocks! Surprise, this is my contribution to the "change drama."

Emotions weave the underlying reality of all our interactions and they are triggered, heightened, harnessed during transformations. As American cooking teacher, author, and television personality Julia Child said it, "Drama is very important in life.... Everything can have drama if it's done right. Even a pancake."[96] Emotions are oftentimes proof of things done right. As long as people feel something, it means they care. Acknowledge their feelings, as well as your own, and constructively use that energy within your organizational transformation.

Be [fill in the blanks...], don't just do [fill in the blanks...]. Speaking of embracing drama, it took me quite a while to be able to constructively repurpose frustration whenever the first question in a change conversation was "So, what tools will you use?" Another recent "victim" of this approach is "agile." Breaking news: having meetings every other week doesn't make your project agile. No, standing around the flip chart instead of sitting around a desk doesn't make that much of a difference, either... Filling in a stakeholder analysis spreadsheet or running a change readiness assessment survey doesn't make you a change maker. It is never about the tools. It is about the mindset, beliefs, willingness to listen, (self-)awareness, skills, attributes, knowledge, compassion, the energy you bring into your work and all the interactions it requires. Using "agile tools" doesn't make you agile. Using "change management tools" doesn't make you a change manager.

One thing I found quite useful for igniting meaningful conversations on this topic is using a quote from a surprising change management figure—American actor and producer Samuel L. Jackson. This is the quote that proudly claimed one slide in all my workshop supporting decks: "Just 'cause you pour syrup on something doesn't make it pancakes."[97] I always ask participants to take a few extra seconds to read it again in Samuel L. Jackson's voice and freely sprinkle in his "signature sentence enhancer." Here, take a few seconds and do just that—it won't make you Samuel L. Jackson, but it will be good fun.

Because of how crêpes, pancakes, waffles, blinis and aebleskivers came into my life, they speak to me about love and discovery. On some Sundays throughout my life (the last one included), they spoke to me about the love needed for self-(re)discovery. Also, about courage. The courage to call a burnt pancake burnt, not spread Nutella on it and call it "chromatically synced dessert." Life is too precious and short to waste it on burnt pancakes. We all deserve love, discovery, and awesome pancakes!

Until next week, keep calm and remember: the best topping for a pancake is more pancakes. I don't know how Samuel L. Jackson orders pancakes for breakfast, but I imagine it is something like: "And drown that MF in maple syrup!"

What Choosing Poster Frames Teaches Me about Change Management

First published on September 14, 2021

After many years and many different addresses, it felt like the walls of my home needed something to make them my own. I ordered posters before any of the furniture, and little did I know how complicated it would get! Choosing and getting the posters delivered turned out to be a walk in the park compared to getting the frames. Those with more or less standard sizes were easier to sort out. Finding and getting frames for the posters with custom sizes, however, became an adventure in itself.

And, just like any good adventure, it created meaningful memories. Two of them are particularly special to me. Totally by accident, I saw a business card with contact details for a frame workshop while paying for a load of houseplants at one of my favorite flower shops. Two emails later, I was in the attic of an old building, talking with a kind and good-for-the-soul-warm lady. It turned out she inherited the shop from her parents and kept it alive as a side business while going about her profession as a nurse. I heard myself thinking out loud, "What a surprisingly complementary way to take care of people and their well-being!"

She has been helping me with quite a few frames over the past couple of months and there is a deeper sense of "care" in her work than meets the eye.

Along one of my usual walking routes, I have been passing by a shop with a name that was meant to catch my attention: "Changemaker." One day, I had to go in. That burst of curiosity brought a most unexpected addition into my life. There, I discovered that there are two brothers in Cape Town, South Africa, who built a business based on handcrafting shabby chic picture and photo frames from reclaimed distressed timber. Whether from the deck of a ship, a vintage ceiling or an antique fence, each piece tells its own story. And now, one of their frames tells me a story every single time I come home or walk out the door. I choose to hear a story about passion, hope, unexpected journeys and life started anew.

This past weekend was a beautiful, Indian summer sunny one. As I walked toward the kitchen to get a glass of water, I couldn't help but stop and look at my hallway poster in the sunlight. And a random question popped up in my head: "What story about change management is it trying to tell me?" I stood there for a while, running my fingers along the frame, and the ideas below started to surface.

Honor the "integrity of the moment." One of the greatest lessons in vulnerability and compassion I have ever learned came through my communication and journalism training—"the integrity of the moment." It is about staying mindful and intentional about the "inner life of the message or story" to which everybody involved is contributing. No matter how good and detailed your communication plan or your interview framework is, open it up to sync into the frequency of those you interact with as well as the energy of the environment. It is not just about the message you came to deliver; it is equally about the message people came to experience. Be vulnerable and compassionate to sync these two dimensions. A piece of art is made vulnerable to its frame—whether to potential damages during the framing process or to impact on attention focus due to the color, patterns, textures of the frame. And we can argue that a frame is the artistic and design expression of compassion if we accept its definition as "empathy and caring in action." The weekend sunlight contributed to the integrity of the moment by stirring unexpected thoughts and emotions. These became integral parts of the story just like the poster, its frame and me being there to experience all of it.

"**It's the frames which make some things important and some things forgotten.**"[98] What a poster-worthy quote from American artist and author Eve Babitz! What kind of frame would best go with it? This makes me think about the importance of focus, but even more so about the significance, impact and value of boundaries. As I tried to stay in the moment while feeling the frame with my fingers, it dawned on me how terribly ironic it was to think about frames and boundaries when life "sent me back to school" to relearn to be comfortable with saying "No," and considering it a full sentence.

In my change management work, one of the most meaningful conversations about boundaries is the one when, as a project team, we define and agree on what feedback—and particularly actionable feedback—is from within the organization. Whenever transformation happens, people give input—through any and all channels known to humankind. It comes down to the project team to set boundaries based on which input is filtered and sorted into noise, information and actionable feedback. This "framing" practice is what reconfirms on an ongoing basis the scope of the project, its strategic intent, as well as the focus of its resources (time, energy, capability and capacity, money).

Like frames guide and prepare the eyes to see the art, the boundaries of actionable feedback contribute to expectations and impact management. Take a moment and think about what frames you use for your "change art." Keep these words from Hawaii-based "Happy Guy" strategist and coach Richie Norton in mind: "Like creating a masterpiece, quitting is an art: you have to decide what to keep within the frame, and what to keep out."[199]

What do you remember: the art or the frame? Can you describe them separately? In all honesty, after hearing the story behind the frame, I now pay more attention to it. But, in the shop, what caught my eye was the art within it: the Holstee Manifesto in the unmistakable design of Rachael Beresh. The Holstee Manifesto was created by the Holstee company founders, Dave, Mike and Fabian. They gathered at Union Square in New York and described how they defined personal success; they wanted to make something they could look back on if they felt trapped or unfulfilled in their lives. After it took the internet by storm, it inspired and encouraged people to chase their dreams, live their best lives and redefine success in their own terms.[200] What is really magic for me is this combination of two amazing stories about how, based on hope, passion and compassion and positive intent, everything is possible. Even creating the perfect consistency between New York inspiration and Cape Town reclaimed wood to bring joy and comfort in Basel.

Probably more so than in any other work, consistency is fundamental to change management—consistency among intent, words and actions. It might very well have been a sign from the Universe when I accidentally found this quote from American doctor Charles F. Glassman, best known under his designation as "Coach MD": "Thoughts frame your portrait, action paints it."[201] We can substitute "words" for "thoughts" and it would still hold true. Or, even better, maybe "words" are the colors and the paints… Consistency is at its best when we can no longer describe the art and its frame separately. It is one single wholesome experience. Hopefully, inspiring. I would love to hear people talk about their change experiences like this. Wouldn't you?

At some point during the weekend, I got curious about the history of frames. According to an article by Mark Rogers, Owner of Frame Destination, on framedestinations.com, "...nowadays, picture frames are used merely to 'frame' beautiful pieces of art, photography, archival documents and treasured mementos. However, when they were first developed, frames were included in the art and even considered a piece of art themselves."[202] And actually, according to "A Survey of Frame History" in *Picture Framing Magazine*, in the past, people were more concerned with purchasing frames that matched the "architectural setting;" frames were not simply made to complement paintings.[203] While reading this, I got a bonus inspiration for change management and, quite frankly, life overall. I realized that frames have been teaching me to be humble but not timid, to be proud but not arrogant.

Until next week, keep calm and "frame" yourselves consistently.

What Watching the Moon Teaches Me about Change Management

First published on September 21, 2021

One of the best benefits of my chronic insomnia is having extra opportunities to watch the moon during the night. It still puzzles me why I never entertained the idea of getting a telescope. I just love looking up into the night sky and watching the moon. No telescope. Almost like a mutual understanding of respecting our secrets from afar.

Every now and again, I get a question about how I manage my creativity. In all honesty, there is no method to my madness. What helps is watching the sky and any kind of water, especially a sea or ocean. Watching the Rhine in my new home city also helps. And somehow, from somewhere, ideas pop up.

I opened the laptop with no idea what this Tuesday Change Management Random Thought would be about. Then I looked up and saw the moon. I remembered reading that we were literally hours away from the "Harvest Moon," a very special full moon in September. It refers to the full, bright moon that occurs closest to the start of autumn. The name dates from the time before electricity when farmers depended on the moon's light to harvest their crops late into the night. And it so happens this full moon is in my birth sign—Pisces.

While mindlessly reading what this means following the first astrology website link Google provided, this is what I learned: "It's time for a little enchantment, as the 2021 Pisces full moon holds ceremony in our deepest psyches. These mystical moonbeams are known for causing miracles. Flowy, dreamy Pisces softens our resistance to change. Do you need to let go and let it flow? Tune in. Under these esoteric moonbeams, your intuition is the most potent voice in the chorus."[204]

Taking a double spoonful of my own medicine, being both a Pisces and a change manager, I turn up the volume while listening to one of my absolute favorites, Shivaree's "Goodnight Moon," and try to put together "the harvest of my lunacy" below.

"Every man is a moon and has a side which he turns toward nobody: you have to slip around behind it if you want to see it."[205] This quote from American writer Mark Twain, the father of Tom Sawyer and Huckleberry Finn, has been a good companion for years and years. It reminds me that there is always more to anyone we meet than meets the eye. Just as there is always more than meets our own eye in the mirror. It is a most useful reminder in change management work.

This quote also pops up in my head every single time I happen to be in a conversation about "shadow work," meaning diving into the unconscious material that shapes our thoughts, emotions and behaviors. It makes me smile that I mention "shadow work" while watching the moon in psychiatrist Carl Jung's country of birth, life and work... I am also thinking about this quote in the context of today's unprecedented mental health and well-being challenges we all navigate. Over the past weeks, I lost people in my life to suicide. It makes me wonder what could have been on that side that nobody could see. What is on the side of myself that I don't see?

There is a quote often associated with American actor Robin Williams: "People do not fake depression. People fake being ok."[206] Maybe we all have a small telescope we carry around with us, ready to be used—it is a simple question that requires nothing but our full presence and compassion in the moment: "How are you?" Say it like you mean it; don't just use it as a longer version of "Hi!"

Trust the process. And let its energy push and pull you forward. According to a great read in National Geographic, the lunar cycle occurs every month partially because "moonlight" is actually just a reflection of sunlight. While the Earth, moon, and sun move in their orbits, the part of the moon reflecting sunlight shifts, creating the eight lunar phases.[207] An anonymous pearl of wisdom describes it beautifully: "And like the moon, we must go through phases of emptiness to feel full again."[208]

For some reason, this made me think of the change curve, the Kubler-Ross model of shock, denial, frustration, depression, experimentation, decision and integration. And just like the moon goes through its phases every 29.5 days, we navigate the change curve as life happens, personally and professionally. Whether it is an international relocation, a breakup, an organizational redesign or a digital transformation, the change curve is there. Oftentimes, we have to trust the process—it is the only certainty we have. The phases are there, and we have to go through them, mindfully and intentionally—not always in a straight and linear manner, and that is okay. A random Google search under this Harvest Moon turned up an inspiring quote from essayist and blogger Cristen Rodgers: "The moon doesn't consider one phase better than another; she just glows, equally stunning at each turn. Why should we be any different?"[209]

In a world where everybody dreams of being a sun, be a moon! According to NASA, the moon actually helps to stabilize the Earth in its axis, which provides a livable climate and creates tides.²¹⁰ If I were the Ruler of the Universe for one day, I would turn this into a "Change Oath" that anyone going into change management work would have to take, then live and work by. Change managers are there, especially in the dark times, to serve and support organizations and their people as they wobble on their journey, (hopefully) leading to a relatively stable organizational environment. They should cause tides of leadership role-modeling, stakeholder engagement, communication, training, creating a comforting, although not always comfortable, rhythm to guide people along. In a world where everybody dreams to be a sun, I want to be a moon!

It got dark and eerily quiet as I sat here with my laptop under the Harvest Moon. And I can think of no better closing thought than a few words from Henri Frédéric Amiel, a Swiss moral philosopher, poet and critic: "Tell me what you feel in your room when the full moon is shining in upon you and your lamp is dying out, and I will tell you how old you are, and I shall know if you are happy."²¹¹

Until next week, keep calm and go be someone's moon!

What Being Totally and Crazily in Love with Penguins Teaches Me about Change Management

First published on September 28, 2021

Penguins are the cutest beings out there! From the very first time I saw one in a documentary decades ago, I have been in love. My favorite movie ever is *Happy Feet*, and the best pick-me-up for me is the bit from the Graham Norton Show where Benedict Cumberbatch admits to not being able to correctly pronounce "penguin." Which only makes both Cumberbatch and the "pengwings" even more adorable. Just in case you were wondering... *Madagascar* is high on my favorite movies list, together with *March of the Penguins*. And one of my strongest beliefs is that there are simply not enough gifs with penguins available.

There is a famous photo taken by Tobias Baumgartner in Melbourne, Australia that won *Oceanographic Magazine*'s Ocean Photography Award in 2020. Baumgartner was told by one of the volunteers with the St. Kilda Pier colony of fairy penguins that two penguins who had recently lost their partners were often seen comforting each other. The photographer spent three nights with the colony before being able to catch a photo of the two lovely beings standing together for hours and watching the dancing lights of the city. This photograph has stayed with me, and it makes me believe that it's not only books find people when they need them most; photographs have their own healing magic like that, too.

The final nudge to write this piece came yesterday as I was aimlessly walking around on my first day of vacation. At one moment I looked up, and the first thing I saw in the window of a bookstore was a 2022 wall calendar with photographs of penguins. Of course, it came home with me.

We are better together, especially under extreme conditions. Penguins possess distinct personalities and many of their traits are adorably human. Did you know that penguins laugh hysterically when tickled? I must have been a penguin in a previous life. They propose with a pebble, they get "penguin married" and also "penguin divorced"… Moving on… They also enjoy a soothing, warm embrace. Whether they hug their baby, their life partner or maybe even you (if you're lucky), it's guaranteed to melt the heart.

During extreme storms, penguins engage in a group hug known as a huddle that often gets so hot they have to eat snow afterward in order to cool down. The center of a penguin huddle, a form of social thermoregulation, can reach temperatures of up to 37° Celsius (98.6° Fahrenheit). The center penguins keep moving through the huddle so they don't overheat, while penguins on the outside move inward to get warm. Huddling is particularly important, as the penguins don't eat for up to 115 days and need to conserve as much energy as possible.

Take a moment to think about what goes on during an "organizational transformation storm." What "huddling" procedures do you have in place to make sure you make the most out of your resources while nurturing a sense of belonging? How do you make sure that organizational "warmth" is a collective accountability, while also offering personal comfort?

If we look beyond immediate expectations, we are all built for extraordinary things. An ongoing dilemma: are penguins birds or fish? Scientifically, penguins belong to a group of birds that cannot fly; their wings are adapted for swimming. For this reason, people often mistakenly think of them as fish. Beyond them being incredibly cute, the main reason why I totally and crazily am in love with penguins is that they do not fulfill immediate expectations. They do not fly, and they do not swim. What they do is something extraordinary: they fly underwater.

A penguin has to work harder than other birds to fly. They move very fast underwater, especially when they are chasing food such as fish. They use the muscles in their chest to bring their special wings, called flippers, downwards. But then they use the muscles between their shoulders to bring their flippers upwards. Most birds only use the muscles in their chest for what scientists call a "powered downstroke." Penguins have both powered downstroke and upstroke. And this is how they can fly underwater.

Look at the people in your organization and push beyond your immediate expectations. Create a space where they can be extraordinary, a space where they can use all their "muscles." When we have that space, we are all built for extraordinary things. When you do Change Management work, don't think inside the box. Don't think outside the box. Think like there is no box!

Bring joy to those around you just by being yourself. Penguins have an altogether infectious waddle that helps them keep their balance on ice. You might have noticed, though, that said waddle isn't very fast. When a penguin wants to pick up the pace, they use their belly to travel instead. Seeing them shimmy face first down snowy landscapes is enough to brighten anybody's day. Penguins hug, kiss and blow bubbles underwater. As English writer John Ruskin put it: "One can't be angry when one looks at a penguin."[212] Please do not start to exercise your own waddle!

Let penguins inspire you to be yourself, perfectly imperfect, built for extraordinary things. Just be yourself and bring warmth and joy to those around you. There is a lovely quote from American actress Carla Gugino: "You can't not be happy around penguins. You're unfortunately happy and cold, but the happiness makes up for the coldness."[213]

It's not that big of a stretch for the imagination to see change managers as the transformation penguins. We do not take away the cold. Hopefully, we bring something that makes up for it. I also like to believe that we stand upright and "wear tuxedos," meaning we are able to meaningfully code-switch (the practice and/or necessity of moving back and forth between two or more languages, cultural norms, social or style environments at one time). The black and white "tuxedo" look donned by most penguin species is a clever camouflage called countershading. It is my personal choice to interpret the "camouflage" bit with a positive twist—more along the lines of blending in, like in an anthropology dimension, rather than hiding and disguising. Everybody has a bright side and a dark side. That's why the human soul closely resembles a penguin. We all just waddle on and hope for a good huddle when the storm comes.

At one point during my lifelong love for penguins, I came across a wonderful piece of wisdom that I will leave here as a closing thought:

"Advice from a Penguin™'
Dive into life
Find warmth among friends
Appreciate snow days
Take long walks
Stand together
Go the extra mile
Keep your cool!"*[1]

Until next week, keep calm and may you waddle joyfully and purposefully!

---

[1] Used with permission ©Ilan Shamir 2023 MYADVICEFORLIFE.COM

What Cooking and Eating Spaghetti Teaches Me about Change Management

First published on October 5, 2021

My first movie ever at the movie theater was *Lady and the Tramp*. I was about five, and we got front-row seats in the balcony section of the best theater in my hometown. Because I was too small to be able to watch the movie above the railing of the balcony, I stood the entire time and watched through the space between the railing and the balcony wall. It felt like I had my own little window into magic.

Without a doubt, the "Bella Notte" scene has always been my favorite—they gaze into each other's eyes as they slurp a strand of pasta into a fateful kiss. Two people meant for each other, yet as different as they can possibly be, one single bowl of spaghetti, no cutlery, any sauce will do—to me, that's AMORE!

Staying within the movie dimension, I must admit that one of the most inspirational quotes for me comes from Italian actress Sophia Loren: "I'd much rather eat pasta and drink wine, than be a size 0. . . . Everything you see I owe to spaghetti."[215] As I keep myself safer and safer from size 0 by opening a bottle of wine and gently stirring a simple tomato and basil pasta sauce, I challenge myself to figure out what cooking and eating spaghetti teaches me about change management. Here below is today's serving. Buon Appetito!

Change work is like a bowl of spaghetti. You can't take one piece out without rubbing it against many others, losing some sauce along the way, and most probably splashing some around. Based on my lifelong empirical research, the whiter the tablecloth, the bigger the stain… There is no way to tell how long the pasta strand is going to be, so you are basically playing tasty draw and hoping for the best. And although you have all the table etiquette knowledge and needed cutlery, you are almost irresistibly tempted to follow Sophia Loren's advice: "Spaghetti can be eaten most successfully if you inhale it like a vacuum cleaner."[216]

Any change you make within an organization, no matter how insignificant or small-scale it seems, has rippling effects, oftentimes along the most surprising dimensions. When working with perceptions, emotions and people experiences, there is always some rubbing and splashing going on, and there is nothing you can do to avoid that. As for the draw, we have all been drafting risk management and change resistance management plans and come across moments when we pushed forward based on nothing else but our own intuition and experience-honed reflexes. What Sophia Loren teaches me with her spaghetti-eating technique is to infuse some joy into it, to stay mindful in the moment of having a great meal, go for it and just savor it with your taste buds, heart and soul alike.

Take time to define what pasta you need and never ever ever break spaghetti. There is a wonderful article on seriouseats. com called "10 Common Crimes Against Pasta You Don't Have to Commit," a delightful read for all pasta lovers out there in this big, tasty world, aimed at tackling the terrible atrocities that people commit with pasta. One of the capital crimes listed is breaking long pasta. There are different types of pasta for a reason; if you want short pasta, you should go get short pasta! Breaking long pasta is absolutely never okay.[217]

Every time I read this article, it makes me laugh out loud. It also makes me think of…the right sauce. While there are no hard and fast rules, food-loving Italians do have a few guidelines for matching shapes with a suitable sauce. For example, fine delicate strands work best with light, smooth sauces, while twisted shapes and wider ribbons can support chunkier ones. And it's not just a manners thing; pairing sauces and shapes well can make it a lot easier to enjoy!

The combination of pasta and sauces makes me think of talent acquisition. How do we define what "meal" we are after, and then describe what kind of "pasta" we need in the role descriptions and the job ads? How much room for "changing the pasta shapes" do we really build into our "organizational menus"? I remember a job interview where I was asked to give examples of talent acquisition projects I was involved in. After saying a little bit about a couple of them, I ventured into admitting that one of the most meaningful talent management interventions for me is building change communities and networks. We define the baseline and the desired outcome, then the roles, we look for the right people, we onboard them, create space for them to fill it with their own aspirations and experience and, hopefully, we are there to share the joy of the journey, the achievements and the lessons.

A change community is a reflection of the people it serves and supports—you have long pasta, curly pasta, short pasta, elegant pasta, free-form pasta, as well as many varied "sauces" created within teams, business units, organizational entities and layers. A good change manager acknowledges, protects and nurtures the wonderful reality that "each pasta shape has its own soul." And one key accountability within any transformation work is to make sure that we don't mess with that.

"If the only tool you have is a hammer, it's hard to eat spaghetti."[218] I totally love this quote from American productivity consultant and creator of "Getting Things Done" time management method David Allen. "The law of the instrument is a cognitive bias that involves an over-reliance on a familiar tool," usually exemplified by the overuse of a hammer.[219] Psychologist and personality theorist Silvan Tomkins wrote about how jobs are usually adapted to tools rather than tools to jobs; someone with a hammer is more likely to look for nails.[220] Kenneth Mark Colby, an American psychiatrist dedicated to the theory and application of computer science and artificial intelligence to psychiatry, wrote in the same book about the First Law of the Instrument. If a boy is given a hammer, he'll begin pounding everything. He claimed that the computer was our "hammer" (in 1963 when the book was published) and must be tested first before it could prove its value.[221]

With all the accelerated digital transformation going on around us, I would distribute a copy of this work to all involved and spark conversations about implementation and adoption. Those of you who know me well and/or have worked with me will not be surprised by my following confession: the only thing that gives me a worse rash than "We have always done it this way" is the question "So, what methodology and tools will you use?" raised within the first five minutes of a change conversation.

When it comes to Italian eating endeavors—with the exception of pasta in broth which requires a spoon—the only utensil you need to enjoy a plate of pasta is a fork! Italians never cut their pasta, so leave the knives for something else, per favore. I so dearly wish it were that simple when it came to change management tools! One particularly meaningful instance of discussing the law of the instrument is within the future of work, and specifically targeted toward the workplace and workplace features moving forward. In many conversations, the highlight on collaboration areas and quiet work areas, furniture and plug-and-play IT equipment steal the thunder from a deeper disruption. There was an amazing statement made during a recent talk I had the privilege of attending: "It is easier to prepare the office for the return of people than it is to prepare the people for the return to the office." Take a moment to let that sink into the "bowl of spaghetti" change work you do.

Before moving to dessert—gelato, of course!!!—I will leave you with a closing thought from American military legend General George S. Patton: "A piece of spaghetti or a military unit can only be led from the front end."[222] Replace "military unit" with "organization," "team," even "change community," and it still holds true.

Until next week, keep calm, have some spaghetti and vino, stay safe from size 0. La vita e bella!

What Drinking Prosecco Teaches Me about Change Management

First published on October 12, 2021

Almost two years ago, a very unexpected change of plans in Rome ended up as one of my favorite memories. I was visiting a friend, and our intention was to go see the celebration of Santa Maria Immaculata at the Column of the Immaculate Conception in Piazza Mignanelli, where the Pontiffs had been offering flowers at the base of the column with the help of Roman firefighters since 1953. This plan was the result of a good laugh over Prosecco back in July, also in Rome, when we came up with a yearly schedule of visits, and this—for some reason none of us remembers—seemed like a good ceremony to witness. Plus, it involved men in uniform…

It took us forever to get done with lunch, so by the time we got ourselves organized, there was no way we could make it closer to the actual location of the ceremony because of masses and masses of people, all of them much better planners than us, apparently. Instead, we walked around the Vatican, then took random turns on the streets of Rome, spent some time at the

Torre Argentina Cat Sanctuary, walked, talked and laughed for hours. On our way home very late that evening (or quite early in the morning, depends on how you interpret time), we got ourselves some pizza and Prosecco, then spent the rest of the night eating and drinking while watching romantic comedies and laughing until our faces hurt. I consider that day as a (very) late celebration of my 40th birthday. It certainly felt most appropriately celebratory!!

Two weeks ago, right before my vacation, there was a great deal on Prosecco at the online supermarket I had been using and it seemed like a good investment. It made me think of Rome and it most definitely helped me with a deeper understanding of "dolce far niente" during my days off. Just like in Rome two years ago, all the plans I had for the week off changed into "more being, less doing." I can always blame it on Prosecco.

With all this "celebratory hydration" going on, I guess trying to see what drinking Prosecco teaches me about change management is a natural progression. Allora, cin cin, alla nostra!

Celebrate forward. Maybe it is just me, but celebrations have always felt somehow..."backward looking." It is about an achievement, a milestone, something that happened, was done, reached fruition, completion, fulfillment. They do not feel very "forward looking" to me. I have yet to receive an invite to a project kick-off meeting that has some celebratory vibe in addition to a pure working session.

Ever since I was little, one type of ceremony has fascinated me: ship launching. In Ancient times, Egyptians, Greeks and Romans called on their gods to protect seamen. Jews and Christians customarily used wine and water as they called upon God to safeguard them at sea. Ship launchings in the Ottoman Empire were accompanied by prayers to Allah, the sacrifice of sheep and appropriate feasting. The religious aspect of ship christening died off in Protestant Europe after the Reformation, especially in Great Britain. Some member of the royalty or nobility would instead join the crew for a secular ceremony of drinking from the "standing cup"—a large goblet, usually made of precious metal and fitted with a foot and a cover—and solemnly calling the ship by her name. After taking a drink, the presiding official would pour what liquid was left onto the deck or over the bow and then toss the cup over the side of the vessel to be caught by a lucky bystander or sink into the sea.

As Britain became a maritime power and its growing navy required more ships, the practice of discarding the expensive cups fell out of favor. For a while, they were caught in a net for reuse, but eventually, the whole ceremony was replaced by the breaking of a wine bottle across the ship's bow. Nowadays, it is usually a bottle of champagne, although I do hope some Prosecco is involved every now and again… The ship launching speaks to me about celebrating future voyages, the courage to sail away, about discoveries, hope and a sense of direction. About celebrating forward! I often think that organizations could use more of this.

Nurture effervescence and look for your bubbles. Without a doubt, "effervescence" is one of my favorite words ever, and I always look for opportunities to use it in change-related conversations. Looking at the joyous movement inside a glass of Prosecco is a fundamental part of enjoying the experience of… celebrating forward. There is no "map" or "plan" to the effervescence, it just happens. And all the bubbles are moving upwards.

How can we replicate, encourage and nurture that same movement inside organizations? How do we create and use upward-moving bubbles? As I am pouring myself another glass just to watch the "show" again, I am thinking about some potential "organizational bubbles": conversations, teams, a coach or mentor, meaningful learning experiences, all characterized by psychological safety, authenticity, commitment, intent, compassion, genuine and full presence and joy. Be someone's bubble, and the effervescence will help you rise, too!

Define identity by itself, not by comparison. It always makes me sad to hear people describing Prosecco as "cheaper champagne." Although "effervescent with best of intentions," one random article on a dedicated website is forever labeling Prosecco as a…well, cheaper champagne. Champagne is a sparkling wine from France and Prosecco is from Italy. While both are pretty popular choices, champagne takes longer to make and is much older than Prosecco, which explains the price difference. The general perception that champagne is "expensive" and "luxurious" is a factor as well. Meanwhile, Prosecco is seen as the cheaper option, which keeps its price more affordable. But outstanding Prosecco wines are out there![223]

We oftentimes get so attached to what we know, to our past experiences, to our comfort zones, that everything new gets defined by comparison, and becomes something "more" or "less." It takes intentionality and mindfulness to simply discover and experience, not just assess and judge, no matter how well intended. Like the ship launching ceremony, change and transformation work should be more about future voyages and destinations than familiar shores.

As counterintuitive for a change manager as it may be, I hope nothing will change my plan to enjoy the Italian Prosecco Road—hopefully soon!!—and get bubbly with joy in my kind of heaven. The Prosecco region stretches out across 20,000 hectares of the Italian countryside, with grapes growing everywhere from 50 to 500 meters above sea level. Sun, Prosecco, laughter—as good as it gets. It makes for an awesome four-item bucket list: buy bucket, buy Prosecco, fill bucket with Prosecco, drink bucket. No change management work needed there. Unless you want to change the bucket…

Until next week, keep calm and celebrate forward!

What Playing Tetris Taught Me about Change Management

First published on October 19, 2021

There have been two moments in my life (so far!) when I felt painfully disconnected from my friends. One of them happened when *Legends of the Fall* came out and E.V.E.R.Y.B.O.D.Y. went totally crazy about Brad Pitt. I have always been more of a Johnny Depp kind of girl…

The other one was triggered by Tetris being launched and taking the world by storm. I was never hooked, just tried it out a few times. Most of my friends got obsessed, and all conversations were about tips, tricks and personal bests. Here is a refresher, courtesy of Wikipedia: "Tetris, created by Soviet software engineer Alexey Pajitnov in 1984, is primarily composed of a field of play in which pieces of different geometric forms, called 'tetrominoes,' descend from the top of the field. During this descent, the player can move the pieces laterally and rotate them until they touch the bottom of the field or land on a piece that had been placed before it. The player can neither slow down the falling pieces nor stop them, but can accelerate them in most versions. The objective of the game is to use the pieces to create as many horizontal lines of blocks as possible. When a line is completed, it disappears, and the blocks placed above fall one rank. Completing lines grants points, and accumulating a certain number of points moves the player up a level, which increases the number of points granted per completed line."[224] I do hope it brought back memories for some of you and I'm not the only one experiencing a blast from the past.

A few weeks back, during a lovely dinner, Tetris was mentioned, and the idea to see what it taught me about change management was born. Apparently, American former professional boxer Mike Tyson also found some inspiration in the game: "You should sit in meditation for 20 minutes a day, unless you're too busy, then you should sit for an hour. If Tetris has taught me anything, it's that errors pile up and accomplishments disappear. Everybody has a plan until they get punched in the mouth."[225]

Challenge accepted, and here are my three rounds of takeaways for change work— which, for the record, has its "punch in the mouth" moments…

Protect empty spaces. With technology feeding the expectation that we are all "ever available and present," our days feel like a game of Tetris. Meeting requests keep falling, we can neither slow them down nor stop them, and we need to move and rotate them around until they fit. Once all time slots fit together, one more day disappears. Oftentimes, there are two or three requests piling up for the same slot, and no matter what we do, we just know we will not score extra points at the end of this life and organizational Tetris game.

With everything going on, our minds and souls feel like playing endless Tetris, eagerly waiting for the next fitting piece to feel complete. Empty spaces are so important in personal and organizational life. They bring huge extra points in rest, readjustment, refocus, restart. Protect empty spaces; consider them "tetriminoes" in their own right, and match them intentionally. But with one exception: never leave empty spaces that people can fill in with confusion or question marks regarding who you are, what you stand for, the meaning, purpose and intent behind your interactions. Fill those spaces with matching tetriminoes of your words, behaviors and actions.

Once you fit in, you disappear. The best advice I have ever received during an onboarding conversation was "Stay new for as long as possible." It is almost tattoo material! "Disruption" seems to be a new favorite word in corporate bingo, yet disrupters do feel the pressure to fit in on many occasions. My key takeaway from Tetris for my change management work is that once you fit in, you disappear. For meaningful change, get comfortable with being uncomfortable, raising questions, staying new for as long as possible. "Different" is such a powerful word! Such meaningful feedback. Stay intentionally curious, learn, unlearn and relearn to make sure "new" and "different" fit together in your own game.

Writing this, I had a weird feeling like I am disappearing in my own game of Tetris, fitting in too much into change-related work. "Disrupting" myself, a different perspective is that we are all the missing piece and the perfect fit to a greater whole, and I am the first one to admit to not (always) feeling whole or complete without the company of others that fit my world.

Mistakes are hardly permanent and can be fixed with time and new opportunities. I have recently been part of a conversation about how organizations could create learning programs that mimic learning in life, and this statement stayed with me: "Failing is learning." There are very few mistakes, in life and business, which cannot be undone—and even if they are more or less "permanent," we can still build success around them. One lesson from Tetris is that practicing delayed gratification can keep us safe from many potential mistakes. We are constantly working toward a bigger picture, sometimes holding little regard for individual pieces unless they are of immediate convenience or use to us. Protecting empty spaces and keeping a different view to be able to rotate and move pieces around ultimately help us create new opportunities to fix mistakes while fitting in new pieces. As one anonymous Tetris player said, the only mistake you cannot undo is forgetting to enjoy the game of life, with all its matching pieces, empty spaces and piled up learnings: "Life is an endless pursuit of successes, all of which ultimately mean nothing in an endless competition against time and yourself."[226]

The only version of Tetris I infinitely enjoy (and am impressively good at!) is fitting ice cream in my freezer. Not so much getting my clothes in the closets, and I am definitely not implementing the "one new in, one old out" principle… This is one mistake that is, quite literally, piling up.

Wanting to leave you with a positive closing thought, here is some online wisdom, signed "the saiKology": "Life is like a game of Tetris, you could always see which brick is coming, but still, it is all a last-minute dangle in between planning and decision. Whatever may come, the only choice is to play on and have fun!"[227]

Until next week, keep calm and don't fit in!

What Struggling with Chronic Insomnia Teaches Me about Change Management

First published on October 26, 2021

It all started back in my early twenties, and it felt like a blessing. I worked three jobs at the same time, all of them creative, to get through college, so not sleeping was an unexpected help. It gave me additional time to write more, read more and even to enjoy life more. The only thing that seemed "less" back then in retrospect was the time I needed to recuperate after sleepless nights.

Two decades later, I am no longer so sure about the "blessing" quality of my chronic insomnia. It does give me extra time, yet it also takes time and peace away from me. I need more time now to manage the side effects of losing sleep. It gives me more time with my thoughts, which is not always a good thing.

It would take me one entire night to make a list of all the things I have tried over the years—cures, remedies, treatments, holistic, ayurvedic, traditional, scientific, trial drugs and experiments, self-care, therapy—you name it, I tried it. Some work for a while, some don't. Instead of losing sleep over this inventory, I'd much rather use the extra time this night offers to make a list of some takeaways for change management work. Much less "tricky" thoughts, I hope!

"I prefer insomnia to anesthesia."[228] I have been carrying this quote from Italian writer Antonio Tabucchi with me for years, and it never ceases to fascinate me! Insomnia makes me tired, edgy, scared of yet another night where I will watch the clock and start calculating how much sleep I could get if I fell asleep right then. And how I wish I could blame this fear on my lack of mathematical skills!!! My mind races back and forth between thoughts and fills up voids of info with scenarios.

All of these have their equivalent in organizational life, especially within high-paced environments. I would take tired, edgy, scared, under-deadline-pressure people on any given day rather than people who don't feel anything, who stopped caring. I would rather listen, explain, care for, nurture and support than endlessly justify, oftentimes to no avail.

Assumptions breed extreme scenarios. There have been only a handful of cases when people, hearing about my sleeping problems, reacted with, "Oh, tell me more, what do you mean?" Two reactions are most common: "You are super lucky, all that extra time you have!" and "How do you survive? How do you manage to function at all?" It is never this clear-cut into extremes. I do not have an almost full extra day every day, and I have certainly learned to live with it in a manageable way so that I am not a fully-fledged zombie all the time.

In all honesty, I am just as guilty as the next person of letting my assumptions push me into extreme scenario-building. And I do get reminded of this in loads of conversations about tech or AI implementation when people ask, "And will I get to keep my job?" Or the latest hype with offices redesigned based on future of work principles: "How cool, it will be like working for Google or Facebook!" Well, not really, no.

Assumptions have a way of staying clear from the middle

ground and creating extremes all on their own. Armed with our own incomplete information, we connect dots that aren't there. And what happens when we add emotions into the mix? The scenarios we come up with could very well keep us awake for nights on end. I remember a dare I read in an article—and yes, it happened one night when I had some extra time to surf the internet. If you think you are pretty assumption-free, try this. Make a note of every assumption you make during an average day. And double it to count the ones you don't notice. Add a few more if you are a fellow insomniac; you have extra time to make them...

There might be such a thing as organizational insomnia. Simply put, insomnia is defined as repeated difficulty with sleep initiation, maintenance, consolidation, or quality that occurs despite adequate time and opportunity for sleep, and results in some form of daytime impairment. Anyone who has worked within transformation and change, or even project or portfolio management can definitely relate to all of these when looked at through an organizational lens—especially within contexts aimed at trying to understand concurring initiatives and their interdependencies. Could the increase in mental health challenges and burnout be effects of "organizational sleep debt"? Is the "Great Resignation" a built-up, collective expression of self-care?

I have also learned that insomnia is a lonely companion. You are awake when your "immediate world" is asleep. And every single time I hear someone casually using "So, what keeps you up at night?" as a conversation starter, I wonder if they are able, willing and ready to hear the 3:00 AM raw, real version of my own self.

Until next week, keep calm and get some good sleep. And if it so happens that you have some extra time to fill, please do not build extreme scenarios.

What Collecting Swatches Teaches Me about Change Management

First published on November 2, 2021

With the time change this past weekend, I got to thinking that I needed to adjust all my Swatches (as in, a brand of Swiss watches) before I wore them next. I have been collecting Swatches for more than two decades, so I think that it's always been a matter of…well, time, really, for me to end up in Switzerland.

The obsession all started with wanting to combine color and discipline, and what better way to do that than with a watch? The tradition to get a new scarf, a new coffee mug and a new Swatch from every new place I got to visit naturally emerged. And I felt fully and genuinely welcomed into my new home when I took some of the Swatches (some, in this case, meaning around 40) to have their battery changed at a Swatch shop in downtown Basel. It was done free of charge, all part of the brand's after-sale service. I celebrated this special "homecoming" with lots of cheese and chocolate.

Over the past three months, prompted by more or less friendly life nudges, I decided to make some adjustments to my focus and commitment, and it came down to an underlying upgraded time management challenge. "Time is a created thing. To say 'I don't have time' is like saying 'I don't want to,'" as the Ancient Chinese philosopher Lao Tzu said.[229] So, as I looked into my Swatches drawer to choose the one for today, I decided to create time to ponder over any takeaways for change work from my decades-long collection.

A change journey is like a drawer full of watches. At the end of September, I was in a conversation with a close friend and we somehow ended up talking about our collections of watches. It was also one of those "What has happened with you lately?" painfully honest talks, and the overlap between these two seemingly unrelated topics triggered a random thought.

I do have a collection of Swatches, but I also have one special watch; that is "my watch," the one that I feel tracks "my time. It is a classic Tissot I got from my grandfather as a birthday gift when I turned 30. It is true that I do wear Swatches most of the time, and the newer it is to the collection, the more visible it is in my drawer. Yet, whenever life gets rough and/or my inner self is unsettled, I go for the Tissot.

Maybe this is something we do with our own selves, too. We have our innermost core stored safely somewhere, so we go for other versions that are more recent, more colorful, more "visible in the drawer," until we need to live in our truest time. We don't misplace it, hopefully we never lose it, it just gets pushed further into the drawer. And in the meantime, some watches run out of battery, get stuck in a different timezone until they get worn again, the armband gets broken; they all need some "loving service care" to function properly again.

If I try to look at this through the lens of organizational life, there are some equivalents that come to mind: the portfolio of transformation initiatives with something new going on all the time and the opportunity and challenge, equally, to stay true to the core. And also, an inventory of my own Change

Management "drawer" of tools and tricks, where new additions complement time- and battle-tested fundamental interventions.

1,440 is one of the most meaningful numbers in our lives. This is the number of minutes in any day we are given on this journey. 1,440. This is it, not one minute more, not one minute less. Each and every one of us has 1,440 minutes every day to "create time." Whatever we decide to focus on builds up within this amount. And equally, whatever we ask, expect and request from others around us takes minutes from their daily allocation.

I keep this number in mind when I perform stakeholder management. I challenge myself and those around me to consider "meaning" and "purpose" as the most important decision-driving return on investments in any conversation.

Let the ticking of your watch become the "sound of purpose," above and beyond whatever deadline you are working toward. Make sure you use your 1,440 minutes every day in such a way that you can share in Dr. Seuss's surprise with a smile on your face: "How did it get so late so soon?"[230]

"Time does not end when your watch stops."[231] This wonderful quote from Indian American scientist and researcher Dr. P.S. Jagadeesh Kumar fascinates me. I grew up being told to always, always, always keep an eye on the watch and never, ever, ever be late. Getting (myself) a watch is an occasion to enjoy something nice, and also a reminder of that "capital accountability." I am no exception to the fact that a wristwatch shapes the way its wearer experiences and perceives time.

My love for watches brought me to an amazing online article from *The Ontarian* newspaper, "The Significance of a Timepiece" by Emil Ghloum, that made me realize why we choose to "carry time": "How does a watch perform its duty? The watch . . . is a reminder that humans are inseparable from time. With each passing movement of a ticking hand, we are forced to confront our situation as human beings, completely and irrevocably immersed in a domain of decision-making. The watch, in a fascinating way, provides humans with the ability to 'carry time' and become physically accompanied by it. The idea of time being something that we are choosing to carry is particularly captivating – it demonstrates the basic human desire to be alive. By situating ourselves in time, the recognition of oneself existing is possible."[232]

As I take one more look at my collection of (S)watches, I can't help but smile as I think about all the possible meanings of "being on time." I also make a decision to create time to re-read a fabulous book about how people's perceptions of things can change as wisdom is shared: *A Million Doorways* by K. Martin Beckner. Here's a teaser: "People create all kind of fancy watches and clocks, never stopping to realize they're building monuments to the greatest of all thieves."[233]

Keep calm and don't count the minutes; make the minutes count!

What Sewing Buttons Teaches Me about Change Management

First published on November 9, 2021

For the past couple of years, I have been working with a number of student associations as a volunteer advisor. During a recent online get-together, the icebreaker made me realize just how much I was influencing the age average of that call. We were prompted to name one "old people thing" we do, and hearing the answers made me feel…ancient. I straightforwardly admitted to proudly following in the footsteps of my family elders by treasuring a plastic bag filled with plastic bags. Because, you know, you could never allow life to surprise you with an opportunity to use a plastic bag you have been saving for this particular chance.

This past weekend, I had to do some "maintenance work" on my favorite winter jacket that was missing a button. While looking for a replacement in my "sewing box"—yes, a Danish biscuit tin!!!—I realized I have been collecting quite an impressive quantity of buttons. And from this paragraph alone, you can add two more items under my name on the "old people things" list.

As my hands got busy with reflex movements sewing buttons, my mind started wondering and wandering. It didn't take long until it picked up the challenge to see whether there are any takeaways for change management work in this souvenir activity from my early childhood.

Small things keep big things together. Buttons are a useful fastening device while also serving as a statement of innovative design. Ever since they were invented, they have been varying in sizes, colors, materials and shapes, and have been placed on different types of garments, serving a decorative function to add a fashionable statement to clothing. The oldest known button relic was found in modern-day Pakistan, in Asia, and is believed to have belonged to the ancient Asian civilization of the Indus Valley, dating back to almost 3000 B.C.

Buttons were used for the purpose of fastening fabric that was used for clothing in Ancient China, Ancient Rome, and also Ancient Greece. Functional buttons with buttonholes for fastening or closing clothes appeared in Germany in the 13th century. They soon became widespread with the rise of snug-fitting garments in 13th- and 14th-century Europe. Ever wonder why men's suit coats have non-functioning buttons sewn on the sleeves? Some say they are just for decoration, but there is also the story that King Frederick the Great of Prussia started the practice in the 18th century. The rumor goes that after an inspection of his troops, he ordered that buttons be sewn on the sleeves of their coats to discourage them from wiping their noses and mouths on them.

Back to more civilized nowadays, buttons are the small things that keep big things together. Have you ever wondered what "buttons" you have in your work? Those small roles and tasks that quite mistakenly seem insignificant, yet hold everything together? Pay attention to them, check and secure them before you run the risk of having them fall off. And also use them mindfully, as German poet Johann Wolfgang von Goethe cautioned change managers: "Once you have missed the first buttonhole, you'll never manage to button up."[234]

Overstatements are dangerous. When used for decoration purposes, buttons have been known to lead their wearers into exaggeration. In the Middle Ages, precious buttons in impressive (more like excessive) amount on clothing was an indicator of the noble origin of man. For example, Philip the Good, Duke of Burgundy (1396-1497) ordered Venetian glass buttons decorated with pearls, and Francis I of France (1494-1547) is said to have ordered a set of black enamel buttons mounted on gold from a Parisian goldsmith. The same French king had a parade costume with 13,600 buttons sewn on it.

The story involving the heir to the Austro-Hungarian throne, Archduke Franz Ferdinand, presents a dangerous side of this supposedly functional piece of adornment. In 1914, he was assassinated in the city of Sarajevo. While all the buttons were unbuttoned, precious time was lost. A few minutes later, Franz Ferdinand passed away. When combining functionality with decoration, the risk of overstatement is real. Get the functional part right; you can always increase the decoration. It might turn out to be slightly more difficult to balance things from the other end.

The simplest of things can have the most meaningful of purposes. The history of this most common item in our life is simply fascinating, and it turns out that a button is not always just a button. During the World Wars, the British and U.S. military used button lockets, which were buttons constructed like lockets to store compasses. On men's coats in China, the five buttons on their front could represent either the five virtues recommended by Confucius (humanity, justice, order, prudence and rectitude) or the branches of China's government (executive, legislative, judicial, examination, control).

About 12 years ago, while working on a corporate social responsibility program, I crossed paths with an organization supporting visually impaired people. Attending one of their workshops for independent living, I learned that they teach participants to get buttons sewn on their clothing by people supporting them so that they can mix and match their garments. Pieces with matching buttons in shape, size or texture are within matching chromatic domains, and they can feel confident in looking their best.

Ever since that moment, a button has been a reminder for me about how the simplest of things can have the most meaningful of purposes. Whenever navigating change and transformation, personal and organizational alike, I often think that the perception of dealing with confusion and lack of visibility could feel like matching clothes without being able to properly see them. What "buttons" can we use as "sense-making anchors" by which we can make sure that we mix and match appropriately? And whom do we trust enough to ask for help with sewing them on?

As you button and unbutton your clothing or sofa cushion covers, I hope you will get to smile and think about the power of small things, the fragile balance between functionality and decoration, and most of all, about the comforting meaning of everyday things. And be mindful of not taking things for granted, not even seemingly insignificant ones like buttons.

Until next week, keep calm and button on!

What Living Right Next to a Tram Stop Teaches Me about Change Management

First published on November 16, 2021

Out of all the (urban) means of public transportation, the tram is my absolute favorite. Maybe because it reminds me of trains or my childhood trips around my hometown with my grandma. Trams "flow" through cities, marking distance and time quite loudly and shakily.

The only question I had before moving into my new home was how I would get used to living right next to a tram stop after years of having a park as my neighbor in Luxembourg, especially a very silent park as it was closed because of the COVID restrictions. It turned out that trams became a very comforting part of my everyday life in record time, as I realized this past weekend. Saturday evening marked the inauguration of my dining room with having some new friends over for a late dinner, and when they wondered whether to order a taxi or not, I said, "Trams are still running, I have been hearing them around this time of the night for the past few months." A quick look out the kitchen window at the timetable board confirmed I was right, and it left a smile on my face as I realized the settling-in process just hit a milestone.

As I was "lazying around" on Sunday, I started thinking about ideas for the weekly article. And as my mind was still hooked on the homey sound of trams, the dots got connected. A random conversation over Monday morning coffee prompted me to start writing about what living right next to a tram stop teaches me about change management. I hope you will enjoy the ride, as loud and bumpy as it may seem.

Make information visible, not just available. One thing I became aware of during this past weekend was how little time I have been spending at the tram stop waiting for the tram to arrive since I moved here. As I can literally see the timetable board from my kitchen window, one look is all it takes for me to know when I should get going to catch the next one. This did not happen before, although the information had always been available through the internet or the public transport app. The key difference now is that information is visible, not just available. According to the dictionary, "see" can be used figuratively to mean "understand," some of the meanings of "see" being to "perceive mentally," "realize," or "determine with certainty."[235] One can always argue that, depending on the context, "I see" doesn't have the same connotation of agreement as "I understand" in a given conversation.

It also made me think about the "seeing is knowing" metaphor theme. We trust vision and eyewitness testimony (notice, not "earwitness"—significantly, "hearsay testimony" is barred in court) more than other sense modalities, even though visual memory is as fallible and suggestible as aural. But vision is a very rich sensory system with enormous bandwidth, lots of details and loads of sense-making around it. A very famous saying that is an abbreviated version of a quote by Indian lawyer and political ethicist Mahatma Gandhi goes, "Be the change you want to see in the world."[236] For the longest time, I believed the keyword in this was "change." As I read more and more about behavioral design, I've started to lean more toward "see." We perceive, decode, understand and communicate change through the behaviors we observe in others and the ones we exhibit ourselves. So, ask yourselves how can you make change visible, not just available, in your personal and professional life alike. What change is visible through the behaviors of the people around you?

Be intentional about "creating your own sunshine." There is one great divide between my best friend and me that will never be bridged: she is a "subway person" while I am a "tram person." She is amazing at getting things planned and organized; speed and efficiency are sacrosanct to her. I am, well, a change manager at work and a master of disaster outside of work, and I always enjoy the context and any additional ways to simply savor the experience. I tremendously enjoy looking out the window at the people on the streets, the shop windows, the traffic going by. I also enjoy watching the people inside the tram itself (in such a way that it is not straightforward staring).

What speaks to me through the change management lens is that just like I can look outside while riding the tram, others can look inside the tram, something that is not possible with the subway. This "two-way transparency" makes the tram special to me. The subway is fast and efficient, while the tram is richer in experience for what it lacks in speed. One great argument I found a few years ago is a wonderful quote from Turkish playwright and novelist Mehmet Murat ildan: "Tramway is more close to human soul than the subway because it touches to the passengers' souls with a sweet sunshine!"[237]

This fell short of settling our debate; if anything, it made it richer by introducing the weather variable... What I am rambling toward here is how you stay intentional about what the overall transformation is about—speed, efficiency, experience, inward-focus or outward-looking perspective, transparency. And most of all, irrespective of the "means of transportation," what kind of "sunshine" can you create to touch your organizational passengers' soul with?

More than any other means of transport, trams run on pre-set paths and influence the entire traffic overall. What "trams" do you have running in your life and organization? As I became more mindful of the presence of trams in my life, I spent some time just watching them pass by under my windows, and this is what I observed. Trams run on set tracks, and they have restricted freedom of movement—much less than any other participant in traffic, even trolley buses. Quite often, the tram lines are right in the middle of the street. At some stops, people need to cross half the street to get on and after they get off, which means that all traffic stops while the tram is halted. It is almost like the tram is the "great equalizer" of street traffic—no matter how fast the car or how slow the biker, the tram stops, and everything stops.

Because the trams run on pre-set tracks, I always thought tram conductors got loads of attention freed up to enjoy the ride in so many different ways than their fellow public transport drivers. Mehmet Murat ildan said it so meaningfully for change managers out there: "The wisdom of the tram is that if you do your work automatically without thinking about it, then you will save a lot of time for the things you want to think deeply!"[238]

After my tram observation sessions, I am now left with questions I really want to think deeply about: what "trams" do I have in my life? What kinds of work are the organizational trams that need pre-set tracks, run right through the middle of the company and so meaningfully impact the overall traffic with their milestones?

| EVERYDAY INSPIRATION FOR CHANGE

Writing this edition of the Tuesday Change Management Random Thought prompted quite a lot of introspection. As I looked back at the last year and everything that has been happening, I realized that there was a "tram" running right through the middle of my "life-street," and when that stopped, everything else seemed to stop, too. My pick-me-up came from the new co-author of this piece, given how often I've turned to his wisdom, Mehmet Murat ildan: "Trams are not free; their paths are predetermined; they must travel on the pre-designed paths! You are not a tram; your path is not predetermined; you can travel on any path! Fate is nonsense; you are free, you choose your own path with your own mind! . . . A wrong tram cannot take you home; a wrong thought cannot take you to happiness!"[239]

Until next week, keep calm and enjoy the tram rides!

P.S. Just in case you are left wondering what Mahatma Gandhi did say, here it is, the actual quote: "We but mirror the world. All the tendencies present in the outer world are to be found in the world of our body. If we could change ourselves, the tendencies in the world would also change. As a man changes his own nature, so does the attitude of the world change towards him. This is the divine mystery supreme. A wonderful thing it is and the source of our happiness. We need not wait to see what others do."[240]

What Making New Friends Teaches Me about Change Management

First published on November 23, 2021

It was an amazingly beautiful summer day back in 2017, and I was eating a huge ice cream from my favorite gelateria in Valletta, Malta, while giving an interview for an expat magazine. Out of all the questions I was asked, one has stayed with me, and I keep thinking about it to this day: "What is the best thing about moving around, living and working in a new country every few years?" My answer was that the best thing about my wanderlust was also its biggest hurt. As I move around, I get to meet wonderful new people, while also I lose some. Sometimes, it feels like a strange Hansel and Gretel journey where, instead of bread crumbs, I leave pieces of my heart and soul behind. Yet, it brings me into the most mind- and soul-enriching adventures.

    Out of all the challenges of relocation, I find that the one requiring the most fluid combination of grit and grace is making new friends. Building a meaningful life around you from scratch doesn't just happen. And it doesn't get easier with each new iteration. What does get easier is navigating it and getting comfortable with being on your own. In a strange way, all my moving around brought an unexpected friend into my life: myself. I realized that, as I get more comfortable with myself in my new setting, my interactions with the people around me slightly start to change.

Starting anew in Switzerland meant initiating a new cycle of building a life around me. COVID didn't make it any easier—and I will consider this the understatement of the decade. Over the past couple of months, happy milestones started to happen: invitations to dinner, a Saturday evening at the pub, the first time I had people around my table in the dining room. These are such normal moments, and they become so much more meaningful when they happen for the first time in a "new life." To me, these moments don't just say "Welcome." I treasure them as "We trust you." As Danish author Hans Christian Andersen said it: "The whole world is a series of miracles, but we're so used to them we call them ordinary things."[241]

Is there anything that making new friends teaches me about change management? I believe so, and here they are, my key takeaways from my "ordinary things" with a friendship spin.

"There are no strangers here; only friends you haven't yet met."[242] This quote, often (and probably mistakenly) attributed to Irish poet William Butler Yeats, is a beautiful gem of reframing. It does sound like an overused cliché, but it holds true every single time: it all starts with your mindset. Along my own journey, I found that intentional reframing requires grit and loads of grace—mostly towards your own self. It takes effort not to become one of those negative people Albert Einstein warned us about who always comes up with a problem to combat a solution.[243]

Reframing strangers into friends you have not yet met is a great friendship twist to one of my favorite takeaways from the "Shining Eyes" talk delivered by English conductor Benjamin

Zander, author of *The Art of Possibility*. He speaks about a conference where participants are almost literally struggling to breathe from under the oppressive, grim future of the Arts, with the inevitable attrition of donors and supporters who had grown to love classical music. Instead of downward spirals, he chose to reframe it into "everybody loves classical music, they just haven't discovered it yet."[244] Practice intentional reframing, whether in your personal or professional life. Make it a tool in your change management intervention box, and it will make a difference. Go for the unexpected twist! The best friendships are always the ones you never saw coming.

Friendship is a sacred space that must make sense only to the friends inhabiting it. A recent series of conversations made me remember one story that profoundly impacted me as a child: *The Lion and the Dog* by Russian writer Leo Tolstoy. In a nutshell, as a zoo comes to London, people can see the animals if they either buy a ticket or bring small animals that can be fed to the beasts on display. A man takes a puppy off the streets and gets into the zoo as the puppy is thrown into the lion's cage. The puppy cowers into a corner, and when the lion approaches him, he rolls over, paws in the air, tail wagging. The lion smells him, appears disinterested, and retreats. Little by little, they become best of friends. A year later, the little dog dies, and within the week, the lion follows his friend after refusing food and all attempts to make a new friend.[245] Not a happy story—well, no surprise there, as it is Russian prose. I got my "joy fix" from Dr. Seuss later on.

This story started to shape my understanding of friendship, about how it can grow from the most unexpected circumstances and between the most seemingly opposite people. As I grew and revisited it, I could see how full vulnerability and blatant disinterest are just opposite starting points, and people somehow meet each other in "their own middle" which must only make sense to them and no one else. Meaning and purpose are to be shared, treasured and cherished, not justified.

This story also started to teach me about grief and letting go, a lesson that I revisit every single time I relocate. How people react to dramatic changes, in either their personal or professional lives, how they choose to show up in front of strangers and how they turn extraordinary circumstances into a joint comfort zone are the coordinates defining the sacred space of friendship or organizational companionship. Respect and treasure it to the fullest!

The fastest way to make a friend for life is to travel with a stranger. Two of my favorite life coaches are cartoon characters Tiny Dragon and Big Panda. As Big Panda carries Tiny Dragon on his back, he asks his friend if the journey or the destination is more important, and Tiny Dragon responds: "The company."[246] Many of my most meaningful friendships started at an airport, on a train, or a long-distance bus. Some one-day trips marked the beginning of a journey from an acquaintance into a friend. When you travel with someone, it gives you the chance to get to know them a lot faster than when you're at home or within a "static environment." Traveling reveals a person's true nature. How much planning do they need? What do they take with them? How do they react to the unexpected? When you're on a journey, out of your comfort zone, moving from place to place, it's not easy to hide who you are from your travel companions. You'll see aspects of a person's character, learn about their endearing and annoying traits relatively quickly and discover things about them that might take you loads of time in another context.

Don't think about travel as just a geographical journey. Any change intervention is a wonderful trip. How people react to it and how they go through it is all just an amazing "window" into who they are. Regardless of whether it is a two-week hiking trip or a few months operating model reengineering intervention, these are both journeys bringing you opportunities to create meaningful connections. The secret is simple, as explained by British life and business coach Rasheed Ogunlaru: "Be genuinely interested in everyone you meet, and everyone you meet will be genuinely interested in you."[247]

Instead of a closing thought, here it is: a confession from a coffee addict. When there is a "new kid on the block," be that in your project team or in your life, and they say, "Hey, maybe we can grab a coffee and chat sometime," they are not looking just for a caffeine fix. What they are asking for is a tiny bit of hope that they can make sense of everything around them in the comforting, accepting and self-validating company of someone else. This is the adult version of the vulnerable puppy wanting to make friends with his cellmate. Please do not overdo the disinterested lion bit. Above all else, stay mindful of the fact that "A friend is the hope of the heart," as American essayist Ralph Waldo Emerson beautifully summed it up.[248]

Until next week, keep calm and make new friends. Start with your own self.

What Speaking about Silence Teaches Me about Change Management

First published on November 30, 2021

Last week, two unrelated conversations within minutes of each other made me smile and take a moment to reflect on what I heard. The first one was a short feedback chat on one of the classes I delivered: "We particularly enjoyed the part where we talked about silence and listening." Literally five minutes later, a colleague dropped me a note with, "I am particularly interested in talking more about silence and silence management."

I have always been fascinated by figures of speech, oxymoron and paradox being of particular interest to me. Building on this strong foundation of curiosity, the raging extrovert that I am instantly picked up on the requests to speak (even more!) about silence. The idea for this week's article came in a natural progression to create an additional opportunity to keep the conversation about silence going…and going…and going…hopefully proving I have taken English cleric, writer and collector Charles Caleb Colton's advice to heart: "Silence is foolish if we are wise, but wise if we are foolish."[249]

And here below you can find my version of "The Sound of Silence," written as the cover by Disturbed is set on repeat.

"Listen" and "silent" are spelled with the same letters. One of the most meaningful "communication aha moments" for me was when I realized that "listen" and "silent" were spelled using the exact same letters. There really isn't much anyone can say after this, so I will leave you to take a moment and listen to the silent wisdom of spelling.

"Silence is one of the hardest arguments to refute."[250] ...as 19th-century American humorist Josh Billings warned change managers out there. Unless you talk about it to understand what it stands for, silence is the most misinterpreted part of a conversation. It can stand for anything between full and unwavering approval to raging condemnation. Also, in order to make sure you are offering someone a comforting or protecting silence instead of a deafening silence, you need to speak with each other and agree on your interpretations through honest and open conversation.

Our feelings, perceptions and intentions are our own, valid in and of themselves. We manifest them, however, through behaviors, and here is where "semantics" can get crossed— especially when it comes to silence. Who makes you more confident and comfortable in your change management work: someone who intensely expresses disagreement or a silent stakeholder who gives you no visibility into their thoughts, opinions and feelings? If you really mean it, how do you make sure you give people your most "eloquent silence"?

Nudge people to do a double-take. An oxymoron is a figure of speech, usually one or two words, in which seemingly contradictory terms appear side by side. This contradiction is also known as a paradox. Writers and poets have used it for centuries as a literary device to describe life's inherent conflicts and incongruities. In speech, oxymorons can lend a sense of humor, irony, or sarcasm. The word "oxymoron" is itself oxymoronic, which is to say contradictory. The word is derived from two ancient Greek words: "oxys," which means "sharp," and "moronos," which means "dull" or "stupid." Writer, linguist and educator Richard Watson Todd, who began his professional career in the field of accounting, once said: "The true beauty of oxymorons is that, unless we sit back and really think, we happily accept them as normal English."[251] This statement applies to any language, and it stands to advocate for doing a mindful double-take.

Transformation is not about a "minor crisis" where the "only choice" is to engage "cheerful pessimists" to communicate "awfully well" with "cool passion" so that things can move forward at "deliberate speed." Take a step back and really listen, try to understand what people have come to happily accept as normal (organizational) life. Nudge them to do a double take. According to one dictionary, a "double-take" is "a delayed reaction indicating surprise."[252] It might be a "bittersweet" awakening.

One of the questions I get quite often is "How do you talk about change with people who see no reason to change?" And this gives me the opportunity to make the following statement: "for things to remain the same, everything must change," inspired by Giuseppe Tomasi di Lampedusa in his book *The Leopard*.[253] If the numbers are good, they will not stay like that forever by doing the same things over and over again. And when was the last time you looked at retention? Do you have a pocket in your organization with high engagement scores and rampant attrition?

One of my absolute favorite quotes about silence is from Chinese philosopher Confucius: "A seed grows with no sound, but a tree falls with a huge noise. Destruction has noise, but creation is quiet. This is the power of silence. Grow Silently."[254]

Confucius is known as the first teacher in China who wanted to make education broadly available and who was instrumental in establishing the art of teaching as a vocation. It is not a coincidence that he advocated for silence as one of the most powerful learning experiences.

Until next week, keep calm and use meaningful silence instead of meaningless words.

What Getting Lost on the Way to a Memorial Service Taught Me about Change Management

First published on December 7, 2021

This weekend was bittersweet. On Saturday, a memorial service was organized in honor and remembrance of a friend who recently passed away. He was one of those rare connections that forever touched your mind and soul, irrespective of how short the friendship or how few the get-togethers. Being anywhere else on that day, all the more so since he was a dear friend's partner, was never an option.

And yet…life happened. With the service taking place at a location about one and a half hour's drive away from Basel, I had the chance to take the trip with two new friends and their son. We made our entire way through gloomy rain and arrived at a beautiful church. A beautiful and very empty church! One Whatsapp exchange later, we felt like overachievers, since it turned out we arrived 30 minutes early. Oh, how fickle the glory, as soon after we realized we were early at the wrong location!!

It took us a little bit over one hour to get to the right place, and what could have been a tense ride turned out to be one of the most comforting, inspiring and meaningful conversations —the best sign of "the beginning of a beautiful friendship" (I hope you read this in Humphrey Bogart's voice, because I sure typed it that way). We talked about what it means to start a new life from scratch after a relocation, about compassion and the lifelong journey towards self-compassion, about the inner divine spark we all bring with us when we come into this world, everything wrapped in childhood memories and surprising common roots. What were the odds that two Israeli would go to a memorial service in Switzerland with a Romanian, only to discover we all shared Romanian AND Hungarian roots, a deep love for gulyas and everything paprika and an appreciation for dry humor?

An expression of that humor was a random, quite ironic remark made by one of my friends: "This could be a Tuesday article, you know." And what better way to spark inspiration for a "Tuesday Change Management Random Thought" than by making a random challenge-like sounding comment? I found myself starting to think about it immediately after, and here it is—what getting lost on the way to a memorial service taught me about change management.

The celebration is in the intent, above and beyond the protocol. During the close to five-hour-long drive overall, we all came to mention our friend, how we met, how graciously and generously he helped us, and how incredibly vibrant and life-loving he was. In many meaningful ways, it felt like we had our own service, honoring his presence in our lives. And the way in which we came together on this occasion feels like a wholehearted tribute to his legacy. I do feel really bad about missing the actual service, and yet, in all honesty, I do not think I could have honored him more deeply or meaningfully by listening to a service in German, a language I could not understand or resonate with.

This realization made me think about how the celebration

is in the intent, above and beyond the protocol. In change management work, this could mean giving people space and grace to go for outcomes over outputs, to constructively challenge, even bend or break processes and rules, always with positive intent and in pursuit of the intended value.

Lessons learned are forward-guiding, not backward-blaming. While we were back in the car on the way to the right location, we tried to understand what had happened. And although it wasn't the most comfortable of situations, it never felt…uneasy. My feeling was that we were trying to figure out the best way to make sure we got to where we would want to go for our next adventure together. No blame, just curiosity. We chose to talk and laugh and share small moments of thoughtful silence. We chose being present over being perfect. Before too long, while discussing what had happened, we ended up talking about compassion. And self-compassion.

Reflecting on that conversation, it was our own retrospective exercise, one of the best I have ever been part of—forward-guiding, not backward-blaming. It reminded me of a beautiful saying from American singer-songwriter and composer Alex Ebert: "To be lost is as legitimate a part of your process as being found."[255] I believe I will update my change management slides with this quote and see what conversations it sparks.

"Never let a good crisis go to waste."[256] It is said that former Prime Minister of the United Kingdom Winston Churchill said this in the mid-1940s as the world approached the end of WWII. He was referring to Yalta and the alliance forged between himself, Soviet political leader Joseph Stalin and the 32nd President of the United States, Franklin D. Roosevelt—an unlikely trio that would lead to the formation of the United Nations, thus creating opportunities in the midst of a crisis. Undoubtedly under less demanding or critical circumstances than decades ago, Saturday still counts as a crisis for us in the car—missing out on showing up (as in literally) for our friend's service.

Churchill's quote talks to me about staying aware to look for a silver lining during a crisis and keeping an open mind, open heart and open will to make the most of what life has to offer, whatever that might be. No matter what change management work you do, a crisis is just a matter of when and where, not if. Stay curious, stay compassionate and stay courageous— things might turn out even better than initially planned or expected. I left home on Saturday feeling sad and alone and I came back having new friends in my new life and the idea for the weekly change random thought. Not exactly the spark of the United Nations, yet it sure feels infinitely meaningful and life-enriching to me.

Every single person in the car going to and from the memorial service on Saturday had recently gone through tremendous loss—of comfort zone, closeness to family, friends and former plans, of a special friend due to life's journey. Yet we all came together with curiosity, compassion, an open mind and an open heart. Our friend was a healer. And how he gave us the chance to spend time together, getting lost only to have more time to find each other and our friendship, is his way of healing us still.

Until next week, keep calm and celebrate life!

What Dog-Sitting over the Holidays Taught Me about Change Management

*Written with the world's most lovable pair
of Frenchies, Frida and Cleo
First published on January 11, 2022*

This Christmas, I got the best festive magic gift ever: time with the world's loveliest couple of French bulldogs, Frida and Cleo. Two of my friends decided to go spend the holidays with their families back in Mexico, and they had been looking for a dog sitter for their fur-babies with no success. When we met at an event in early December, they mentioned their challenge, and I said, "Hey, if they can move in with me for the holidays, I am up for it." A few days later, after yet another dog-sitting dead-end, I got the job!!!

It really felt like early Christmas when they moved in during the first week of December. Although my couch is an immense 10-seat extravaganza, barely five minutes later we were all three sandwiched in the same corner. No later than that very first evening, I sent a note to their parents wishing them a restful, joyful, festive trip and giving them a heads-up that they would come back to fierce shared custody negotiations.

I have been enjoying our time together immensely; they are sitting by my side as I type this piece. They have the sweetest nature, yet very distinct personalities. Cleo is all about attention, while Frida is more…socially awkward. There are two memories especially near and dear to my heart from our time together so far. One is New Year's Eve. When the fireworks and firecrackers started to go off, Frida got more scared than Cleo. As I was holding and kissing Frida, Cleo was glued to my thigh. When she realized her sister was having a hard time, she started gently licking Frida's paws, then climbed into my lap and covered her as widely and tightly as she could. When Frida's breathing got back to normal, they started to munch on each other's ears, and soon after they were running around the apartment.

The other memory is made up of all the times we went to the "movie theater," or "cinema" as I call it. There is a platform on top of the entrance into the building's garage that offers a nice and safe panorama over the street. The girls love to go there on our daily walks and spend some time watching the traffic. That has been our "cinema" for the past month. To get there, we have to climb a few steps. Frida is a bit curvier than Cleo, and each time we get to the climb, she looks a bit overwhelmed by the task ahead. She then starts to climb, huffing and puffing, more and more determined with each step. She reminds me of The Little Engine That Could, the character created in 1930 by Hungarian-born American writer Arnold Munk under the pen name Watty Piper. Frida's signature Frenchie noises almost sound like "I think I can, I think I can, I think I can," and then finally "I thought I could." She makes me smile every single time, and she is an adorable reminder of optimism and determination.

There are so many things I have learned from them, but I will try to condense my learning into a short collection of key takeaways for change management. So, here we go. I think I can, I think I can, I think I can…

Routines are the guardians of willpower. Research has been proving time and time again that willpower alone is not enough to get us through what we set out for ourselves, regardless of whether we aim for a healthier diet in our personal life or a digital transformation within our organizations. Moreover, according to studies, willpower is not as limitless as advertised by popular belief. It is a finite resource and needs to be used carefully and intentionally. There are also two "willpower vampires" we encounter on a day-to-day basis: avoiding temptations and decision-making. We basically use up a lot of our willpower to control ourselves and make choices. For years now, one of my New Year's resolutions (it is their season, after all) has been to go out for a walk, no matter how short, every single day. How many years do you think I was successful at this? Please answer truthfully, and no worries, I won't take it personally… Yeah, you guessed it correctly!!!

Having the snoring love dumplings for the holidays meant that I had to incorporate their daily walking routine into my own schedule. No more "I am not going out because it is too cold or too rainy or too peopley out there." Every single day, I took them out for their walks, and we went to the "cinema." This made me reflect on the importance of routines over sheer willpower, and I ask myself what routines I could build to keep myself honest to my goals, and equally what routines I could further develop in my change management work. What organizational routines do you have in place to help people move forward? Add to the "where there's a will, there's a way" adage the mission-critical mention "and where there's a routine, there's consistent progress on that way."

Always choose mindful over mind-full. Dogs in particular, and animals in general, are THE masters of mindfulness, according to extensive research. They simply live in the moment. I have no idea what they think, but I guess it might be something like: "Hooman is slow this morning. This bush smells of that poodle on the fourth floor, let me rectify this. Grass is so beautiful. Oh, pigeon, pigeon, pigeon!!! Hooman, catch-up! What a great stick! Enough nature, let's go home." Pets are completely unconcerned with anything other than what is happening now, and when you interact by playing, petting or snuggling them, you can experience that same sense of presence.

Practicing being mindful over mind-full with Frida and Cleo also reminded me of the importance of being present over being perfect in a relationship, be it personal or professional, of suspending judgment and also leaving the past in the past and the future for the future. Change management work is about human connection—igniting it, nurturing it and enriching it above and beyond anything else. And all these reminders are meaningful insights into how to go about touching people's minds and hearts in a way that makes a difference.

"If you don't ask, the answer is always no."[257] Frida and Cleo are the most adorable and lovable furry embodiments of this saying, most often attributed to American novelist Nora Roberts. They always always always ask for what they want, and they do it repeatedly until they get it. They ask for their food, water, walks, toys, best spots on the couch, pieces of carrots, mangoes, bread (they are totally in love with my homemade bread, the best food review ever!!!), and my personal favorites: cuddles, snuggles and kisses. They are constant reminders that persistence does pay off big time! Never assume that people know what you need and want and they just decided not to give it to you or are waiting for the right time to make their offer. Ask for what you need and want in a clear way, and why not in a progressively assertive way. Ask for resources, decisions, help, and take all replies as temporary. Come back and ask again.

This coming Monday, January 17, would have been American actress and animal activist Betty White's 100th birthday. In honor of her memory, here's a lovely quote from her: "Animals don't lie. Animals don't criticize. If animals have moody days, they handle them better than humans do."[258] Frida and Cleo have been honoring this every single day. They also keep on reminding me that family doesn't have to be blood, that play is important and love is unconditional.

Until next week, keep calm and always ask for what you want. Then ask again and again.

What Struggling with an Unstable Internet Connection Teaches Me about Change Management

First published on January 18, 2022

If my life had background music, the only moments when Queen's iconic "Under Pressure" would be blasting full-volume are the ones when a small message pops up on my screen: "Your internet connection is unstable." Over the past few months, I have been volunteering to manage and facilitate panel conversations for an online global conference, and the dreaded message appeared on my screen quite a few times. On a handful of occasions, things got worse pretty quickly and the connection crashed, sending everyone back into the scheduling logistics pain. One instance was particularly frustrating, and I remember standing up from my desk yelling, "Can nothing be stable in this house?????????" Quite a counterintuitive reaction from a change manager…

At some point, my reflex of looking at things through the lens of change management random thoughts potential kicked in, and I started to think about it. Usually, as soon as an idea— as in a "writing challenge"—appears, my desk quickly gets covered in Post-it notes. This time, it felt more "hicuppy" than usual, and I told myself it must have been because I was still easing myself back into the weekly writing routine after the vacation. I mentioned this to one of my best friends when we chatted over the weekend. He smiled and said, "Hey, isn't this the perfect analogy? The frustration of not being sure! Of anything…" The smile his reaction put on my face has been very stable over the last few days; I am still wearing it as I type.

So, here we go. I don't know why the 1999 romantic comedy film *Notting Hill* popped up in my mind, but I felt inspired to say that "I'm just a girl, holding her laptop on the couch, by the router, asking it to love her with some stable Wi-Fi signal."

Anything can unexpectedly come to an end, and there is nothing you can do about it. This was the biggest takeaway from the spring of 2020 when the COVID pandemic hit the world and everything felt like it stood still for a second. Then, as we all found ways to move forward, this teaching started to fade away…until the dreaded "your internet connection is unstable" started to pop up on my screen during some of the most inspiring and uplifting conversations. After one of the instances when the internet crashed, I went outside on the terrace to watch the sky, looking for a new perspective. I started to think about all the things that came to an unexpected end in my life over the past year without me being able to do anything about it: personal relationships, my lease contract in Luxembourg that accelerated my relocation to Switzerland, planning my dream trip to Portugal, projects or parts of ongoing initiatives at my full-time job or within my side projects and volunteering work.

In the absence of the expected, contracted end result, how do you still showcase value? Knowing that the internet could crash and take away the possibility to deliver the end result, how could I still create value throughout the interaction and work together with the panelists? One of my personal answers to this question is "connection"—oh, the irony of it!!!—built and nurtured through how I strive to show up in our interactions, hopefully always with curiosity, compassion and courage (even to a raging extrovert like myself, it feels a little daunting to reach out to over 300 strangers all over the world within a few weeks).

It's just like in any interaction along a change management journey. When personal or organizational life happens and things come to an unexpected end, in the absence of the end result, you can still create meaningful value. Quite possibly because over the last few days I have been seeing the news about the newly minted dollar quarters with American poet and civil rights activist Maya Angelou entering circulation and making history, the theme of one of my favorite quotes came to mind: people may forget everything else, but what they won't forget is "how you made them feel."[259] How can you create meaningful value so that people will feel inspired and committed to give it another go?

Beware of over-accountability. When the technical challenges appeared at my end, I apologized over and over again to everyone involved. Arguably, I made quite a few "deposits" into the "sorry cycle of over-apologizing," as research calls it. I felt really bad and frustrated, and even to some extent responsible. I must have come across as extra wound up during a conversation right after Christmas, and I got the following question: "Why are you so stressed? After all, it is volunteer work, right?" That question triggered sooooo many thoughts. While most of them feed into my inner child and shadow work, some can be shared here.

As I started to draft a keynote on self-leadership for (yet another) volunteer project with The Hague University of Applied Sciences, I revisited my own values and beliefs, and I fundamentally and unwaveringly believe that my word is my word, and it carries the same weight regardless of the context within which I give it. There is also a permanent "mental Post-it note" in my mind now to be extra intentional and mindful to pick up signs of over-accountability in the conversations I will be part of. Especially within the organizational context, during project retrospectives and lessons learned interventions, I will pick up on signs that speak of potential over-accountability as a result of personal and professional journeys coming together within the company culture ecosystem. How accountability and ownership are defined, dispersed and contracted within teams, fulfilled by the people on the project teams became even more important to me, all thanks to my unstable internet connection.

"**May your choices reflect your hopes, not your fears.**"[260] This is one of my all-time favorite quotes, courtesy of South African anti-apartheid revolutionary, political leader and philanthropist Nelson Mandela. As connection challenges became quite serious over the past few days and the absolute, non-negotiable deadline for getting the recordings done approached, the offer to simply cancel panels was put on the table. I could have accepted it. I did not. You want to ask me whether it was only hope fueling my decision, and not also a little bit of over-accountability? We all know the answer to this one; I don't have to type it out, right? I wanted to give it one last shot, gave a heads-up to all the panelists, asked for understanding, patience and help with taking over the facilitator role if needed. I feel infinitely blessed and grateful I only got "Of course, what help do you need?" replies. Our interactions reflect our hopes and not our fears, and this is the best takeaway for my change management work.

When searching for tips to make an internet connection more stable, one stood out in particular: "decongest." This word sounds like a perfect source of inspiration for an entire *Seinfeld* episode, and I imagine Kramer would have a field day with it.

I do not find much comfort or help in it, yet I believe words come into our life for a reason, and maybe this will help some of you. I will just continue to fantasize about crawling back into my cave and playing with my favorite pet dinosaur... I won't be impressed with technology until I can download ice cream!!! And the connection better be stable then.

Until next week, keep calm and enjoy stable connections!

What Being Stuck in Back-to-Back Zoom Calls Teaches Me about Change Management

First published on January 25, 2022

"Apologies for being late, had to jump off another call." "Sorry, need to drop off, got another back-to-back and I'm already late." "I just need one minute for a bio break, been in calls since 7:00 AM." "Will stay off video if that's okay, trying to get lunch." … and many more variations along the same lines. Does this sound familiar? I have been hearing these increasingly often (from others and myself, equally), and not just in work-related calls. With a lot of social connections happening online because of distance, COVID and simply life sometimes, it feels like there are no Zoom-free days anymore. Plus, Teams, Whatsapp, FaceTime, Slack, Skype and all the platforms known to humankind, available to anyone and everyone, display that little green dot next to your name—which of course is an open invitation to connect across all weekdays and timezones.

Barely three weeks back from a one-month-long vacation, I find myself daydreaming about the next out-of-office message. My mind starts to wander off in this direction when I check my calendar and it looks like Tetris with an *Inception* twist. A calendar inside a calendar, dreaming of an extra calendar. So many awesome tips out there on sorting, filtering and prioritizing, and we all know it is not always a clear-cut, frustration- and risk-free decision-making process. Working across timezones makes it even more of an adventure, while navigating priorities, expectations, assumptions, personal preferences, sometimes even egos, within various organizational cultures could seem like a power swim against the current in a troubled sea.

My change management reflex to turn frustration into inspiration kicked in and this piece started to come to life on Post-it notes all over my desk, some of them scribbled while in, you guessed it, Zoom calls. So here we go, a back-to-back list of takeaways below.

Presence is no guarantee for "being present." Just like a green dot next to a name is not a guarantee of availability, (physical) presence in a box on a screen is not a guarantee of mental or emotional bandwidth. And the chances of being "present absent" increase exponentially with the number of back-to-back calls. Add into the mix having Zoom calls on different topics for different projects and—shock of shocks!!!—"zooming multitasking" is not as effective as advertised. I am the first one to raise my hand and admit to sitting in calls and at some point asking myself "What meeting am I in?" And it takes a lot of mindfulness and intentionality to keep myself answering "yes" to a more meaningful question: "Am I in?" One of my absolute favorite memes is of a minion being asked "On a scale of 1 to 10, how focused are you?", and the answer is "Banana!!!" I can totally relate, and I have had some "bananas" in my "calendar diet" over the past several months.

Never assume that people on your screen, even if they have their video on the entire call, are truly, fully present. Make sure the information is available for them in multiple other ways, check for their understanding and try to build in some "Zoom switching buffers" into your meetings so that people can more easily "zoom in" on the topic of the call and "zoom out" respectively. One particular point that I have been paying extra attention to lately is the assumptions people have related to the (perceived) expectations of "visible work," everything heightened within the wider conversation of organizational culture in a flexible or hybrid environment. How high on the list of criteria based on which they "curate" their calendars is their belief that they are expected to be "visible" (even if not always "present"), and what feeds that assumption?

We are all the same height on Zoom. It was a happy coincidence that both one of my best friends and I changed jobs early last year. When we had our celebratory drinks on Zoom, no kidding, we talked about all the things we were curious about in our new roles and how much we were looking forward to meeting our new colleagues in person. Ten minutes and one glass of wine later, we were laughing to tears after admitting to our greatest, most genuine curiosity: how tall everyone really was!! That is one piece of personal data that Zoom keeps confidential.

Beyond human curiosity, Zoom calls triggered another thought. Videoconferencing managed to achieve something that had close to "Holy Grail" status for all organizational design practitioners out there: the flat organization. A lot of the hierarchy markers are absent from Zoom—no corner executive office, no conference room table, no high-up senior floors, no name badges with visible roles and titles. We all have the same size boxes, and "we are all the same height on Zoom."

Trust, confidence and respect are gained, built and maintained in different ways, some of them way more subtle and meaningful than before. It is through the lens of our "Zoom height" that I find more meaning in the "Let's Stop Talking

About Soft Skills: They're Power Skills" article from The Josh Bersin Company, published in October 2019, and updated one year later. The article challenges the distinction between hard and soft skills, defined traditionally as "technical skills" and "people skills," respectively. The part I love most talks about how hard skills are actually soft because they're constantly changing and updating with the times, not to mention you can learn them fairly quickly. And, conversely, soft skills are hard; they're crucial to know and extremely difficult to learn and grow.[261] It is the soft skills, oftentimes upgraded to "human skills," that add "centimeters" to your "Zoom height."

You are always a speaker, even when you just listen. For me, Zoom calls come with a huge challenge. I have never had a "poker face." Even if I don't say anything, my face will provide you with detailed subtitles, sometimes in shouty capital letters… After many years of working on this, I managed to identify certain ways to make it harder for people to get these unfiltered insights, and especially during in-person meetings, I could change my position and the angle of my head depending on who was looking in my direction. Zoom makes that impossible, so I end up watching myself more than anyone else on the call.

As I try to stay silent in more ways than one, I am constantly reminded of one fundamental communication truth: you are always a speaker, even when you just listen. And Zoom makes this all the more obvious. According to research conducted by the Stanford Virtual Human Interaction Lab (VHIL), in a normal meeting, people will variously be looking at the speaker, taking notes or looking elsewhere, but on Zoom calls, everyone is looking at everyone all the time. A listener is treated nonverbally like a speaker, so even if you don't speak once in a meeting, you are still looking at faces staring at you. The amount of eye contact is dramatically increased.

Professor Jeremy Bailenson, founding director of VHIL,

said that fear of public speaking is one of the most universal phobias in our world; standing up in front of people and being stared at is an anxiety-inducing experience.[262] In a Zoom call, you are sitting in front of your computer, most often alone in the room, yet with the additional peek you offer into your own home and private life in the background, you feel even more exposed. All of this while constantly seeing your face, realizing how much of your own self you reveal to everybody in the call. My hope is that other people are just as worried as I am about the subtitles on their faces, and they watch themselves more than others…is anyone really looking at the slides being shared on the screen?

I really wanted to leave you with an inspiring final thought, but I just checked my inbox and found 17 new invites to different Zoom meetings over the next three days, and I am having a "Banana!!!" moment… Now all I can think of is this joke about Zoom I saw on social media the other day: "Turning off your Zoom camera is like getting food from a buffet at a party. You want to do it, but you don't want to be the first, and you definitely don't want to be the only."[263] I told a Zoom joke, it probably wasn't even remotely funny…

Until next week, keep calm and be present!

What Delivering Presentations Teaches Me about Change Management

First published on February 1, 2022

Glossophobia. It sounds ominous, yet it isn't a dangerous disease or chronic condition. It's the medical term for the fear of public speaking. According to research, 75% of people experience some degree of anxiety or nervousness when public speaking and 10% of people are terrified.[264] Speaking in public is one of the most common fears, ranking among heights, death and snakes. To put it in perspective: public speaking is usually ranked as people's number one fear. Death is ranked as number two.

Literally within a couple of hours after pressing "Publish" on this piece, I will be facing my own glossophobia. As an extrovert who is naturally extremely shy, I have to constantly push myself to face my fear of public speaking, and today I am doing it for something that is very near and dear to my heart: sharing knowledge. One of the best news I got toward the end of last year was an invite to go back to the Hague University of Applied Sciences as a guest speaker for their International Week Program, delivering both a keynote on self-leadership and a class on Intentional Curiosity. While I am still pondering on the timeliness of mentioning my delivering the keynote as a milestone on my own self-leadership journey, I decided to keep myself intentionally curious about what delivering presentations teaches me about change management.

The first one who needs to get comfortable with your voice is you. Whenever I hear a recording of myself, or within the first few minutes of a live presentation, it takes all I've got to fight the urge to send everyone I have ever spoken with a text to apologize. My voice sounds terribly off to my own ears. The pitch, the accent—as almost without exception all my public speaking instances happen in a language other than my mother tongue—it all sounds terribly unfamiliar. There is a lot of research available on how your voice not only affects your listeners, but even more so how confident you feel about yourself. What helps me power through the initial few minutes of a public speech is what I hear myself saying, how "familiar" the information feels, how what I say is aligned with who I am and what I stand for. It is about what I use my voice for, above and beyond how my voice sounds like.

I guess this is my first takeaway for self-leadership and overall change management work: the first one who needs to get comfortable with your voice is you. If you are not aligned with what you speak about, if your innermost values, beliefs and principles do not resonate with what comes out of your mouth, if you cannot articulate your own "why" behind your words, no amount of public speaking training will help you get through delivering a presentation meaningfully and in a totally foolproof manner. It is quite fitting that George Orwell, the English novelist known for his *1984* dystopian work, was the one who pointed out that when our true intentions and spoken intentions aren't aligned, our language grows more confusing and exhaustive; it's much more difficult to speak clearly when you're not sincere.[265]

"A presentation is a chance to share, not an oral exam."[266] ...as M.F. Fensholt, author of *The Francis Effect: The Real Reason You Hate Public Speaking and How to Get Over It*, puts it. This is in no way, shape or form a waiver of information accuracy. Those of you who have crossed paths with me heard this as "be present over perfect," listen, speak, engage, touch minds and hearts, be generous with your time, insights, energy, curiosity towards others and their point of view and do not create pressure out of anything else.

Transposed into change work, this speaks about sharing available information, clarifying the distinction between the parts that are clear, certain and pending additional inputs, keeping all communication channels open to multi-directional flow, encouraging different and disruptive points of view. Especially within the overall context we all have been sharing over the past couple of years, we seem to be (collectively and individually) "lost in the right direction" and we got the chance to shift from "know it all" to "learn it all." Always be learning, always be sharing!

People don't care how much you know until they know how much you care. It is never just about what you have to say. It is—arguably even more so—about what people come to hear. "Know your audience" is shorthand for understand, acknowledge and respect why your audience shows up. Some come to learn, others to add insights into a decision-making instance, a few are there to simply be entertained, and I bet you there is no single presentation without a few who show up because "they were told to." Regardless of what kind of presentation or supporting materials you design, build and deliver—whether for a town hall meeting, an engagement session with key stakeholders, a co-creative visioning workshop on whatever the topic might be, a keynote or a class—having your audience in mind and staying intentional about acknowledging their needs, requests, expectations, hopes and constraints is paramount. Here's something to always keep in mind from the late Ken Haemer, formerly Manager, Presentation Research for AT&T: "Designing a presentation without an audience in mind is like writing a love letter and addressing it: To Whom It May Concern."[267]

An unexpected thought popped up in my mind. In high school, I remember something one of the physics teachers I used to talk with told me: "Have a mirror placed by the phone, look at yourself as you get ready to answer the call, and make sure you smile. People can hear a smile, and it makes all the difference in the world." Although this advice was given in the era of landline phones, the reflex to make sure I smile before I say "Hello" has stayed with me to this day. And if people can "hear a smile," they can definitely see it. What I learned over years of delivering various presentations is that there are two additional fundamental elements to any speech besides words: smiling and breathing.

Until next week, keep calm, smile, breathe, and the words will come!

What Coloring My Hair Teaches Me about Change Management

First published on February 8, 2022

While growing up, from early childhood and up to my late teen years, I practiced swimming. For purely practical reasons, I had my hair cut really short, and my favorite comb was a towel. I used to dream about having long hair and started experimenting with longer haircuts in my late high school years. Quite surprisingly, I started getting gray hairs around the age of twenty, and I got almost entirely white by my mid-twenties. So much for my long hair extravaganza fantasies…

Because life happened more intensely than anticipated, I had to cancel my hairdresser's appointment this past weekend. I have never been very interested in or committed to these types of maintenance upgrades, yet it frustrated me a bit. And this feeling made me curious.

Keeping Post-it notes and a pen nearby, I started scribbling bits and pieces of colorful thoughts as I challenged myself to reflect on what coloring my hair teaches me about change management.

Meet people where they are, but don't leave yourself behind. Twelve years ago, my parents got divorced. A few days before the appointment with the notary public, my mom called me and asked me to go with her. I bought a plane ticket right away, flew back to my hometown, and on the day of the appointment we took a cab together. It was a glorious, warm, mid-October day, and the sun shone through the cab windows as we stopped at a red light. My mom looked at me, reached out to caress my hair and started crying. She kept repeating through sobs, "My baby's hair is white, my baby's hair is white." Because I really didn't mind my natural hair, I hadn't dyed it for years. My mom's reaction had a huge impact on me, so after the appointment, I took her home, told her I had some stuff to take care of, went into town and got my hair colored chocolate brown in the first place I found an available hairdresser. Then I went back home and took my mom out for dinner.

I remembered this moment under the strangest of circumstances a few months ago. It was in the middle of facilitating a team debrief on their collective intercultural profiles, talking about preferred work styles and means to bridge distance and difference. When we deep-dived into style-switching (changing one's behavior to align with the behaviors of others), this story just popped up in my head. Was coloring my hair to make my mom more comfortable and comforted an expression of style-switching? Maybe…

What are the organizational equivalents of that? What is it that we can change in our behavior, without changing who we are and what we stand for, to accommodate other people's comfort zones? Particularly in change work, style-switching is a superpower. How do you show up as a superhero, meeting people where they are without leaving yourself behind? And just a personal curiosity: what color is your superhero hair?

What decisions are we making for other people just because we control the resources they need? With very few exceptions, the loved ones I have lost so far left my life because of various types of cancer. One of my choices to honor them is to donate my hair to organizations making wigs for people going through cancer treatments. Every four years or so you might see me with a short(er) haircut, and now you know why.

A few years ago, I was happily seated in a very comfortable hairdresser's chair, looking forward to getting my hair colored—it was my "neon red hair" period, please don't ask!!! As he casually brushed my hair, the hairdresser said: "Your hair is getting really long, are you ready for the change soon?" His question triggered the following thought in my mind: "Who would wear a neon red wig?" I am sure that quite a few people would, yet in that moment, it felt like I was making a decision that would in some way, shape or form restrict access to a resource I had (primary) control over. The donated hair could always be dyed a different color, but why build in an additional step to make something (that is readily available) accessible?

Many change conversations with stakeholders remind me of that thought. Are they having control over information, in both degree of clarity and form of "packaging," that drives them to make decisions for other people who ultimately need that input? Or are there people in their teams with a particular set of capabilities needed across the organization and they make that kind of resource more difficult to be accessed? As my haircuts change across four-year-long cycles, I keep this one question with me in both my personal and professional life: how do I make decisions for other people just because I control the resources they need?

On bad hair days, there is always lipstick. Replaying almost two decades' worth of change conversations in my mind, there is one thing that stands out: sometimes, the pure and simple mention of "change" and "change management" is disruptive in and of itself. "What is coming now, that we need to address it with dedicated change management?" How do we speak about change when even the word itself creates disruption, discomfort and distancing? How do we "color our white hair" to make people see the "right color" of outcomes and outputs that make them most comfortable and comforted? What is the organizational "hair-coloring" equivalent of "covering the gray hairs as wisdom highlights" of change management mindset and approach, dedicated processes, activities and tools, so stakeholders can see only the outputs they are after based on their own assumptions, understanding of change work and expectations (including the expectations around the scale and type of effort required by change interventions)?

What is the alternative when you cannot get away with gray hair or neon red hair or visible roots, or simply when whatever haircut or color you choose rubs people the wrong way? (In full disclosure, I deeply believe that only Shakira can pull it off to look great with visible roots…) As these thoughts rambled around in my head, I remembered a great social media post that goes viral every now and again with a sweet, yet very confused-looking monkey with disheveled hair and red lipstick on, and the text: "On a bad hair day, there is always lipstick."[268] It felt like a good takeaway for change work, with a lighthearted twist… What is your "change lipstick" on bad hair days?

As I pull my hair back in a ponytail and get ready to look for alternatives to reschedule the hairdresser's appointment, here is my closing thought, the most important thing I have ever learned about hair in my life: you can't control everything; your hair was put on your head to remind you of that.

Until next week, keep calm and make comforting decisions!

What Enjoying Candlelight Teaches Me about Change Management

First published on February 15, 2022

Last week, I got a splinter in my eye, courtesy of a gust of wind, and I was forced into tech detox and a very painful "no reading" treatment for a few days. While listening to music and resting my eyes, I tried my best to make peace with an unexpected gap in the weekly ramblings on change…until I got to one of my favorite self-care activities: lighting a candle.

Candlelight always reminds me of an awesome quote from an ancient Chinese proverb: "It is better to light a candle than curse the darkness."[269] And this is when my inner "pirate" rebelled and challenged me to remember the last time I followed any treatment to a tee…yeah, that's right, never!

Two decisions were made on the spot. First and foremost, for my birthday next month, I will order 43 scented candles from my favorite brand, because that sounds like the right amount of festive. Then (promising myself to rest my eyes every few sentences), to give it a go on what enjoying candlelight teaches me about change management… Flickering thoughts below.

Don't burn a new candle for only a few minutes. My favorite candles come in beautiful glass jars, and it took me some time and research to learn how to use them properly. Based on loads of recommendations I have come across over the years, the first time you burn a container candle, you should allow it to form a complete pool of melted wax across the surface of its container, from rim to rim. This is because wax has a memory, and on subsequent lightings, the wax pool will struggle to go beyond the circumference of the previous burn. The candle will most likely tunnel down into the wax from then on. The wick will sink deeper and deeper into the candle and the wax on the sides will never burn, shortening the life of your candle. Whenever I gift a candle, I make sure I tell people to treat it with joy and patience.

It's a great takeaway for change work, too. Many conversations about change management end up revolving around how much time is needed to start seeing meaningful results. Of course, there are low-hanging fruits and quick wins, but meaningful change takes time. And just like a container candle, change has a "memory," and on subsequent interventions, it will struggle to go beyond the previous coverage. It also happens with people— when they are moved from one "burning priority" to another, the "wick" of their motivation and engagement will sink deeper and deeper, shortening their time with the organization.

"Everybody is a candle, true. But not everybody is lit."[270] This wonderful quote from former Indian cricketer Harbhajan Singh has been with me for a while, and it always speaks to me about the fabulous potential in each and every one of us. All we need is a spark to light us up. I just made a mental Post-it note to include this quote in my change management toolkit when doing stakeholder engagement and especially change community-building work. Understanding what inspires, motivates and lights people up is essential in any transformation.

This also triggers a thought about knowledge sharing. Share your passion, curiosity, compassion and knowledge; share your light with people you cross paths with. Always remember that a candle loses nothing by lighting another candle. Use your spark and light to bring out the "inner candle" in those around you.

"To light a candle is to cast a shadow."[271] This takeaway comes courtesy of one of my all-time favorite writers, Ursula K. Le Guin. The entire quote is included in her book *A Wizard of Earthsea*, and to me it is a brilliant reflection on leadership and change.

Shadows from the candlelight have been fascinating me my entire life. I grew up in communist Romania, and I learned to write and read by candlelight. My grandparents used to read me stories by candlelight. The shadows created by the flickering flame were my alternative cartoons, and I imagined they had a life of their own. Every shadow tells a story, and this is a great learning for change, in both my personal and professional lives. As I had to rest my eyes for a little while, I tried to reflect on Ursula K. Le Guin's quote… A candle only casts light from one point, so while it may illuminate some of our surroundings, it leaves others in darkness. I think this can be a metaphor for how relying on a single perspective or source of knowledge can leave gaps in our understanding. Another thought is that when you light a candle, you, the person sparking the flame, are always going to cast a shadow. The lesson there is the inevitability of our involvement in events influencing those events to have a certain outcome.

Candles are believed to contain the gifts of the gods, as the Greek gods gave fire to Prometheus for illumination and progress. In ancient times, candles largely symbolized the divine. The flame is symbolic, as it holds celebration and remembrance. I love candles, for they speak of home, a home for the soul. In many cultures and parts of the world, there is the tradition of putting a candle in the window that dates back to colonial times. It was one-part prayer that a special someone far away would return home safely, and one-part a sign that someone was waiting for them and ready to welcome them home. The flame came to represent home. It is oftentimes believed that the sight of a burning flame brings us back home no matter where we are and quells the nostalgia and homesickness, bringing us peace and tranquility.

Until next week, keep calm and light up the home of your soul.

What Making Peace with Broken Dreams Teaches Me about Change Management

First published on March 1, 2022

Maybe because my birthday is approaching, I am going through an "inventory" phase. It is so easy to look back and smile at the good things. It is harder to look at the…I will call them "wonderings," all those experiences that almost literally brought me to my knees. Yes, I've had quite a few broken dreams, a couple of them hurting fresh, the last one still cracking and screeching from last week.

I call these "wonderings" because sometimes I wonder what my life would have been like if they had turned into reality. I keep this perspective with me from an imagined dialogue created by independent writer Amanda Torroni in her book *Poetic Conversations*, where one of the characters explains they don't have regrets, just "wonderings," as we only consider something a "mistake" in hindsight while wondering what would have happened if things had played out differently; in the moment, we all try to make the best decisions under the given circumstances.[272]

I believe "wonderings" can equally apply to broken dreams. We dream the best dreams we can; we do not set out to intentionally dream broken ones.

Life has a serendipitous magic way of connecting dots. It brought me another lens through which my broken dreams are "wonderings," this one from Buddhist teacher Pema Chödrön in her book *When Things Fall Apart: Heart Advice for Difficult Times*. She says that having space for "not knowing" is important; when something bad happens in our lives, or even something good, we have no idea what the ultimate results of it will be. We simply don't know, and that's okay.[273]

Whenever I am grieving, I find comfort and healing peace in Ernest Hemingway's advice to write about the most difficult things.[274] So here I go, trying to find some larger meaning and maybe learnings for change management.

Be aware of what is, not what you would like to be. There are two excruciatingly painful milestones for me on my journey of healing from a broken dream. One of them is getting closure over something that never really came to be after grieving more over what could have been, not what actually happened. And letting go of the incessant self-doubting questions: "What have I dreamed myself into seeing?", "Where have I lost touch with reality?", "Where did I go so delusionally wrong?" As Pema Chödrön summed it up, "nothing ever really attacks us except our own confusion."[275]

While I try to keep myself anchored in the present and not in the "past future-to-be," there seems to be one lesson I must learn: being aware of what is, not what I would like to be. This makes me think of change work. Nobody sets out into any project to fail. Yet, a significant number of "transformation dreams" get broken. There is a magic balance between hope and courage on one hand and the organizational reality and potential on the other. Create it based on your change readiness assessment, change impact assessment, conversations covering as many different voices within the layers and pockets of the organization as possible and introspection into your own appetite and energy to drive and role model change. Be unwaveringly and uncompromisingly honest with yourself and others and hold the space for the people within your organization to do the same. And if a project fails, make the most out of this opportunity to learn.

Get compassionately and intentionally curious about what broken dreams made possible. Here's a confession: when it hurts, I would give anything and everything to make it go away, to numb my mind and heart, to run away from it. It takes a while for me to remember that nothing really goes away until it has taught us what we need to know, until we learn whatever it has to teach us about where we are separating ourselves from reality.

I try to sit with my broken dream through the pain, the grief, the numbness, the anger, shame, emptiness, the choking sadness, and let it push and pull me into hope and renewed courage—and ever so slowly into curiosity about what is now made possible for me to dream about with what I learned. I hope project retrospectives are less traumatic for anyone going through them and that they fuel organizational hope, courage, curiosity and ultimately, innovation. Use every broken dream to teach you how to dream better and bigger dreams, to diminish and alleviate your fear of failure and to celebrate your imperfections. Dream, undream, redream.

Broken dreams break more than just their dreamers. I experienced the grief of broken dreams not just as a dreamer, but also as someone close to grieving dreamers. As a witness to a loved one's pain, I felt helpless, sad, anguished. I even experienced feelings of self-doubt and guilt, asking myself whether I had contributed to fueling unreasonable dreams or got willfully blind to warning signs. I felt the loss of plans we made together once their dream would come true. I felt robbed of my share of laughter, joy and happiness. There are some bonds that got broken because lessons in compassion and self-compassion were not yet learned. We cannot simply stand and watch unmarked. We cannot help but hurt. Compassion burns, as I have come to learn. Grief is not just overwhelming; it is also overspilling. The takeaway here for my change work is to always follow the rippling effects of a broken project way beyond the project team and the key stakeholders. Also, to ask for help, and accept help offered from within the organization.

Just as I started writing this piece, I realized today was March 1. Back in Romania, my home country, this day is traditionally known as "Mărțișor," literally meaning "Little March," and it marks the first day of spring. The tradition is to gift small trinkets attached to a white and red silky cord with small tassels as an expression of appreciation, respect, friendship or love. In some parts of the country (like where I come from), men offer "mărțișoare" to women, and in other regions, it is the other way around. The white and red thread honors an ancient custom of celebrating passion and wisdom as the vital feminine and masculine forces which give birth to the eternal cycle of nature. Its purpose is to protect the wearer against evil spirits and to invoke nature's regenerative power. My personal preference has always been to tie the entwined string around my wrist and wear it until it decides to leave me. What perfect timing to celebrate renewal while making peace with my "wonderings"…

Until next week, keep calm and let there be room for not knowing.

What Crossing Bridges Teaches Me about Change Management

First published on March 8, 2022

My fascination with water made me fall in love with bridges. There is something magical about them and how they came to bear such rich symbolism. Change and transition, unity, meeting point, farewell, conquering fear and overcoming, trust—there is something for everyone in the notion, purpose and architecture of bridges.

Yesterday I was reminded of this during the first day of the Basel Fasnacht Carnival. I went to see the carnival parades and ended up watching the show standing on the Middle Bridge that connects the Old Town with Little Basel, where I live. At some point, I turned around and started to watch the Rhine. With the happy, festive sounds all around me and with the calm water flowing under the bridge completely oblivious to the celebrations "flowing across the bridge," I felt suspended between realities, enjoying the "best of both worlds."

The collision of these two dimensions sparked the idea to write about what crossing bridges teaches me about change management. The walk home was my creative journey, and here I am, trying to cross the bridge between my mind and the keyboard.

Bridges don't take sides. Have you noticed how in thriller novels and movies there is almost always a meeting between spies or sworn enemies on a bridge? How a bridge is used as a safe, neutral meeting point with a secretive spin? Bridges don't take sides. It is as if bridges suspend judgment, almost literally, between the points they connect, as well as toward those crossing over them.

What bridges do you build between the key stakeholders of your projects? Between the realities within your organization and their expectations? How about between the members of your team? How can you use change management to build a bridge between the current state and the desired result in such a way that you do not create a "bad versus good" comparison, but a journey to a different setting? Every organization has roles and individuals that act as bridges. Do you know these roles and people around you? When you look for these, keep in mind that in order to serve their purpose to unify, bridges need to be and feel safe; people crossing them need to trust the bridge won't collapse. Trust is a critical element in their decision to step on the bridge, to overcome whatever fears might hold them back. Help people crossing your organizational bridge, including yourself, to trust not only the bridge and those who built it, but also their own power and strength to face and manage whatever is at the other end of the bridge.

And here's another thought. The "neutrality" of a bridge can be observed even in its design, in how it balances forces at play. Although there are many kinds of bridges, virtually all of them work by balancing compressive forces in some places with tensile forces elsewhere so there's no overall force to cause motion and do damage. A bridge is safe and stable because all the forces acting on it are perfectly in balance. In short, bridge designers are "force balancers"—remember this when you do change work within your organization.

"Don't burn bridges. You'll be surprised how many times you have to cross the same river."[276] —a wonderful teaching from Horace Jackson Brown Jr., an American author who is best known for his *Life's Little Instruction Book* piece of writing. Change work, just like life, is never a straight line. It pushes and pulls you, your team, your stakeholders and the entire organization in (oftentimes unpredictable) ways. It launches you forward and kicks you backward, too. And repeat.

Burning bridges should not be part of a change plan, regardless of what they connect you to: people, pockets of the organization, resources, past projects, ideas or previous versions of planning. Don't carry this whole load with you—it only adds weight to the bridges you are crossing now. Just don't burn bridges unless that is the absolute best decision and you are fully committed and prepared to deal with any and all consequences.

I did burn some bridges in my life, both personal and professional. Not many, but enough to learn that this is an exceptional solution and it requires an equally exceptional amount of consideration, courage, integrity and painfully honest introspection. On a handful of occasions, I must admit that I agree with American musician and founding member of the Eagles, Don Henley: "Sometimes you get the best light from a burning bridge."[277] In very few cases, there was no burning involved, just…bolts got loosened a little bit every day, and the bridge collapsed under its own weight. Also not recommended. As much as you can, take care of your bridges, and they will take care of your journey.

Beware of resonance, break step. My grandfather was an army officer, and one of my favorite childhood adventures was to go watch the military parades with him. We even had our favorite watching spot on a bridge close to my grandparents' place where I grew up. I remember being intrigued by the soldiers "walking more like normal people" when they crossed the bridge. That must have been the first time I heard about "resonance," although I am quite sure that exact word did not come up back then. All I understood was that the soldiers were taking care of us and the bridge, and my grandfather holding my hand felt safe enough for me. Later, I understood more, and today I am thinking about how this learning can help me in my change work.

You can think of resonance as the vibrational equivalence of a snowball rolling down a hill and becoming an avalanche. When an army marches across a bridge, the soldiers are often ordered to "break step" so that their rhythmic marching will not start resonating throughout the bridge. A sufficiently large army marching at just the right cadence could set the deadly vibration into motion. In a great "How Bridges Work" article on science.howstuffworks.com website, it is explained how, in order to mitigate fully the resonance effect in a bridge, engineers incorporate dampeners into the bridge design to interrupt the resonant waves and prevent them from growing.[278]

Another way to halt resonance is to give it less room to run wild. If a bridge boasts a solid roadway, then a resonant wave can easily travel the length of the bridge and wreak havoc. But if a bridge roadway is made up of different sections with overlapping plates, then the movement of one section merely transfers to another via the plates, generating friction. The trick is to create enough friction to change the frequency of the resonant wave. Changing the frequency prevents the wave from building. And what a great takeaway for change work! Are we taking into consideration the organizational bridges when we set out the cadence of the transformation initiative? Do we have dampeners in place? Are we mindful of overlapping organizational plates creating "safe" friction? Are the right marching orders in place, communicated and understood, so that the project team can break step, keeping themselves and everybody else on the organizational bridge safe?

Bridges are meant to support movement; they are not points where we spend too much time. People don't generally live on bridges. Many bridges include pavilions or other shelters serving pedestrians crossing the bridge, but there are a few exceptions of such structures with houses on them. Spaces of transition are called "liminal spaces," spaces of "in between." Being on the precipice of something new but not quite there yet requires that we be willing to live with the ambiguity of not knowing what's next. We have left what was, but haven't yet inhabited what's next. And in this "realm of pure possibility," as British cultural anthropologist Victor Turner called liminal spaces, is where magic happens.[279] This makes me think of a beautiful Indian proverb that says: "Life is a bridge. Cross over it, but build no house on it."[280]

Until next week, keep calm and cross every bridge with courage, hope and a big smile on your face!

What Celebrating My Birthday Teaches Me about Change Management

First published on March 15, 2022

Yesterday was my birthday. I took the day off and was looking forward to "me time" with nothing really planned other than reading, walking, having some Prosecco and ice cream and getting over a dentist appointment for an extraction scheduled in the afternoon. No birthday cake, as I have developed a new appreciation for British-American entertainer Bob Hope's wise humor: "You know you're getting old when the candles cost more than the cake."[281]

The entire day turned into an awesome surprise.

As I was sitting in the dentist's chair thinking about the ice cream dinner to be savored cuddled up in my favorite spot on the couch, I heard the doctor walking in and saying: "Who in their right mind chooses to spend their birthday at the dentist?"

"You lost me at the 'in their right mind' part," I replied. A few minutes later, he said: "I will band-aid this tooth, and doctor's orders are you go enjoy your day, have loads of cake, come back in April." This surprise treatment came in handy, as one of my best friends planned a business trip so she could be in Basel for my birthday, and now I could join her for dinner at our favorite Thai place.

Dinner started with Prosecco and a confession. I told her I had not written one word for the weekly piece and most likely nothing would go out this week. She smiled and asked me why not write something on celebrating my birthday. Now *I* smiled, because there was a note on my phone with a few rough ideas on this very topic I had played around with earlier in the day. I considered the confirmation of this writing challenge as an awesome surprise gift and decided to give it a go.

Every day is a special day. I took some time to think about what I loved most about my birthday. For many years, I had this expectation of something totally extraordinary about to happen, nothing specific, just a fuzzy anticipation that soon transformed into a tiny lingering feeling of "Hmmm, well, maybe next year…"

Now I realize, even more clearly than in past years, that so many extraordinary things do happen. All the notes and wishes, all the people who take time from everything happening around them to let me know they think of me. Friendships that are strong and safe enough to go on without a note because sometimes life happens more intensely than we would like it. A surprise birthday card in my mailbox. A friend's surprise business trip. A surprise dentist appointment rescheduling. A day with nothing planned. A day when I feel safe, able to enjoy a sunny apartment. A freezer full of ice cream. A bottle of Prosecco in the fridge. A good excuse— as if I need any!!!—to buy books and look for new additions to my Swatch collection.

There is a wonderful quote from Indian author and alternative healing practitioner Sanhita Baruah: "Every day is a gift. But some days are packaged better."[282] Birthdays are packaged in "festive wrapping." Each note or message from people in my life on any day is a gift. Each surprise of any kind on any day is a gift. Each reason to smile or laugh is a gift. Each ice cream is a gift. Each new book. Each conversation.

Major project milestones are like birthdays—better-packaged gifts. Achievements happen every single day. They might seem less significant, mainly through the lens of our "packaging" expectations. Take time to appreciate the gift of trust and courage whenever someone reaches out to you—with news, with a request for advice, with a challenge—needing anything from a safe space to vent up to a joint effort to solve the issue. Appreciate the incredible gift of connections, personal and professional, that do not require constant contact to go on, ready to be resumed whenever needed. Take a moment to appreciate your ability to access a resource you need for your projects. Do not schedule or reserve feeling extraordinary for specific milestones. Every day of your life or project is a gift, so enjoy it, share it, don't take it for granted.

Celebrate the whole you. Feeling festive felt a little bit off because of everything going on—in the world, as well as in my life. I felt happy, and I also felt sad. I felt safe, and also unsettled because of Ukraine and my hometown close to the border. I laughed with my friend last evening and enjoyed amazing food, felt loved and valued, while also painfully missing people no longer in my life, feeling rejected and disappointed.

Trying to reconcile all these feelings, I remembered what I read at some point about ambivalence. Wrestling with opposing feelings is a normal part of being human, and according to Antonio Damasio, author of *Feeling & Knowing: Making Minds Conscious*, there's a natural benefit to it. "Animals that have only positive or negative feelings are very limited because things are too much black or white," but humans can perceive the in-between nuances.[283]

These nuances can help people make good decisions. Ambivalence makes you more cautious during the decision-making process, Damasio says.[284] It can also help you learn from past missteps. So, let's celebrate this extraordinary gift of being human! We can be enthusiastic about a change or transformation and still feel unsettled or even overwhelmed by the process of going through it. We can feel motivated and inspired by our work and still have days when we are tired and all we want to do is take a break from everything. Celebrate the whole you, with all your nuances! Celebrate the whole change, with all its nuances. Neither people nor change work are zero-sum games. Celebrate the whole you on each and every special day you are given!

Embed protection into the celebration. Birthdays first started as a form of protection. It is assumed that the Greeks adopted the Egyptian tradition of celebrating the "birth" of a god when they crowned a new pharaoh. Later on, the Romans appear to have been the first people who celebrated not only the birthdays of divinities and leaders, but also those of prosperous citizens. Many pagan cultures thought that days of major change, such as these "birth" days, welcomed evil spirits. Candles were lit in response to these spirits almost as if they represented a light in the darkness. In addition to candles, friends and family would gather around the birthday person and protect them from harm with good cheers, thoughts, and wishes. They would give gifts to bring even more good cheer that would ward off evil spirits. Noisemakers were also used to scare away the unwanted evil.

This makes me reflect on what "evil spirits" gather for my birthday. The first thought that comes to mind is about all the "inventory work" I do and how I tend to come up short against some expectations, all those instances of "I should have done this by now." Then all the usual birthday party crashers come running: self-doubt, oftentimes with the "plus one" of imposter syndrome, a few regrets, the feeling of running out of time. Sometimes even feeling bad because I don't feel "festive enough" on my birthday... The fact that birthdays started out as protection rituals is such an amazing reminder to celebrate ourselves and those we love and to stay intentionally mindful of our journey. Embed some protection in your celebration of transformation achievements; both people and organizations have "evil spirits" that need to be warded off with cheers and celebrations.

There is a wonderful quote sometimes attributed to American writer Mark Twain: "The two most important days in your life are the day you are born and the day you find out why."[285] Celebrate each day you are given, celebrate the full you, and ward off any evil spirits coming between you and your "why."

Until next week, keep calm and live every day like your birthday!

What Drinking Coffee Teaches Me about Change Management

First published on March 22, 2022

Last week marked an important milestone: the posters I had dreamed about for almost one year finally went up on my kitchen walls. Over the past few days, the "Hello darkness, my old friend!" morning greeting has been putting extra flavor in my coffee and a big smile on my face.

Yesterday I was making coffee and my mind started wandering around, looking for an idea for the Tuesday piece. I caught a glimpse of the poster and it suddenly came to me. How could I not give it a go? Coffee is a fundamental element in my life. I oftentimes say that my birthstone is a coffee bean, and regardless of what historians claim, I strongly believe that "B.C." actually means "Before Coffee."

Coffee also represents values near and dear to my mind and heart. Curiosity—legend says the Ethiopian goat herder Kaldi discovered coffee when he noticed that after eating the berries from a certain tree, his goats became so energetic that they did not want to sleep at night. He reported his findings to the abbot of the local monastery, who made a drink with the berries and found that it kept him alert through the long hours of evening prayer. The abbot shared his discovery with the other monks at the monastery and knowledge of the energizing berries began to spread.

Creativity—think of all the ways in which we get to enjoy coffee today, plus the variety of coffee cups and mug designs.

Courage for change—from the Ottoman Empire to the American and French Revolutions, coffeehouses have offered a place for people to discuss new waves of thought.

And the most important one of all, conversation—by the 16th century, coffeehouses were very popular in cities all across the Near East, becoming centers for the exchange of information to such an extent that they were often referred to as "Schools of the Wise."

Last, but not least, coffee is the "morning wine." It didn't take long for the knowledge of this "wine of Arabia" to spread with the thousands of pilgrims visiting the holy city of Mecca each year from all over the world during the 15th and 16th centuries. We have the word "coffee" today from the Dutch "koffie," through the Turkish "kahveh," inspired by the Arabic "qahwah," which Arab etymologists connected with a word meaning "wine." Bright morning cheers to all!

So, what takeaways for change work are there in drinking coffee? Well, pour yourselves a cup or a mug, and let's start a conversation…

We all are collections of coffee cups and mugs. I have always been fascinated and passionately curious about what makes people tick— for the purpose of this conversation, what "wakes them up and energizes them into action." The types of coffee we enjoy depend on our personal (taste) preferences, our cultural background, curiosity to try new caffeinated experiences, maybe time of day, our geographical location, possibly medical conditions, seasons… And each type of coffee comes with a specific cup or mug, different in size, shape, texture. Sometimes we go for an espresso, sometimes a cappuccino, and some other times we crave a large, self-indulgent iced caramel macchiato.

Now think about change work as "awakening people to new opportunities." What are their coffee preferences? Into what cups and mugs are you pouring? It takes different amounts of information, of different concentration, sweetness, temperature, to wake us up. And just as our coffee-savoring experience is supported by the cup or mug used for serving, our intake of change depends on what and how much we are designed to contain. If we are in an "espresso mode or mood," a latte will overspill. If we get a ristretto in a cappuccino cup, it would look and feel like not enough—and if the service is slow, it could get to "too little, too late." If we look at what inspires, energizes and motivates us into action, we all are collections of coffee cups and mugs.

Change managers are great baristas. The word "barista" comes from Italian and Spanish, documented since 1916, where it means a male or female "bartender" who typically works behind a counter serving hot drinks (such as espresso), cold alcoholic and non-alcoholic beverages and snacks. The native plural in English and Spanish is "baristas," while in Italian the plural is "barista" for masculine (literally meaning "barmen," "bartenders") or "bariste" for feminine (meaning "barmaids"). Nowadays, the term has come to describe someone who prepares coffee and operates an espresso machine.

This makes me reflect on how oftentimes, change managers are perceived primarily through the mechanics, methodologies and tools they use, their initial wider scope being trimmed down and somewhat "lost in translation." Here is additional descriptive information for a barista role that sounds similar to the assumptions and expectations from a change manager in many organizational settings: Baristas are often trained to use the espresso machine in their coffee shop and make coffee drinks based on the specifications of the shop owner. Experienced baristas might be given the freedom to experiment or prepare drinks a bit differently. There are several steps that go into making a coffee drink, each one of them equally important to how the drink turns out: the temperature of the water, grind size and amount of coffee beans, extraction of the espresso, milk frothing, and finally, pouring the milk over the espresso.[286] As they grow into their skill and experience, some baristas can widen their knowledge, pretty much like how a sommelier becomes familiar with the entire process of wine-making and consumption. And "change management similarity alert": baristas can learn these essential skills in classes, but they're usually learned on the job.[287]

"Art it up." Regardless of your coffee of choice, I am sure there is at least one instance when you were impressed by "latte art." It might have been a photo shared on social media, a YouTube video, or even better, a live experience of witnessing a barista producing figures and shapes on the surface of the foam of espresso-based lattes and cappuccinos. With so many awesome tutorials available, I gave it a try some time ago. The only notable achievement of this exercise was a slight increase in kitchen cleaning products sales… Moving on…

Latte art is basically an artistic or more personalized way of making and serving coffee. "Perfect symmetry, high contrasts and consistently made patterns are the trademarks of highly experienced baristas."[288] Anything in this statement reminding you of change work? How latte art is made is so similar to how change management work is performed to drive a personalized transformation experience. There are two basic ways to art coffee up. One is free-pouring the steamed milk into the espresso while jiggling the pitcher to create ripples that turn into an image. The other consists of "drawing" the image onto the steamed milk and coffee crema with a special pen. There are change management interventions that an experienced change practitioner can perform in a "free-pouring" manner, whereas some require a more precise design and delivery. Whatever the technique, personalizing the experience makes a huge difference.

A few years ago, I found a page on social media called "Sweatpants and coffee," and their posts resonated with me. Sometimes funny, other times serious, they are good "food for thought" as I savor my coffee. As a "thank you" for reading this far, here is one of my absolute favorites: "May we be anchored in love and empathy. May each step we take forward be mindful. May we appreciate each moment of joy, big or small, and may we find rest in those cool, sweet places. May we find our common ground, and may it be firm enough to stand on. May we remember who it is we'd like to be, and may there be good coffee to sustain us as we do the work."[289]

Until next week, keep calm and let coffee wake you up to curiosity, creativity, courage for change and awesome conversations!

What Learning to Meditate Teaches Me about Change Management

First published on March 29, 2022

Over the past several years, I have tried to learn how to meditate countless times. Sitting still has always been impossible for me. With a personal best of 43 seconds spent cross-legged with my eyes closed, I was sure meditation would forever elude me. Three years ago, I had a really bad experience at a yoga center with their "Meditation for Beginners" class. After 40 minutes of torture, I walked out and signed up for a Krav Maga introductory session as soon as I had access to my phone. Definitely more enjoyable than the meditation experience, but still not my thing.

This past Saturday, I gave meditation another go and it turned out to be one of the best things ever. The conversation during the class at the Buddhist center near my home was about all sorts of meditation techniques, including active meditation. Being able to explore mindfulness meditation, especially in ways that do not require physical stillness, opened a whole new world for me. I know I am quite late to the meditation party, but hey, better late than never, right? And yes, I did pick up on the fact that my mind wandered straight into judgment mode there…

TUESDAY CHANGE MANAGEMENT RANDOM THOUGHTS

While walking along the Rhine over the weekend, enjoying new thoughts and wonderful spring sunshine, one idea popped up: how about a Tuesday random thought on what learning to meditate teaches me about change management? And as the takeaways started to flow through my mind, the challenge was accepted. I did try my best to practice mindful walking for the rest of the afternoon, but my mind would go to writing. And below are my mental wanderings...

Doing nothing takes a lot of doing. It is incredibly hard to just...be. The amount of dedication, consistent practice and self-compassion needed to get better at simply being in the moment, quieting your mind and focusing on your breath is daunting. It is hard to learn to simply be—harder than to do anything requiring movement. Although so natural, it oftentimes feels like it goes against all acquired reflex behaviors. I could not help but smile when I realized how similar this train of thought was to some recent conversations about change work within organizations.

What would be the organizational meditation equivalent? How could organizations and their leaders create spaces of seemingly no action that would allow them to focus and move from reacting to responding? What "judgments" should organizations suspend in order to be able to meditate? How can leaders hold space before jumping into reflex solution and fixing modes? What ways can we go beyond corporate mindfulness programs and elevate meditation as an organizational practice? What is organizational mindfulness? And could it yield the organizational equivalents for individual benefits such as lower blood pressure and improved blood circulation?

Meditation is one "T" away from mediation. I discovered this by pure accident when I came across a typo in an article about meditation techniques. When I realized I was looking at "mediation techniques," something in my mind clicked. Putting it simply, meditation balances our mind, soul and body; it "mediates" between different states. I have been hearing increased talk within the recruitment and sourcing communities about the value of "T-shaped professionals," also known as "versatilists," given the current work reality. Professionals who are able to bring both depth of skills and expertise in a single field and have the ability to collaborate across disciplines are critical to high value-added, innovation-focused, cross-functional teams.

It might very well be a pure coincidence that this letter turned out to be the difference between "mediate" and "meditate," but it got me thinking that meditation creates the space to mediate between breadth and depth, where breadth could stand for our "doing" while depth is our "being"… Or, through a different lens, by suspending judgment and simply focusing on awareness, meditation mediates our decision-making. As former Buddhist monk Andy Puddicombe, Headspace co-founder, explains: "… True freedom is when we are equally content, no matter what arises in the mind…"[290] Binary thinking and zero-sum games are finite, mediation-driven settings. Meditation elevates "T"hinking into a space of judgment-free possibilities.

We need so much less than what we think we do. With decluttering and minimalism becoming so popular over the past few years, I did give them a go… My achievement is perfectly described by a post on social media from a while back: "I tried that Japanese decluttering trend where you hold every object that you own and if it does not bring you joy, you throw it away. So far, I have thrown out all the vegetables, the electric bill, the scale, a mirror, and a pair of old socks."[291] My relationship with Marie Kondo got very tense when she started to discuss the optimal number of books in a home. It is not hoarding if it's books!!!

One thing I collect to the point of "borderline hoarding" is synonyms, which brings me back to our conversation about meditation. Some common synonyms of "meditate" are "muse," "ponder" and "ruminate." While all of these words mean "to consider or examine attentively or deliberately," "meditate" implies a definite focus of one's thoughts on something so as to understand it deeply.

"Ruminate" caught my attention and made me think of "mental clutter," especially within decision-making contexts. We gather information, facts and figures, SWOT analysis, risks, and then we try to make a decision. The best decision. The safe decision. Because we crave certainty. How much time, energy, joy get lost in "mediating" between courses of action? How much input do we really need for our decision-making process, and how much is just mental clutter? The more I think about meditation and its principles, the more I see "clarity" as a feasible and sustainable goal over "certainty." We need so much less than what we think we do. As I learn more about meditation and think about mental decluttering, I have a feeling that clarity of being ensures certainty of doing.

One thing that I found out this past weekend is that according to Buddhist tradition, "meditation" is not just a single activity. Similar to how we think of sports, meditation is actually a whole group of activities, and "different meditation practices require different mental skills," as University of Wisconsin neuroscience lab director Richard J. Davidson, Ph.D., told *The New York Times* in an article on meditation techniques.[292] Whatever kind of meditation or grounding mindfulness practices you enjoy, may it "mediate" your thoughts, ideas, inner struggles and decisions. Even self-perceptions. Suspend judgment, and suspend self-judgment first. As one of my best friends recently encouraged me: "When you do the dishes, just do the dishes. That is mindful enough, more will come from it."

Until next week, keep calm and be present over perfect in your mind, body and soul.

What Experiencing Moments of Being Absent-Minded Teaches Me about Change Management

First published on April 5, 2022

The Universe has a wicked sense of humor. Proof of that is the fact that I am now writing about being absent-minded one week after advocating for being present and practicing grounding mindfulness techniques.

Last Friday, I had a total "Minola Signature Moment." I used to call them "moments that don't matter," only this one proved to be an inspiration spark. As soon as I got the notification that two packages were delivered, I grabbed a jacket, went out of the apartment and took the elevator to the ground floor. Oh, it felt like a small Christmas all over again—one big box of books and a smaller one with candles and water bottles. Priorities, priorities…

I grabbed (more like "hugged") the boxes, stepped back into the elevator, pressed the button. Once. Twice. Oh, joy, just my luck, what were the chances of something happening to the elevator during the last 28 seconds??? Three floors worth of stairs later, as I reached out to open the apartment door, seeing my hand on the handle triggered a strange, out-of-body experience. I could see my finger pressing the elevator button. As in the ground floor button while standing in the elevator on the ground floor... Not the first time, most definitely not the last!

Still laughing, I dropped a note about it to one of my friends and he jokingly replied: "That's definitely a change post idea." Challenge accepted. I looked for the closest block of Post-it notes, and thankfully I still remembered why I needed them by the time I found the pen...

How can you be sure of where you go and how to get there if you don't pay attention to where you are? It never ceases to amaze me how much resistance there is to investing time, focus and energy into a baseline study within organizations at senior stakeholder level. When it comes up in conversations, regardless of how "light-touch" it is positioned—"Let's just make sure we are all within the same book, if not exactly on the same page" for clarification and confirmation purposes only—the reply oftentimes comes as "We are all clear on where we are, this is precisely why we need this change. Can we get things started already?" I am sure the next time I hear this, I will have a very vivid picture of me standing in the elevator on the ground floor, hugging the boxes, and eagerly pressing the ground floor button.

Over the years, I have always found solace after my moments of being absent-minded in a wonderful quote from English writer and journalist Gilbert K. Chesterton: "I am not absent-minded. It is the presence of mind that makes me unaware of everything else."[293] Reading it again these days, it brought a new line of reflection: what is this "presence of mind" focused on? And when my mind is present in a particular space, where is it absent from? One takeaway from the failed elevator ride is to not be so present in the future that it makes me absent from the present.

"The secret motive of the absent-minded is to be innocent while guilty. Absent-mindedness is spurious innocence."[294] This piece of wisdom from Canadian-born American writer Saul Bellow, winner of both the Pulitzer and Nobel Prize for Literature, made me think about our sense of agency, how we use it for self-validation, and equally how readily we write it off when we need someone or something else to take the blame. In an article called "What Is the Sense of Agency and Why Does it Matter?" published in *Frontiers in Psychology* back in August 2016, James W. Moore from the Department of Psychology, Goldsmiths, University of London, talked about the sense of agency and how, as with other aspects of conscious experience, it is not an infallible reproduction of objective reality:

"You might think that you are immune to such cognitive foibles, but you would almost certainly be mistaken. I would bet that most of us have fallen foul, at some point, of so-called 'placebo buttons.' These are buttons that we encounter every day that we think do things, but actually do nothing. Buttons at pedestrian crossings are a common example of placebo-buttons. Most of these buttons are ineffective and instead the changing of the traffic lights are linked to timers.... Intriguingly, most of us fail to notice the causal inefficacy of our button presses. Other examples of placebo buttons include 'close door' buttons in lifts and even thermostats in offices (many of which, apparently, do not work). There are two reasons for flagging up the occasional lapses in our sense of agency. The first is to show that the accuracy of this experience is not a given. Instead, the brain appears to actively construct the sense of agency, and because of this, our experiences of agency can be quite divorced from the facts of agency. The second reason is that these lapses reveal something quite remarkable about our sense of agency: its impressive flexibility.... we see over and over again that people come to experience control over outcomes in many weird and wonderful situations."[295]

It came so naturally for me to conclude that the elevator must have broken down within the space of a few seconds rather than assume I had done something wrong. How often are we witnessing and going through equivalent behaviors in our work environment? We are in control when the outcomes are positive, and the first reflex is to conclude that something must have gone wrong when they are less than ideal... Where is our "presence of mind" when it comes to analyzing our sense of agency? How does this influence our decision-making? I made a Post-it note to look at future change conversations and project retrospectives through the lens of the participants' sense of agency. And I will keep a great quote from American aphorist Mason Cooley, Professor Emeritus of French, speech and world literature at the College of Staten Island, as a conversation prompt close by: "Most of my decisions in life seem absent-minded but inevitable."[296]

Never stop wondering what your mind might bring back from its wanderings. There are countless rewards on a personal level that come from mind wandering, as research has proved. In a post on the "Beautiful Minds" blog in September 2013, it's pointed out that many gifts come from being absent-minded, including greater self-awareness, better planning, and more compassion and understanding, among many other things. It makes sense, then, why so many people allow their minds to wander every single day: it gives us meaningful rewards. For example, forgetting to purchase the item you went to the store to get in the first place is only a minor nuisance if, somewhere along the way, you came to a monumental choice or realization.[297]

I wonder now how becoming more intentionally aware of these rewards might influence our sense of agency... The brain balances remembering and forgetting gracefully to facilitate optimal use of memory and its processing power. Moments of being absent-minded can actually be a byproduct of rigorous thinking, smooth decision-making or heightened creativity, and it can enable us to think more clearly by eliminating interference from competing thoughts. As research shows, a judgment call on absent-mindedness is influenced by outcomes, personal meaning and context. Does any of this remind you of change management? Oh, your mind has already wandered in that direction...

What was I saying? Ah, yes, the closing thought for today. Over the past couple of weeks, almost without exception, the change conversations I have been part of touched on ways to increase people's sense of control and influence. Believe it or not, a powerful one-liner comes from Christopher Robin: "You're braver than you believe, stronger than you seem, and smarter than you think."[298] It is all a matter of perspective. And, equally, of full accountability and ownership. American comedian George Burns agrees with Christopher Robin from a slightly different angle, yet equally meaningful for change work: "I must be getting absent-minded. Whenever I complain that things aren't what they used to be, I always forget to include myself."[299]

Until next week, keep calm and pay attention to not being so present in the future that you become absent from the present.

What Knitting and Crocheting Teach Me about Change Management

First published on April 12, 2022

The most comforting sound of my childhood was my grandmother's knitting needles hitting the armrests of her favorite armchair. When she wasn't cooking something out-of-this-world delicious, she would knit. She used to sit in a red armchair with a smile on her face, a coffee cup within arm's reach and yarn at her feet, and magic was made with clock-like precision ticking as her metallic knitting needles hit the wooden armrests.

She taught me to knit and crochet, cook, savor coffee and equally enjoy the company of people or of a colorful ball of yarn. More than two decades since she passed away, I still feel like we are talking when I have a pair of knitting needles or a crochet hook in my hands. Over the weekend, I had a revelation. After an amazing long morning walk on Sunday, I was sitting in my favorite spot on the couch, crocheting with a coffee mug close by, waiting for the oven timer to let me know my apple pie was done. It dawned on me that, slowly but surely, I was becoming my grandmother. What a great transformation to look forward to!!

Still smiling with anticipation, I got to thinking that Tuesday was approaching, and the article would not write itself. While looking for inspiration, I realized I was looking at it. Literally. The turquoise yarn by my side, the orange crochet hook in my hand, my grandmother's birthday just a few days away... And here I am, trying to stitch random thoughts together.

Work is gradual, awareness is sudden. Knitting, crocheting, and Tunisian crochet (as I recently learned), happen one stitch at a time. I cannot describe it in words, but there is a moment in every project when I pick up whatever it is I am making and it feels almost done—surprisingly so! It feels "almost-finished" heavy, I suddenly realize how it fills my lap, I find myself checking I have enough yarn left to make the final touches. I have been there every stitch of the way, yet the awareness of (almost) completion takes me by surprise.

This is the "Hemingway effect," as described in a dialogue from Ernest Hemingway's *The Sun Also Rises*. One of the characters asks another how he went bankrupt, and the answer is, "Gradually, then suddenly."[300] This is how knitting and crocheting happen, and it is strikingly similar to how change works. Gradually, then suddenly. Although unnoticeable, gradually eventually leads to suddenly. It builds momentum. It succumbs to the compound effect. While we're doing our thing, our daily acts—both good and bad—work toward a grand result that can take us by surprise. The initial effects happen unnoticeably, gradually. We don't notice the gradual change occurring until it becomes "surprisingly obvious." Awareness is sudden, not the work and its effects. Next time you hear "How have we got here?" or "How will we get there?", just smile and know you have an awesome answer: gradually, then suddenly.

Do you identify yourself by what you are or what you do? About two weeks ago, I was invited to a podcast on how to hire a "Change Enthusiast." The first question I was asked was why

I had listed "Change Enthusiast" as my primary job title on my LinkedIn headline. That gave me a wonderful opportunity to say: "A Change Enthusiast is what I am, it just so happens that at the moment I am an enthusiastic Change Manager. I believe we are always more than what we do."

As I was thinking about knitting and crocheting, I tried to incorporate this side of me into my description in a parallel with my change work, especially for people who do not do crafts, or at least not these ones. It is not as straightforward as one might think. Sometimes as someone who crochets, there are some interesting conversations that happen with people who don't crochet. Of course, the classic question from a non-crocheter is "Oh, what are you knitting?" Crocheter grits teeth and responds: "IT'S CROCHET!"

In a wonderful article on the desertblossomcrafts.com blog from early last year, it is explained that knitters and crocheters give themselves different titles depending on who they're talking with. Those who crochet have their own lingo, so crocheters will give themselves a title easily understood by their crocheting kin. When talking to people who don't crochet, most crocheters find it easiest not to give a title at all but simply say that they crochet.[301]

Things are different when we talk with "our tribe," as we would call ourselves "crafter," the most generic term; "yarnie"— let's be honest, hoarding yarn is our favorite way to include fiber in our diets; "knitter;" or, very lovingly and totally decently so, "hooker" (that is NOT a needle, and it is not sharp, people!!). So, are you a "Change Enthusiast" regardless of what role you have? Do you believe change work is the exclusive responsibility of a "Change Manager"? Do you identify, describe and give yourself different titles depending on who you are talking with?

Never interrupt a crafter when they are counting. I'm a good person, but don't interrupt my stitch count. I don't know whether it is the frustration of discipline or the overwhelming pressure of doing something even remotely math-related, but counting stitches is a nightmare for me. The only answer you will get from me if you ask me anything while I am counting will be LOUDER counting—yes, shouty capitals! The takeaway here is to overcome frustration—my own when interrupted (especially from a task I dislike, and it means extra work with doing it again, plus making amends for my behavior while "under the math influence"), and other people's (who do not get their requests heard or fulfilled because I am fighting some other evil at the moment...)

Regardless of how much you enjoy change work, and any kind of work for that matter, there are tasks required by that work that are simply frustrating. Learning to overcome frustration is a critical ability. Also, be clear about the boundaries within which you deal with the frustrating activity. Respect your boundaries, respect other people's boundaries and respect those who respect yours. And keep in mind that different people have different boundaries around different things and tasks, as well as different ways to uphold them. When boundaries are pushed or crossed, you will get an unusual reaction. Truth be told, I am not sure what is strangest: me counting, me ignoring other people asking something or me counting in your face even louder. Come to think of it, maybe I should follow my own advice, and next time someone asks me "So, how do you get to the desired length and width of your project?", simply smile and say, "Well, you know, gradually, then suddenly."

Weaving in loose ends is a fundamental step in any project. So, it feels important that I leave you with a meaningful closing thought. It comes courtesy of Vickie Howell, one of my favorite craft authors and knitting and crochet experts, who talks about how crochet fulfills our craving for balance: "We want to work hard without losing touch with our creative selves; we want to earn money without losing our souls; and we want to be part of a larger picture of human progression while still maintaining our individuality."[302]

Until next week, keep calm and celebrate what you are above and beyond what you do.

What Repotting Plants Teaches Me about Change Management
First published on April 19, 2022

These past few days have been quite "grounding," as in literally, with a lot of gardening and repotting going on. Every year, I officially declare "terrace season open" after a serious gardening episode takes place. I have been blessed with generous windowsills and terraces in all the homes I have lived in over the past several years. All my plants are special to me, yet there is one with an extraordinary place in my heart: Pablo, a seven-year-old cactus in a Mexican turquoise ceramic pot. Pablo, just like me, is a "serial immigrant," and we have relocated across four countries together. He seems to enjoy adventure just as much as I do, and he is now making new friends: Karen and Denys, two small coffee trees named after the main characters in *Out of Africa*, one of my favorite movies of all time.

Encouraged by the sunny and warm days, I decided to go for the spring repotting and also give the terrace a Mediterranean twist with some citrus trees. A handful of shopping trips and a full-day repotting episode later, I am now the proud owner of a terrace that makes me really sad I have to go inside during the night.

While surrounded by pots, plants, bags of soil and bottles of fertilizer, I felt inspiration coming. I ran inside, grabbed some Post-it notes and a pen, went back outside and started scribbling ideas about repotting and change work. I hope some of my random thoughts will take root in your mind and you will water them with your own ideas and perspectives.

Not all repotting must be up-potting. Repotting is beneficial and an important part of growing plants that are healthy and happy. But you should only do it at the right time and for the right reasons. If the only reason you want to repot a plant is to put it into a prettier planter or because it's something you just do every year...well, those are the wrong reasons. These habits can end up causing problems with your plants. It struck me how "naturally" most people associate repotting with moving the plant into a larger pot. It is almost automatic. Plants benefit greatly from being repotted when they need it. The key benefits are refreshing the soil and nutrients, improving water retention and absorption, helping to avoid soil compaction and giving the roots more room to grow. None of these require a larger pot by default. A pot of the same size, even the same pot with fresh soil, does the trick! Without compacted soil around them, even the roots have more room to grow. Yet, we automatically equate repotting with up-potting, moving the plant into a larger container.

While gardening this weekend, repotting made me think of career paths, succession planning, organization design and the overall focus on providing "growth opportunities"—sometimes without even checking the assumptions around how much and what kind of growth people are open to or genuinely interested in. For years, "up or out" was the norm in most organizations, and the work environment equivalent of repotting has been almost automatically an "up-potting." Does this sound familiar?

A few years ago, I found one of my colleagues crying in the office bathroom right after the end-of-year letters with promotions and bonus news were handed out. Between heartbreaking sobs, she told me she was sure she would be called to HR to be let go, as this was the first time she did not get a promotion every two years for the past decade. After sitting with her for a while, I started asking questions like: "Is there anything in that letter, or in recent conversations, that points towards this conclusion?", "What is your performance rating?", "Have you noticed different behavior patterns around you?" At one point, she looked at me and said: "You don't understand, if I can't do better and bigger, I am not relevant!"

That statement still haunts me, and I remember it during many performance management-related conversations. Not all repotting is automatically up-potting. Please be mindful and intentional about the embedded message the performance management gives to the organization. Create options for different experiences, not just for "growth opportunities." Not all people want to "move up," and they most definitely do not want to do it all the time. Organizational repotting can be a new project, a new team. "Compacted soil" triggered a thought about how we can constructively challenge statements like "We are such a tightly-knit team by now!" It can even be two smaller pots, in case people want to pursue spin-off interests or feel the need to re-balance different priorities. Just remember: not all repotting is automatically up-potting.

Pace yourself during the "transplant shock" and do not over-help. Plants are not designed to move from one place to another. If we try to move them around to a new home or uproot them, it is bound to cause some problems. A plant that is newly dug up and shifted to another place or into a new pot may show signs of wilting leaves, dying branches or it might die altogether. It is called transplant shock. The transplant shock is caused by harm to the plant roots during the repotting process. After re-potting or potting up, plants tend to enter a period of shock. Don't worry—it's normal! Plants may appear wilted and thirsty, but take care to refrain from watering until about a week after repotting to ensure that any roots damaged during the process have healed. It might also help to place the plants in a cooler, shadier spot while they recover. Most potting soil contains fertilizer. To prevent from over-fertilizing and damaging your plant, you can hold off on fertilizing for about six weeks after repotting.

All this information can be read through the lens of humans going through change. Danger of damaging roots? Yes. Showing signs of not doing so great, at least not as well as before? Yes. Finding ourselves in danger of being "over-helped"? Oh, yeeees!!! Although coming from a place of best intentions, deep care and genuine compassion, some help can be too much. Maybe even too soon. And this happens equally in our personal and professional life. Be there for your people going through change, help them when and how they need it. Pay attention to the signs and be patient. Your help is for and about them, not for or about your need to be useful and helpful. Acknowledge, respect and honor people by helping, not over-helping.

Pay attention to the nursery line. When you're repotting, it's important that the surface of the soil around the plant stays at the same level. Often called the "nursery line," this is the point where the stem emerges from the soil. If you cover the stem in compost, it will rot away. The nursery line should be about a centimeter below the edge of the new pot so there's space for watering. We all have our own equivalent of a nursery line. And we definitely feel when it is covered or overwhelmed by new soil. Try to identify your people's and your organization's nursery line and pay attention to it.

Summing up the learnings for my change work from these past gardening days, it really comes down to three mental Post-it notes. First: size up slowly, if you absolutely must. Move your plant up just one pot size at a time. A pot that's too big for your plant won't suit its watering needs, so you'll be more likely to over- or under-water.

Second: be gentle. Never pull the plant out by the stems! If the plant isn't releasing easily from the pot, squeeze or shake the pot gently to loosen the roots and soil.

And last, but not least: mind the roots. If the roots have grown through the old pot's drainage holes, anchoring the root ball inside, gently untangle them and tuck them back through the holes. Only cut roots if absolutely necessary. If you must, make sure to use a sharp, clean knife.

Until next week, keep calm and give yourselves space to grow "into unfamiliar territory of the heart, of the mind and of the spirit."[303]

What Shopping at Farmers Markets Teaches Me about Change Management

First published on April 26, 2022

This weekend was special. It felt festive. And it just dawned on me that I celebrated freedom and homecoming, all in one. It was the first weekend that felt like the ones before the pandemic, only...better. It started with a trip into France to a farmers market, then lunch at a friend's place, a loop into Germany on our way back to stop at a gardening center, just as I realized I was literally a few days away from my one year of living in Switzerland anniversary!

    Although it looks like there was a lot of moving around and traveling involved, to me it actually felt like "settling down." Being born and raised in a mixed family on the border between Romania and Hungary, "crossing borders" has always been part of my identity. It got more intense as I started traveling and relocating for work and life. When I lived in Tallinn, I used to take the ferry on Saturday morning, go to Helsinki to my favorite bookstore, then have a salmon soup at one of the food stalls in the Market Square by the South Harbor. Weekends in Luxembourg oftentimes started with a short train ride into Germany for the farmers market and small shopping, followed by some great food at a place I loved specializing in "everything potatoes," then a trip to IKEA in Belgium and either Saturday dinner or Sunday lunch at a friend's place in France. I guess "home" has always been at some kind of "intersection" for me. And, as you probably realized by now, it does involve sharing meals!

As I stood in the middle of the farmers market in Mulhouse on Saturday, I felt my heart ache—for all the marketplaces I could not visit anymore and all those I had yet to discover, for all the people I could not take with me to farmers markets on the weekends and all those I had yet to meet. Back in Bucharest, I lived across the street from one of the largest farmers markets in Eastern Europe and I realized how much I missed it. I remembered a few lines from Nigerian poet Ijeoma Umebinyuo's book *Questions for Ada* where she describes the struggle of not quite fitting where you are but not quite fitting at home anymore, either.[304]

Then I felt one of my friends taking my hand, looked over my shoulder and saw her smiling: "Come on, we go now to get some pies from an Afghan lady, she makes amazing things!!" That pie tasted awesomely delicious, and my friends reading this now will know why it was one of the best pies of my life—it had a very special spice sprinkled all over it called "you are never alone."

The farmers market gave me some "fresh produce" for the change random thoughts, and I hope you can use them to create your own freedom and homecoming experiences in life and work alike.

It is about the interaction, not the transaction. Farmers markets are said to have originated in Egypt over 5,000 years ago. Farmers and craftsmen met in urban spaces to sell their goods. Purchases were usually trades rather than money transactions and goods are said to have been valued by weight. Up until the middle of the 20th century, farmers markets were the main means of selling and buying food as well as facilitating social interaction across urban and rural communities and different social layers. In the 1950s and 60s, with improved roads, high-speed transportation and the influx of grocery stores, farmers markets began to disappear. It was estimated that in the 1990s, food in the United States traveled an average of 1,300 miles and changed hands six times before being eaten. In the 1970s, farmers markets became increasingly more popular again. The research shows that behind this comeback was the combined benefit of high-quality, fresh produce, and most of all, the social atmosphere!

Farmers markets are a "meeting place," a "social intersection" where customers who are concerned about food safety can ask questions about production practices, farming techniques and business policies. In large cities, the farmers market may be the only access to fresh produce for low-income inner-city residents. Farmers markets are also excellent educational tools concerning our local economies, farming in general, food systems, environmental issues relating to food production and general knowledge of food: how to prepare it, eat it and much more.

The history of farmers markets is proof that humans crave interaction. Transaction is necessary, but not enough. The comeback after improved infrastructure and grocery stores makes me think of any technology implementation. Availability is necessary, but not enough. Access supports transaction. Interaction serves purpose, meaning and belonging, and it feeds connection. That gives you adoption. Don't bring home just the ingredients. Ask sellers and fellow shoppers about new recipes, tips and tricks for preparing and preserving different foods, their diets, their stories associated with the produce. You will learn so many wonderful new things, and you will get something invaluable: something to look forward to next weekend, a place and a community that feed your mind, soul, heart and body equally. That is adoption in so many different meanings of the word.

Taste and appearance can sometimes be in an inverse proportion relation. Shopping at farmers markets keeps me mindful of my own "superficial tendencies" that prompt me to go for appearance over anything else. Fresh produce reminds me over and over again that we all are perfectly imperfect. The most flavorful tomato is not necessarily the winner of the "Miss Tomato of the Universe" beauty pageant. Some slightly battered apples will give you the best tarte Tatin ever! The mint bundle doesn't look like a bridal bouquet? Take it home nevertheless, sprinkle some on lamb chops, turn the oven on and enjoy life. Well, if it still bothers you, throw a few leaves in a shaker and go for a mojito or a saint if you also got a bundle of that awesome basil!

Writing this makes me think about—surprise!—PowerPoint slides. Some of the most "insipid" decks came in an impressive design, and other times three simple bullet points on a random, "designless" slide started a meaningful conversation. Some of the deepest, life-changing feedback I received did not come gift-wrapped and with a pretty bow. Years ago, my most successful addition to my team started with an almost eye-hurting formatted CV. Go to the farmers market often; it is good practice to keep you honest on some of your (un) conscious biases.

Celebrate the unexpected "bigger wholes" you are part of. One of my absolute favorite things to do is to go to the farmers market without a shopping list and just let inspiration come. As I look at the offerings, I start to recall or imagine recipes that would combine different ingredients. An apple is not just an apple, but a great spin to "something with red cabbage," or an eggplant will become a trigger for getting some bell peppers, red onions, a chunk of Feta cheese and some thyme honey... The ingredients get their identity at an unexpected intersection, out of "isolation" and oftentimes it feels surprising.

I do carry isolated elements of my identity to the farmers market, and there I become so many other expressions of who I am: a spice fanatic, a cheese lover, an artichoke hater (nobody is perfect!!!), an herbs collector, a fruit hoarder, a Brussel sprouts detractor, a chili addict. I also feel like I'm part of an ancestral fundamental value chain. As I learn more about the produce, the people selling it, the people buying it, I feel like I belong to unexpected bigger wholes than before. I discover new facets of my own identity at the intersection of tastes, cultures, countries, experiences. Maybe one of my most meaningful takeaways from the farmers market is to use curiosity to allow myself to belong. That I become "more" at intersections, not in isolation. That I grow through each interaction. That we all are perfectly imperfect.

In the middle of the Mulhouse farmers market filled with seasonal produce, I realized we are always presented with new starts—to a soul-nourishing meal, a heart-warming friendship, a life-changing relationship, a humanity-celebrating world. Farmers markets speak to me about staying open to constant new starts while standing at intersections, based on interactions, never on transactions.

I will leave you with a quote from the same powerful Nigerian voice, Ijeoma Umebinyuo: "Start now. Start where you are. Start with fear. Start with pain. Start with doubt. Start with hands shaking. Start with voice trembling but start. Start and don't stop. Start where you are, with what you have. Just… start."[305] This past Saturday, I started with a cheese-filled pie from an Afghan, a batch of ginger beignets from a Senegalese, a bunch of mint from a Moroccan, a packet of butter from a French, a bowl of Italian mango sorbet and two hugs around a friend's table.

Until next week, keep calm and find your new starts that feel like coming home.

What Getting Scars Teaches Me about Change Management

First published on May 3, 2022

This past weekend was particularly social. And it felt quite good. "Homey" kind of good. As I bent over to tie my shoelaces to get going to a Sunday dinner, I saw the scar on the back of my left hand. It's been there for two decades, a souvenir from when Dada, my most gorgeous, blue-eyed Ragdoll cat, was coming back from anesthesia at the vet's after a surgery and got scared by a very curious Rottweiler. The scar is barely noticeable, crossing the entire back of my hand, and it always reminds me of how, when we are confused and struggling to make sense of our surroundings, even the friendliest of best intentions could be misinterpreted as scary and distressing.

The idea to see whether there were any lessons in scars for change work popped up instantaneously. And I remember thinking to myself "Why not?" After all, I do have enough scars to consider it a relevant "learning experience."

When I was about five, I was running around in my great-grandmother's yard, tripped and fell face-first into a pile of barbed wire. This episode left a now-faint scar on my left cheek. There is a burn mark on my upper left arm from an iron, as I lifted my right hand to scratch my nose while ironing a frustratingly difficult pair of trousers and forgot to set down the said appliance… Imagine if it had been the phone ringing!!!!! My best friend makes fun of me when I wear short sleeves because she can see the scar I gave myself on the left elbow with a pair of newly sharpened scissors while attempting to cut my cuticles… We were talking about something, I started explaining a particular point I felt very passionate about while moving my hands and arms, interrupting the already dangerous and slightly bloody attempt at self-manicure… Me and sharp or hot objects is a no-no combination!

And oh, all those mental and emotional scars…a whole different conversation! In honor of May being the mental health month, here is a wonderful insight, a deep accountability reminder from writer Napoleon Hill: "Think twice before you speak, because your words and influence will plant the seed of either success or failure in the mind of another."[306]

I hope the takeaways below will leave a mark in your mind, anything but a scar.

What do you see in a scar: the wounding or the healing? A scar is a mark left on the skin after a wound or injury has healed. Scars are a natural part of the healing process. Most will fade although they never completely disappear. When the skin is wounded, the tissues break, which causes a protein called collagen to be released. Collagen builds up where the tissue is damaged, helping to heal and strengthen the wound. New collagen continues forming for several months and the blood supply increases, causing the scar to become raised and lumpy. In time, some collagen breaks down at the site of the wound and the blood supply reduces. The scar gradually becomes smoother and softer. Although scars are permanent, they can fade over a period of up to two years. It's unlikely they'll fade any more after this time.

I wish emotional scars were this easy to explain. I never ever ask people about their scars, but I am always fascinated by what they choose to share. Some stories are of the wounding, some of the healing. Many conversations about change contain stories of scars, if you listen carefully. Especially the ones about resistance to change. When you ask people about their past change journeys, listen for their "scars stories," try to understand whether they are about the wounding or the healing. That will inform your strategy and plan, and it will help you direct focus as well as pace rhythm.

Think of the change readiness assessment as your "stories inventory" and "scars check" —oftentimes, change initiatives should start with some healing of previous wounds so that the new work will not inflict fresh ones. The stories people choose to share with you are precious. Arguably, the sharing itself is a sign of ongoing healing. I am totally with Japanese fashion designer Yohji Yamamoto on how perfection is overrated: "I think perfection is ugly. Somewhere in the things humans make I want to see scars, failure, disorder, distortion."[307]

"The scars of others should teach us caution."[308] I so so soooooo love this small piece of huge wisdom from Saint Jerome, a Christian priest and historian, born in Croatia around the middle of the 4th century, recognized (by the Catholic Church) as the Patron of archaeologists, Biblical scholars, librarians, students and translators. Whenever it is time to give a message of caution, I prefer this one to a much more popular version coming from former German Chancellor Otto von Bismarck: "Only a fool learns from his own mistakes. The wise man learns from the mistakes of others."[309] Over the years, I realized that some people take the von Bismarck quote quite literally and use it to "shorthand" their own judgment. Other people's journeys should not be the basis for denying your own experiences. Also, I prefer to talk about "scars" rather than "mistakes" as learning milestones.

It so happened that over the past week I was in a handful of conversations about how, more or less consciously, we are running the risk of absorbing other people's experiences and judgments as our own, especially when it comes to negative aftereffects. Changes and failures they went through, relationships they had with other people and the betrayals and disappointments. Each and every one of us is different from everyone else, and there is absolutely no "guarantee" that going through the same experience or interacting with the same people will yield the same results as it did for someone else. Do be cautious, by all means, especially when more stories overlap in significant elements, but never ever ever shorthand your own judgment and refuse yourself your own journey.

It is the absolute same when we speak about organizations or teams. No one organization is like the rest, no one team is the exact replica of another. Each is different in big or more elusive and subtle ways. Take with you Saint Jerome's advice and use the scars of others for caution, not for inaction.

Show your scars so that others know they can heal. Sharing your own stories is one of the most powerful ways to heal yourself and others. It took me decades to realize this and to get the courage to share my own scars stories. Looking back, a few years ago, they were still mostly stories of wounding. With each telling, they transformed into stories of healing, and I am forever grateful to all who listened and shared their own stories.

Sharing stories is one of the most wonderful ways to say: "You are not alone." It doesn't have to happen through a keynote or a speech to thousands. A walk with your best friend can be the perfect setting for storytelling. And who knows, maybe your sharing is the best healing aid for their own wounds that they haven't shared with anyone before. My favorite reminder to honor scars comes courtesy of writer Rasmenia Massoud: "Maybe I should find another doctor; one who realizes the importance of scars."[310] Let's all be "the other doctor," especially when we do change work—in our personal and professional lives alike. Let's honor scars and prescribe a treatment based on healing (self)storytelling.

For years and years, looking at my scars and thinking about how they came to be felt like...picking at scabs—until I realized that I was looking at them with judgment, echoing all the toxic "should haves" as in "it should have healed, more or less, by now," or the equally noxious "should have nots" like "I should have not done that."

One thing that helped me turn stories of wounding into stories of healing was judgment-free reflection. *Newsweek* contributor and recipient of the Daniel Pearl Investigative Journalism Fellowship Cameron Conaway speaks about childhood wounds (maybe because "first cut is the deepest?"), yet his words equally apply to wounds of all kinds from any age: "...real childhood scars heal, but not when band-aids replace self-reflection."[311] Sit with your scars, honor them, be proud of them, share them to help yourself and others heal. And when it becomes hard, remember: we may have a scar, but this also means we have a story.

Until next week, keep calm and tell yourself and others stories of healing.

What Loving Watching Waves Teaches Me about Change Management

First published on May 10, 2022

Maybe because I am Pisces, I have always been fascinated by watching waves—or at least listening to their sounds. More than anything else, the sea and the ocean speak to my soul. I could sit on the sand and watch the waves forever and ever.

Toward the end of last year, I found "my painting," or maybe I should say it found me when I needed it most. It is a painting of waves coming to a shore in glorious hues of turquoise and blue. My eyes were just drifting around the hairdresser's place as I was waiting to pay, and this painting was hung on a wall. And just like the Metallica song goes, "nothing else mattered." It turned out it was painted by my hairdresser's mom, and a couple of weeks later, I welcomed it home. I oftentimes look at it and hear the sound of waves in my mind.

This past Sunday, as I was going around my bed to open the door to the terrace, I looked at the painting out of reflex. The sun was shining right on it, and two decisions were made on the spot: to look for flights to get to a beach and think about the "waves of change" for a random thought in the Tuesday series.

TUESDAY CHANGE MANAGEMENT RANDOM THOUGHTS

So, here I am, sitting on my couch at 4:00 AM, pretending to be on a beach, listening to ocean sounds on YouTube and secretly wishing for waves of coffee to wash over me. Hopefully, the ebb and flow of early morning inspiration will send some good change insights to your mind shores.

"There is no new wave, only the sea."[312] French film director Claude Chabrol might have given me a new opening for future change conversations with this quote. Over the past year, I have been thinking and speaking more and more about how change has been changing, trying to figure out ways to make people get comfortable with change as a constant. I have been playing with the idea of "breaking up" the "change management" denomination because it feels to me that it might promote and contract the expectation that change work is just a specific body of labor that can be carved out from project activities and tasks, put through a methodology and done in blissful isolation by a change manager. Maybe if we could break the label up, then it would be easier to speak about change managed through projects, and less and less about projects with an added change management work stream (oftentimes added when things start to go off track, or at best only at the start of the actual implementation.)

And this is why this quote is so appealing to me. It might help with questions like "So, when is this change going to end?", "Is this the last change?", "Why are we changing again? We just had another change finished early last year." How would "There is no new wave, only the sea" shift the conversation? Would it make change as the "sea" and turn the projects into the "waves" instead of the other way round? And would this make the waves… "easier to surf"?

It is not what you think you see. The ocean is never still. Whether observing from the beach or a boat, we expect to see waves on the horizon. Waves are most commonly caused by wind. Wind-driven waves, or surface waves, are created by the friction between wind and surface water. As wind blows across the surface of the ocean or a lake, the continual disturbance creates a wave crest. Waves are created by energy passing through water, causing it to move in a circular motion. Waves transfer energy, but not mass. When we watch waves coming into shore, it's easy to think that individual water particles are moving toward us, but that's not actually the case. The particles involved in waves move back and forth perpendicularly to the way the wave is going but don't move significantly in the direction of the wave. The particles "take part" in the wave by bumping into one another and transferring energy. This is why energy can be transferred, even though the average position of the particles doesn't change.

There are so many takeaways for change work in this simple physics demystification of waves! How often do we look at organizations and mistakenly see "water" moving instead of energy being transferred? For stakeholders engagement purposes, I find the following explanation even more fascinating: particles in a water wave exchange kinetic energy (the energy that an object or a particle has by reason of its motion) for potential energy (the latent energy in an object at rest, also explained as the energy held by an object because of its position relative to other objects, stresses within itself, its electric charge or other factors). When particles in water become part of a wave, they start to move up or down. This means that kinetic energy has been transferred to them. As the particles move further away from their normal position (up toward the wave crest or down toward the trough), they slow down. This means that some of their kinetic energy has been converted into potential energy; the energy of particles in a wave oscillates between kinetic and potential energy.

It dawned on me that too often we only concentrate on the kinetic energy of our stakeholders, harnessing their movement, and we reserve the lens of potential energy for the senior executive layer through the capital of their "position" (quite literally). Although they have crests and create troughs, waves have no "water particles hierarchy" and all particles balance kinetic with potential energy. And this is how the magic of the waves is created—by each and every particle transmitting energy.

"It's a wonderful metaphor, catching a wave, for how you can look at other challenges in your life."[313] Oh the sweet, sweet, wonderful irony of having this quote about seizing an opportunity that is presented to you, especially an opportunity to do something new, from "The Dude" himself, American icon actor Jeff Bridges (and one of my hugest crushes of all times!!!). According to rave reviews for *The Big Lebowski* at its launch and ever since, the movie's biggest joke is that it's truly perilous to try to make anything make sense. If you have ever done any kind of change work and you caught yourself smiling just now, yes, The Dude's Magic is still going strong!

According to a "thought experiment" published on the *NBC News* website back in March 2018, "Dudeism" and "abiding" have gained popularity, as a low-effort, laid-back lifestyle sounds increasingly appealing in our busy world. In the movie, The Dude's ultimate goal is to "abide" in life with little to no effort, and it's brought him to the place he wants to be: nowhere.[314] Reading this made me reflect on how we sometimes "abide" by the changes, either in our personal or professional lives. The etymologic journey of the word itself is great food for thought. This phrase "to abide by" comes from the verb "abide," which today means "tolerate," although it originally meant "wait," from a root meaning "remain, wait, or dwell."

But back to catching waves... One could argue there will always be new waves to catch. True. But no wave is like another. No one chance is like the one before it, or the one right after. Each and every wave is singular, unique, and it only comes once. If you see it and feel it is "your wave," surf it, ride it on The Dude's carpet if you must, swim with it, do not let it wash over you.

Thinking about how we experience change, I got to make an inventory of the phrases we use to describe how a wave hits the beach and fades away. Big waves pound on the shore, small waves lap at the shore. They roll and crash into the shore. They wash over sand and rocks. Waves break on the beach and then ebb away… A great inspiration for change work comes courtesy of Shunryu Suzuki, also referred to as Suzuki Roshi, a Sōtō Zen monk and teacher who helped popularize Zen Buddhism in the United States and is renowned for founding the first Zen Buddhist monastery outside Asia: "Waves are the practice of water. To speak of waves apart from water, or water apart from waves is a delusion."[315] Let's think about how we can reframe the "waves of change" into something that is not disruptive in and of the words themselves…

Until next week, keep calm and catch your wave!

What Enjoying the Solar Lanterns on the Terrace Teaches Me about Change Management

First published on May 17, 2022

It was a glorious summer-ish evening this past Saturday, and I got to enjoy it on the terrace in the company of two new additions: flower-patterned solar lanterns. Ever since I saw the photos of this apartment, I knew the terrace would be my happy spot. And it is just about the only part of the house that is somewhat finished based on initial dreams and plans.

Last week marked one year in this home. I wanted to celebrate it by getting rid of the last five or six relocation boxes. Okay, maybe there are eight left… Who am I kidding, there are eleven of them… In all honesty, I am much closer to naming them than throwing them out. So, I am extra grateful for the terrace; it gives me a good refuge from my own unboxing failure.

Back to my happy spot! As I was enjoying some midnight quiet time, my attention was drawn to the light from the solar lanterns. I found them by total surprise while out on Friday to get food for lunch. Because I was chasing some random thoughts in my mind, I took the escalator upward, instead of down to the food floor. As I walked around this new floor I had never visited before, there they were waiting for me on a shelf. I bought two, for a balanced lifestyle, you know, one solar lantern in each hand. When I got home, I decided to go for ice cream for lunch, and it felt like quite a festive preparation for the weekend.

No surprise by now, late Saturday evening (or it might have been very early Sunday morning already…) I started thinking about what enjoying the flower-patterned light was teaching me about change management. There must have been more to finding them so unexpectedly, pretty much like how inspiration for the random thoughts series hits… Here below, sharing some of their light with you.

Stay close to whoever and whatever feels like sunshine. Because solar lanterns work based on the light they receive from the sun, it is immensely important that they receive a plentiful amount and are in a position where the sunlight reaches them without any obstruction. This means any shade or coverings that can cause the solar light to not get enough sunlight will result in the solar light not working or will cause a very dimmed light.

The combination of May, which is Mental Health Awareness Month, and that time of the year when you start to get reminders for confirming your vacation days made me think quite a lot about the importance of charging and recharging. As I tried to find the best spots with the most direct sunlight to charge the lanterns, I started asking myself what my equivalent of sunshine was. How do I look for it, how do I capture it, and how do I turn it into "light" when it gets dark? How does all this happen in my personal life? And in my work? Are there similarities that intensify the light I shine, and what differences take up energy and dim it?

My sunshine is made up of all the wonderful people in

my life. It is sometimes a book, other times music and dancing around the house. Always meaningful conversations, every now and again alone time and silence. A good laugh, and equally a good cry. A heartfelt hug. A looooong walk, or simply sitting on the sand and watching the waves. Hitting "buy now" on an order for books, or repotting citrus trees on the terrace. Always plane tickets. An impromptu birthday dinner, like this past Sunday, with two amazing humans and their "amazinger" furry babies. Lately, I have found that what "dims my light" is the energy consumption with reconciling who I am with what I (am expected to) do, between my deepest beliefs and my irrepressible need for safety. What is the equivalent of sunshine in your organization? How can the organization and its people charge and recharge? Is there enough "direct sunlight exposure?" How do you capture sunlight, and what dims your light?

Keep the solar panels of the lanterns clean. Ever since I got solar panel fairy lights last summer, a new cleaning task was added to my domestic to-do list. It is not necessarily my favorite thing to do, but it is necessary. The lights can gather dust and debris on their solar panels which can cause obstruction to the sunlight and prevent them from working. I even had to clean pigeon droppings off of one small solar panel— what impressive marksmanship!!!—and it did make me laugh out loud, as it reminded me of something I often say during change work: "shift happens."

What dust and debris do we gather on our solar panel equivalents? Assumptions, beliefs, stereotypes, expectations that we absorb as initial sense-making shortcuts and never intentionally go back to challenge and recontract. The same happens with and within organizations. The organizational solar panels collect dust and debris, but is there an intentional cleaning? It could be the best practice of retrospective sessions, lessons learned sharing, holding space for conversations. And I am just wondering what the best cleaning product is... Psychological safety gets good "customer reviews," but the real deal one, role-modeled and lived, not the declared and professed replicas.

Combine energy sources. Some of the solar lanterns on my terrace have batteries, some a USB charging port. I try to use them with solar power only, but sometimes that is simply not enough. The fairy light jars only have the solar panels to recharge, and that means that sometimes they simply do not work.

Writing about this makes me think about the importance of combining energy sources. We find energy, motivation and inspiration in different things, at different times, for different purposes. It is the case for people just as it is the case for organizations. One particularly insightful takeaway from my solar panel lanterns is how important it is to have the possibility of combining energy sources as a matter of choice and efficiency, rather than a case of unavailability and necessity.

There is solid evidence that American inventor and businessman Thomas Edison, the "Father of the Light Bulb," believed that sunshine, wind and tides should be employed to generate energy for humankind. In a book called *Uncommon Friends: Life with Thomas Edison, Henry Ford, Harvey Firestone, Alexis Carrel, & Charles Lindbergh* by James D. Newton, there is a story about what must have been an amazing conversation amongst Thomas Edison, automobile manufacturer Henry Ford and tire manufacturer Harvey Firestone. Edison purportedly said to his friends a little before he died in 1931, "I'd put my money on the sun and solar energy. What a source of power! I hope we don't have to wait till oil and coal run out before we tackle that. I wish I had more years left!"[316] In addition to the power of vision, this speaks to me about the power of choice. One of the best, most intense "sunlight" as energy for change I have ever seen is giving people the power, freedom and control of their choices.

TUESDAY CHANGE MANAGEMENT RANDOM THOUGHTS

What I noticed over this past weekend was that the solar lanterns on the terrace started to shine at different times. The small jars with fairy lights inside came on first, then the new flower-patterned solar lanterns followed about half an hour later. Also, the two small lanterns at the ends of the terrace were quite dim, and one of them started flashing weakly. That made me think of "not enough"—not enough sunlight during the day in one case, and not enough darkness in the other. Just as we have different sensors with different sensitivity levels for light, there are significant and meaningful differences in how we perceive darkness. Pay attention to these differences in both your personal and professional life. Understand them, honor them, harness them—they are part of your superpower!

Until next week, keep calm and clean your solar panels!

What Taking Myself Out to Restaurants Teaches Me about Change Management

First published on May 24, 2022

Last week, a friend traveled to Seville for work and decided to extend her stay over the weekend. As she went out for dinner, she dropped me a note saying: "I'm sitting in a restaurant all by myself." Without thinking, I texted back something I have learned over the past two decades: "I love taking myself out on my own. There is immense power in that, enjoy!" This small exchange reminded me of many conversations I have had with friends, and even with my mom, about going out on my own—to a restaurant, to the movies, to a new travel destination. Enjoying my own company started as a necessity because of traveling and frequent relocation, and I ended up loving it tremendously. I lost count of how many times I heard "I could not do it," accompanied by looks covering the entire spectrum, from pity and admiration to dismay, disapproval, envy and inspiration.

Solo dining, as eating out on your own came to be coined, tackles "the stigma of loneliness" and brings into the conversation a phobia with a name just as frightening as its meaning and implications: solomangarephobia, defined as the fear of eating alone in public, especially at the restaurant. Those who have solomangarephobia have absolutely no problems eating alone at home, but it's almost impossible for them to eat alone in public at a restaurant. Less so when it is a pub or fast food, and the worst meal of all to have alone in public is dinner. People who have solomangarephobia don't necessarily want to have someone with them, either. No, the problem comes from what other people might think. Those who have solomangarephobia think people look at them like a sad, friendless person, someone who got stood up—basically, the losers, those who are stigmatized. And research shows that women eating out on their own are being judged more harshly and get more sympathy from onlookers. They also get seated away from restaurant windows, usually by the kitchen or restroom, the areas where restaurants wouldn't put a large party of diners they want to keep for longer and for larger bills.

There is a wonderful quote from actor Keanu Reeves—the fact that his iconic *Matrix* character, Neo, also had the alias "The Anomaly" is particularly ironic for this conversation, and I do say it to myself quite a lot when I enjoy my own company: "Someone told me the other day that he felt bad for single people because they are lonely all the time. I told him that's not true; I'm single and I don't feel lonely. . . . Once you know how to take care of yourself, company becomes an option and not a necessity."[317] I have come to love eating out on my own. And if you think that is a tell-tale sign of me being single, think again! I also take myself out when I am in a relationship, and it happens equally when my partner is away or otherwise enjoying other plans. I take myself out to eat as an intentional practice to know who I am above and beyond circumstances, contexts, situations, as a precious reminder of the power and freedom to make life choices over needing solutions to life's necessities.

As I enjoyed a lovely early dinner this past Saturday at one of my favorite restaurants, I started thinking about what eating out alone has been teaching me about change management. I hope you will get a generous serving of inspiration, curiosity, courage, motivation, support and unwavering celebration from the thoughts below. Bon appetit!

Intentionally practice making your own choices and decisions. Thinking back over conversations about planning going out to eat, it surprises me how often the phrase "I don't mind" comes up. Not minding the restaurant choice, the menu, the "allocation" of food, as it is decided to either "I will have the same, thank you," or "Oh, if we are sharing, I will just order something different than you, please go ahead." There you go, decision made. Eating alone means that you don't have anyone to double-check your decisions—where to eat, what to order from the menu and where you want to sit (that is, if you choose to challenge the staff's decision to keep your "misery" safe from the world by seating you in the "safe corner" next to the kitchen). You have to trust your own gut and intuition and not run through the should have, could have and would haves in your head.

Solo dining fights something that research in the field calls "poverty of enthusiasm and ideas," and what a great takeaway for change work that is!!! Looking back at my journey of getting comfortable with eating out on my own, I now realize that, in addition to my love for it, something else has changed. I used to be hesitant to send food back or give less-than-stellar feedback when on my own. As if they couldn't do the same "funny business" to my plate behind the kitchen doors with ten other people with me around the table... I am totally fine with doing that now, but it took practice. Eating out on my own has made me more and more comfortable and confident in making my own choices and decisions, a fundamental "tool" for any change work. It also taught me to be comfortable sitting through uncomfortable situations of being looked at and judged, oftentimes misjudged, as well as looooong moments of silence, accompanied by the "free side" of incredulous stares. Eating out on my own made me totally and delightfully comfortable with standing out (technically, "seating down") like a sore thumb.

When doing meaningful change work, you inevitably come to challenge beliefs, habits, processes, statuses, comfort zones, and I have learned that it can oftentimes feel like…well, solo dining. The more you are used to making and standing by—or should I say "sitting by?"—your choices and decisions, taking the silence and judgmental looks with an inner smile, the better change-maker you become. Now take yourself out for dinner and celebrate that!

See people above and beyond their circumstances. Many restaurants are simply not set up to cater to dinner for one. Restaurants themselves might see those eating alone as a smaller bill or a hindrance to turning over tables to larger parties. However, restaurants should cater to patrons eating alone. Every guest is an opportunity to demonstrate your restaurant's ability to offer not just tasty food, but a wholesome experience, too, and to continually bring in business down the line. If this reminds you of stakeholder engagement, please keep on reading.

In a wonderful blog post on webstaurantstore.com, the case for meaningfully accommodating solo dining is built as follows: Even though some restaurants might see solo diners as a nuisance because they take up space that a larger party (with a larger bill) could have had, even these lone eaters can turn out to be a valuable opportunity for a restaurant in the long run. First of all, hospitality should be paramount in a restaurant, no matter who the customer is; it should always be more important to be accommodating and courteous than to make a big profit. Secondly, there's a high likelihood that a satisfied solo diner will become a regular and/or bring others with them in the future. Finally, a one-person table is simply easier to take care of. Instead of seeing it as a loss, think of the server who is getting a well-deserved breather during the dining rush when serving a simple table of one amid the other four, five, and six-person tables. Keep these points in mind when you go through your stakeholder engagement strategy and plan.

One of the things I enjoy most is coaching people for their writing and public speaking engagements. Recently, I had a conversation that basically came down to one question: "Who do you think got the invitation to speak at this conference: you as a person or you as a role within your company? If you quit tomorrow, how many invitations will you still receive?" And that touches on our dining conversation with the takeaway question: who do we primarily engage through our stakeholders management—the person, their current organizational context, intentionally both? We look at people and see not necessarily who they are, but rather where they are within a given social construct (a group of diners, an organizational hierarchy). In dining terms, who do we serve: the person or the "company of their company"?

Take the compliment, with a bonus on top. When solo diners come to your restaurant, take the compliment of them liking your food and service. And look for the bonus on top: they also feel safe. When you do change work and someone comes to you especially with something that "stands out" like a solo diner, be that information, opinion, observation, comment or feedback, take the compliment of being a safe, trusted space.

Solitude, the kind we elect ourselves, is met with judgment and enslaved by stigma. It is also a capacity absolutely essential for a full life. We think about storytelling, having conversations and going out to eat as (almost) exclusively linked to other people, outward-looking. Yet the most meaningful stories, conversations and meals are those we have with our own self. Change work is all about people, and yet it gets terribly lonely every now and again. As in work, so in life…or the other way around, whatever way it applies. Use solo dining to fill the following with your own deeply personal and special meaning: "I know what I bring to the table, so trust me when I say I'm not afraid to eat alone."[318]

Curiously—and importantly—mastering the art of solitude doesn't make us more antisocial but, on the contrary, better able to connect. Take this piece from Rainer Maria Rilke with you as a "dessert" from this reading, which applies to life and work relationships equally: "I hold this to be the highest task for a bond between two people: that each protects the solitude of the other."[319]

Until next week, keep calm and take yourself out to a nice restaurant.

What Renewing My Passport Teaches Me about Change Management

First published on May 31, 2022

About three weeks ago, while looking for a plane ticket, I had a surprise: I discovered my passport would expire in less than two months. I've heard of many similar stories recently, so I do feel I am in good company, and I guess this is one side effect of the COVID pandemic.

Gathering all the necessary documents and some patience, I started the process of renewing my passport through the Romanian Consulate in Bern. And yesterday was the day! As I traveled to Bern and back home, I had time to watch the sky out the train window and the more I tried to empty my mind, the more intense thoughts about travel and identity got. Maybe because the appointment was at noon and a couple of times my focus got hijacked by thoughts about the Hungarian dinner I'll be hosting this coming Saturday, food was the backdrop of my reflection. So, it should not be a total surprise that one of the quotes I remembered was from American chef and travel documentarian Anthony Bourdain about how "travel changes you." Throughout life, you leave your mark on the world. "And in return, life—and travel—leaves marks on you."[320]

While waiting to have my photo taken at the consulate, my weekly reflex kicked in and I started wondering whether there was some food for thought in my travel and identity reflection, maybe just enough for a change random thought. And here it is, also a welcome distraction from the outcome of the photoshoot... Have you heard of the saying that goes: "If you look like your passport photo, you probably need the trip"?

You never really "travel light." While thinking about takeaways for change work, I remembered this piece of news that every now and again triggers my curiosity: the most powerful passports in the world. This ranking used to be all about access, meaning passports have been ranked on their mobility score—in essence, how many countries or territories you can get visa-free access to with a certain passport. As I started reading about this topic, I discovered that the parameters got more and more complex. The access element now goes beyond simply counting the number of countries or territories that the passport provides immediate access to, ranking instead from restricted travel, through to visa on arrival and unlimited visa-free access. The "desirability of countries" is also included here, based on the quality of life score. The investment and business opportunities are now a factor counting for the strength of a passport, covering global competitiveness, gross national income per capita and personal income. The "quality of life" dimension factors in six indicators for the passport ranking: sustainable development, the cost of living, the protection of personal freedom, the happiness of the citizens, environmental performance, and migrant acceptance.

On the surface, this ranking of passports speaks about the thrill of access. On a closer look, it bears the accountability of representation. What are the equivalents of all these in organizational change work? Your role? Your title? Your position within a specific team, function, unit? As someone doing change work, you are oftentimes granted a powerful passport across the organization, and your "change travels" will take you to many places. Keep in mind you never really travel light, and you have with you all these factors of representation. You should stand for current and future opportunities, and all the elements defining the "quality of life" should be top of mind.

Have faith. This is not an expression I use often, so I got intrigued when it popped in my mind and refused to go away. Bearing some inertia from the previous takeaway, one clue comes courtesy of "to have faith in someone" definition: to believe someone, to trust someone to do or be what is claimed. Then, I stumbled upon a nice short read on psychologytoday.com, called "Why Faith Is Important" published back in September 2012. It speaks of how faith comes from our hearts; it's a hope that defies description. "We act in faith when there is no guarantee, no certainty."[321]

If I read this through the lens of traveling, then requesting or renewing a passport is a sign of faith, of hope for adventure, discovery, and—why not?—awakening to new possibilities. We plan with our mind and we travel with our heart. A lot of faith is required in change work. Any transformation, be it personal or organizational, is an expression of hope for something better. Can anyone else resonate with "we act in faith when there is no guarantee, no certainty" within the dimension of organizational change?

And if this takeaway triggered some religious or spiritual connotations, it might not be purely by accident. Passports are an invaluable document dating back to biblical times when individuals could be granted safe conduct letters requesting that the governors of foreign lands bestow them safe passage. The first mention of a passport is in the Bible's Book of Nehemiah from approximately 450 BC. In the 13th century, Venetian merchant Marco Polo's father became the first European to receive safe conduct from Kublai Khan—the grandson of "The Unifier of the Mongolian Steppe" Genghis Khan and the founder of the Yuan Dynasty in China—granting him safe passage and access to the entire Mongol Empire.

Etymological sources show that the term "passport" is from a medieval document that was required in order to pass through the gate (or "porte") of a city wall or to pass through a territory. In medieval Europe, such documents were issued by local authorities to foreign travelers (as opposed to local citizens, as is the modern practice) and generally contained a list of towns and cities the document holder was permitted to enter or pass through. On the whole, documents were not required for travel to sea ports, which were considered open trading points, but documents were required to travel inland from sea ports. The transition from private to state control over movement was an essential aspect of the transition from feudalism to capitalism. Communal obligations to provide poor relief were an important source of the desire for control on movement. Traveling and identity were finally officially merged in the early 20th century. The British Nationality and Status Aliens Act of 1914 produced the first modern British passport. By 1920, the League of Nations had adopted a standard passport format.

Travel and identity are forever linked. It fascinates me how the passport, a document that links travel and identity, must be requested. And it is mandatory when traveling internationally. For the purpose of this random thought, could we agree that "traveling internationally" could represent "stepping out of one's comfort zone"? With every trip we take, especially to foreign lands, our identity gets a new layer. Those passport stamps are proof of that. I sometimes think of those stamps as "graduation certificates." As Chef Bourdain said, every travel, personal or professional, "leaves a mark."[322] Stepping out of our comfort zones, whatever those might be, is a choice. Requesting or renewing a passport is a choice. Stepping into the accountability of never really traveling light is a choice. Having faith is a choice. Our identity is continuously shaped by our traveling choices. Similarly, an organizational identity is continuously shaped by its change choices.

Since we had the "starter" from Chef Bourdain, it makes sense to leave a final "dessert for thought" from him here: Travel is all about diving into the unknown. It isn't straightforward, it's messy, and it can even hurt, but the important thing is that it changes you. The journey is something you'll carry with you always, and the hope is that you make a mark on wherever you've been, too.[323]

As I now wait to get my new passport in about one month (like I mentioned, renewing my travel document required original documents and patience!), I choose to have faith, I think about what makes my "change passport" strong and I keep my mind and heart open to all future "identity travels."

Until next week, keep calm and check the validity of your passports!

What Putting Things in Storage Teaches Me about Change Management

First published on June 14, 2022

For a few years now, every mid-month I get an invoice for storage services for some of my belongings that were left behind in Bucharest. And without exception, every time I see the new invoice in my inbox, I ask myself what the chances are of ever needing something that has been stored for years and years and years and one month. And one more month, and one more month, and one more month… Then I press the "pay now" button in the online banking application, tell myself it is not a big expense anyways and move on… Or am I really?

Earlier this year, I finally got the few boxes I left behind with some friends when I left Malta four years ago. If I remember correctly, there is at least one box stored in a friend's attic in Luxembourg—and in all honesty, since my memory is quite fuzzy on having a box stored in his attic, I sure can't remember what is stored inside…

It seems like I have left a "trail of storage" over the years. Research calls it "lock and leave culture." Some of my friends regularly mention decluttering, and I do seem to remember there is at least one copy of *Goodbye, Things: The New Japanese Minimalism* by Fumio Sasaki in one of the boxes stored in one of the places… Since a new invoice landed in my inbox a few days ago, I started thinking about any takeaways for change work "stored" in this experience. I can only hope the unboxing below will bring some inspiration and not mental clutter.

Clean it before you store it. If you do not follow any other storage best practice, please please please follow this one! No matter what you store—clothing, appliances, books, furniture—always clean it before you store it. It is quite stressful and depressing to look for something in your storage space when you really need it—do not let yourself get carried away by the mirage of the archaeology sites you see in all of those wonderful documentaries, it is not glorious at all!!!—only to find it dusty, dirty, deteriorated by something you could have prevented with a little bit of time, water or a simple wipe.

There are quite a few "organizational storage facilities and practices" that come to mind while writing this. Knowledge management is one of them—how is information collected, sorted, cleaned and stored in our organizations? Then, even more generically, whenever we go through a change or transformation initiative, how do we sort, clean and store retired or replaced information, processes, platforms, structures, roles and accountabilities no longer needed? How do we clean all this, making sure no "bad smell" or "mold" hazards are left around the organization? Throughout the years, I have found honest—and sometimes uncomfortable—conversations to be the greatest and most efficient "cleaning products"— whether it is a simple conversation with stakeholders or a series of lessons learned, make sure you clean whatever organizational artifact you put in storage.

Make it easy to search and sort through it. It is sooooooo frustrating to search for something in a crammed storage space through what feels like an infinite number of boxes, and it only gets worse when you have no clue or way of approximately telling where it might be!!! As one of my mentors used to say: "It is very difficult to find a black cat in a dark room, especially if the cat is not there." Whenever possible due to specific regulations and procedures, I try to store my stuff in transparent boxes. It does save me from making extra detailed inventory lists, and it also helps me with searching and retrieving time when needed. Which reminds me that I need to get some extra transparent boxes to store some stuff in the basement...

It also makes me think about the organizational equivalents of transparent storage boxes. How do we make stored information easily searchable and retrievable? How do we allow, encourage, use, enforce and safeguard transparency? And when that is not possible, how do we register and label organizational information or any other relevant artifact? American organizing consultant Geralin Thomas, who makes regular appearances on the TV show *Hoarders*, once said: "Proper storage is about creating a home for something so that minimal effort is required to find it and put it away."[324] Especially during transitions of any kind, be it a home move or an organizational change, proper storage of clean items is critical.

Be honest: is it really temporary or forever and ever? A good friend of mine is fascinated by astrology and she keeps telling me the Universe always sends us messages, especially around full moons. We have one today, the "Strawberry Moon," so she might be right about this, as a few days ago, I came across an article by Karen Kingston called "The deeper implications of putting your stuff in storage." Here is what triggered some painfully honest introspection: "Self-storage facilities are eerie places. Some owners try to make them more cheerful by painting the doors bright colors or playing piped music through the corridors, but there's no getting away from the lifeless energy of tons of stagnant stuff. The problem with being in one place while your stuff is in another is that you're neither here nor there. You're energetically stretched between the two locations.... The bottom line is, can you truly get on with life when you have stuff in storage? And the answer, I'm sorry to say, is no. Some part of you will be disconnected, neglected, unconscious or just plain waiting until you and your stuff are united in one place. This puts an interesting new slant on that well-known phrase 'getting yourself together'."[325]

This hit pretty deep, especially as I have been struggling to decide between "storing" or "closing" a chapter in my own life—which made me reflect on the meaning of the boxes in my "storage trail." Some of them I haven't even thought about, seen or opened in years. My only (perceived) connection to them is the monthly invoice for storage services. When have they transitioned from being boxes full of "not knowing (what to do)" into boxes full of "not wanting (to make a definite decision)"? What boxes are we storing for too long or indefinitely? And are we really that unaware of whether it is temporary or indefinitely? As I look back at my change work, the same questions apply within organizations. What boxes keep your company in limbo? What organizational boxes are full of "not knowing" and which ones are storing decisions waiting to be acknowledged? Are these boxes transparent?

There is a post on social media that made me think: "Put your stuff in storage. Book a one-way ticket. Explore our world. Your old life will be waiting for you... If you even want it back."[326] I know I will not want or need anything from the boxes in storage back in Bucharest. Yet, I know I will pay the next monthly invoice, and the next one, and the next one, and it will take some time before I finally hit "reply" and write an e-mail to check for options to close that chapter of my life. More than an "anchor," my stuff in storage used to speak to me about hope. Temporary hope feels comfortable, and now the question to myself is: "When has this comfortable temporary hope changed into uncomfortable indefinite hope?"

Until next week, keep calm and acknowledge the decisions in your storage boxes.

What Eating Ice Cream Teaches Me about Change Management

First published on June 21, 2022

Is it possible to live on ice cream, coffee, books and a touch of Prosecco? Well, based on extensive research I have conducted over the years, the answer is a most definite YES. I can't think of any other main food group that is so versatile as ice cream—great for breakfast, awesome for lunch, perfect for dinner and totally amazing for the snacks in between... And if you get some kind of craving every now and again? Ice cream! Coffee ice cream?

As American author Abbi Waxman put it, "Sometimes life is what it is, and the best you can hope for is ice cream."[327] While struggling with the heatwave in Switzerland over the past few days, I put all my faith and hope in ice cream (and the ceiling fans I had installed last year). Under severe weather conditions, the small size of my freezer turned out to be quite life-endangering. I also remembered one of my most painful memories: parting ways with my ice cream machine and sending it to storage a few years ago. I just looked for a new one online, and I feel like my life will take a turn for the better (and definitely sweeter!)

TUESDAY CHANGE MANAGEMENT RANDOM THOUGHTS

Nothing like starting the day with ice cream at 5:00 AM to ignite inspiration for the Tuesday writing. And here we go, a few takeaways for change work before the ideas melt away...

To scoop or not to scoop? That is the question. Let me start off by saying that, based on wide-ranging research, there is enormous wisdom in the advice to never ask a woman who is eating ice cream straight from the carton how she's doing. Some people say that the secret to enjoying ice cream is the perfect scoop. To each their own, I say. I was reminded of this about two weeks ago when I had some friends over for dinner. We had apple pie for dessert with ice cream on top, of course. As it turned out, patience in the presence of ice cream was not one of our virtues, and we had a "scoop incident."

While looking for a new set of ice cream scoops, I started thinking about the use of tools in change work. Not so much about the tools themselves (I have been known to bend spoons and break plastic utensils in fresh-out-of-the-freezer ice cream), as the timing and skillfulness of their use. Right timing is essential if you aim for the perfect scoop and not biceps training. You should wait for the ice cream to get slightly soft around the edges, until you can squeeze it lightly.

The next step triggers debates. Some say a dry, room-temperature scooper is always the way to go. Using a wet scoop glazes ice cream with a thin layer of ice, while hot water will melt ice cream too much, causing ice crystals to form faster when you return the carton to the freezer. Others will swear by the magic powers of a wet scoop and will have none of this dry scoop talk. And did you know there are professional scoops out there with the handle filled with a liquid that transfers heat from your hand to the aluminum scoop, which melts just a little bit of ice cream as you run it over the surface and cleanly releases the ice cream from the metal?

Sometimes, a spoon is all you need, really! A spoon and

commitment. Or an honest craving. How you time your change interventions is key, above and beyond the actual tools that you use. How you use them comes down to context, personal preferences and experience, organizational realities and stakeholders' expectations.

Enjoy it before it melts. This seems like such straightforward advice. But is it really? It makes me reflect on the merits of simplification and how easy (or should I say "simple"?) it is to misuse it. Following a methodology, a method or a "how to" guide without intentional curiosity, deep awareness and granular understanding of the organization, its people and their realities is just as "meaningful" as giving someone advice to eat ice cream before it melts. Is it summer or a colder season? That will dictate how fast this should happen. Is your throat more on the sensitive side and you prefer slightly melted ice cream like my mom does? Are you going for an ice cream cone, stick or carton? One scoop or the "gigantino" cup? And don't be so quick to discard melted ice cream. I am totally with American actor Chris Pratt on "You can pour melted ice cream on regular ice cream. It's like a sauce!"[328]

When you do change work, look for…"melted projects" on purpose. They can yield amazing insights and additional resources: lessons learned, knowledge and information, requirements, deliverables, pointers regarding stakeholder dynamics, patterns and behaviors. What a great "sauce" for your endeavor!

Do you care about the seasons? Many would argue, yours truly included, that this question is the one true filter between amateur and professional ice cream eaters. "It is a grave error to assume that ice cream consumption requires hot weather."[329] Take it from American writer and journalist Anne Fadiman! While enjoying ice cream over the recent hot days, I could not help but miss having a gooseberry-flavored ice cream cone for breakfast on my way to the office through snow and temperatures of -27°C when I lived in Tallinn... Oh, good times!

In many change conversations, the question about what the right time for change is pops up almost without exception. Is there such a thing as the right time for change? Especially in the realities we have been navigating over the past few years, personally and professionally? Reflecting on people's preference to "timebox" their ice cream consumption based on seasons and the recent scoop incident, I would encourage everyone doing change work in some way, shape or form to turn the "right time for change" challenge into an "appropriate timing of relevant change work" conversation.

In a recent conversation, I was asked if I saw myself doing change work for the rest of my life. Hmmmm, I don't know. What I do know is that my love and fascination for this kind of work shows no signs of melting in the near future... I recently stumbled upon rap music icon Snoop Dogg's career change goals: "When I'm no longer rapping, I want to open up an ice cream parlor and call myself Scoop Dogg."[330] I would give up my change work to go into a business partnership with Scoop Dogg! Anyone got a lead?

Until next week, keep calm and eat ice cream!

What Watching Water Teaches Me about Change Management
First published on June 28, 2022

My absolute favorite neighbor by far is the Rhine. It is a short walk from my home down to the river, and that means I am often on one of its banks, sitting and watching the water, while my thoughts feel like they swim upstream, downstream, and get caught in wild whirlpools…

I wrote about watching waves a few weeks back, and as I stared at the blank page in front of me this morning, I asked myself: "Is this going to be much different? And if yes, why don't you clarify it is about watching flowing water?" These questions reminded me of change work-related conversations: "Is this change going to be much different than the one(s) before it? And if yes, why not clarify it as such from the get-go?"

As I think back to the better part of my Sunday morning when I sat by the Rhine at one of my favorite spots and watched it flow, I have a "yes, and" answer. Yes, this random thought is different than the one about watching waves, and although it will mainly be about watching flowing water, I would not make that differentiation so clear-cut binary. Arguably, it would even be misleading. Ocean water is constantly moving, and not just in the form of waves and tides. Ocean currents flow like vast rivers, sweeping along predictable paths. Some ocean currents flow at the surface, others flow deep within water. So, the only clarification I could make at this point would be between watching "saltwater" and "freshwater," and that would not make for an enticing title, would it?

Watching the Rhine on Sunday flow silently and totally oblivious to its spectators reminded me of a passage from *The Penelopiad*, a novella by Canadian author Margaret Atwood published in 2005 as part of the first set of books in the Canongate Myth Series where contemporary authors rewrite ancient myths. In it, a character talks about how water is gentle yet powerful, assertive yet patient. When you touch it, you only feel a caress, but it is strong enough to go around and wear away the toughest obstacles with time.

I can only hope reading the below thoughts will feel like a "mental caress," and it will take you into a pleasant change flow.

"What is soft is strong." This is part of a wonderful piece of wisdom from Ancient Chinese philosopher Lao Tzu that goes like this: "As a rule, whatever is fluid, soft, and yielding will overcome whatever is rigid and hard. This is another paradox: what is soft is strong."[331] The first thing coming to my mind is how oftentimes change work is considered "soft" work, and yet it is expected to do the "heavy lifting" of paradigm shifts, challenging rigid, deeply entrenched (individual and organizational) patterns and beliefs. It also makes me reflect on how it actually comes down to the "soft" part of change labor to truly work its magic. I am talking about what happens before, in between, and after applying the visible, structured tools: all the interactions, conversations, observations, reflections, all the connection work.

All of these are fluid, soft and yielding in change work, and they make for the strength of it. Part of the trick is to do it not only fluidly, but also consistently, persistently. We all have witnessed the power of a persistent drop of water and how it can wear away even the hardest stone. Stay fluid, stay persistent.

Stay open to meandering. Very rarely, if ever, do change interventions unfold according to plan. Most of the time, they... well, meander, in real life and actual implementation. There must have been a little change worker inside American singer, actress and comedian Eartha Kitt that made her leave us with this quote: "The river is constantly turning and bending and you never know where it's going to go and where you'll wind up. Following the bend in the river and staying on your own path means that you are on the right track. Don't let anyone deter you from that."[332]

In the April issue of his newsletter, MIT researcher and author of *Questions Are the Answer: A Breakthrough Approach to Your Most Vexing Problems at Work and in Life* Hal Gregersen shared one of his learnings from a 2015 trip to Everest. Invited by American mountaineer David Breashears to accompany him on this expedition, Gregersen asked him what leading multiple expeditions to the top of the mountain had taught him about leadership. Here it is: "Plans don't think." Breashears stressed that good plans are important, but they are not the end all, be all. When it comes down to it, the most successful people are those who are able to adapt when plans go astray.[333]

A river's meandering speaks to me about its constant sensing, adapting, "thinking" above and beyond the initial plans. It is not about giving in or up to obstacles, but rather about finding a way around them.

Close your eyes for a second and picture your change work like a river. What do you see: just a river or a river AND floodplains? When was the last time your change initiative stayed "safely within its riverbed" and maybe it only meandered a little bit at most? No flooding? Ever? Really? Flooding is usually associated with devastation, damages, disruptions and everything gloom and doom. The case of an "organizational flooding" is no different from a river overflowing, which makes me think about floodplains, their merits and their organizational equivalents.

Simply put, a floodplain is an area of flat land alongside a river that gets covered in water when the river floods. Floodplains have an important positive impact on flooding. Flood waters can spread over a large area of flat open land. This reduces flood velocities and provides water storage to reduce flood depths downstream, decreasing flood damage risks to communities. By offering rivers more room when they rise, floodplains reduce pressure on other manmade flood protection structures such as dams and levees. When filled with water, floodplains work like natural filters, getting rid of a lot of excess sediment and other nutrients that can worsen water quality and increase the costs of treating the water and preparing it for human use. On the disadvantage side, problems arise when floodplains are urbanized or used inappropriately. These pieces of land do come with obvious restrictions for use, and non-compliance incurs devastating costs.

One potential equivalent that comes to mind is a project pilot. That is an "organizational land" where you can give it your all, stress test, experiment, filter and sort, let it run in a safe environment. And oh, how the soil gets more fertile for it! If a pilot is not possible, at least do loads of scenario planning. Be intentional about allowing for floodplains in your change initiatives and your "organizational soil" will be all the richer for it. Also, do not be quick to judge an initiative by one "flood" or "waterfall." As Russian writer Mikhail Lermontov said in his 1840 novel *A Hero of Our Time*, "Many a calm river begins as a turbulent waterfall, yet none hurtles and foams all the way to the sea."[334]

I feel like meandering back to the "watching water" point and taking it a bit more granular. Watching a river is a distinct experience from watching an ocean, a stream, a lake, or...a puddle. And just as being specific about what kind of water you watch is important in describing an experience, it is critical you clarify and contract the right "change endeavor" with and for your stakeholders. Most of the time, the request sounds like this: "We need/The project lacks/I am looking for change management support." What does that mean? Never assume that "change management" stands for the "same kind of water." Clarify not just the type of the water body, width, depth, "the organizational river course," speed of flow, but also whether it is about a (main) river or a tributary.

A recent conversation made me reflect on how change/change management, communication and training, are used interchangeably depending on stakeholders' prior experience with and exposure to change work, their (subsequently influenced) initial needs assessment and little, if any, appetite and energy for clarification, vocabulary alignment and baseline setting... And now I have this question in my head: when people say "Oh, but I do love change and change work," if we keep the change as water analogy, what do they mean? Do they like swimming in the open sea? Floating down a river, or "city swimming" as the Swiss call their signature free river entertainment during summer? Jumping from rock to rock across a creek? Doing laps in a swimming pool? Taking a bubble bath? Watching the Rhine flow peacefully while sipping a glass of wine at one of the terraces on its banks?

Before I get carried away by another rivulet of thought, here is a closing takeaway for life and change work, courtesy of martial arts icon Bruce Lee. In one quote, he talks about how we should be like water, adjusting to whatever vessel we find ourselves in. "Now, water can flow or it can crash. Be water, my friend."[335]

Until next week, keep calm and "be water."

What Having Surprise Late-Night Conversations Teaches Me about Change Management

First published on July 5, 2022

Almost a decade ago, it so happened that my best friend and I lived in the same building in apartments one above the other. We used to joke about installing one of those fire poles between my kitchen on the seventh floor and hers just below and wondered whether having this would have made the short journey up the stairs a bit more frustrating...

One of my favorite memories from that time is a surprise late-night conversation. I stopped by her place for a quick chat after work, and one story turned into another and another and another and another... It was late fall and the night outside turned into a foggy, all-engulfing darkness, yet we never felt like turning the light on. I sat in my favorite spot on her couch, she was seated in her favorite armchair, two glasses and a bottle of wine on the coffee table between us. As it got darker and foggier outside, our stories got deeper, the moments of silence between them a little longer and more comforting.

I was reminded of this over the weekend when a dinner invite turned into a surprise late-night conversation. And because the terrace lighting did not work properly, we ended up chatting the night away in comfortable and comforting darkness, two glasses and a bottle of wine on the garden table between us. I seriously doubt our stories would have been just as deep had the lights been on...

Last night, a mild stomachache and the prospect of four more workdays ahead cut a deep conversation with an amazing friend shorter than either of us wanted it to be. It was a lovely summer night, we were on my terrace, the darkness was just the right amount of inviting and comforting for sharing stories. No wine this time, but two glasses of water, and a bit of light from the solar lanterns and citronella candles. Just enough to make me think that there might be some takeaways for change work in surprise late-night conversations.

Surrounded by the dark outside, you tread lightly in the dark within. I remember reading somewhere that people are more honest when physically tired, and this is why confessions oftentimes happen during late-night conversations. There definitely is some truth in this. Looking back at my late-night conversations, I can honestly confess in the glorious morning light as I type this that the stories shared were let out into the "anonymity of darkness" and they would not have happened in such an honest, raw way had the lights been on. It makes me smile to think that this almost sounds like the adult version of sharing scary stories around the campfire...

We have this instinct of going to the light, of turning the lights on, yet somehow sitting in the dark can be just what we need at times. As counterintuitive as it may sound, sitting in the dark on these occasions brought things into the light. Surrounded, embraced, protected by the dark outside, we treaded around lightly and felt our way through the dark within. This makes me think about how we can create the organizational equivalent of late-night conversations. How can we "snooze" the instinct to "turn the lights on" long enough to allow the honest, raw and most vulnerable stories to surface in safe, comforting conditions?

Who does the darkness create anonymity for and from? I cannot help but think about the role of darkness in late-night conversations. To me, it feels like it might have given me this…"cloak of anonymity." Maybe mostly from my own self, my self-judgment, self-doubt, self-blame, as I shared stories I safely kept in the dark within. As I was reflecting on the meaning of darkness and anonymity, I asked some of my closest friends—some native speakers, some not—what this idea meant to them. The words they came up with were: "obscurity," "namelessness," "confidentiality," "secrecy," "objectivity," "impartiality" and "knowledge."

The last one in particular, "knowledge," triggered a spin-off thought. I was reminded of a series of conversations around the advantages and disadvantages of allowing anonymous answers in surveys and, more recently, anonymous questions on Zoom webinars and calls. I fully agree it is important to trace input to its source for meaningful stakeholders engagement. Yet, I bet we can all think of at least a handful of times when the "Who said this?" question prompted by the results of a survey, a change readiness or impact assessment had nothing to do with…straightforward stakeholders engagement intentions.

On occasion, I find that this question says more about the people raising it, the environment that prompts it and the reasons behind choosing the anonymous question feature than it does about anything or anyone else. And that is insightful "knowledge" in anonymity. One of the best challenges in change work is turning insights, information and knowledge into forward-guiding, not backward-blaming, and how we respond to "Who said this?" might give us a great tipping point.

Late-night conversations should overpower the tiredness in the morning. Don't miss out on them. One of the things I love most about surprise late-night conversations is how much more deeply, truly and refreshingly awake I feel after losing some sleep. Not physically, and especially even less so with every year I am getting further away from being twenty... Mentally, emotionally and spiritually, late-night conversations turn "sleep loss" into "mind, heart and soul investment." Whatever the equivalent of late-night conversations is within your organization, acknowledge it, protect it and harness it as an essential part of change work superpower. Whether in life or business, we can catch up on lost sleep much easier than on lost awakening. Create anonymity in whatever way, shape or form is needed, resist the urge to turn the lights on for a tiny while longer and welcome the stories that come out.

Late-night conversations speak to me about courage and compassion—to speak them, to listen to them, to share them, to tread around in the outside and inside darkness. And sometimes, compassion is the only light we have. The only light we need. According to Henry S. Haskins, American stockbroker and man of letters from the first half of the 20th century, that is enough: "The darkness around us might somewhat light up if we would first practice using the light we have in the place we are. . . . There is not an ounce of our former strength which is not doing some sort of job, right now."[336] Maybe this "ounce of former strength" is the courage doing the job of keeping the light of compassion on.

Until next week, keep calm and tread lightly in the dark within.

What Cooking with Chocolate (and Eating It!) Teaches Me about Change Management

First published on July 12, 2022

July 7 is a very important day. Since 2009, it marks World Chocolate Day, sometimes referred to as International Chocolate Day, or just Chocolate Day, and this annual celebration commemorates the introduction of chocolate to Europe in 1550. And just in case you feel particularly festive when reading about chocolate, please know there are other special days to look forward to like White Chocolate Day (September 22), Milk Chocolate Day (July 28), Chocolate Covered Anything Day (December 16), Bittersweet Chocolate Day (January 10).

Many modern historians estimate that chocolate has been around for about 2,000 years, but recent research suggests that it may be even older. According to the "A Brief History of Chocolate" article in the *Smithsonian Magazine* dated March 2008, it's hard to pin down exactly when chocolate was born, but it's clear that it was cherished from the start. Etymologists trace the origin of the word "chocolate" to the Aztec word "xocoatl," which referred to a bitter drink brewed from cacao beans. The

Latin name for the cacao tree, "Theobroma cacao," means "food of the gods." American author Richard Paul Evans has a slightly different spin on the meaning of chocolate, yet equally touched by the divine: "Nothing heals the soul like chocolate. . . . Chocolate is God's excuse for broccoli."[337]

For several centuries in pre-modern Latin America, cacao beans were considered valuable enough to use as currency. One bean could be traded for a tamale, while 100 beans could purchase a good turkey hen, according to a 16th-century Aztec document. Both the Mayans and Aztecs believed the cacao bean had magical, or even divine, properties, suitable for use in the most sacred rituals of birth, marriage and death. Legend has it that the Aztec king Montezuma welcomed the Spanish explorer Hernando Cortes with a banquet that included drinking chocolate, having tragically mistaken him for a reincarnated deity instead of a conquering invader.

July 7 also happens to be the birthday of one of my dearest, best friends—and as soon as you get to know him, you see it is NOT a coincidence. Since we had our usual "Sunday chosen family dinner" this past weekend, chocolate ganache and raspberry tart seemed like an appropriate item on the menu. As I was waiting (and hoping) for the ganache to set, I started thinking about any tasty takeaways for change work from cooking with chocolate, and hopefully, they will make for some sweet treats below.

"Oh, you should never, never, doubt what nobody is sure about."[338] A recent conversation reminded me of this wonderful one-liner from Willy Wonka, the owner of the chocolate factory in Roald Dahl's *Charlie and the Chocolate Factory*. We were speaking about and brainstorming around the change vision for a project and one of my colleagues said: "We are not just making something new here. We are dreaming a dream, and we need to help people dream this dream and make it happen."

The moment of silence that followed this was the best sign that people on the Zoom call started dreaming.

Less than one day after the chocolate and raspberry tart, this "call to dream" made me think of Willy Wonka's wisdom and how that had always spoken to me about how essential it is to believe in the impossible. Oftentimes, change work is about turning things on their head, so why not start by never doubting what nobody is sure about? Just in case you need more encouragement, take some more from the same Willy Wonka, what feels like a special chocolate glaze dedication to anyone and everyone doing change work: "We are the music makers, and we are the dreamers of dreams."[339] Grab some chocolate and read the wonderful poem that gave us this line: British poet Arthur O'Shaughnessy's "Ode" from *Music and Moonlight* (1874).

No wishy-washy when it comes to chocolate. Or change. You're either all in, or all out. Whether large or small, quick or time-consuming, you cannot be "watery" about change. You can't go with half-measures either. Using chocolate as inspiration and an accountability buddy, here is a great takeaway from Italian writer and aphorist Fabrizio Caramagna: "A bar of chocolate. You don't have to just try it. You have to choose it with curious and impatient eyes. You don't have to just taste it. You must have it. You don't have to just swallow it. You have to bring it up in the mind."[340] I absolutely love this idea of a choice made with "curious and impatient eyes," and if there is such a thing as "ideal change readiness," I believe this would be the perfect description for it.

And since we are talking about sight, I can't help but confess to being highly susceptible to hypnosis by the luscious shine of good chocolate. There is a patisserie technique called "chocolate tempering," which consists of heating and cooling chocolate to stabilize it for making candies and confections. It gives chocolate a smooth and glossy finish, keeps it from easily melting on your fingers, and allows it to set up beautifully for dipped and chocolate-covered treats. To all intents and purposes, tempering chocolate is all about heat handling, and this is what links this technique to change work. It comes down to balancing skill, patience and good quality ingredients so that the final product retains its shiny gloss and snap. And if this sounds to you like balancing time(line), quality and resources on your projects, well, that's because heat handling is heat handling, whether for chocolate or change.

Stay close. Change work is not about supervising, it is about observing. It is not so much about communicating as it is about connecting. No one can do meaningful, deep, sustainable change work from an "ivory tower," from "the headquarters," from behind an e-mail address or from a dedicated, closed-off conference room. And for anyone needing a structured, phased approach, here is an easy-to-follow, foolproof tutorial courtesy of American cartoonist Terry Moore: "The 12-step chocolate program: Never be more than 12 steps away from chocolate!"[341]

In case you got to reading this far and are thinking all the responsible diet thoughts, please allow me to give you a belated World Chocolate Day gift. It comes in the form of my favorite definition of strength, a piece of wisdom from American writer, newspaper journalist, and psychoanalysis researcher Judith Viorst: "Strength is the ability to break a chocolate bar into four pieces with your bare hands and then eat just one of those pieces."[342] I wish you strength, my friends!

Writing this piece gave me inspiration for today's perfect evening plan. I will cuddle up on the sofa and watch for the gazzilionth time one of my all-time favorites, the 2000 *Chocolat* with Johnny Depp and Juliette Binoche. Mindful of spoiler alerts for those of you who haven't seen it—I know I pleaded earlier for believing in the impossible, but really? Is this possible???— here is the final takeaway for change work, some wise advice from the character Father Henri, played by Hugh O'Connor: "We can't go around measuring our goodness by what we don't do. . . . I think we've got to measure goodness by what we embrace, what we create…and who we include."

Until next week, keep calm and measure goodness in the good way.

What Changing Bed Sheets Teaches Me about Change Management

First published on July 19, 2022

Just as I was making peace with my resolve to write about being melted into oblivion by the heatwave, a spark of inspiration and energy ignited a timid creative push. Ironically, the heatwave bears most of the responsibility and, therefore, the credit for it!

My survival instinct (which sounds so much more constructive than "retail therapy craving") pushed me to buy a cooling gel mattress protector, which turned out to be one of my best investments yet. I was…how should I put it…"hopefully skeptical and skeptically hopeful" when I hit that "add to cart" button, but now I can say that I am "almost truly happy." This being said, my recent purchase turned out to be quite an accurate analogy for technology acquisitions. Simply getting and installing it did not (completely) solve the problem, and it actually created additional challenges. The fabric of the mattress protector is very silky and smooth (I know, I know, it starts to sound like an advertisement), which made it impossible to use with my regular flat bed sheets. The solution presented itself as one item I have spent most of my adult life hating passionately and skillfully avoiding up to this point: the fitted sheet!!!

As I struggled under the ceiling fan to put the fitted sheet on my previously-loved-for-its-sheer-size-but-not-anymore-because-of-the-fitted-sheet-torture bed, (in case you are wondering, a Euro Super King size bed, which makes for an approximate US California King), I wanted to find a deeper meaning to this effort. The thought of starting a series of unconventional fitness advice crossed my mind, and I could have launched it with this prompt: "Skipped gym today and put on a fitted sheet instead. Follow me for more guilt-free alternative fitness tips." Maybe as I was subconsciously processing the guilt of skipping a Tuesday random thought issue, the question popped into my mind: what if the whole point of this human-versus-fabric struggle was to bring inspiration for change work?

Still enjoying the somewhat cooler morning in one of my favorite bedding sets now complete with a fitted sheet, lying comfortably on the cooling mattress protector, here we go with a few takeaways, celebrating one (temporary and utterly vain) victory for human over fitted sheet this past weekend.

Arguably, the only thing more frustrating than a fitted sheet is a fitted sheet that doesn't fit. A few years ago, one of my best friends came to visit me in Tallinn. As she helped me put on new bed sheets and we folded the edges of the flat sheet under the mattress, she asked me why I didn't buy fitted sheets. Now please bear with me and suspend judgment for a second as you read my reply: "Because I don't know what bed I will sleep in next, so it makes no sense. The only thing more frustrating than a fitted sheet is a fitted sheet that doesn't fit." Relocating so often over the years meant that it made no sense for me to buy my own furniture, and one thing I really did not need to be strict about was the mattress size in the new home. Small fitted sheets are useless on a larger bed, while the larger ones need to be folded under the mattress, so what's the difference in using a flat one? At least, this was my reasoning…

Last year, I finally gave in and decided to settle for a little longer than usual and bought furniture for the first time in my life, which meant a mattress of my own choosing. And now, the cooling protector challenge made me reassess my surprisingly strong, and (slightly) irrational, standpoint against fitted sheets. I am not a full convert, and I believe this is yet another example of how things in life and business are never simply clear-cut binary. Fitted sheets helped me address a very specific immediate need under (stable) medium-term good visibility and control conditions, while flat sheets give me full flexibility for any future "bed changing decisions." Which leaves me with a question for change work: what is the "organizational bedding" equivalent for balancing long-game flexibility needs with clear(er) visibility over solutions for immediate requirements?

Bridging the great divide: ironed bed sheets or not ironed bed sheets. Is making time for it the solution to iron this one out? My relationship with my mom has slightly improved over the years, yet despite our best efforts, there is still one great divide that simply cannot be bridged: ironing the bed sheets. She sits firmly on the "You MUST iron the bed sheets to get a good night's sleep" edge, while I am on the "Oh, PLEASE!!! Can we just move on from this already?" side. When I used to go visit her, I felt really bad every single time the pristine-looking freshly ironed bed sheets would wrinkle the very moment I sat my pajamas and toiletries bag on the bed. Conversely, when she was over at my place, I could see her trying to take out the slightest creases in the pillowcases with the back of her hand before getting into bed.

For a brief time, we bridged this divide with the absolute textile abomination: the crepe cotton bed sheets!!! As life gave me new additions to my collection of natural wrinkles, the "beauty sleep" in crepe cotton bed linen started to turn me into a Shar-Pei, so thankfully that came to an abrupt halt a few years ago. When catching up over the phone this weekend, my mom told me that, among other things, she ironed some bed sheets… in red alert heatwave… Mumbling to myself something along the general lines of "Give me strength and Prosecco!!!", I quickly changed the subject.

Now, I can't help but think there is value for change work in this conversation. Apparently, the main challenge is having the time to iron and making the decision to allocate time to this activity (based on individual preferences, generational conditioning and other factors.) There is an interesting article on pedestrian.tv from back in April 2020 looking into empirical research conducted at the beginning of the pandemic about how people reallocated their time at home and whether they kicked ironing bed sheets up on their to-do lists. Titled "Apparently Some of You Iron Your Sheets & I Need to Know Where You Get The Fkn Time," it said that the results leaned toward "Team No Iron," with "Team Iron" winning extra points for strength of conviction—it turns out that most people on this team not only iron their sheets, but all of their bedding. They claim it's a luxury that adds even more satisfaction to fresh bedsheets, but even still, "Team No Iron" continues to question how some people have the time to pay such special attention to their bedding.[343]

This debate reminds me of countless change work conversations when, faced with the probability of not getting the exact expected (ideal) outcome and the necessity to reassess, executive sponsors and stakeholders come up with the solution to "put more hours into it." According to extensive research (no kidding!), getting the impeccable "hotel room-like look" for a bed comes with much more than just ironing time. It is about the (correct) choice and combination of fabric, size, washing cycle, detergent and softener, drying method, overall bedding skills of hospitality staff and so much more. Not every problem can be solved by "putting more hours into it;" sometimes you need to go back and make different choices and decisions.

Pro-tip to change bed sheets easier and faster: do it when you are NOT tired and impatient to just get into bed already. While mindlessly browsing the internet for tips and tricks to change bed sheets easier and faster, I ended up going down a rabbit hole on this topic on social media. Who knew that changing bed sheets is one of the most frustrating things ever and such a social unifier? I got fascinated by how many tips rely on turning things inside out, like the duvet cover or the pillowcases. At one point, I discovered this gem of advice from someone who introduced themselves as "working for a high-end bedding company": "...At work, we tend to turn the duvet cover inside out, secure the ends in the corner, then fold the cover over the filler and button that one up, then fluff and pray nothing moves."[344] Is it just me or does this sound a little bit similar to change work?

But then, oh my, in an ocean of tips and tricks related to "methodologies" and "interventions," this one shone bright as anything: change your bed sheets when you are not already tired, and everything seems so much harder because you just want to get into bed and call it a day! We tend to get so focused on the process and the steps and the tools that we oftentimes miss out on plain common sense and a little bit of forethought.

I read somewhere that the reason it is so difficult to neatly fold a fitted sheet is that you are actually folding five different sheets at the same time. This sounds borderline impossible to me, and not just because math is involved! In addition to making me understand the saying "Being an adult is like folding a fitted sheet" on a deeper level, it also prompted me to make a promise to myself. If, by some twisted science fiction development, humankind becomes required to iron bedding and fold fitted sheets, I will promptly open the door to the closest wardrobe. Not to take out the bedding to comply, but to run to Narnia!

Until next week, keep calm and think about what decisions and choices you can make differently before you get tired.

What Getting to the ER Teaches Me about Change Management

First published on September 6, 2022

All I wanted for this past Sunday was a calm day with nothing to do other than write the comeback article after the creative vacation for the #tuesdaychangemanagementrandom-thought series. It was not meant to be. Not in my wildest dreams did I imagine I would spend it in the emergency room of the Basel University Hospital, but hey, life happens in the most unpredictable ways!

Ever since I can remember, writing has been my go-to coping and self-healing mechanism. Those of you who know me well won't be surprised to know that there were Post-its and a pen in my backpack (my regular, everyday backpack that follows me everywhere), so I made good use of them during waiting times—while my papers were being processed, my health insurance card checked, and especially while I waited for the yummy IV cocktail to get into my body through the happiest-looking green cannula I have ever seen in my life. And when I could not write on Post-its because of tubes, wires, and EKG monitoring stuff, I did my best to write notes on my cell phone—and yes, those of you who know me well will be surprised to read this. It looks like you can teach an old dog new tricks after all!!! I was not ready to totally let go of my initial plan to write a change random thought, so there it was: what getting to the ER teaches me about change management.

It took me a lot longer to write this one, as it seems like all I can do since I got home is sleep, sleep, sleep, take the meds, sleep, drink water, sleep some more. It felt important to me that I write this as a way to process the last few days, to distract my brain from the pain, to guide my mind and body through healing and also to say THANK YOU to the wonderful hospital staff and all of you who have been sending lovely notes and thoughts my way!

So here we go, one takeaway at a time between naps, and I can only hope you find something inspiring, comforting and healing in this.

Aim to do the most for the most, and know you cannot do everything for everyone. Ever since the TV series *M*A*S*H*, I have been fascinated by the triage system in emergency situations. It felt like an indescribable and elusive means to "tame the chaos." The word "triage" originated in the French language and means "to select or sort." The French trace the meaning and use of the word back to the days of Napoleon when it was necessary for medical workers to determine who to see first in cases of mass injuries among wounded soldiers. The system has developed over the years to include several levels of determining priority to ensure that all patients receive the best possible service. There are many regulations, principles and procedures in place, yet it feels to me that there is a bit of art in this science, too. In an article published in *BMC Emergency Medicine Journal* in October 2011 titled "Emergency department triage: an ethical analysis," the authors mention "the four principles of biomedical ethics: respect for autonomy, beneficence, non-maleficence and justice," and these resonate so deeply when I think about them within the context of any change work.[345]

The article goes on to point out that "In emergency department triage, medical care might lead to adverse consequences like delay in providing care, compromise in privacy and confidentiality, poor physician-patient communication, failing to provide the necessary care altogether, or even having to decide whose life to save when not everyone can be saved."[346] Apart from the last consequence listed which thankfully is not present to such a life-threatening degree in projects, all the others fully apply in their organizational equivalents. Delays are project and change work realities, sensitive information leaks often occur, albeit without any ill intent, communication is not always the most efficient no matter how much effort goes into it and sometimes organizations and projects teams "fail to provide the necessary care altogether."

Boiled down to its core purpose, ER care aims to do the most for the most, and it comes with the hard reality that it cannot do everything for everyone. Above and beyond any strategic and operational ER drivers, the ethical principles are deeply meaningful for change work in today's organizations.

Information improves care. Hospital walls are often built with materials that obstruct cellular signals, including concrete, brick, and steel, to be able to withstand extraordinary conditions, and also to mitigate interference with critical care equipment. Hence "No Service" will oftentimes be displayed on your cell phone screen when in a hospital. As soon as I could, I logged into the guest Wi-Fi network so I could still connect with a couple of my best friends and, in all honesty, to feel less alone. Although not my first rodeo, ER is a mysterious, frightening and frustrating place (sounds a bit like change work, right?), and any connection helps, no matter how remote.

While waiting for the blood test results, I kept my mind busy and stumbled on a wonderful article: "6 Tips for Getting the Most Out of Your Emergency Room Visit, From an ER Doctor," written by Esther Choo, M.D., M.P.H., Professor of Emergency Medicine at Oregon Health & Science University, and published on self.com. She explains how having as much available information as possible regarding your medical history, current medication and routine healthcare setup, allergies, as well as insurance details, can make a huge difference in enabling ER staff to provide the best care for you in the shortest time.[347]

This point sparked a train of thought around the absolute criticality of organizations and stakeholders to open up about previous experiences and projects, blockers and failures and equally things that worked well, success stories, competing agendas, underlying "political currents" or "organizational conditions" of any kind, resourcing commitments and constraints, when entering conversations about expectations, needs and requirements from change work. My Sunday adventure reminded me there is no room for judgment in an emergency room, and no room for shame or blame either. Disclose freely and fully, in the comfort of knowing that information improves care. Also, keep in mind that organizations can also have "thick walls blocking signals" and information does not flow as freely and seamlessly as we oftentimes assume it does.

"Care shouldn't start in the emergency room."[348] I won't be using this quote from American politician Jim Douglas who served as the 80th Governor of Vermont to start a political or social discussion around access to healthcare. Rather, it felt like a good prompt to raise some questions within both the personal and organizational dimensions about how we define "care." What is our threshold for pain and discomfort? Where are we, as in our own selves, on our priority and monitoring list?

What symptoms, and for how long, are we willing to ignore until it is too late?

One of my professional "crusades" is to take conversations about change management upstream from the implementation and execution phase in an attempt to make it more than just transactional, operational, mechanistic and, quite frankly, directional and corrective. More often than not, change management feels like the ER of project management, and a lot of value is lost—for the people involved and impacted, for the project, for the project team and for the organization. "Care shouldn't start in the emergency room," and organizations should be more intentional with embedding preventive and diagnostic care, using change work mindset and principles before setting themselves up to becoming over-reliant on methodologies and tools.

Reflecting on my ER experience, above and beyond all these takeaways, the main thought in my mind is about the importance of the quality of staffing in the ER. People made the difference. They made me feel safe, comforted, heard and valued. The American College of Emergency Physicians mentions the following strategic drivers when speaking about the staffing of an ER: quality of care, patient safety, and the level of service you want to deliver.[349] It reads to me as great drivers for staffing an organization, and especially a project and change team.

Out of everything that happened on Sunday, I am most grateful for a wonderful nurse. I can only remember her first name, Andrea, who took exquisite care of me. She is the first nurse ever who managed to get the cannula up and running on the first attempt—quite an achievement, as my veins aren't any nurse's best friends. While she was connecting me to the medical equipment, I asked her whether she liked her job. Without skipping a beat, she said: "Oh, I totally love my job, I am in love with it. But it is a tough one. Not because of the workload or the crazy hours. Not at all. But because…[she paused for a second, searching for words] you have very high highs, and very low lows, and almost no 'just okay' in between, and somehow the low of the lows seems 'more' than the high of the highs, because that means we lost someone."

Until next week, keep calm and be safe!

What Loving Thunderstorms Teaches Me about Change Management

First published on September 13, 2022

Hi, my name is Minola and I am a ceraunophile. "Ceraun" is from the Greek word "keraunos," meaning thunderbolt. So, a ceraunophile is a person who loves lightning and thunder. I am a lover of thunderstorms.

There is something absolutely majestic about thunderstorms. I always felt frustrated and even somehow "punished" when I had to come inside during thunderstorms when I was little. All I wanted to do was stay outside and laugh with the clouds. That is what I imagined the skies were doing: letting out deep-belly, bray, guffaw laughter. As I have been enjoying adulthood for a couple of decades now, my take slowly changed. If you asked me why I enjoy thunderstorms, on some days I might reply, "Because it shows that even nature needs to scream sometimes…"

My second summer in Basel is coming to an end and I am happy to report a better understanding of what people meant by "Oh, you are here just in time for thunderstorm season" last year when I arrived. June and July are famous for intense weather phenomena in this region. Summers in Switzerland are known for their unpredictable, violent thunderstorms. This is especially true during periods where it is relatively hot by Swiss standards, like this year with three consecutive heatwaves. According to MeteoSwiss, lightning strikes around 150,000 times yearly in Switzerland, including secondary lightning.[350]

Several of my friends who visited me this summer were totally blown away by the sheer unpredictability and violence of thunderstorms, and that only made me pay closer attention. On Saturday, during a lovely brunch with friends, we somehow ended up speaking about the thunderstorms over the recent months, and that's when I felt there was some #tuesdaychangemanagementrandomthought inspiration in here somewhere… Should I try out introducing myself as a "lover of thunderstorms" when I join the next project as change lead? Hmmm, I would definitely give it a go…

Understand the movement of thunderstorms, and harness this knowledge on your change journey. A post on Britannica.com demystifies the movement of thunderstorms. They're mainly influenced by updrafts and downdrafts, as well as "steering winds in the middle layer of the atmosphere."[351] Maybe I should blame it entirely on my memory not being what it used to, but I did not remember this part of "steering winds in the middle layer of the atmosphere" from what I was taught in school. The "updrafts" and "downdrafts" sounded familiar, yet it was the mention of the steering winds that made me think about organizations.

Explained like this, the movement of thunderstorms is pretty similar to how change occurs in organizations. We have downdrafts from the senior stakeholders (the famous "top down"), updrafts from within the organization (the much sought-after "bottom up"), yet the steering winds happen in the middle. This could be, as an overall generalization, the middle management taking the strategic input from the "downdraft" and making it actionable and operational, then taking the insights from the "updrafts" and using them to inform decision-making. Within a team, the middle layer can be a team leader or a team assistant. I have witnessed HR and (Internal) Comms generating "steering winds." I am sure that anyone who has ever done a bit of change work has a small smile on their face reading this—yeah, you caused some "steering winds," you little wonderful thunderstorm rebel! Thunderstorms reminded me to be more mindful and intentional in engaging the "middle layer" so that the "steering winds" can be "winds of change…" And now I have Scorpions on heavy rotation in my head…

Embrace the release. Thunderstorms are a great way for the atmosphere to release energy. They also help keep the Earth in electrical balance. Did you know that without thunderstorms and lightning, the earth-atmosphere electrical balance would disappear in five minutes? We aren't really sure what would happen if this balance wasn't maintained… Psychologist Bruce Tuckman came up with the memorable phrase "forming, storming, norming, and performing" in his 1965 paper "Developmental Sequence in Small Groups."[352] It describes the path that teams follow on their way to high performance. Later, he added a fifth stage, "adjourning" (also known as "mourning"), to mark the end of a team's journey.[353]

Of all five of these stages, "storming" is consistently perceived as the most difficult to navigate. In the storming stage, people start to push against the established boundaries. Conflict or friction can also arise between team members as their true characters—and their preferred ways of working—surface and clash with other people's. At this stage, team members may challenge authority or management style, or even the team's mission. Just like thunderstorms release energy and keep electrical balance, the storming within a team helps its members along on their journey. In his book *The Five Dysfunctions of a Team*, Patrick Lencioni mentions "fear of conflict."[354] This dysfunction is an interesting alternative to the "storming" stage in the Tuckman model of team development. Whereas Tuckman suggests that all teams go through a period of conflict, Lencioni points out that if team members are lacking in trust they will not engage in robust debate. When different working styles, beliefs and values clash, you often look at your coworkers and think, "I thought I trusted you, but now I'm not so sure." Weather the storm together, and you will find out.

Let thunderstorms put things in perspective. When I was thinking about ideas for this piece, I remembered an excerpt from American writer David Levithan's novel in verse *The Realm of Possibility* about how incredible it is to fully experience a thunderstorm.[355] There is an increasing body of research that proves that for some, thunder and lightning are like magic pills against anxiety, depression and loneliness. The totality and power of the elements have a way of showing us our troubles are relatively small. "Stormy weather reminds people that the world is made up of forces bigger than they are, which makes their woes pale in comparison," says Laurel Steinberg, a New York City-based psychotherapist and a professor at Columbia University.[356] When overpowering nature does interrupt the course of one's life, it's hard not to be taken outside the self in its presence.

Psychologists also believe that thunderstorms positively impact our mental health and overall well-being. Our brain craves sensory input and the sound of rain or a thunderstorm can appease the brain's demands, which then calms us down. Sun, on the other hand, doesn't do anything to diminish sensory input and keeps our brains wanting more stimulation.

One other thought that came running into my mind is related to the perspective we gain when we reflect on how we react and respond during a thunderstorm. How much is instinct and reflex and how much is structure and planning? When thunderstorms happen unexpectedly, meteorologically and equally in our personal or professional life, what and who do we want to keep safe? Where—and who—is our safe shelter? What hesitations do we conquer?

Almost every ancient culture had its own interpretation of lightning and why it happened, and it's normally connected to the earliest known stories of humankind. In most cases, lightning earned a godlike reputation and was believed to be owned by the gods. Because of its raw power and the fact it comes from the sky, lightning is often associated directly with the gods' wrath, and it symbolizes some kind of divine punishment. There is one lesser-known meaning attached to lightning, loss of ignorance, and a post on symbolismandmetaphor.com describes it in a way that links it beautifully to change: "Throughout history, people believed that God invoked lightning strikes because people became too ignorant and lazy. It was meant as this wake-up call to do something and to change the way they lived. That's why we sometimes connect the lightning to loss of ignorance, which was employed by people who witnessed it in the past. It acted as a reminder to change and to stop making God angry, or else these strikes would continue to be threatening."[357]

As a closing thought, I will leave you with a wonderful reflection from Criss Jami, an American poet and essayist known as "The Killosopher," included in his book *Killosophy*: "The weather is nature's disruptor of human plans and busybodies. Of all the things on earth, nature's disruption is what we know we can depend on, as it is essentially uncontrolled by men."[358]

Until next week, keep calm and embrace the release.

What Visiting the Zoo Teaches Me about Change Management

First published on September 20, 2022

In a recent post, I confessed to suffering from the "saving things for a special occasion" affliction. It turned out it was not just "things," but also experiences. I had been wanting to visit the Basel Zoo ever since I moved here a year and a half ago, but somehow it just didn't feel like…the perfect time.

This past weekend, a very special friend was in Basel in between business trips and we ended up visiting the zoo on Sunday. The company and the sunny day made this "the perfect time" to do it. I must say I enjoyed it tremendously, while I also remembered—and fully agreed with—Ernest Hemingway, who once said that he didn't like going to the zoo on Sunday because people would make fun of the animals when in reality, the animals should be the ones making fun of us. It was a bit too "peopley" for my taste, but nothing could have ruined spending the day in my friend's company, speaking about anything and everything, sharing moments of silence and also deep belly laughs.

While we were visiting the vivarium, he jokingly said at one point: "I feel like there is a Tuesday article in here." I smiled and replied: "Funny you said that, as I just jotted down a couple of notes on the phone while you were watching the yellow fishes." We laughed and laughed, and now I am having a very early morning coffee and writing.

Make balancing and reconciling between opposing thoughts, opinions and feelings an exercise of self-awareness, not of judgment. Zoos always trigger me in two very different ways simultaneously. As American writer and journalist Thomas French once put it: "What's the reality of being inside a zoo, for the animals and for the people who love and care for those animals? There's a lot of joy, and there's a lot of loss."[359] I totally see and appreciate the value and benefits of zoos, while caged up animals always stir up a very deep, inner growl within me. This ambivalence reminded me of change work. Experiencing different, oftentimes opposing feelings and thoughts is an every change journey reality, whether it is a personal or professional change. Sometimes, I caught myself thinking "I am such a hypocrite," or "I should be able to pick one side," judging either side of the ambivalence and even myself for experiencing it.

There is a bit of comfort (and, in full honesty, it feels a little vain every now and again—potential self-judgment alert!) courtesy of American novelist F. Scott Fitzgerald: "The test of a first-rate intelligence is the ability to hold two opposed ideas in mind at the same time and still retain the ability to function."[360] I sometimes use this in change conversations when people talk about their own encounters with ambivalence all the way into cognitive dissonance. The Sunday visit to the zoo made me think about a different approach to ambivalence than judging it: acknowledging it, embracing it, exploring it with endless intentional curiosity. Making it a place where "there's a lot of joy, and there's a lot of loss."

"Zoo: an excellent place to study the habits of human beings."[361] I must give full credit for this takeaway to American humorist Evan Esar. Maybe because it was impressively (I wanted to write "overwhelmingly" here) crowded on Sunday, I found myself observing people almost a bit more than the animals. And I realized what zoos, airport luggage claim conveyor belts and rugby have in common: huddling like there is no tomorrow!! The thought triggered by this realization was around the importance of not keeping focus exclusively one-directional. I came to the zoo to see the animals, but what a wonderful place to observe humans, too!

Since then, I've kept on thinking about one-directional focus in change work and how sometimes the very practices and behaviors we focus on instilling and embedding in an organization during change are enacted the opposite way within the project team and environment. Here's what I mean: we aim for timely, in time, streamlined communication within the organization, yet somehow within the project team… We aim for clear contracting of expectations, roles, mandates from our stakeholders and wider organization, yet somehow within the project team… We aim for staying mindful and intentional about not "overwhelming" and "over-flooding" the organization, yet somehow within the project team… Not the best expression of ambivalence, I want to say elegantly. Someone once told me it was like being in a restaurant and the different experience depending on whether you are a diner or one of the kitchen staff…not entirely convinced, I must say.

On Sunday, I made a commitment to myself to stay intentional about what I choose to focus on and constantly challenge the directions of my attention. To the best of my ability, I will aim to make the project team and environment a role model of what we aim to create within the overall company. After all, the project team can be a great pilot environment for behaviors and engagement styles we want to drive within the wider organization. Go visit the nearest zoo and use this trip to also observe human beings. Stay self-aware, and as much as you can, create and nurture "huddle-free" bubbles of experiences around you—at the zoo and beyond. Stay intentionally and multi-directionally protective of mutual respect, civility, patience, understanding, care and support.

Are we aware of the organizational equivalent of "visitor attraction model"? In an amazing article on frontiersin.org called "What Is the Zoo Experience? How Zoos Impact a Visitor's Behaviors, Perceptions, and Conservation Efforts" dated July 30, 2019, the authors talk about studies suggesting that visitor behaviors are influenced by "both the presence of a zoo animal and the behaviors it displays. These studies have analyzed and tested the 'visitor attraction model;' the theory that active animals attract visitors and have used observable measures such as pointing, stopping, and length of time facing the exhibit. Results suggest visitors attend more to animal behaviors the more visible and active the animal is, and also tend to spend more time in exhibits when an animal is visible and active."[362]

This made me reflect on how much "visitor attraction model" is baked, more or less consciously, into our stakeholder engagement strategies and plans. Are our leading and managing change behaviors influenced by the "visibility" of the stakeholder group (sometimes by sheer size) and by the "visibility and activity levels of their behaviors"?

Inside the vivarium, I had the opportunity to witness a special moment. A wide-eyed kid was intently watching one of the seemingly empty displays while his family kept pressuring him to move on since "There is nothing here, come on, you are wasting time, look, there is a big snake over there." This wonderful little human would not move. A few minutes later, a breathtakingly beautiful blue-green snake appeared out of nowhere, uncoiling itself from a tree branch and gifting the little boy with a moment of pure joy! I got curious and checked the info; it was a rhinoceros snake, native to Northern Vietnam and Southern China. How can we embed some of that little boy's sense of unwavering, patient curiosity and wonder into our change work? How can we safeguard pockets of stillness, patience and waiting, when everyone pushes to move on and focus on the "more visible and active"?

One of my all-time favorite movies, up there with *Happy Feet* and *Chocolat* is *We Bought a Zoo*, a 2011 American family comedy-drama film loosely based on the 2008 memoir of the same name by Benjamin Mee. There is a quote in it that is my go-to whenever life or work (or life *and* work) get a little too close to being overwhelming: "You know, sometimes all you need is twenty seconds of insane courage. Just literally twenty seconds of just embarrassing bravery. And I promise you, something great will come of it."[363] May this also be an inspiring and comforting takeaway for change work.

Until next week, keep calm and go visit a zoo.

What Loving (and Eating!) Pizza Teaches Me about Change Management

First published on September 27, 2022

On a lovely Friday summer afternoon, I enjoyed an early pizza dinner with a couple of friends. Before we even arrived at one of my friends' places, there was a lively conversation, more like a "negotiation," on the topic of sharing food. We were trying to agree on the order so we could place it as soon as possible and pick it up on our way. There was a tense moment when one of us said: "Let's just order four different ones and we share." Do you remember the "Joey doesn't share food!!!" moment from the TV series *Friends*? Well, it turned out I was friends with some Joeys… Maybe because I have been doing change work for so long, my inner Joey comes out to play with a twist: I don't share food, but I am open to exchanging food. This is why I try to be the last one to place the order. If the exchange option is not available because somebody ordered something I do not like, then I revert to "full Joey default setting."

It was during our pizza exchange dinner that the thought of writing a #tuesdaychangemanagementrandomthought about pizza first came to mind. Many pizzas later, as in a few months later, it popped back up on my writing radar. Last week I ordered one of those oven stands that allows you to bake three pizzas at the same time, a wonderful kitchen toy for future Sunday family dinners. As I put it together for a quick test, the idea of looking at pizza through the lens of change work came back and I could not shake it off. So here we go, some "slices of thought" I hope you will enjoy. They also come with a confession: I can't turn water into wine, but I can turn pizza into breakfast. Bon appetit!

In the crust we trust. This is the pizza equivalent of "change happens at the edges." Have you noticed how at any gathering of people, the awesome conversations and interactions almost always happen around the edges? Somewhere away from the spot where the music is loudest, voices are highest, around the edges where people can actually hear each other? Those smaller groups create a sub-party all of their own, like a more personal, meaningful alternative to the main event. And, more often than not, the food stands are on the sides, anyways, so there's an "edge perk" for you!

From a different perspective, any habit change contains a step focused on small, simple actions that slowly, but surely, chip away at the core of the pattern from its "edges." Even when we think about a human body cell, its edge, the membrane, is where interaction and exchange with the outer environment happens. Everything that is innovative, disruptive, different in any way, shape or form is perceived and deemed as risky, and the "middle of anything," be it an organization, a political party, a college party, might think there is too much to lose to something that feels dicey. Thinking about the edges of change, "underdog" came to mind. Change oftentimes starts at the edges, with the underdogs, and moves toward the center. In pizza words, in the crust we trust.

Sometimes, no sense makes most sense. Have you ever wondered how come we enjoy triangle(ish) slices of a round piece of magical deliciousness that comes in a square box? I know pizza does come in different sizes and shapes, and all of them are fabulous and critical to maintaining happy life on Earth. However, I am sure we can all agree that the most commonly known and enjoyed variety is the round pizza. I stumbled upon a wonderful read on crustkingdom.com on "Why Is Pizza Round? The Box Is Square, And It's Cut Into Triangles" and will take a few lines to share some of its fascinating knowledge with you. Pizza is round because, before cooking, the dough is shaped into a ball to rise. It is easiest to shape and stretch a ball of dough into an evenly thick base, and later on, a circular pizza is easier to cut into equal pieces like a pie. Let's not forget that sometimes dough is stretched by spinning and throwing it, which naturally makes it circular. Also, traditional Neapolitan pizza has clear and set rules, and one of them says it must be round.

Moving on to the square box. Square boxes are much easier to make, needing only one piece of cardboard. Round boxes need a few pieces. One piece of cardboard can be unfolded flat and so boxes take up less space when being stored. Square boxes are stacked in freezers and shelves easily, and flat edges stop the box from falling. A circular box takes up the same width and length, so there's no space-saving improvement. Last, but not least, it's cheaper to make square boxes as they are common and so don't need bespoke production. At this point, you might ask "Why not a square pizza for a square box then?" Here's a possible answer: "It is simply easier to make a pizza round from its dough ball to its stretching technique. So, this has become well known and traditional. There is the argument that square pizza would be harder to get out of a square box, so a round pizza is actually easier to eat."

Getting closer to actually eating a pizza, we come to the point of cutting it into its iconic triangle slices. Pizza is cut into triangle slices because that is the most common way to equally divide a circle. Plus, by slicing it from the crust to the center to make a triangle, every slice gets an equal portion of toppings and crust. In the spirit of full disclosure, it needs to be mentioned that "Some pizza is cut into squares, a good example of this is the Chicago thin crust pizza which is popular in Midwestern United States. The pizza usually has toppings pushed right to the edge and so there is little or no crust. A portion will therefore have toppings on the whole square. This cut can sometimes be referred to as 'party-style'. This is because it is easier to cut and serve a large pizza in squares than slices – the slices become too long to manage from crust to center."[364]

In summary, pizza is easier to make round rather than any other shape. And pizza boxes are easier and cheaper to make square than circular. It's cut into triangles as that is the natural way to divide a circle. That is why we get a mismatch of all these different shapes. Take a second to think about how this resonates with change work. Sometimes, things do not have to make sense. They just need to…come together and feel right. And make you feel good. Triangle slices of a circular thing coming in a square box; it looks like a series of perfectly rational, common-sense decisions made in blissful isolation from each other, which make weirdly perfect sense together—when it comes to pizza, at the very least!!! Allow apparently mismatched change items to come together and you might be surprised at how sometimes no sense makes most sense, based on a magic all of its own.

"**Every pizza is a personal pizza if you try hard and believe in yourself.**"[365] Cannot thank American actor and comedian Bill Murray enough for this gem!!! I do change work, which is quite lonely work, and brings me disapproving looks on a daily basis. The absolute most disapproving look I ever got in my life was a few years ago when I ordered pizza in Italy and asked for extra mozzarella topping. Apparently, that is a big no-no, as each pizza in Italy is made with the "perfectest" amount of mozzarella from the get-go. I imagine asking for pineapple topping would have ended with me getting escorted out of the country by the carabinieri…

In retrospect, this small story makes me think about how we react to feedback, especially during change work. I guess it is quite difficult to get to the disruption level of ordering pizza with extra mozzarella within an organizational transformation, but how strongly and steadily we feel about our preferences, choices and end outcomes is a fascinating element in change work. A friend of mine oftentimes says: "Feedback is like pizza. You choose what toppings you keep and which ones you discard."

Here's a twist I had the joy of hearing recently during a team development workshop. We were unpacking a "slice" of a voice of the customer feedback, and one participant remarked that some inputs did not feel as directly addressed to this particular team. And, here it comes: "I agree, this might not be directly about our team and our role. But if I read it, I still learn something important about what my internal clients find valuable and meaningful in our interaction." There we have it: feedback made relevant through intentional effort to stay curious and open-minded as well as unwavering self-awareness and improvement. Had this workshop been in-person, I would have celebrated this with ordering pizza for everyone. My treat! "Every pizza is a personal pizza if you try hard and believe in yourself," just as every feedback, no matter how directly or indirectly targeted at you, your role or your team, holds a meaningful nugget if you try hard and believe in your power to change yourself, your work and those around you.

Right after I press "publish" on this week's piece, I will place an order for pizza. With extra mozzarella. And if you wonder where I stand in the polarizing, society-cutting discussion about whether I love or hate pizza crust? As intense a debate as the ones around cilantro or licorice. My answer is I LOVE CRUST. And I also love cilantro and licorice. Not on pizza, though. By the way, did you know there is a 2021 movie called *Licorice Pizza*? It is an American period comedy-drama film set in 1973 that follows the development of a young couple's relationship. Look for it, order some pizza and enjoy!

Until next week, keep calm and do good, be nice, order pizza, repeat.

What Looking for Daily Celebrations Teaches Me about Change Management

First published on October 11, 2022

There is a short list of websites I check each morning with the first sips of coffee—there's no news site among them, I keep those for when I am properly caffeinated to deal with the world. Instead, the list is made up of a handful of daily "pick-me-ups," reliable go-tos for chuckles, reflections, oftentimes full-on laughing out loud—as in "coffee spilling alert"—laughter! The "Sarcasm as a Second Language" Facebook group is one of them. Followed closely by "Moms Who Drink and Swear," a wonderful gem of safe venting, ranting, unwavering support and an infinite supply of moral and emotional hugs, even for those of us who do not have children (as they describe their audience: "any woman with a huge heart and a mouth that sometimes needs washing out with soap")—now also available as a book, by the way.[366] It gave me the best definition to date of "political correctness;" please reach out to me directly if you are curious to hear/read it and you can handle a good laugh. Set your coffee safely aside before you do that, please!

A while ago, this carefully curated morning routine got an upgrade: I started looking for the daily celebrations by simply searching for "what do we celebrate on [*insert date here*]." It is a great curiosity exercise and quickly turns into wonderfully unexpected learning journeys. I remember waking up to a particularly gloomy day, then looking for the daily celebrations, and guess what? Happy World Nutella Day!! I sent a couple of "Happy Nutella Day" notes to my friends and the day turned into a sweet, festive blur of laughter and calories. This past weekend, I had no ideas for the Tuesday piece, but one came to me as I learned we celebrated World Curious Events Day on Sunday, a day to wonder about everything we've ever wondered about. So why not wonder about what looking for daily celebrations teaches me about change management?

Curiosity is the best celebration finder. I was thinking about the organizational equivalent of my morning routine of searching the daily celebrations. And it might very well be an amazingly innovative method (disclaimer: I just read "Sarcasm as a Second Language" before writing this piece): asking—simply and, most importantly, genuinely asking people about their experiences and journeys. The small joys, sometimes the small mercies, too, the everyday wins that steadily pile up, the Big Bang moments also. You find so many wonderful daily celebrations if you simply ask and listen. And who knows, you might even help those around you put a celebration spin on their everyday life, too.

A clarification is in order: I do not advocate for forced or false positivity (trying to be positive about *everything*, even if the situation is tragic or serious). Sometimes, the best thing to celebrate is the compassionate and courageous curiosity to look at things and acknowledge they went off track, terribly wrong or totally and unexpectedly different than planned.

Do not drown the celebration under the preparation.
Some of my worst childhood memories are related to family reunions preceded by enthusiasm-killing extensive preparation. Cleaning, cooking, "Remember to do this!", "Do not, I repeat, do not do this!", "Please remember to say this!", "Delete those words from your vocabulary over the next few days!" In hindsight, I am fascinated by how much longer the list of don'ts was in comparison to the one with the "approved and allowed items." By the time the actual celebration happened, I was so tired, and equally sick and tired of everything (and some people) that I just wanted it to be over and done with.

I sometimes have flashbacks of these moments when looking at project and change plans. There is a ton of research available on the risks of under-planning and under-preparing when doing project management and change work. Unjustly so, there is significantly less focus on the pitfalls of over-planning and over-preparing. We all, personally and organizationally, have different milestones and thresholds on the under-planning, planning and over-planning spectrum. I firmly believe that preparation is essential. I have also witnessed resounding failures prompted by over-preparation, most of the time resulting from building false expectations and depleting enthusiasm. Sensing and negotiating the thresholds is as much art as it is science. And it takes years of practice and exposure to different realities to eventually learn to lean into your intuition and trust the calling of spontaneous curiosity. The best thing about my daily celebrations is how spontaneous they feel—it is like being surprised by a "daily special" every day.

A gem of change work advice comes courtesy of Henri Nouwen, a Dutch Catholic priest, professor, writer and theologian: "Each day holds a surprise." But we must be willing and open to receive it, no matter what it brings.[367] Plan and prepare, expect the surprise, celebrate. Repeat.

We open two gifts every morning. For years, American author Zig Ziglar's "I opened two gifts this morning. They were my eyes"[368] has been stored in my memory. Something made it more present in my mind in recent times. Maybe it was the COVID pandemic. Maybe a more mindful approach to compassion and gratitude. Maybe age. Maybe the combination of all of these and much more.

A couple of days ago, I stumbled upon an online conversation and one of the speakers mentioned the famous "None so blind as those who will not see," pointing out the fundamental change in meaning it held from the other existing version of "those who cannot see;" "cannot" removes responsibility, "will not" implies choice. This conversation made me think about willful blindness and, strangely enough, about Zig Ziglar's quote. Every morning is a celebration. We receive the gift of doing, and equally undoing. Of learning, and equally unlearning. Of looking ahead, and equally looking back. Of preparing, and equally expecting a surprise. As in life, so in change work.

This edition of #tuesdaychangemanagementrandomthought goes out into the wide world web on October 11. Do you know today's celebrations? It is the International Day of the Girl, based on a resolution passed by the United Nations General Assembly in December 2011—a day seeking to bring awareness and solutions to the unique challenges that girls around the world face every day, a celebration aimed at empowering girls and amplifying their voices. It is the anniversary of the inauguration of the University of Sydney in Australia back in 1852. This year, October 11 also marks the Boat Racing Festival in Laos and National "Face Your Fears" Day in the USA.

I was trying to find words to best express how celebration is a choice. A choice of being and equally doing. And how can it be said any differently than a wonderful thought from the legacy of Abraham Joshua Heschel, a Polish-born American rabbi and one of the leading Jewish theologians and philosophers of the 20th century? He said we are forgetting "the power of celebration" as we choose to be entertained instead. "Celebration is an active state, an act of expressing reverence or appreciation. To be entertained is a passive state—it is to receive pleasure afforded by an amusing act or a spectacle…" A celebration is really a "confrontation;" it gives voice to the meaning of our actions.[369]

Until next week, keep calm and celebrate every day!

What Making Sense of a Breakup Teaches Me about Change Management

First published on October 18, 2022

A little bit over a year ago, on an early Thursday night in August, my world came crashing down. You know those special effects in movies that make everything spin at nauseating speed, then explode into billions of tiny shards, the screen goes black, and you get this ringing in your ears that makes it hard to even breathe? That is the closest I can get to putting how it felt into words. We were laughing and talking about anything and everything like we always had, even making our usual inside jokes about "the COVID-special third party in our relationship—the internet connection," searching for plane tickets to finally resume and enjoy our new life together in Switzerland after the logistics nightmare of the pandemic, looking forward to filling all our dreams and plans made for two, as well as the new home, with vibrant life and play and laughter. With us. And then, two hours later, nothing. Literally. And nothing ever since.

Today's #tuesdaychangemanagementrandomthought has been in the making for a long time. Not in writing, but in the making of the decision to publish it. It took me the least amount of time to write in comparison to all the other editions in the series; maybe I have been carrying it in me all along.

Three separate occurrences over the past two days prompted me to publish it today.

First, over the weekend, I got a connect invite from someone who happened to find a recording of a talk on self-rejection I gave a couple of years ago. The presentation started with "Hello, my name is Minola, and I am a self-rejection subject matter expert." By pressing the "publish" button today, I want to change that into "Hello, my name is Minola, and I am a recovering self-rejection subject matter expert."

Yesterday, I started working on the content of a leadership team development workshop and I looked for some samples of leadership stands. I was reminded of my own, one I wrote a few years back when we launched an organizational culture think tank with a handful of awesomely inspiring people. By pressing the "publish" button today, I want to be able to confirm it is still valid: "I stand for unwavering authenticity that creates a safe space for those around me to feel inspired, empowered and accepted to live in and by their full and unaltered truth."

Lastly, I realized this morning that this would be edition no. 99 in a series of 100, my self-imposed limit. So, it is befitting to talk about endings so close to the wrap-up, and yet at a safe distance to still be able to end it on a positive note. By pressing the "publish" button today, I want to role-model the last takeaway of this issue as best as I possibly can.

Find a safe space to just "talk it out of your system." I found out that, for me personally, simply putting fuzzy thoughts and feelings and "the knot in my stomach" into words, as coherently as possible (I had to teach myself not to have rigid expectations of coherence all the time) made everything more bearable and got me one infinitesimally tiny step at a time closer to making sense out of what happened. Hearing it said out loud also helped me with putting it into perspective. I have found it easier to listen to myself while speaking with others.

Change work comes with a huge load of distressing, unsettling, deeply disruptive and oftentimes soul-crushing information and action, for both those who lead it and those experiencing it. It comes with its own sense of loss and grief in different ways, shapes and forms for each of us. It makes a hugely positive difference if we have a safe space to just "talk it out of our system" with a person or small group of people in a safe environment with no rigid expectations of full academic-level coherence. Just talk it out. And if the same words and things come out over and over again, let them come out. Over and over again, until they hold no more power over your mind and heart and soul. Talk them out into nothingness. Remember: if you're not speaking it, you're storing it, and that gets heavy.

Ask for help and learn to ask for the help that helps you. It has been feeling like an infinite rollercoaster. Some days it feels like a distant, hazy memory; I even question whether any of it actually happened. Some other days, I wake up and the first thing I feel is like all the million small pieces that my heart broke into get broken into infinitely smaller ones. It is excruciating. And sudden. It is excruciatingly sudden and suddenly excruciating. There have been days when I could not, still cannot "hear" solutions, I don't want to "learn the lesson," "trust the process," "practice gratitude," "say affirmations," "change the door nameplate, burn his s**t and move on" (definitely more tempting than the affirmations), "stay kind and compassionate."

Honestly, I just want to breathe, like really breathe, simply breathe a full, deep breath. People want to help, or at least say something helpful, and I truly and deeply believe this drive comes from a place of genuine care and love. Yet, sometimes I need to push back on it because...well, the help is not helping.

The challenge is to push back in such a way that I still make my hurt heard and keep the (positive) relationship with the person who offered help the best way they knew how or in a way that they found helpful for themselves in similar situations. It is often said that we comfort others in the ways we want(ed)/need(ed) to be comforted, so an offer of help is more about the person who makes it than ourselves. Which makes the accountability and ownership of asking for help—and even more importantly, of asking for the help we need—our very own prerogative.

I also know there is a fine, fluid line between "love" and "tough love," but I am not speaking about that. A very good friend of mine calls it the "List of Toxic Shoulds and Should-Haves." You know what I mean, that "Instructions Manual" that apparently is out in the world and you didn't get your copy, with clear regulations and descriptions regarding the length, intensity and manifestations of your grief, the correct sequencing of feelings, emotions and thoughts, all the steps and tools for the mental, emotional and residential, if applicable, cleansing, culminating with the ultimate exorcism of any shred of self-doubt, self-judgment and carbs-fueled self-pity for all eternity evermore.

My takeaway for change work is that while good intentions and genuine caring are all-encompassing and infinite, the needs and requirements for help are exceptionally individually specific and have boundaries. Help and support should be offered as most meaningful and helpful, not simply as readily available, "time-tested," and with an impressive collective track record.

Turn shame into courage. Pain, hurt, longing, sadness, regret, loss, anguish, confusion, hope, denial, more hurt, yearning, loads more hope, mind-numbing and soul-crushing grief—I have been feeling them all. On an endless repeat loop. I struggle with anger. I can't feel it. It comes very easy to feel angry at myself, though. Somehow, along the journey, an overwhelming feeling started to form, drowning all the others. Shame. I caught myself ruminating: "What was I thinking??? I wasn't some 15-year-old naïve innocent shielded from the world in a remote, disconnected settlement in the virgin forests along the Amazon… How have I let this happen? How have I fallen for it?"

Well, it did happen. And although this wasn't my first breakup, it is definitely the first such event of its kind that counts as a "before and after" delineating moment in my life. Maybe I will never fully understand why, maybe I am not even supposed to get that understanding. I went on a walk recently with one of my friends, and I confessed struggling with shame. She listened to me, then asked me: "What is the opposite of shame?" As I was letting out a deep sigh (secretly bracing myself for an excerpt from the "Instructions Manual"), she said "It's courage. Think about it! Just let it settle in your mind and heart, it is courage."

I have been challenging myself ever since to think about it like this and replace "shame" with "courage." I have been keeping Post-it notes close by, and every single time I feel a shame-thought creeping up, I reach for a Post-it and write it out, replacing "shame" with "courage." Courage to feel everything I have been feeling. Courage to speak about it. Courage to try again. Courage to simply listen and be there for someone else. Courage to say, "I know, me too." Courage to ask for help. Courage to ask for the help that helps me.

I have come across shame in change work, it usually follows right after a "blame game." More usual occurrences are those of embarrassment, discomfort, unease. I have seen them manifested in people around me and I have also experienced them within organizational settings. There should be a "change oath" mandatory for anyone going into change work binding them to turn and help people around them transform shame into courage. It takes courage to initiate a change. It takes infinitely more courage to try again after a failure. It takes courage to ask for change support. It takes even more courage to push back and ask for change help that actually helps. It takes courage to speak about your organizational change journey. It takes courage to simply listen and be there for someone else. It takes courage to say, "I know, me too."

We have been speaking about imposter syndrome in our professional lives for years now. In full honesty, I have been experiencing some sort of imposter syndrome in my personal life after the breakup. It feels like carrying around huge chunks of self-doubt, self-judgment, deafening echoes and heavy inertia of all the "not enough" self-assessments… It takes safe space to talk it out of my system, loads of help that helps, and… something else that I have yet to earn the right to call "courage."

There is a bit of dialogue in *The Wonderful Wizard of Oz* that perfectly describes my feeling. The Wizard is telling the Tin Woodman that he should be thankful that he doesn't have a heart because they are not "practical," at least until the day "they can be made unbreakable."

The Tin Woodman's reply is simple: "*But I still want one.*"[370]

Until next week, keep calm and courageously hold on to "But I still want one."

What Hosting People in My Home Teaches Me about Change Management

First published on October 25, 2022

For the best part of my childhood, my dream career was being a guest. When people asked me what I wanted to become when I grew up, "a guest" came out without skipping a beat. It seemed like the coolest thing to be—welcomed everywhere, exposed to new things, everyone seemed really interested in knowing my favorite things to do, what I liked to eat and drink and dedicated themselves to fulfilling my every wish. When my family hosted, everything had to be perfect for the guests. Being a guest quickly won a magic kind of status in my mind, coming infinitesimally close to being like Santa Claus—after all, there was always that element of "getting something nice for the host" on top of everything else.

A few days back, I mentioned to someone this would be my last #tuesdaychangemanagementrandomthought and they said, "Oooooh, it's a big one, I bet it will be something special." I have been thinking about this ever since, and somehow writing about hosting people in my home popped up. After all, it feels like this is what I have been doing every week for the past two years: welcoming you into my mind and heart and trying to offer you some of the best bits of my life and work experience. I am deeply grateful for all of your "visits," and equally for allowing me to be a guest in your lives by offering me the most generous gift of time and attention. After all, this is the very best gift a host can offer their guests.

So, as I am hosting you for the 100th time, here are the "thank you for visiting" takeaways of today. I can only hope they will make for nice souvenirs.

A guest sees more in an hour than a host in a year. I fell in love with this Polish proverb the first second I heard it. Every single time I host someone, it is like I get to see my home with new eyes. Sometimes, it is because of something they say about the layout, the light, the colors, the sounds, the smells. Other times, I just pay attention to what they seem to naturally enjoy—a spot on the couch, the hanging chair on the terrace, the bookshelves, a particular seat at the dining table. I rediscover my home through their experiences.

Doing change work makes you a guest within organizations, teams, people's lives and work environments. Go into it with wonder, awe and respect. Discover their "homes" enthusiastically, and equally humbly and dutifully, and share what you experience with them in a way that creates comfort, understanding, safety, acceptance and mutual gratitude. And, hopefully, the desire to welcome you again.

"A guest is really good or bad because of the host or hostess who makes being a guest an easy or a difficult task."[371] This quote from the longest-serving First Lady of the United States Eleanor Roosevelt makes me reflect on whether, when and how we get to "one rule too many." I remember visiting a great aunt when I was little, and she seemed like a tireless generator of rules. Of course, I was labeled as a "naughty guest" on some (most, actually…okay, all!!!) occasions. And once in history

I was considered a "wonderful guest"—I was actually scared of doing anything, so I ended up spending an entire summer weekend reading on the sofa, too afraid to "discover on the go" the endless list of rules and regulations regarding inside and outside shoes, meal schedules and table etiquette, interactions with the neighbors, dress code, proper conversation topics, most efficient use of lights, going to bed routine... I forgot most of the mind-boggling rules, but the one feeling that has always stayed with me was how unfair it all seemed because I was in constant "breach of rules" simply because I could not keep up and, most of all, did not know them upfront.

Every now and again I am reminded of this "Hostzilla" great aunt when I look at change strategies and plans. I challenge myself and those around me to assess the rigidity of the initiative. Are all rules and regulations necessary? Are all of them equally firm? Are all of them rules or can we "downgrade" some to (strong) personal preferences or expectations? And are all rules made known upfront? Whenever I host people in my home, I always tell them there is only one single rule: make sure the curtains cover the terrace access when the doors are open so that bees cannot come in. It is difficult to get them back out without hurting them, so let's make sure they cannot come in in the first place. We can work around anything and everything else and find our joint balance in the flow.

One amazing lesson I learn every single time I host someone in my home is how unspoken expectations or personal preferences cannot be considered requests or requirements. Whenever something happens that triggers me in a certain way, I challenge myself on whether that is a hard boundary or simply an instance of the good old "this is not how I do things around here"—which, to make things even more interesting, was never explicitly "laid out as the law." And if this sounds familiar, then I am sure you have been in senior stakeholder conversations where statements like "I did not expect this," "This wasn't supposed to happen," "This wasn't supposed to happen like this" sound like expectations, maybe not even fully and clearly expressed or contracted, that somehow grew into their own life as unwritten rules. Please, don't be like my "Hostzilla" great aunt. You are sooooooo much better change hosts!!!

Honor the vulnerability and create a safe space for it. No matter how considerate, mindful and intentional we are about creating and ensuring privacy, having people in our home is a deeply vulnerable experience for both host and guest. We get a peek into each other's most personal routines, we get "behind the scenes" tickets to everyday life performances, we expose so many of our subconscious reactions and reflexes. I have always believed that, regardless of whether we're a host or a guest, sharing a personal space is a sign of trust and it has an unspoken, yet unwavering "suspend all judgment" contract that comes with it.

In change work, you constantly shift between being a host and being a guest. You welcome people and organizations into new ways of thinking, doing, asking, learning, ultimately being, while also visiting them in their work life and organizational settings. Always honor the vulnerability, regardless of what side of the hosting or visiting you are on, and create a safe space for it.

It is difficult, and very emotional, to bring this piece and the series to an end. But, as the late Prince Philip, Duke of Edinburgh, taught us: "The art of being a good guest is to know when to leave."[372] You have been hosting me in your lives for two years, and it has been the most amazing guest experience of my life. It looks like, after all, I did get to live my childhood dream and become a guest. I will forever host you in my heart with wonder, awe, respect and gratitude.

Until next week, keep calm and welcome people in your mind, heart and soul.

Oh, wait, there is no next week!!!

EVERYDAY INSPIRATION FOR CHANGE

Let me rephrase this…

On any given week, keep calm and live life with an open mind and an open heart, with curiosity, courage and compassion. And please, please, please, never stop looking for the magic in everyday life that gets us through the most wonderful and challenging of changes.

What Writing 100 Tuesday Change Management Random Thoughts Taught Me about Change Management

First published on November 1, 2022

This is the "inertia edition" of the #tuesdaychangemanagementrandomthought, which was not in the plan. I canceled the recurrent Tuesday 4:00 AM alarm, celebrated the 100 editions, kept telling myself a creative break was one of my best ideas yet…and still, here I am, typing away, feeling like there is one more issue that wants to go out. Jokingly, yet very honestly, I keep saying I have always been better at "hello" than "goodbye," so I guess this is irrefutable proof.

The Tuesday change thoughts have gone on for a little over two years, and it's one of the most consistent journeys in my life. At some point, I started lovingly calling them my "sanity milestones." Regardless of what was going on in my life or work, I kept on waking up on Tuesdays at 4:00 AM, listening to music for about one hour, then sitting down in front of the laptop and letting out whatever popped up in my mind by 8:00 AM. Some say this was discipline. Others, myself included, do not see the "method in the madness," yet it worked. In more ways than one. I kept telling myself that if I could do it every Tuesday, with everything else going on within and around me, then I could definitely get through whatever happened until the next Tuesday. One more week. And one more week. And one more week. Every week.

I have been reflecting on what this journey has taught me, and my random thoughts are below. Hopefully, there is still a drop of inspiration in them for you; I sure know they will stay with me forever.

Find your voice and never ever let it go quiet! The first post came totally out of nowhere. I was baking bread during one of the lockdowns and I just felt this pull to write about it through the lens of change management. For the first time in a looooooong time, I did not stop to self-reject. It felt right, it came naturally, and I did it for me. Could I have written it better? Of course! But what makes that tentative, even awkward piece of writing perfect is the sheer fact it happened. And regardless of the views and likes and comments, what I call the "vanity metrics," I kept going.

Does this sound like change work? Good, because it is very much like it. You have doubts, yet you do it anyway. It could have been done better, yet it feels the best you could do within your current circumstances. Most importantly, is it true to what you think, believe and feel in the moment, based on all the facts and your deepest, unfiltered gut feeling? Then it is perfect. If I had a cent for every single time I heard the most popular question of my childhood in my mind—"What would people say?"—I could write this while enjoying my very own private island in the sun!

I have been blown away and infinitely humbled by how many people resonated with my random thoughts. There have been instances when people who never even engaged with the posts mentioned something from my writings with a smile or a thoughtful expression on their faces. Such precious gifts to me! Comforting, healing, validating, humbling and motivating!!!

One of my biggest takeaways from this journey is that we sometimes sacrifice authenticity for safety until we realize the only real, true safety we have is our authenticity. Find your voice and never ever let it go quiet! Is it shaky? Use it anyway. Is it raspy? Use it anyway. You feel like you have nothing to say? Then just show up. Be present over perfect, and please know that simply showing up is the most meaningful—and oftentimes the loudest—statement you can make.

Put your heart and soul into it because your mind will run out of solutions sooner or later. Soooooo many times I just sat in front of the laptop and felt like nothing could be squeezed out of my mind. Maybe I could have really used the time to catch up on sleep. Or sorting out those two drawers in the home office filled with "stuff" that I never really got to organizing. My mind kept telling me about all these tasks I could repurpose my time and energy into, yet there was this little voice coming from somewhere around my sternum whispering: "Come on, listen to one more song, turn the volume up, go get a glass of water, maybe dance a little by the fridge, then come back and just let your fingers caress the keyboard. It is not the first time this happens. Plus, water is good for you."

One of my all-time favorite communication models is the "Rider – Elephant – Path," originally developed by Dan and Chip Heath in their book *Switch: How to Change Things When Change Is Hard*, which basically advocates for an intentional shared focus on the rational (the rider), emotional (the elephant) and practical (the path).[373] The model has been adapted into a wider known framework of "Head – Heart – Hands"—I personally find that this adaptation loses the meaningful impact of the sheer difference in both size and agility between the "rider" and the "elephant," our rational and emotional dimensions. My "elephant" got me through the "jungle" of writer's block every single time, as well as across many of life's rough terrains.

As in life, so in change work. There is a wonderful piece of inspiration from social media writer JM Storm: "Magic happens when you don't give up, even when you want to. The universe always falls in love with a stubborn heart."[374] Keep intentional shared focus across the rational, emotional and practical, and if you come to a point where you have one single unit of extra effort to give, please please please touch people's hearts. Their minds will follow, and they will find a way.

You must close some chapters, even if you don't know what is next. This is a big one for me, in both life and work. Closing chapters comes with excitement for future discoveries, but also with loss, no matter how grateful and "complete" (sometimes just simply "done") I might feel. Everything gets infinitely more complex when I have to close chapters not knowing what is next. There is an amazing gift and power in "not knowing yet," but still… And while my "rider" might feel lost and confused, I can sense my "elephant" curiously poking around and pulling me to just explore a new "path."

Is not knowing what comes next a good enough reason to simply continue with the current chapter? Whether dealing with a personal or organizational change, I have found that the answer is "no," almost without exception. There is a quote from American novelist Ann Patchett's book *The Dutch House*, a finalist for the 2020 Pulitzer Prize for Fiction, which I oftentimes use in change workshops to create the space for different kinds of reflections and conversations. It speaks of how sometimes, you take a leap of faith and the past falls away, but the future is not yet certain, so you find yourself in a strange place between the two, not really knowing who you are.[375] That moment of suspension is filled with infinite possibilities. To fall or to soar. Choose to soar. The "fall(back)" might be only an illusion of safety.

Well, I guess that's a wrap! Thank you, dear reader, for indulging me with one extra Tuesday change random thought.

On any given week, keep calm and live life with an open mind and an open heart. And please, please, please, never stop looking for the magic in everyday life that gets us through the most wonderful and challenging of changes.

What Getting Obsessed with Jamón While in Spain Teaches Me about Change Management

First published on February 7, 2023

Have you ever made one of those bucket lists of things you want to do before you die? I spent the last week of January in Madrid traveling for work, and I realized I must make a special list, a bucket list with a twist: countries I want to visit before I diet. Spain made it all the way to the top, as I realized I had been harboring an inner jamón-obsessed alter ego my entire life!!! It was a super busy week, packed with awesome conversations with wonderful people, all wrapped up in a blur of jamón, some Manchego cheese and a handful of olives...

As I was enjoying dinner with some of my colleagues, a question was raised my way: "So, Minola, are we going to see what jamón teaches you about change management any time soon?"

"Challenge accepted," I replied, hoping that keeping the conversation flowing would help me go (almost) unnoticed while reaching for another slice of cured meat awesomeness.

There is such a thing as "the perfect time and place for something," the perfect set of circumstances. I cannot, simply cannot understand why this sudden craving for jamón took over my life while in Madrid. I had had it before, and yes, I did like it a lot. It had never, ever, ever happened that I would look at a table, and everything else but jamón would simply vanish into the insignificant background. Maybe it was the way the word sounded pronounced in that wonderful accent among other mouthwatering-sounding tapas. Maybe it was a week-long delayed effect of Blue Monday. Maybe it was a strange reaction to being in glorious sunshine after weeks of gloomy weather. Or a yet undocumented side effect of flying and the cabin pressure after not traveling for sooooo long. Maybe all of these and so many more tiny and huge seemingly unrelated things coming together. The perfect time and place. The perfect time and place for jamón.

As I look back on my change work, there are moments that can count as "jamón moments," instances when things that had been dragging for a long time or just simply would not happen suddenly clicked. Information that had been out there on any and all channels and platforms known to humankind got delivered by a specific someone within a specific context and suddenly, it got magic traction. A decision that just would not get its buy-in becoming an instant outcome of a chance meeting among people who never walked along the same hallways on a daily basis… Can we truly create/recreate and replicate this ineffable "perfect time and place" within our organizations, and even our life overall? Or is it more about creating as many opportunities for it to occur, as in doing things and communicating information in as many ways as possible until something, somewhere, somehow it just clicks for someone?

How (and why) do we linger? Are you wondering how much jamón I stuffed into my checked-in luggage? Or how much I bought at the airport from the duty-free shops? I was tempted, soooooooo infinitely tempted, but I didn't do it. As I was reflecting on my jamón craving for inspiration for this piece, the question of how and why we linger came to mind. How do we hold on, hang on, or, as the definition goes: "remain long, drawn out in time," reluctant to leave? It crossed my mind that bringing jamón back with me could have been my way of lingering, of holding on to that "perfect time and place" feeling.

I also realized that childhood triggers are still going strong. Growing up in an everyday reality of food shortages, it does take a lot of intentional focus to reign in irrational reflexes of hoarding food, telling myself, "Hey, this will be here later, this will be here tomorrow, or you can buy or order it whenever you want." There is always something along our journey through both life and work that makes us linger. Sometimes, it escalates into sheer resistance to change. And it always speaks about a fear. Or a loss. Or a craving.

If I were the Master of the Universe for one day, by the power of jamón, I would forever banish a set of two letters and a full point. After my reign, there would never be "vs." again! Okay, I would allow it for very specific circumstances, but never ever in situations where it drives binary "either/or" judgments. Here's what I mean. While confessing my jamón craving to one of my friends, she said, "Oh, I guess no more prosciutto for you when you go to Italy for your birthday, then." And I remember thinking, "How has this become a jamón vs. prosciutto international predicament?" I am always fascinated by how quickly binary thinking gets triggered!

My heart sinks a little (please read "I scream inside") every single time I see or hear "management vs. leadership," "x mindset vs. y mindset" or my absolute favorite in change work, "old vs. new"! While I agree that there is a "content"/meaning key component to the notions/concepts/tasks, I also believe that "context" plays a fundamental role when it comes to getting a deeper understanding and reaching a conclusion on any given matter. There should be no place for "vs." in change work. Unless, maybe, it is "understanding vs. judging"… So please do expect a spike in prosciutto sales in Italy in about a month. And I will also very happily make my humble contribution to the Spanish economy by attending the Campillos Fiesta del Jamón in November, a wonderful festival of ham a short drive away from Málaga. There, "jamón vs. prosciutto" international conflict averted! You're welcome!

While I do not advocate for lingering, I am all for keeping wonderful moments and experiences alive. My learning-unlearning-relearning journey for this year is not to live in the past, but to fill the present with the joys of all past experiences and the hope for all future discoveries. As Spanish actress Paz Vega said: "I cook croquetas, and I eat jamon. I keep my diet 100% Mediterranean and drink my Rioja. In that sense, I have a piece of Spain in West Hollywood."[376] So, I will post this #tuesdaychangemanagementrandomthought, then order some jamón from a great online store with Spanish products in Switzerland. Oh, don't worry, I did get a bottle of Rioja from the duty-free!

On any given week, keep calm and live life with an open mind and an open heart. And please, please, please, never stop looking for the magic in everyday life that gets us through the most wonderful and challenging of changes.

More Change before Change Management

Just before Christmas last year, my best friend came over for a full week. What a treat it was, after six years of not having seen each other because of life, COVID and everything in between! One evening, we ended up having a very deep conversation, one of those exchanges that touches on all the big questions in life, and when answers come more easily if you just keep on talking without even turning the lights on. We had ice cream, Prosecco, and decades of friendship to keep us going. At one point, she said: "Hey, there's something on my mind. You have been doing this change management thing for two decades now, and I am still not sure I fully understand what you actually do." "Well, that makes two of us. Cheers!" I replied, and we started laughing.

A few minutes later, I said: "You actually know more about this change management thing than you think, and you do it more consistently and more meaningfully than you give yourself credit for. You just do not label it as such. You have high-stakes communications almost every day. You do perform senior executive stakeholder engagement strategies. You have visioning sessions and change readiness assessments. You even run change impact assessments and implement corrective and mitigating measures. I am sure you even do risk management. You might call it 'Spending Christmas with the In-Laws,' while the way these are packaged within organizations is called 'Transformation Initiative' or 'Digital Evolution.' The principles are the same to their very core." I then shared with her what I lovingly call my "personal and professional crusade."

I have been fascinated with why change is perceived as so much more disruptive and even menacing within the organizational environments while we all navigate far more sophisticated and impactful transformation journeys in our lives. One element of the answer could be that many of us still anchor a big part—maybe the defining part—of who we are in what we do, in our work. Any change to that source of identity, (self-)validation and security impacts us to our very core. Pay attention next time you are within a context where there is a round of introductions, and see how many people start with "Hi, I am [name], and I am the [role]." One small thing I have been doing for years, mostly to keep myself honest and grounded, is this: "Hi, I am Minola, and I currently serve as [role]." My work is a fundamental expression of who I am, but it does not define me. I am a change enthusiast. It just so happens that I had many roles of an enthusiastic change manager.

Another hypothesis I have been testing over the past several years is that in life we don't say "change management." We use that expression or label only within the workplace, and what I have learned is that people hear "management" the loudest. The whole vocabulary we use to talk about change at work is based on and developed around tools. It is as if we skip over "change" straight into the (illusion of) control-creating "management." I recently heard somebody saying that we "fluffify" conversations in a totally different context from change work. It made me think that the opposite might be true when it comes to change work within organizations: we "toolified" it, and we ended up over-reliant on frameworks, methodologies, tools and the promises of linear, smooth, structured processes they hold.

There is a "stigma" now associated with change management. It makes it sound corrective, transactional, mechanistic, purely and exclusively implementation-oriented. If you pardon me an informal confession, I sometimes feel it is used as the blue pill to project management. It is also almost obsessively concerned with resistance to change and exclusively purposed to address it at all costs. One of the most under-rated, under-used and misunderstood questions in change work is "What needs to be preserved?" There is huge value in understanding what that change resistance is trying to protect. Just as there is massive risk in over-enthusiasm for change and overselling its benefits. About two years ago, I was speaking with someone, and they said something to me right off the bat: "I don't think we will get a lot of opportunities to work together. I don't need change management, I have no burning platform." I smiled, and then I said: "I am so happy to hear this! What is your burning ambition?"

The requests I normally get sound like "We need a toolkit to manage this big change coming," "What is the methodology you recommend, and can you do a maximum half-day workshop to equip people to manage the disruption we are facing?" While I believe there is immense power in frameworks, methodologies and tools, I also see time and time again how, in the words of Abraham Maslow's "Law of the Instrument:" "To a man with a hammer, everything looks like a nail." It is never just about the toolset. It is always about the mindset and skillset, too. There is always a deeper request beyond "I need a toolkit." Meaningful and sustainable change work happens when we address the deep(er) problem, not the first problem.

All this to bring me back to my "crusade." Whenever I can, I avoid saying "change management," replacing it with "change work." It has helped me open some amazing conversations. In everyday life, we say we "deal with change," in organizations we "manage the change." And while it might seem more like a semantics-driven conversation, the mental and emotional contexts we create around "dealing with change" and "managing the change" are subtly but fundamentally different.

I can only hope this book will inspire you to bring some of the "dealing with change" into "managing change," and equally reversely. Maybe some ways in which we "deal with change" would benefit from disciplined common sense inspired by how we experience change being "managed" within our organizations. Get comfortable with change, first as a word, then as a process and ultimately as the very fabric of our life and work. Create spaces of curiosity over places of certainty. Know that even change is changing.

And always remember: there is no other journey worthier of our curiosity, courage and compassion than living everyday life with awe, wonder, grace, purpose, intention and joy.

Endnotes

1. Bloch, Arthur. "A conclusion is the place…" n.d., quoted in www.goodreads.com. "A Quote by Arthur Bloch." https://www.goodreads.com/quotes/1607-a-conclusion-is-the-place-where-you-get-tired-of.
2. St. Francis of Assisi. "Preach the Gospel at all times…" n.d., quoted in "Quote by Francis of Assisi." n.d. Www.goodreads.com. Accessed July 22, 2023. https://www.goodreads.com/quotes/8119941-preach-the-gospel-at-all-times-when-necessary-use-words.
3. "Someone called me 'pretty' today…" n.d., quoted in DBadLeprechaun. *Someone Called Me "Pretty" Today...* January 13, 2018. Digital image. https://boldomatic.com/p/FrJYMQ/someone-called-me-pretty-today-well-they-actually-said-pretty-annoying-but-i-onl.
4. Gino, Francesca. *Rebel Talent*. HarperCollins, 2018.
5. Grant, Adam M. *Originals: How Non-Conformists Move the World*. London: Viking, 2017.
6. Gladwell, Malcolm. *Outliers: The Story of Success*. New York: Back Bay Books, 2008.
7. Hari, Johann. *LOST CONNECTIONS : Uncovering the Real Causes of Depression and the Unexpected Solutions*. Bloomsbury Publishing, 2019.
8. Millman, Dan. *Way of the Peaceful Warrior : A Book That Changes Lives*. Readhowyouwant.com, Limited, 2009.
9. Hoffman, Eva. "There is nothing like a gleam of humor…" n.d., quoted in A-Z Quotes. "Eva Hoffman Quote," n.d. https://www.azquotes.com/quote/533961.
10. *Happy Feet*. Film. Warner Bros. Pictures, 2006.

11 Nossel, Murray. *Powered by Storytelling : Excavate, Craft, and Present Stories to Transform Business Communication*. New York: Mcgraw-Hill Education, 2018.
12 Fitzgerald, Isaac, and Wendy Macnaughton. *Pen & Ink : Tattoos and the Stories behind Them*. New York: Bloomsbury Usa, 2014.
13 Rinaldi, Karen. *(It's Great To) Suck at Something : The Unexpected Joy of Wiping out and What It Can Teach Us about Patience, Resilience, and the Stuff That Really Matters*. New York: Atria Books, 2019.
14 Kottke, Jason. "The Dunning-Kruger Effect: We Are All Confident Idiots." kottke.org, June 27, 2018. https://kottke.org/18/06/the-dunning-kruger-effect-we-are-all-confident-idiots.
15 Wallace, Jade Sandberg. "Tidying up with Marie Kondo." TV series episode. Netflix, January 1, 2019.
16 *The Pursuit of Happyness*. Film. Columbia Pictures, Sony Pictures Releasing, 2006.
17 *Ibid.*
18 Zenni Optical. "Tips for Adjusting to New Glasses." The Zenni Blog, April 10, 2018. https://www.zennioptical.com/blog/tips-for-adjusting-to-new-glasses/.
19 Hill, Aaron. "Don't call the world dirty..." n.d., quoted in *Aaron Hill Quotes*. n.d. Online image. *Brainy Quote*. https://www.brainyquote.com/quotes/aaron_hill_391831.
20 De Saint-Exupéry, Antoine. *The Little Prince*. United States: Reynal & Hitchcock, 1943.
21 "Some talk to you in their free time..." n.d., quoted in Quotes About Everything. *Some Talk to You in Their Free Time...* n.d. Online image. Pinterest. https://www.pinterest.co.uk/pin/470555861060352534/
22 Kramer, Steven. *The Progress Principle: Using Small Wins to Ignite Joy, Engagement, and Creativity at Work*. Harvard Business Review Press, 2011.
23 Tzu, Lao. "Nature does not hurry..." n.d., quoted in www.goodreads.com. "A Quote by Lao Tzu," n.d. https://www.goodreads.com/quotes/34644-nature-does-not-hurry-yet-everything-is-accomplished.
24 Tomasi, Giuseppe. *The Leopard*. New York: Pantheon Books, Stampa , Cop, 2015.
25 Atcheson, Sheree. "Allyship - the Key to Unlocking the Power of Diversity." Forbes, November 30, 2018. https://www.forbes.com/sites/shereeatcheson/2018/11/30/allyship-the-key-to-unlocking-the-power-of-diversity/?sh=1d6a5fe849c6.
26 "Sometimes I feel like throwing in the towel..." n.d., quoted in the folde. *Sometimes I Feel like Throwing in the Towel...* n.d. Online image. Instagram.

27 "Irony is the opposite of wrinkly," n.d., quoted in Rice, Wendy. *Irony Quotes*. n.d. Online image. *Pinterest*. https://www.pinterest.com/pin/grammarly-timeline-photos--108227197271238020/.
28 "Whoever said death and taxes…" n.d., quoted in Laundry Chutes. "Whoever Said Death and Taxes…" June 20, 2023. Online image. Facebook.
29 Einstein, Albert. Letter to Otto Juliusburger. Letter, September 30, 1942.
30 Einstein, Albert. *Ideas and Opinions / by Albert Einstein*. New York: Dell Pub. Co, 1954.
31 *The New York Times*. "ASSAILS EDUCATION TODAY; Einstein Says 'It Is Miracle' Inquiry Is Not 'Strangled.'" March 13, 1949, sec. Archives. https://www.nytimes.com/1949/03/13/archives/assails-education-today-einstein-says-it-is-miracle-inquiry-is-not.html.
32 William Bruce Cameron. *Informal Sociology*. Random House, 1963.
33 "If Plan A didn't work…," n.d., quoted in Akhtaboot. *Plan A*. n.d. Online image. *Pinterest*. https://www.pinterest.com/pin/67554063136502637/.
34 Daniel Todd Gilbert. *Stumbling on Happiness*. London: Harper Perennial, 2007.
35 Leydesdorff, Loet, 'Interaction' Versus 'Action' in Luhmann's Sociology of Communication (June 14, 2013). Colin B. Grant (Ed.), Rethinking Communicative Interaction: New Interdisciplinary Horizons. Amsterdam, John Benjamins, Forthcoming, Available at SSRN: https://ssrn.com/abstract=2279672 or http://dx.doi.org/10.2139/ssrn.2279672
36 Campbell, Joycelyn. "The Anticipation Machine Isn't All It's Cracked up to Be." Farther to Go!, December 8, 2014. https://farthertogo.com/anticipation-machine-isnt-cracked/.
37 *Ibid.*
38 Burbank, Luther. "Flowers always make people better…" n.d., quoted in www.goodreads.com. "A Quote by Luther Burbank." https://www.goodreads.com/quotes/31061-flowers-always-make-people-better-happier-and-more-helpful-they.
39 Brown, H. Jackson Jr. "Remember that children…" n.d., quoted in www.goodreads.com. "A Quote by H. Jackson Brown Jr.," n.d. https://www.goodreads.com/quotes/528013-remember-that-children-marriages-and-flower-gardens-reflect-the-kind.
40 Hobson, David. "I grow plants for many reasons…" n.d., quoted in A-Z Quotes. "TOP 7 QUOTES by DAVID HOBSON." https://www.azquotes.com/author/25366-David_Hobson.

41 Krkić, Bojan. "It is important to find…" n.d., quoted in *Bojan Krkic Quotes*. n.d. Online image. *Brainy Quote*. https://www.brainyquote.com/quotes/bojan_krkic_1025850#:~:text=Bojan%20Krkic%20Quotes&text=It%20is%20important%20to%20find%20a%20place%20where%20you%20feel,you%20feel%20belonging%20and%20stability.
42 Hemingway, Ernest. *Across the River and into the Trees*. London Vintage, 2017.
43 Vonnegut, Kurt. "Laughter and tears are both…" n.d., quoted in HuffPost. "Here's What Kurt Vonnegut Can Teach You about Life," November 11, 2013. https://www.huffpost.com/entry/kurt-vonnegut_n_4241283#:~:text=Laughter%20can%20cure%20just%20about%20anything.&text=He%20says%2C%20%22Laughter%20and%20tears
44 D'Angelo, Anthony J. "Realize that if you have time…" n.d., quoted in www.goodreads.com. "A Quote by Anthony J. D'Angelo," n.d. https://www.goodreads.com/quotes/79180-realize-that-if-you-have-time-to-whine-and-complain.
45 "I wish my life had…," n.d., quoted in Delitonik. *I Wish My Life Had…* December 7, 2016. Online image. *Boldomatic*. https://boldomatic.com/p/QnjFAg/i-wish-my-life-had-background-music-so-i-could-understand-what-the-hell-is-goin.
46 Wikipedia. "Underground Music." Wikipedia, June 4, 2023. https://en.wikipedia.org/wiki/Underground_music#:~:text=The%20term%20%22underground%20music%22%20has.
47 Tolstoy, Leo. "Music is the shorthand…" n.d., quoted in www.goodreads.com. "A Quote by Leo Tolstoy," n.d. https://www.goodreads.com/quotes/65861-music-is-the-shorthand-of-emotion.
48 Ocean, Frank. "When you're happy…," n.d., quoted in quotefancy.com. "Frank Ocean Quote: 'When You're Happy You Enjoy the Music, but When You're Sad You Understand the Lyrics.'" https://quotefancy.com/quote/1350812/Frank-Ocean-When-you-re-happy-you-enjoy-the-music-but-when-you-re-sad-you-understand-the.
49 The Tunedly Team. "The Role of Music in Human Culture." Tunedly, April 3, 2019. https://www.tunedly.com/blog/musicandculture.html.
50 Bonaparte, Napoléon. "Music is what tells us that…" n.d., quoted in quotecatalog.com. "Napoléon Bonaparte Quote - Music Is What Tells Us That the Human Ra… | Quote Catalog." https://quotecatalog.com/quote/napoleon-bonaparte-music-is-what-t-b1ryWea.
51 Buhl, Hermann. "Mountains have a way…" n.d., quoted in stuckinindiana. *Hermann*. n.d. Online image. *Pinterest*. https://www.pinterest.com/pin/90072061276563308/#:~:text=%22Mountains%20have%20a%20way%20of,Words%20of%20wisdom%2C%20Favorite%20quotes.

52 Thoreau, Henry David. *The Writings of Henry David Thoreau.* Vol. 10. The Riverside Press, 1906.
53 Proust, Marcel. *The Captive.* Grasset and Gallimard, 1923.
54 Hillary, Sir Edmund. "It's not the mountain…" n.d., quoted in Outdoor Vancouver. *Bible Quotes.* n.d. Online image. *Pinterest.* https://www.pinterest.com/pin/it-is-not-the-mountain-we-conquer-but-ourselves-sir-edmund-hillary-qotd-quotes-explore-climb--281897257905151338/.
55 Corneille, Pierre. Le Menteur, Comedie. Based on "La Verdad Sospechosa" of J. Ruiz de Alarcon Y Mendoza, the Authorship of Which Is Wrongly Attributed by Corneille in His Preface to Lope de Vega, 1868.
56 Mauss, Marcel. *The Gift: The Form and Reason for Exchange in Archaic Societies.* 1925. Reprint, New York: W.W. Norton, 2000.
57 Bregman, Peter. "The Real Point of Gift-Giving." Harvard Business Review, December 15, 2010. https://hbr.org/2010/12/the-real-point-of-gift-giving.
58 Digh, Patti. *Life Is a Verb : 37 Days to Wake Up, Be Mindful, and Live Intentionally.* Guilford, Conn.: Skirt, 2008.
59 Brooks, Norman W., "Let Everyday Be Christmas." 1976.
60 Ward, William Arthur. "A warm smile is…" n.d., quoted in www.goodreads.com. "A Quote by William Arthur Ward." https://www.goodreads.com/quotes/115144-a-warm-smile-is-the-universal-language-of-kindness.
61 Tzu, Lao. "Kindness in words…" n.d., quoted in www.goodreads.com. "A Quote by Lao Tzu." https://www.goodreads.com/quotes/46874-kindness-in-words-creates-confidence-kindness-in-thinking-creates-profoundness.
62 Valencia, Jordana. "How to Convince Your Boss You Need Time Off." Harvard Business Review, June 2, 2020. https://hbr.org/2020/06/how-to-convince-your-boss-you-need-time-off.
63 *Ibid.*
64 Dobra, Eric. "Taking a break…" n.d., quoted in www.goodreads.com. "A Quote by Russell Eric Dobda," n.d. https://www.goodreads.com/quotes/7254308-taking-a-break-can-lead-to-breakthroughs.
65 Suzman, James. *Work : A History of How We Spend Our Time.* Bloomsbury Circus, 2020.
66 Celeste Anne Headlee. *Do Nothing : How to Break Away from Overworking, Overdoing, and Underliving.* New York: Harmony Books, 2020.

67 Lamott, Anne. "Almost everything will work again…" n.d., quoted in www.goodreads.com. "A Quote by Anne Lamott," n.d. https://www.goodreads.com/quotes/6830146-almost-everything-will-work-again-if-you-unplug-it-for.
68 Epicurus. "We should look for someone…" n.d., quoted in www.goodreads.com. "A Quote by Epicurus." https://www.goodreads.com/quotes/1291739-we-should-look-for-someone-to-eat-and-drink-with.
69 Chang, David. "To eat well…," n.d., quoted in *David Chang Quote*. n.d. Online image. *Quote Fancy*. https://quotefancy.com/quote/1695176/David-Chang-To-eat-well-I-always-disagree-with-critics-who-say-that-all-restaurants.
70 Oldenburg, Claes. "I like food because you can change it…," n.d., quoted in *Claes Oldenburg Quote*. n.d. Online image. *Quotefancy*. https://quotefancy.com/quote/1627732/Claes-Oldenburg-I-like-food-because-you-can-change-it-I-mean-there-is-no-such-thing-as-a.
71 Schwartz, Tony, and Catherine McCarthy. "Manage Your Energy, Not Your Time." Harvard Business Review, October 2007. https://hbr.org/2007/10/manage-your-energy-not-your-time.
72 *Ibid.*
73 *Ibid.*
74 *Ibid.*
75 Gikas, Mike. "Plugging Old Phone Chargers into Fast-Charge Smartphones." Consumer Reports, October 20, 2016. https://www.consumerreports.org/smartphones/plugging-old-phone-chargers-into-fast-charge-smartphones/.
76 Schwartz, Tony, and McCarthy. "Manage Your Energy."
77 Boom, Corrie Ten. "When a train goes through…" n.d., quoted in www.goodreads.com. "A Quote by Corrie Ten Boom." https://www.goodreads.com/quotes/583815-when-a-train-goes-through-a-tunnel-and-it-gets.
78 "Don't let the train of enthusiasm…," n.d., quoted in www.wisesayings.com. "Train Sayings and Train Quotes | Wise Sayings." Accessed July 5, 2023. https://www.wisesayings.com/train-quotes/.
79 Bonhoeffer, Dietrich. "If you board the wrong train…" n.d., quoted in www.goodreads.com. "A Quote by Dietrich Bonhoeffer." https://www.goodreads.com/quotes/22812-if-you-board-the-wrong-train-it-is-no-use.
80 Dickens, Charles. "Railway Dreaming." *Household Words* XIII, no. 320 (1856).
81 Hanley, A.W., Warner, A.R., Dehili, V.M. *et al.* Washing Dishes to Wash the Dishes: Brief Instruction in an Informal Mindfulness Practice. *Mindfulness* **6**, 1095–1103 (2015). https://doi.org/10.1007/s12671-014-0360-9

SOURCES | 461

82 "You know you are an adult…" n.d., quoted in Cool Funny Quotes. *Funny Quote.* n.d. Online image. *Pinterest.* https://www.pinterest.com/pin/humor--455708056028724026/.

83 Kanter, Rosabeth Moss. "I've found that small wins…" n.d., quoted in *Rosabeth Moss Kanter Quote.* n.d. Online image. *Quotefancy.* https://quotefancy.com/quote/1264863/Rosabeth-Moss-Kanter-I-ve-found-that-small-wins-small-projects-small-differences-often.

84 Baxter, Cecil. "You don't get anything clean…" n.d., quoted in The Quotations Page. "The Quotations Page: Quote from Cecil Baxter." http://www.quotationspage.com/quote/27673.html.

85 Kalman, Maira. *The Principles of Uncertainty.* New York: Penguin Books, 2009.

86 "If you have to wear glasses…," n.d., quoted in nJoy Vision, Twitter post, February 17, 2021, 11:40 AM, https://twitter.com/nJoyVision/status/1362079468932759553.

87 Hippocrates. "The chief virtue…" n.d., quoted in A-Z Quotes. "Hippocrates Quote." https://www.azquotes.com/quote/892665#:~:text=Hippocrates%20quote%3A%20The%20chief%20virtue%20that%20language%20can%20have%20is%20clarity..

88 Rubin, Marty. "Behind every mask there is a face…" n.d., quoted in AllAuthor. "Behind Every Mask There Is a Face and Behind… - Quote," n.d. https://allauthor.com/quotes/280615/.

89 Abraham, Amit. "We have always been wearing…" n.d., quoted in www.goodreads.com. "A Quote by Amit Abraham." https://www.goodreads.com/quotes/10365807-we-have-always-been-wearing-masks-it-s-just-that-it.

90 Rubin, Marty. "The desire to change…" n.d., quoted in www.quotemaster.org. "The Desire to Change Things Must Begin with Accepting Things as They Are. Marty Rubin." https://www.quotemaster.org/qcd0d3d0333e437eb7e4a007a840af5e1.

91 de Botton, Alain. "'Writer's block' is an emotional…" n.d., quoted in Writing Routines. "37 Famous Author Quotes about Writer's Block," November 27, 2018. https://www.writingroutines.com/writers-block-quotes/.

92 No source recovered.

93 Rogers, John. "You can't think yourself out…" n.d., quoted in www.goodreads.com. "A Quote by John Rogers," n.d. https://www.goodreads.com/quotes/1305134-you-can-t-think-yourself-out-of-a-writing-block-you.

94 Trapani, Gina. "Jerry Seinfeld's Productivity Secret." Lifehacker, July 24, 2007. https://lifehacker.com/jerry-seinfelds-productivity-secret-281626.

95 Saintcrow, Lilith. "Discipline allows magic…" n.d., quoted in www.goodreads.com. "A Quote by Lili St. Crow." https://www.goodreads.com/quotes/417747-discipline-allows-magic-to-be-a-writer-is-to-be.
96 Hemingway, Ernest. *A Moveable Feast*. London Arrow Books, 2011.
97 Belinda_MSC. "Benjamin Zander Shining Eyes Clip." www.youtube.com, September 22, 2011. https://www.youtube.com/watch?v=ZS-YYhoyBMo&t=71s.
98 Fey, Tina. "The thing that always fascinated me…" n.d., quoted in *Tina Fey Quote*. n.d. Online image. *Quotefancy*. https://quotefancy.com/quote/921915/Tina-Fey-The-thing-that-always-fascinated-me-about-improv-is-that-it-s-basically-a-happy.
99 Rumi. "As you start to walk…" n.d., quoted in www.goodreads.com. "A Quote by Rumi." https://www.goodreads.com/quotes/811906-as-you-start-to-walk-on-the-way-the-way.
100 Close, Del. "Don't bring a cathedral…," n.d., quoted in Nyfors, Margret. "Bring a Brick." Margret Nyfors, March 5, 2016. http://www.margretnyfors.com/2016/03/04/bring-a-brick/.
101 Poehler, Amy. "No one looks stupid…" n.d., quoted in A-Z Quotes. "Amy Poehler Quote." https://www.azquotes.com/quote/591310.
102 Rosamund Stone Zander, and Benjamin Zander. *The Art of Possibility*. London: Penguin Books, 2002.
103 Anderson, Robert J, and W A Adams. *Scaling Leadership : Building Organizational Capability and Capacity to Create Outcomes That Matter Most*. Hoboken, New Jersey: John Wiley & Sons, Inc, 2019.
104 Adenauer, Konrad. "We all live under…" n.d. quoted in www.goodreads.com. "A Quote by Konrad Adenauer." https://www.goodreads.com/quotes/286452-we-all-live-under-the-same-sky-but-we-don-t.
105 Buddha, Gautama. "In the sky there is no…" n.d. quoted in www.goodreads.com. "A Quote by Gautama Buddha." https://www.goodreads.com/quotes/145776-in-the-sky-there-is-no-distinction-of-east-and.
106 Buddha. "Develop a mind …," n.d., quoted in *Buddha Quote*. n.d. Online image. *Quotefancy*. https://quotefancy.com/quote/1705724/Buddha-Develop-a-mind-that-is-vast-like-space-where-experiences-both-pleasant-and.
107 Kalam, A.P.J. Abdul. "Look at the sky…" quoted in www.goodreads.com. "A Quote by A.P.J. Abdul Kalam." https://www.goodreads.com/quotes/7636094-look-at-the-sky-we-are-not-alone-the-whole.
108 Jain, Sanya. "The Heartwarming Story behind Nike's First Hands-Free Shoe." NDTV.com, February 2, 2021. https://www.ndtv.com/offbeat/the-heartwarming-story-behind-nikes-first-hands-free-shoe-2361922.

109 Norman, Donald A. *The Design of Everyday Things*. 1988. Reprint, Massachusetts: Mit Press, 2013.
110 Daily-Diamond, Christopher A., Christine E. Gregg, and Oliver M. O'Reilly. "The Roles of Impact and Inertia in the Failure of a Shoelace Knot." *Proceedings of the Royal Society A: Mathematical, Physical and Engineering Sciences* 473, no. 2200 (April 2017): 20160770. https://doi.org/10.1098/rspa.2016.0770.
111 Higdon, Hal. "I double-not my shoelaces…" n.d., quoted in A-Z Quotes. "Hal Higdon Quote." https://www.azquotes.com/quote/1221697.
112 No source recovered.
113 Brown, Brené. "FFTs". Produced by Parcast. *Unlocking Us*, March, 2020. Podcast, 37:52. https://brenebrown.com/podcast/brene-on-ffts/
114 Peters, Tom. "Leaders win through logistics…" n.d., quoted in joelynch. "Famous Logistics Quotes - the Logistics of Logistics." The Logistics of Logistics, July 15, 2011. https://www.thelogisticsoflogistics.com/famous-logistics-quotes-2/.
115 Kelly Williams Brown. *Adulting: How to Become a Grown-up in 468 Easy(Ish) Steps*. New York: Grand Central Pub, 2013.
116 Rosenberg, Eric. "Settling the Great Toilet Paper Debate Once and for All: A Practical and Visual Analysis Based on Science | Eric Rosenberg." ericrosenberg.com, October 28, 2014. https://ericrosenberg.com/great-toilet-paper-debate/.
117 Sherman, Erik. "individuals can generate bad ideas…" n.d., quoted in Butler, Jen. "Group Decisions: Avoiding Disaster." JB Partners, July 3, 2020. https://jbpartners.com/lessons/group-decisions-avoiding-disaster/.
118 Cicero, Marcus Tullius. "More is lost by indecision…" n.d., quoted in A-Z Quotes. "Marcus Tullius Cicero Quote." https://www.azquotes.com/quote/1447345.
119 Ambridge, Ben. "What Your Toilet Paper Says about You." *The Guardian*, December 27, 2015, sec. Life and style. https://www.theguardian.com/lifeandstyle/2015/dec/27/what-your-toilet-paper-says-about-you-quiz.
120 Vedder, Eddie. "I feel like we have to keep our eyes on the road…" n.d., quoted in *Eddie Vedder Quote*. n.d. Online image. *Quotefancy*. https://quotefancy.com/quote/798766/Eddie-Vedder-I-feel-like-we-have-to-keep-our-eyes-on-the-road-Being-nostalgic-is-like.
121 Book, William Frederick. "A man must drive his energy…" n.d., quoted in A-Z Quotes. "William Frederick Book Quote." https://www.azquotes.com/quote/1522887.

122 *Something's Gotta Give*. Film. Warner Bros., Columbia Pictures, Warner Bros. Pictures, Sony Pictures Entertainment Motion Picture Group, 2003.
123 Hemingway, Ernest. "Write hard and clear..." n.d., quoted in www.goodreads.com. "A Quote by Ernest Hemingway," n.d. https://www.goodreads.com/quotes/248820-write-hard-and-clear-about-what-hurts.
124 Bridges, William. *Transitions : Making Sense of Life's Changes*. Boston: Da Capo Lifelong, 2020.
125 Eliot, T. S. *Four Quartets*. S.L.: Faber And Faber, 2019.
126 Tamir, Shira. "Anyone who thinks fallen leaves...," n.d., quoted in Ella Patrice. "Affirmation Mondays 177 – Anyone Who Thinks Fallen Leaves Are Dead Has Never Watched Them Dancing on a Windy Day." Lawhimsy, October 23, 2017. https://lawhimsy.com/2017/10/23/monday-mantra-177-anyone-who-thinks-fallen-leaves-are-dead-has-never-watched-them-dancing-on-a-windy-day/.
127 Kessler, David. *FINDING MEANING: The Sixth Stage of Grief*. Simon and Schuster, 2020.
128 Brown, Brené. *Rising Strong: How the Ability to Reset Transforms the Way We Live, Love, Parent, and Lead*. New York: Random House, 2017.
129 Seneca. "Every new beginning..." n.d., quoted in *Seneca Quotes*. n.d. Online image. *Brainy Quote*. https://www.brainyquote.com/quotes/seneca_405078.
130 Jain, Prem. *Buffett Beyond Value : Why Warren Buffett Looks to Growth and Management When Investing*. Hoboken, N.J.: John Wiley & Sons, 2010.
131 Kwon, Jennie. "Jewelry has the power..." n.d., quoted in Kivotos Jewelry. *Make You Feel*. n.d. Online image. *Pinterest*. https://www.pinterest.com/pin/759701030865878817/.
132 Adigard, Erik. "Design is in everything we make..." n.d., quoted in A-Z Quotes. "Erik Adigard Quote." https://www.azquotes.com/quote/667807.
133 von Fürstenberg, Diane. "Jewelry is like the perfect spice..." n.d., quoted in DelBrenna Jewelry. *Tuscany Italy*. n.d. Online image. *Pinterest*. https://www.pinterest.com/pin/jewelry-is-like-the-perfect-spice-it-always-compliments-whats-already-there-diane-von-furstenberg-de--552465079280677820/.
134 Amabile, Teresa, and Steven Kramer. *The Progress Principle: Using Small Wins to Ignite Joy, Engagement, and Creativity at Work*. Boston, Mass: Harvard Business Press, 2011.

135 Hicks, Dusty. "I've been told that swimming…" n.d., quoted in www.coolnsmart.com. "Quote: It's Been Told That Swimming Is a Wimp Sport, but I Don't... - CoolNSmart." https://www.coolnsmart.com/quote-its-been-told-that-swimming-is-a-56025/.

136 Thorpe, Ian. "For myself, losing is not coming in second…" n.d., quoted in *Ian Thorpe Quote*. n.d. Online image. *Quotefancy*. https://quotefancy.com/quote/1444223/Ian-Thorpe-For-myself-losing-is-not-coming-second-It-s-getting-out-of-the-water-knowing.

137 Thorpe, Ian. "This is why relays are so important…" n.d., quoted in *Ian Thorpe Quote*. n.d. Online image. *Quotefancy*. https://quotefancy.com/quote/1444229/Ian-Thorpe-This-is-why-relays-are-so-important-because-you-can-find-more-in-yourself-for.

138 Colapinto, John. *This Is the Voice*. New York, Ny: Simon & Schuster, 2021.

139 Colapinto, John. "Accents, Dialects, and Discrimination." The Walrus, February 22, 2021. https://thewalrus.ca/accents-dialects-and-discrimination/.

140 "If you talk to a man in a language he understands…" n.d., quoted in Noah, Trevor. *Born a Crime : Stories from a South African Childhood*. New York: One World, 2016.

141 Colaptino. "Accents, Dialects, and Discrimination."

142 Quintilianus, Marcus Fabius. "One should not aim…" n.d., quoted in Ute's International Lounge & Academy. "Intercultural Communication." https://utesinternationallounge.com/intercultural-communication/.

143 Wittgenstein, Ludwig. *Logisch-Philosophische Abhandlung*. W. Ostwald's Annalen der Naturphilosophie, 1921.

144 Lewis, Flora. "Learning another language…" n.d., quoted in A-Z Quotes. "Flora Lewis Quote." https://www.azquotes.com/quote/611490.

145 Smith, Frank. "Language is not a genetic gift…" n.d., quoted in A-Z Quotes. "Frank Smith Quote," n.d. https://www.azquotes.com/quote/671566.

146 Mackesy, Charlie. *The Boy, the Mole, the Fox and the Horse*. London: Ebury Press, 2020.

147 Wikipedia Contributors. "Imagination." Wikipedia. Wikimedia Foundation, November 12, 2019. https://en.wikipedia.org/wiki/Imagination.

148 "I don't care about Disney lying about…" n.d., quoted in Someecards. *I Don't Care about Disney Lying About...* n.d. Online image. *Pinterest*. https://www.pinterest.com/pin/69524387971732305/.

149 Zander and Zander. *The Art of Possibility*.

150 Mackesy, Charlie. *The Boy, the Mole, the Fox and the Horse.* London: Ebury Press, 2020.
151 Carpenter, Dave. *Project Finance.* n.d. Online image. *Pinterest.* https://www.pinterest.com/pin/209839663861700473/.
152 Quelch, John. "Mention health in most companies..." n.d., quoted in BrainyQuote. "John Quelch Quotes," n.d. https://www.brainyquote.com/quotes/john_quelch_757983.
153 Churchill, Winston. "Healthy citizens..." n.d., quoted in www.goodreads.com. "A Quote by Winston S. Churchill," n.d. https://www.goodreads.com/quotes/97948-healthy-citizens-are-the-greatest-asset-any-country-can-have.
154 "There is no such thing as scope creep..." n.d., quoted in www.oreilly.com. "Chapter 10: How Do I Avoid Scope Creep? - Change with Confidence: Answers to the 50 Biggest Questions That Keep Change Leaders up at Night [Book]." https://www.oreilly.com/library/view/change-with-confidence/9781118556573/9781118556573c10.xhtml.
155 Holzwarth, Aline. "Decrease Friction and Add Fuel for Health Behavior Change." Center for Advanced Hindsight, March 1, 2019. https://advanced-hindsight.com/blog/decrease-friction-and-add-fuel-for-health-behavior-change/.
156 Change Designers. "The Ikea Effect: Accepting Change by Creating It," April 13, 2021. https://www.changedesigners.eu/blog/the-ikea-effect-accepting-change-by-creating-it/.
157 Bryson, Bill. *Neither Here nor There.* Anchor Canada, 2012.
158 Melville, Herman. *Moby Dick.* London: Richard Bentley, 1851.
159 *My Big Fat Greek Wedding.* Film. IFC Films, Hollywood Pictures, 2002.
160 Proust. *The Captive.*
161 Longfellow, Henry Wadsworth. "The best thing one can do..." n.d., quoted in A-Z Quotes. "Henry Wadsworth Longfellow Quote." https://www.azquotes.com/quote/178503.
162 "Some people feel the rain..." n.d., quoted in Metris Leadership. "Some People Feel the Rain, Others Just Get Wet," May 8, 2017. https://metrisleadership.com/some-people-feel-the-rain-others-just-get-wet/.
163 Henry David Thoreau. *Walden.* London Vintage, 1854.
164 Clark, Frank A. "Criticism, like rain..." n.d., quoted in www.goodreads.com. "A Quote by Frank A. Clark," n.d. https://www.goodreads.com/quotes/1009681-criticism-like-rain-should-be-gentle-enough-to-nourish-a.
165 Barrett, Tom. "If the rain spoils our picnic..." n.d., quoted in in A-Z Quotes. "Tom Barrett Quote." https://www.azquotes.com/quote/19060.
166 *The Equalizer.* Film. Sony Pictures Releasing, 2014.

167 Weingarten, Randi. "Good tests can help teachers…" n.d., quoted in Brainy Quote. "Randi Weingarten Quotes," n.d. https://www.brainyquote.com/quotes/randi_weingarten_776443.
168 "Know why an empty bottle…" n.d., quoted in goldhunter. *Know How an Empty Bottle…* February 11, 2022. Online image. *America's Best Pics.* https://americasbestpics.com/picture/know-why-an-empty-bottle-of-wine-is-per-than-reIWNFcJ9.
169 Viorst, Judith. "Strength is the ability to…" n.d., quoted in BrainyQuotes. "Judith Viorst Quotes," n.d. https://www.brainyquote.com/quotes/judith_viorst_390004.
170 Poe, Edgar Allan. Letter to J. Beauchamp Jones. Letter, August 8, 1839.
171 Shriver, Lionel. "Reading time is precious…" n.d., quoted in BrainyQuote. "Lionel Shriver Quotes," n.d. https://www.brainyquote.com/quotes/lionel_shriver_886446#:~:text=Lionel%20Shriver%20Quotes&text=Please%20enable%20Javascript-,Reading%20time%20is%20precious.,you%20off%20the%20activity%20altogether..
172 "Friends." TV series episode. NBC, February 25, 1999.
173 Cumberbatch, Benedict. "I can feel infinitely alive…" n.d., quoted in www.goodreads.com. "A Quote by Benedict Cumberbatch." https://www.goodreads.com/quotes/581122-i-can-feel-infinitely-alive-curled-up-on-the-sofa.
174 Nool, Erki. "The hardest distance…" n.d., quoted in *Erki Nool Quote.* n.d. Online image. *Quotefancy.* https://quotefancy.com/quote/1622939/Erki-Nool-The-hardest-distance-is-always-from-the-sofa-to-the-front-door.
175 Martin, Demetri. "The sofa…" n.d., quoted in A-Z Quotes. "Demetri Martin Quote." https://www.azquotes.com/quote/1432668.
176 Scottoline, Lisa. "Let's talk about a decision…," n.d., quoted in *Lisa Scottoline Quote.* n.d. Online image. *Quotefancy.* https://quotefancy.com/quote/1406339/Lisa-Scottoline-Let-s-talk-about-a-decision-that-women-have-to-make-every-morning-Big.
177 Beverley Edmondson Millinery. "Mother of the Bride Outfit: Getting It Right," February 6, 2017. https://www.beverleyedmondsonmillinery.co.uk/mother-of-the-bride-outfit/.
178 Marinelli, Gina. "Here's the 2020 Way to Match Your Shoes and Bag." Who What Wear, January 9, 2020. https://www.whowhatwear.com/matching-shoes-and-bags.
179 Angelou, Maya. "I've learned that people will forget…" n.d., quoted in Goodreads.com. "A Quote by Maya Angelou," 2019. https://www.goodreads.com/quotes/5934-i-ve-learned-that-people-will-forget-what-you-said-people.

180 Princeton University "About WordNet." WordNet. Princeton University. 2010.
181 Rose, Aaron. "In the right light..." n.d., quoted in www.goodreads.com. "A Quote by Aaron Rose." https://www.goodreads.com/quotes/238363-in-the-right-light-at-the-right-time-everything-is.
182 Harari, Oren. "The electric light did not..." n.d., quoted in Tan, Ashley. "Designing Image Quotes." Another dot in the blogosphere?, December 5, 2016. https://ashleytan.wordpress.com/tag/quotes/.
183 Serling, Rod. "There is nothing in the dark..." n.d., quoted in www.goodreads.com. "A Quote by Rod Serling." https://www.goodreads.com/quotes/128320-there-is-nothing-in-the-dark-that-isn-t-there-when.
184 Renkel, Ruth E. "Never fear shadows..." n.d., quoted in Omved Natural Living. *Light Wave*. n.d. Online image. *Pinterest*. https://www.pinterest.com/pin/83387030571945641/.
185 Proenneke, Richard, and Sam Keith. *One Man's Wilderness : An Alaskan Odyssey*. Anchorage: Alaska Northwest Books, 1999.
186 Shaw, George Bernard. "Better keep yourself..." n.d., quoted in www.goodreads.com. "A Quote by George Bernard Shaw." https://www.goodreads.com/quotes/31191-better-keep-yourself-clean-and-bright-you-are-the-window.
187 Eckhart, Meister. "Stillness is where creativity..." n.d., quoted in A-Z Quotes. "Meister Eckhart Quote." https://www.azquotes.com/quote/1385728#:~:text=Meister%20Eckhart%20quote%3A%20Stillness%20is%20where%20creativity%20and%20solutions%20are%20found..
188 Holiday, Ryan. *Stillness Is the Key: An Ancient Strategy for Modern Life*. London: Profile Books, 2019.
189 Drabble, Margaret. "When nothing is sure..." n.d., quoted in www.goodreads.com. "A Quote by Margaret Drabble," n.d. https://www.goodreads.com/quotes/27752-when-nothing-is-sure-everything-is-possible.
190 "A bird sitting on a tree...," n.d., quoted in jRachelle. *Always Believe*. n.d. Online image. *Pinterest*. https://www.pinterest.at/pin/262475484510853433/.
191 Eckhart, Meister. "If the only prayer you said..." n.d., quoted in www.goodreads.com. "A Quote by Meister Eckhart." https://www.goodreads.com/quotes/81720-if-the-only-prayer-you-said-in-your-whole-life.
192 Benson, Ezra Taft. "You are free to choose..." n.d., quoted in www.goodreads.com. "A Quote by Ezra Taft Benson," n.d. https://www.goodreads.com/quotes/230871-you-are-free-to-choose-but-you-are-not-free.

193 Conan O'Brien. "Mitch Hedberg: Waffles Are like Pancakes with Syrup Traps | Late Night with Conan O'Brien." www.youtube.com, July 30, 2021. https://www.youtube.com/watch?v=WNi8BnmhRDk.

194 "Never let your toes…" n.d., quoted in Victoria. "100+ Pancake Quotes and Instagram Captions - Go Cook Yummy." Go Cook Yummy, August 18, 2022. https://gocookyummy.com/instagram-pancake-quotes-captions/.

195 Tosh, Daniel. "No matter how flat…" n.d., quoted in A-Z Quotes. "Daniel Tosh Quote." https://www.azquotes.com/quote/1439299.

196 Child, Julia. "Drama is very important…" n.d., quoted in www.goodreads.com. "A Quote by Julia Child." https://www.goodreads.com/quotes/8691149-drama-is-very-important-in-life-you-have-to-come.

197 *Juice*. Film. Paramount Pictures, 20th Century Home Entertainment, 1992.

198 Babitz, Eve. "It's the frames which make…" n.d., quoted in A-Z Quotes. "Eve Babitz Quote." https://www.azquotes.com/quote/1181529.

199 Norton, Richie. "THE ART of QUITTING: THE ONE QUESTION to ASK YOURSELF." The Blog of Richie Norton, May 5, 2014. https://richienorton.com/2014/05/art-of-quittin/#:~:text=Like%20creating%20a%20masterpiece%2C%20quitting.

200 Holstee. "The Holstee Manifesto | This Is Your Life.," n.d. https://www.holstee.com/pages/manifesto.

201 Glassman, Charles F. *Brain Drain : The Breakthrough That Will Change Your Life*. Mahwah, Nj: Rts Publishing, 2009.

202 Rogers, Mark. "A Brief History of Picture Frames." Frame Destination Blog, October 30, 2014. https://www.framedestination.com/blog/picture-frames/a-brief-history-of-picture-frames.

203 Day, Diane. "A Survey of Frame History." *Picture Framing Magazine*, December 12, 2012.

204 No source recovered.

205 Twain, Mark. "Every man is a moon…" n.d., quoted in www.goodreads.com. "A Quote by Mark Twain." https://www.goodreads.com/quotes/237641-every-man-is-a-moon-and-has-a-side-which.

206 "People don't fake depression…" n.d., quoted in Health, Lightfully Behavioral. "People Don't Fake Depression; They Fake Being OK." Lightfully Behavioral Health, March 9, 2023. https://lightfully.com/people-dont-fake-depression-they-fake-being-ok-how-to-recognize-depression-in-a-loved-one/.

207 Jaggard, Victoria, and National Geographic Staff. "Learn about the Full Moon and Its Many Names." National Geographic, June 15, 2019. https://www.nationalgeographic.com/science/article/full-moon.

208 "And like the moon…" n.d., quoted in QuotesToEnjoy. "And like the Moon, We Must Go through Phases Of… - Author Unknown," January 13, 2023. https://quotestoenjoy.com/and-like-the-moon-we-must-go-through-phases-of-emptiness-to-feel-full-again/.
209 Rodgers, Cristen. "Poetry." Cristen Writes, July 8, 2017. https://cristenwrites.com/poetry/.
210 NASA Solar System Exploration. "Earth's Moon," n.d. https://solarsystem.nasa.gov/moons/earths-moon/overview/#:~:text=The%20brightest%20and%20largest%20object.
211 Ariel, Henri Frederic. "Tell me what you feel…" n.d., quoted in A-Z Quotes. "Henri Frederic Amiel Quote." https://www.azquotes.com/quote/6865.
212 Ruskin, John. "One can't be angry…" n.d., quoted in www.goodreads.com. "A Quote by John Ruskin." https://www.goodreads.com/quotes/7603690-one-can-t-be-angry-when-one-looks-at-a-penguin.
213 Gugino, Carla. "You can't not be happy…" n.d., quoted in A-Z Quotes. "Carla Gugino Quote." https://www.azquotes.com/quote/1436827.
214 Advice For Life. "Advice from a Penguin Greeting Card." https://myadviceforlife.com/products/advice-from-a-penguin-greeting-card-blank-1.
215 Loren, Sophia. "I'd much rather eat pasta…" n.d., quoted in Twitter Inc. *Beautiful Sophia!* n.d. Online image. *Pinterest.* https://www.pinterest.com/pin/592082682238520584/.
216 Loren, Sophia. "Spaghetti can be eaten…" n.d., quoted in www.goodreads.com. "A Quote by Sophia Loren." https://www.goodreads.com/quotes/82885-spaghetti-can-be-eaten-most-successfully-if-you-inhale-it.
217 Gritzer, Daniel. "10 Common Crimes against Pasta You Don't Have to Commit." Serious Eats, March 7, 2021. https://www.seriouseats.com/crimes-against-pasta.
218 Allen, David. "If the only tool you have…" n.d., quoted in A-Z Quotes. "David Allen Quote." https://www.azquotes.com/quote/1123424.
219 Wikipedia. "Law of the Instrument," September 2, 2020. https://en.wikipedia.org/wiki/Law_of_the_instrument.
220 Tomkins, Silvan, and Samuel Messick. *Computer Simulation of Personality.* New York: Wiley & Sons, 1963.
221 Tomkins and Messick. *Computer Simulation.*
222 Patton, George S. "A piece of spaghetti…" n.d., quoted in A-Z Quotes. "George S. Patton Quote." https://www.azquotes.com/quote/226602.
223 Puckette, Madeline. "Champagne vs Prosecco: The Real Differences." Wine Folly, n.d. https://winefolly.com/deep-dive/champagne-vs-prosecco/.

224 Wikipedia Contributors. "Tetris." Wikipedia. Wikimedia Foundation, October 12, 2019. https://en.wikipedia.org/wiki/Tetris.

225 Tyson, Mike. "You should sit in meditation..." n.d., quoted in A-Z Quotes. "Mike Tyson Quote." https://www.azquotes.com/quote/1446749.

226 No source recovered.

227 No source recovered.

228 Tabucchi, Antonio. "I prefer insomnia..." n.d., quoted in Gibby-Brown, Sckylar. "Restless Insomnia Quotes for When You Can't Sleep." Everyday Power, March 10, 2021. https://everydaypower.com/insomnia-quotes/.

229 Tau, Lao. "Time is a created thing..." n.d., quoted in www.goodreads.com. "A Quote by Lao Tzu." https://www.goodreads.com/quotes/36323-time-is-a-created-thing-to-say-i-don-t-have.

230 Dr. Suess. "How Did It Get so Late so Soon?", n.d.

231 Kumar, P.S. Jagadeesh. "Time does not end..." n.d., quoted in JewelryCult.com. "The Best Quotes about Watches and Clocks of All Time," April 1, 2023. https://www.jewelrycult.com/watches/the-best-quotes-about-watches-and-clocks-of-all-time.

232 Ghloum, Emil. "The Significance of a Timepiece." The Ontarion, March 26, 2015. https://theontarion.com/2015/03/26/the-significance-of-a-timepiece/.

233 K. Martin Beckner. *A Million Doorways*. Createspace Independent Publishing Platform, 2016.

234 von Goethe, Johann Wolfgang. "Once you have missed..." n.d., quoted in A-Z Quotes. "Johann Wolfgang von Goethe Quote." https://www.azquotes.com/quote/946128.

235 Princeton University. WordNet.

236 "Be the change..." n.d., quoted in Ranseth, Joseph. "Gandhi Didn't Actually Say 'Be the Change You Want to See in the World.' Here's the Real Quote": Joseph Ranseth, August 24, 2017. https://josephranseth.com/gandhi-didnt-say-be-the-change-you-want-to-see-in-the-world/.

237 Murat ildan, Mehmet. "Tramway is more close..." n.d., quoted in www.goodreads.com. "A Quote by Mehmet Murat Ildan." https://www.goodreads.com/quotes/9655120-tramway-is-more-close-to-human-soul-than-the-subway.

238 Murat ildan, Mehmet. "The wisdom of the tram..." n.d., quoted in www.goodreads.com. "A Quote by Mehmet Murat Ildan." https://www.goodreads.com/quotes/10081643-the-wisdom-of-the-tram-is-that-if-you-do.

239 Murat ildan, Mehmet. "Trams are not free…" n.d., quoted in www.goodreads.com. "Tram Quotations Quotes (4 Quotes)." https://www.goodreads.com/quotes/tag/tram-quotations.
240 Gandhi, Mahatma. "We but mirror the world…" n.d., quoted in www.goodreads.com. "A Quote by Mahatma Gandhi," n.d. https://www.goodreads.com/quotes/760902-we-but-mirror-the-world-all-the-tendencies-present-in.
241 Andersen, Hans Christian. "The whole world is a series…" n.d. quoted in www.goodreads.com. "A Quote by Hans Christian Andersen." https://www.goodreads.com/quotes/324050-the-whole-world-is-a-series-of-miracles-but-we-re.
242 Yeats, William Butler. "There are no strangers here…" n.d., quoted in *William Butler Yeats Quotes*. n.d. Online image. *Brainy Quote*. https://www.brainyquote.com/quotes/william_butler_yeats_383082.
243 Einstein, Albert. "Stay away from negative people…" n.d., quoted in www.goodreads.com. "A Quote by Albert Einstein." https://www.goodreads.com/quotes/9816201-stay-away-from-negative-people-they-have-a-problem-for.
244 Zander, Benjamin. "The Transformative Power of Classical Music." Video. 2008. https://www.ted.com/talks/benjamin_zander_the_transformative_power_of_classical_music/transcript.
245 Tolstoy, Leo. *The Lion and the Dog*. Progress Publishers, 1975.
246 Norbury, James. *Big Panda and Tiny Dragon*. U.K.: Michael Joseph, 2021.
247 Ogunlaru, Rasheed. "Be genuinely interested in…" n.d. quoted in www.goodreads.com. "A Quote by Rasheed Ogunlaru." https://www.goodreads.com/quotes/612717-be-genuinely-interested-in-everyone-you-meet-and-everyone-you.
248 Emerson, Ralph Waldo. "A friend is the hope…" n.d., quoted in www.quotedb.com. "A Friend Is the Hope of the Heart. By Ralph Waldo Emerson." https://www.quotedb.com/quotes/3131.
249 Colton, Charles Caleb. "Silence is foolish…" n.d., quoted in www.goodreads.com. "A Quote by Charles Caleb Colton." https://www.goodreads.com/quotes/442594-silence-is-foolish-if-we-are-wise-but-wise-if.
250 Billings, Josh. "Silence is one of the hardest arguments…" n.d., quoted in *Josh Billings Quotes*. n.d. Online image. *BrainyQuote*. https://www.brainyquote.com/quotes/josh_billings_100690.
251 Todd, Richard Watson. "The true beauty of oxymorons…" n.d., quoted in Nordquist, Richard. "100 Awfully Good Oxymorons." ThoughtCo, June 21, 2023. https://www.thoughtco.com/awfully-good-examples-of-oxymorons-1691814.

SOURCES

252 Princeton University "About WordNet." WordNet. Princeton University. 2010.
253 Tomasi, Giuseppe. *The Leopard*. New York,: Pantheon Books, Stampa , Cop, 2015.
254 Confucius. "A seed grows with no sound…" n.d., quoted in Kilbourn Avenue. "'Grow Silently.'" Medium, September 3, 2019. https://medium.com/@kilbournave/grow-silently-316acc6c68f6.
255 Ebert, Alex. "To be lost…" n.d., quoted in *Alex Ebert Quotes*. n.d. Online image. *Brainy Quote*. https://www.brainyquote.com/quotes/alex_ebert_609151.
256 "Never let a good…" n.d., quoted in Family Zone Team. "'Never Let a Good Crisis Go to Waste.'" www.familyzone.com, n.d. https://www.familyzone.com/anz/families/blog/never-let-a-good-crisis-go-to-waste.
257 Roberts, Nora. "If you don't ask…" n.d., quoted in www.goodreads.com. "A Quote by Nora Roberts." https://www.goodreads.com/quotes/442499-if-you-don-t-ask-the-answer-is-always-no.
258 White, Betty. *If You Ask Me (and of Course You Won't)*. New York: Berkley Pub. Group, 2012.
259 Angelou, Maya. "I've learned that people will forget…," n.d., quoted in Goodreads.com. "A Quote by Maya Angelou," 2019. https://www.goodreads.com/quotes/5934-i-ve-learned-that-people-will-forget-what-you-said-people.
260 Mandela, Nelson. "May your choices reflect…" n.d., quoted in www.goodreads.com. "A Quote by Nelson Mandela." https://www.goodreads.com/quotes/956662-may-your-choices-reflect-your-hopes-not-your-fears.
261 Bersin, Josh. "Let's Stop Talking about Soft Skills: They're PowerSkills." JOSH BERSIN, October 31, 2019. https://joshbersin.com/2019/10/lets-stop-talking-about-soft-skills-theyre-power-skills/.
262 Metadot Corporation. "Zoom Fatigue: How to Beat the Burnout of Remote Work Meetings." metadot.com, April 14, 2021. https://metadot.com/blog/zoomfatigue/#:~:text=.
263 "Turning off your Zoom camera…" n.d., quoted in leslistes.net. "Top 41 Camera Jokes for National Camera Day | Les Listes," June 9, 2021. https://leslistes.net/top-41-camera-jokes/.
264 Zauderer, Steven. "31 Fear of Public Speaking Statistics (Prevalence)." www.crossrivertherapy.com, January 11, 2023. https://www.crossrivertherapy.com/public-speaking-statistics.
265 Orwell, George. *Politics and the English Language*. 1946. Reprint, London: Penguin, 1946.

266 Fensholt, M.F. "A presentation is a chance..." n.d. quoted in Allison, Kelly. "25 Public Speaking Quotes That Will Change Your Life - Ethos3 - a Presentation Training and Design Agency." Ethos3. https://ethos3.com/25-public-speaking-quotes-will-change-life/.

267 Haemer, Ken. "Designing a presentation..." n.d. quoted in Boone, Amy. "3 Important Quotes from Presentation Experts - Ethos3 - a Presentation Training and Design Agency." Ethos3. https://ethos3.com/3-important-quotes-from-presentation-experts/.

268 "On a bad hair day..." n.d. quoted in *On a Bad Hair Day...* n.d. Online image. *Pinterest.* https://www.pinterest.com/pin/on-a-bad-hair-day-there-is-always-lipstick-8x10-wall-art-instant-download--359936195231199884/.

269 "Better to light a candle..." n.d., quoted in Quote Investigator. "Better to Light a Candle than to Curse the Darkness – Quote Investigator®," March 19, 2017. https://quoteinvestigator.com/2017/03/19/candle/.

270 Singh, Harbhajan. "Everybody is a candle..." n.d., quoted in A-Z Quotes. "Harbhajan Singh Quote." https://www.azquotes.com/quote/720748.

271 Le Guin, Ursula K. *A Wizard of Earthsea.* Harmondsworth: Penguin, 1971.

272 Torroni, Amanda. Poetic Conversations, 2015.

273 Chödrön, Pema. *When Things Fall Apart: Heart Advice for Difficult Times.* Boulder, Colorado: Shambhala, 2016.

274 Hemingway, Ernest. "Write hard and clear..." n.d., quoted in www.goodreads.com. "A Quote by Ernest Hemingway," n.d. https://www.goodreads.com/quotes/248820-write-hard-and-clear-about-what-hurts.

275 Chödrön, Pema. "Nothing ever goes away..." n.d., quoted in www.goodreads.com. "A Quote by Pema Chödrön." https://www.goodreads.com/quotes/1521676-nothing-ever-goes-away-until-it-has-taught-us-what.

276 Brown, Horace Jackson Jr. "Don't burn bridges..." n.d., quoted in A-Z Quotes. "H. Jackson Brown, Jr. Quote." https://www.azquotes.com/quote/1352374.

277 Henley, Don. "Sometimes you get the best light..." n.d., quoted in *Don Henley Quotes.* n.d. Online image. *Brainy Quote.* https://www.brainyquote.com/quotes/don_henley_193059.

278 Lamb, Robert, Michael Morrissey, and Patrick J. Tiger. "How Bridges Work." HowStuffWorks, April 1, 2000. https://science.howstuffworks.com/engineering/civil/bridge.htm?srch_tag=uboqipqixak7iw37mfbyv4qjia2ljfbn.

279 Turner, Victor. "... realm of pure possibility..." n.d., quoted in Cleto, Sara. "Liminality and the Realm of Pure Possibility." Enchanted Living Magazine, July 23, 2021. https://enchantedlivingmagazine.com/liminality-and-the-realm-of-pure-possibility/.
280 "Life is a bridge..." n.d. quoted in *Bruce Chatwin Quotes.* n.d. Online image. *Quotefancy.* https://quotefancy.com/quote/2262231/Bruce-Chatwin-Life-is-a-bridge-Cross-over-it-but-build-no-house-on-it.
281 Hope, Bob. "You know you're getting old..." n.d., quoted in www.goodreads.com. "A Quote by Bob Hope." https://www.goodreads.com/quotes/119988-you-know-you-re-getting-old-when-the-candles-cost-more.
282 Baruah, Sanhita. "Every day is a gift..." n.d., quoted in www.goodreads.com. "A Quote by Sanhita Baruah." https://www.goodreads.com/quotes/10160043-every-day-is-a-gift-but-some-days-are-packaged.
283 Damasio, Antonio. "Animals that have only..." n.d., quoted in Watson, Galadriel. "Perspective | It's Natural to Feel Happy and Sad at the Same Time. Here's When It Can Become a Problem." *Washington Post,* August 4, 2021. https://www.washingtonpost.com/lifestyle/wellness/ambivalence-nostalgia-unhealthy/2021/08/04/73289c3c-f0b2-11eb-a452-4da5fe48582d_story.html.
284 Damasio, Antonio. "... more likely to be cautious when you make the decision..." n.d., quoted in Watson, Galadriel. "Perspective | It's Natural to Feel Happy and Sad at the Same Time. Here's When It Can Become a Problem." *Washington Post,* August 4, 2021. https://www.washingtonpost.com/lifestyle/wellness/ambivalence-nostalgia-unhealthy/2021/08/04/73289c3c-f0b2-11eb-a452-4da5fe48582d_story.html.
285 "The two most important days..." n.d., quoted in Quote Investigator. "Two Most Important Days in Your Life: The Day You Were Born and the Day You Discover Why – Quote Investigator®," June 22, 2016. https://quoteinvestigator.com/2016/06/22/why/.
286 MorBeans Coffee Company. "Traditional Barista Coffee Machines." https://www.morbeans.co.uk/equipment/traditional-barista/.
287 Rethlake, Bill. "The Branch Needs Baristas." Greensburg Daily News, February 4, 2021. https://www.greensburgdailynews.com/news/local_news/the-branch-needs-baristas/article_fce3c456-6723-11eb-82b2-97430d4e9221.html.
288 noccoffeeco.com. "The History of Latte Art - NOC COFFEE CO.," May 30, 2019. https://noccoffeeco.com/en/blog/history-of-latte-art/.
289 No source recovered.
290 Puddicombe, Andy. "It is not that thinking is bad..." n.d. quoted in Headspace. "33 of the Best Meditation Quotes," 2021. https://www.headspace.com/meditation/quotes.

291 No source recovered.
292 Hall, Stephen S. "Is Buddhism Good for Your Health?" *The New York Times*, September 14, 2003, sec. Magazine. https://www.nytimes.com/2003/09/14/magazine/is-buddhism-good-for-your-health.html.
293 Chesterton, G.K. "I am not absent-minded..." n.d., quoted in www.yuni.com. "Gilbert Keith Chesterton Quotes and Quotations, Famous Quotes by Authors." https://www.yuni.com/quotes/chesterton.html.
294 Bellow, Saul. "The secret motive..." n.d., quoted in A-Z Quotes. "Saul Bellow Quote." https://www.azquotes.com/quote/1074532.
295 Moore JW (2016) What Is the Sense of Agency and Why Does it Matter? Front. Psychol. 7:1272. doi: 10.3389/fpsyg.2016.01272
296 Cooley, Mason. "Most of my decisions..." n.d., quoted in A-Z Quotes. "Mason Cooley Quote." https://www.azquotes.com/quote/1251486.
297 Kaufman, Scott Barry. "Mind Wandering: A New Personal Intelligence Perspective." Scientific American Blog Network, September 25, 2013. https://blogs.scientificamerican.com/beautiful-minds/mind-wandering-a-new-personal-intelligence-perspective/.
298 *Pooh's Grand Adventure: The Search for Christopher Robin*. Film. Walt Disney Studios Home Entertainment, 1997.
299 Burns, George. "I must be getting absent-minded..." n.d., quoted in A-Z Quotes. "George Burns Quote." https://www.azquotes.com/quote/583241.
300 Hemingway, Ernest. *The Sun Also Rises*. Scribner's, 1926.
301 Rachel. "What Do You Call Someone Who Crochets? Crocheter Definition + Alternatives." Desert Blossom Crafts, February 18, 2021. https://desertblossomcrafts.com/crocheter-definition/.
302 Howell, Vickie. "We want to work hard..." n.d., quoted in Rachel. "What Do You Call Someone Who Crochets? Crocheter Definition + Alternatives." Desert Blossom Crafts, February 18, 2021. https://desertblossomcrafts.com/crocheter-definition/.
303 Cochran, Heather. The Return of Jonah Gray. MIRA, 2007.
304 Umebinyuo, Ijeoma. *Questions for Ada*. Charleston, South Carolina: Createspace, 2016.
305 Umebinyuo, Ijeoma. "Start now..." n.d., quoted in www.goodreads.com. "A Quote by Ijeoma Umebinyuo." https://www.goodreads.com/quotes/3247698-start-now-start-where-you-are-start-with-fear-start.
306 Hill, Napoleon. "Think twice before you speak..." n.d., quoted in www.goodreads.com. "A Quote by Napoleon Hill," n.d. https://www.goodreads.com/quotes/715079-think-twice-before-you-speak-because-your-words-and-influence.

307 Yamamoto, Yohji. "I think perfection is ugly…" n.d., quoted in www.goodreads.com. "A Quote by Yohji Yamamoto," n.d. https://www.goodreads.com/quotes/346078-i-think-perfection-is-ugly-somewhere-in-the-things-humans.
308 St. Jerome. "The scars of others…" n.d., quoted in A-Z Quotes. "St. Jerome Quote," n.d. https://www.azquotes.com/quote/146384.
309 von Bismarck, Otto. "Only a fool learns from his own mistakes…" n.d., quoted in Goodreads.com. "A Quote by Otto von Bismarck," 2019. https://www.goodreads.com/quotes/294225-only-a-fool-learns-from-his-own-mistakes-the-wise.
310 Massoud, Rasmenia. *Human Detritus*. Lulu.com, 2011.
311 Conaway, Cameron. *Caged*. Threed Press, 2011.
312 Chabrol, Claude. "There is no new wave…" n.d., quoted in A-Z Quotes. "Claude Chabrol Quote," n.d. https://www.azquotes.com/quote/976960.
313 Bridges, Jeff. "It's a wonderful metaphor…" n.d., quoted in A-Z Quotes. "Jeff Bridges Quote," n.d. https://www.azquotes.com/quote/36007.
314 Johnson, J.C. "Opinion | the Dude Abides. But Is Aspiring to Do Nothing Still Funny?" NBC News, March 9, 2018. https://www.nbcnews.com/think/opinion/dude-abides-20-years-after-big-lebowski-aspiring-do-nothing-ncna855176.
315 Roshi, Suzuki. "Waves are the practice of water…" n.d., quoted in *Waves Are the Practice of Water…* n.d. Online image. *Pinterest*. https://www.pinterest.ca/pin/649151733761486715/.
316 Newton, James D. *Uncommon Friends : Life with Thomas Edison, Henry Ford, Harvey Firestone, Alexis Carrel, & Charles Lindbergh*. San Diego: Harcourt Brace Jovanovich, 1989.
317 Reeves, Keanu. "Someone told me the other day…" n.d., quoted in www.goodreads.com. "A Quote by Keanu Reeves," n.d. https://www.goodreads.com/quotes/10154001-someone-told-me-the-other-day-that-he-felt-bad.
318 "I know what I bring to the table…" n.d., quoted in www.treasurequotes.com. "Famous Quote: 'I Know What I Bring to the Table. So Trust Me When I Say I'm Not Afraid to Eat Alone.,'" n.d. https://www.treasurequotes.com/quotes/i-know-what-i-bring-to-the-table-so-trust-me.
319 Rilke, Rainer Maria. *Letters to a Young Poet*, 1929.
320 Bourdain, Anthony. *The Nasty Bits : Collected Varietal Cuts, Usable Trim, Scraps, and Bones*. New York: Bloomsbury, 2007.
321 Dobrin, Arthur. "Why Faith Is Important | Psychology Today." www.psychologytoday.com, September 28, 2012. https://www.psychologytoday.com/us/blog/am-i-right/201209/why-faith-is-important#:~:text=Faith%20is%20an%20expression%20of.

322 Burdain. *The Nasty Bits*.
323 Bourdain, Anthony. *No Reservations: Around the World on an Empty Stomach*. New York ; London: Bloomsbury, 2011.
324 Thomas, Geralin. *Decluttering Your Home : Tips, Techniques & Trade Secrets*. Richmond Hill, Ontario: Firefly Books, 2015.
325 Kingston, Karen. "The Deeper Implications of Putting Your Stuff in Storage." Karen Kingstons Blog, October 31, 2017. https://www.karenkingston.com/blog/the-deeper-implications-of-putting-your-stuff-in-storage/.
326 "Put your stuff in storage..." n.d., quoted in *Travel Terms*. n.d. Online image. *Pinterest*. https://www.pinterest.com/pin/107945722293409637/.
327 Waxman, Abbi. "Sometimes life is what it is..." n.d., quoted in Irina. "201 Ice Cream Quotes and Sayings." Baking Like a Chef, May 12, 2022. https://www.bakinglikeachef.com/ice-cream-quotes-and-sayings/.
328 Pratt, Chris. "You can pour melted ice cream..." n.d., quoted in A-Z Quotes. "Chris Pratt Quote." https://www.azquotes.com/quote/235805.
329 Fadiman, Anne. "It is a grave error to assume..." n.d., quoted in A-Z Quotes. "Anne Fadiman Quote," n.d. https://www.azquotes.com/quote/1020294.
330 Snoop Dogg. "When I'm no longer rapping..." n.d., quoted in Headley, Sandy. *Ice Cream Parlor*. n.d. Online image. *Pinterest*. https://cz.pinterest.com/pin/734157176741830406/.
331 Tzu, Lao. "Water is fluid..." n.d., quoted in www.goodreads.com. "A Quote by Lao Tzu," n.d. https://www.goodreads.com/quotes/365687-water-is-fluid-soft-and-yielding-but-water-will-wear.
332 Kitt, Eartha. "The river is constantly turning..." n.d., quoted in BrainyQuote. "Eartha Kitt Quotes," n.d. https://www.brainyquote.com/quotes/eartha_kitt_331304.
333 Gregersen, Hal. "Inquiry-Driven Leadership at Work and in Life | Testing a Newsletter Prototype." www.linkedin.com, April 1, 2022. https://www.linkedin.com/pulse/inquiry-driven-leadership-work-life-testing-prototype-hal-gregersen/?trackingId=D2bKolXKSrOKe%2B3Pjk926g%3D%3D.
334 Lermontov, Mikhail. *A Hero of Our Time*. Iliya Glazunov & Co, 1840.
335 Lee, Bruce. "Be like water..." n.d., quoted in www.goodreads.com. "A Quote by Bruce Lee," n.d. https://www.goodreads.com/quotes/29138-be-like-water-making-its-way-through-cracks-do-not.

336 Haskins, Henry S. "The darkness around us…" n.d., quoted in Svoboda, Martin. "The Darkness around Us Might Somewhat Light up If We Would…." Quotepark.com, n.d. https://quotepark.com/quotes/1816904-henry-s-haskins-the-darkness-around-us-might-somewhat-light-up-if/.

337 Evans, Richard Paul. "Nothing heals the soul…" n.d., quoted in Irina. "195 Best Chocolate Quotes and Sayings." Baking Like a Chef, May 6, 2022. https://www.bakinglikeachef.com/chocolate-quotes-and-sayings/.

338 Dahl, Roald. *Charlie and the Chocolate Factory*. London: Puffin, 1964.

339 *Willy Wonka & the Chocolate Factory*. Film. Paramount Pictures, 1971.

340 Caramagna, Fabrizio. "A bar of chocolate…" n.d., quoted in "195 Best Chocolate Quotes and Sayings." Baking Like a Chef, May 6, 2022. https://www.bakinglikeachef.com/chocolate-quotes-and-sayings/.

341 Moore, Terry. "The 12 step chocolate program…" n.d., quoted in www.goodreads.com. "A Quote by Terry Moore." Accessed July 5, 2023. https://www.goodreads.com/quotes/143709-the-12-step-chocolate-program-never-be-more-than-12-steps.

342 Viorst, Judith. "Strength is the ability…" n.d., quoted in philosiblog. "Strength Is the Ability to Break a Chocolate Bar into Four Pieces with Your Bare Hands and Then Eat Just One of Those Pieces.," March 31, 2016. https://philosiblog.com/2016/03/31/strength-is-the-ability-to-break-a-chocolate-bar-into-four-pieces-with-your-bare-hands-and-then-eat-just-one-of-those-pieces/.

343 Fry, Courtney. "Apparently Some of You Iron Your Sheets & I Need to Know Where You Get the Fkn Time." PEDESTRIAN.TV, April 2, 2020. https://www.pedestrian.tv/entertainment/do-you-iron-your-sheets-who-does-this/.

344 No source recovered.

345 Aacharya, R.P., Gastmans, C. & Denier, Y. Emergency department triage: an ethical analysis. *BMC Emerg Med* **11**, 16 (2011). https://doi.org/10.1186/1471-227X-11-16.

346 *Ibid.*

347 Nast, Condé. "6 Tips for Getting the Most out of Your Emergency Room Visit, from an ER Doctor." SELF, November 30, 2017. https://www.self.com/story/6-tips-for-getting-the-most-out-of-your-emergency-room-visit.

348 Douglas, Jim. "Care shouldn't start…" n.d., quoted in A-Z Quotes. "James Douglas, Lord of Douglas Quote." https://www.azquotes.com/quote/1182470.

349 www.acep.org. "Policy Statements," n.d. https://www.acep.org/patient-care/policy-statements.

350 www.meteoswiss.admin.ch. "Thunderstorm and Lightning Frequency in Switzerland - MeteoSwiss," n.d. https://www.meteoswiss.admin.ch/weather/weather-and-climate-from-a-to-z/thunderstorms/thunderstorm-and-lightning-frequency-in-switzerland.html.
351 Encyclopedia Britannica. "Thunderstorm - Movement of Thunderstorms," n.d. https://www.britannica.com/science/thunderstorm/Movement-of-thunderstorms.
352 Tuckman, Bruce. "Developmental Sequence in Small Groups." *Psychological Bulletin* 63, no. 6 (1965): 384–99. https://doi.org/10.1037/h0022100.
353 Tuckman, Bruce W., and Mary Ann C. Jensen. "Stages of Small-Group Development Revisited." *Group & Organization Studies* 2, no. 4 (December 1977): 419–27. https://doi.org/10.1177/105960117700200404.
354 Lencioni, Patrick. *The Five Dysfunctions of a Team*. San Francisco, Calif.: Pfeiffer, 2012.
355 Levithan, David. *The Realm of Possibility*. New York: Knopf, 2012.
356 Steinberg, Laurel. "Stormy weather reminds people..." n.d., quoted in Keppler, Nick. "Stormy Weather Is Great for Anxiety." www.vice.com, August 17, 2017. https://www.vice.com/en/article/a33ena/why-bad-weather-soothes-your-anxiety.
357 Chris. "What Is the Symbolism of Lightning? (5 Meanings)." Symbolism and Metaphor, January 16, 2021. https://symbolismandmetaphor.com/lightning-symbolism-meaning/.
358 Jami, Criss. *Killosophy : Original Aphorisms & Poetry*. Criss Jami, 2015.
359 French, Thomas. "What's the reality of..." n.d., quoted in *Thomas French Quotes*. n.d. Online image. *Brainy Quote*. https://www.brainyquote.com/quotes/thomas_french_621636.
360 Fitzgerald, Scott F. "The test of a first-rate intelligence..." n.d., quoted in www.goodreads.com. "A Quote by F. Scott Fitzgerald," n.d. https://www.goodreads.com/quotes/6736446-the-test-of-a-first-rate-intelligence-is-the-ability-to.
361 Esar, Evan. "Zoo: an excellent place to..." n.d., quoted in A-Z Quotes. "Evan Esar Quote," n.d. https://www.azquotes.com/quote/550154.
362 Godinez AM and Fernandez EJ (2019) What Is the Zoo Experience? How Zoos Impact a Visitor's Behaviors, Perceptions, and Conservation Efforts. *Front. Psychol.* 10:1746. doi: 10.3389/fpsyg.2019.01746.
363 *We Bought a Zoo*. Film. 20th Century Studios, 2011.
364 Hambly, Tom. "Why Is Pizza Round? The Box Is Square, and It's Cut into Triangles." Crust Kingdom, April 6, 2019. https://www.crustkingdom.com/why-is-pizza-round-the-box-is-square-and-its-cut-into-triangles/.

SOURCES | 481

365 Murray, Bill. "Every pizza is a personal pizza..." n.d., quoted in A-Z Quotes. "Bill Murray Quote." https://www.azquotes.com/quote/783159.
366 Knepper, Nicole. Moms Who Drink and Swear. Penguin, 2013.
367 Nouwen, Henri. "Each day holds a surprise..." n.d., quoted in Henri Nouwen. "Expecting a Surprise." Accessed July 5, 2023. https://henrinouwen.org/meditations/expecting-a-surprise/.
368 Ziglar, Zig. "I opened two gifts..." n.d., quoted in *Zig Ziglar Quote*. n.d. Online image. *Quotefancy*. https://quotefancy.com/quote/94378/Zig-Ziglar-I-opened-two-gifts-this-morning-They-were-my-eyes.
369 Heschel, Abraham J. *The Wisdom of Heschel*. Farrar, Straus And Giroux, 1985.
370 Baum, L. Frank. *The Wonderful Wizard of Oz*. George M. Hill Company, 1900.
371 Roosevelt, Eleanor. "A guest is really good or bad..." n.d., quoted in *Eleanor Roosevelt Quote*. n.d. Online image. *Quotefancy*. https://quotefancy.com/quote/800039/Eleanor-Roosevelt-A-guest-is-really-good-or-bad-because-of-the-host-or-hostess-who-makes.
372 Prince Philip, Duke of Edinburgh. "The art of being a good guest..." n.d., quoted in 5sk. *Quotes about Being a Good Guest*. n.d. Online image. *Pinterest*. https://www.pinterest.com/pin/the-art-of-being-a-good-guest-is-toknow-when-to-leaveprince-philip-duke-of-edinburghquotedcombritish-noble--599893612870490251/.
373 Heath, Chip, and Dan Heath. *Switch : How to Change Things When Change Is Hard*. Random House US, 2013.
374 Storm, JM. "Magic happens when..." n.d., quoted in www.goodreads.com. "Quote by JM Storm." https://www.goodreads.com/quotes/9546059-magic-happens-when-you-don-t-give-up-even-when-you.
375 Patchett, Ann. *The Dutch House*. London Bloomsbury Publishing, 2019.
376 Vega, Paz. "I cook croquetas..." n.d., quoted in A-Z Quotes. "Paz Vega Quote." https://www.azquotes.com/quote/742900.

Made in the USA
Middletown, DE
08 September 2023